State of Emergency

Nine out of ten constitutions contain explicit emergency provisions. During the pandemic, half of the governments with such constitutions made use of these provisions by declaring a state of emergency. *State of Emergency* is the first book to analyze the factors that led to such provisions being included in newly drafted constitutions. It explores their use – as well as their misuse – and explains the effects of using emergency provisions. Declaring a state of emergency is particularly challenging in federally constituted states as it endangers the balance of powers between the federal level and the states. This book, therefore, pays special attention to this topic. Focusing on two of the most important recent cases relating to emergency provisions, the Covid-19 pandemic and acts of terrorism, this book uses numerous examples to analyze emergency provisions with a rigorous empirical approach.

CHRISTIAN BJØRNSKOV is Professor of Economics at Aarhus University in Denmark, as well as affiliated researcher at the Research Institute of Industrial Economics in Stockholm, Sweden. He is the author of more than 100 articles in journals including the *American Journal of Political Science* and *Public Choice*.

STEFAN VOIGT is Professor of Law and Economics at the University of Hamburg and the Director of its Institute of Law and Economics. His research focuses on the economic effects of institutions. He is one of the editors of the journal *Constitutional Political Economy* and author of *Institutional Economics: An Introduction* (2019, Cambridge University Press) and *Constitutional Economics: A Primer* (2020, Cambridge University Press).

State of Emergency

An Economic Analysis

CHRISTIAN BJØRNSKOV
Aarhus University

STEFAN VOIGT
University of Hamburg

CAMBRIDGE
UNIVERSITY PRESS

CAMBRIDGE
UNIVERSITY PRESS

Shaftesbury Road, Cambridge CB2 8EA, United Kingdom

One Liberty Plaza, 20th Floor, New York, NY 10006, USA

477 Williamstown Road, Port Melbourne, VIC 3207, Australia

314–321, 3rd Floor, Plot 3, Splendor Forum, Jasola District Centre, New Delhi – 110025, India

103 Penang Road, #05–06/07, Visioncrest Commercial, Singapore 238467

Cambridge University Press is part of Cambridge University Press & Assessment, a department of the University of Cambridge.

We share the University's mission to contribute to society through the pursuit of education, learning and research at the highest international levels of excellence.

www.cambridge.org
Information on this title: www.cambridge.org/9781009372084

DOI: 10.1017/9781009372138

First published 2024

A catalogue record for this publication is available from the British Library

Library of Congress Cataloging-in-Publication Data
Names: Bjørnskov, Christian, author. | Voigt, Stefan, author.
Title: State of emergency : an economic analysis / Christian Bjørnskov, Aarhus University, Denmark, Stefan Voigt, University of Hamburg.
Description: Cambridge, United Kingdom ; New York, NY : Cambridge University Press, 2024. | Includes bibliographical references and index.
Identifiers: LCCN 2023047144 | ISBN 9781009372084 (hardback) | ISBN 9781009372138 (ebook)
Subjects: LCSH: Economics – Political aspects. | Emergencies – Law and legislation. | Constitutional law – Economic aspects. | Economic policy.
Classification: LCC HB74.P65 B526 2024 | DDC 330–dc23
LC record available at https://lccn.loc.gov/2023047144

ISBN 978-1-009-37208-4 Hardback
ISBN 978-1-009-37210-7 Paperback

Contents

Figures

Tables

Acknowledgments

A book – especially if it contains as many chapters as this one – is the result of many influences, comments, criticisms, suggestions, ... Back in 2013, the Minerva Center for the Rule of Law under Extreme Conditions was established at the University of Haifa – and Stefan was one of its founding members. When reflecting upon his possible input to the Center, the idea of analyzing how extreme conditions are dealt with in constitutions took hold. The regular exchange with my colleagues in Haifa was not only important but always very pleasant. Thanks are due to Gad Barzilai, Amnon Reichman, Eli Salzberger, and Deborah Shmueli. It was a lucky coincidence that I was invited to spend a couple of months as a senior fellow at the Institute of Advanced Study at the University of Notre Dame in 2013. This gave me the room and time to do some basic reading on states of emergency. Special thanks go to the then director of the Institute, Vittorio Hösle.

Likewise, it was a lucky coincidence that the two authors came to discuss the concept of "constitutional crime," which morphed into the themes covered in this book. While Stefan could draw on having a central role in European law and economics research, Christian was grateful for much input from colleagues in public choice. Peter Kurrild-Klitgaard, Jacob Mchangama, and Martin Rode deserve special mention as well as the Jan Wallander and Tom Hedelius Foundation for funding part of the research.

While we are responsible for the research going into this book, it would have been impossible without the help of a number of colleagues. Most specifically, the original research for Chapter 10 was a joint effort with Mahdi Khesali who coauthored the article in the *The Journal of Legal Studies*. Likewise, much of the impetus for Chapter 13 and the ideas behind the chapter are the result of work by our excellent master's student, Emily Johnson. We feel privileged to have worked with such talented young researchers and are grateful to them for including their work in this book. Also, Chapter 9 has benefited a lot from our cooperation with Abishek Choutagunta and Shruti Rajagapolan. We have also been very fortunate to have some long-term colleagues who have been willing to produce constructive comments on pretty much any idea: Although they do not appear as co-authors in any of the chapters, Jerg Gutmann and Niclas Berggren have contributed immensely to the project.

Bits and pieces of this long-term project have been presented at many conferences. In a sense, we were almost regulars at the Public Choice Society meetings (e.g. San Antonio 2015), the European Public Choice Society Meetings (Freiburg 2016, Budapest 2017, Jerusalem 2019), the meetings of the European Association of Law & Economics (e.g. Vienna 2015, Bologna 2016, Tel Aviv 2019), the annual meetings of the Italian Law & Economics Society (e.g. Naples), the Southern Economic Association, and the Danish Public Choice Society conference. But we were also fortunate to have been invited to nonregular events such as the jubilee conference of the Eucken Institute (Freiburg, June 2014), the conference "State of Exception – an Overview" organized by Matthias Lemke at the German Historical Institute in Paris (2017), the Future of Federalism Conference at the NYU Law School in November 2016, the Law & Economics workshop in Florence, the Political Economy Workshop of the University of Indiana (at Berlin) and others.

And of course, we presented single chapters of this book to many regular department workshops including those in Ankara (Bilkent), Bonn, Freiburg, Hamburg (Helmut Schmidt University), Hannover, Lugano, Lund, Marseille, Milan (Bicocca), Munich (TU), Paderborn, Prague (University of Economics), and Stellenbosch. We thank all the convenors for inviting us and all the participants for raising interesting and intriguing questions.

A long list of other people have helped to improve our work: Dagmar Ahlgrimm, Daniel Arce, Dan Brinks, Francisco Castellanos, Adam Chilton, Kevin Cope, Matthias Dauner, Nora El Bialy, Marek Endrich, Benjamin Engst, Lars Feld, Paula Herm, Daniel Hicks, Sven Höppner, Sina Imhof, Jean Michel Josselin, Rola El Kabbani, Hartmut Kliemt, Tim Krieger, Tommy Krieger, Patrick Leyens, Katerina Linos, Mariana Llanos, Brian Loveman, John Matsusaka, Katarzyna Metelska-Szaniawska, Stephan Michel, Peter Nannestad, Konstantinos Pilpilidis, José Reis, Roee Sarel, Janina Satzer, Thomas Stratmann, Agnes Strauss, Alois Stutzer,

Rok Spruk, José Tavares, Mark Tushnet, Viktor Vanberg, and Mila Versteeg.

At the end of the day, dozens and dozens of colleagues have commented on various aspects of this book during the years of work on the project. However, we cannot blame any of them for the mistakes and shortcomings in the rest of this book, which are entirely ours. We also cannot blame them if we decide to continue research on this topic. This book is the beginning of our understanding of states of emergency, but far from the end.

1 *Introduction*

Nine out of ten constitutions contain explicit emergency provisions (Elkins et al. 2009). These provisions are not dead letters but are regularly invoked by national governments with both honorable and dubious rationales. Between 1985 and 2019, at least 137 countries around the world called a state of emergency (SOE). During the COVID pandemic and lockdowns of 2020–22, a previously unlikely situation arose when every second government in the world made use of constitutional emergency provisions by declaring an SOE: At the beginning of May 2020, 99 countries were simultaneously in a constitutional SOE, and several more were in a de facto although undeclared emergency. The inclusion of emergency provisions – those legal rules specifying who can declare an emergency, when they can do so, and what actors have what powers once it has been declared – in constitutions has become the norm.

This is the first book to analyze the factors that make constitutional conventions include such provisions in newly drafted constitutions, to analyze their use (as well as their misuse), and the effects that using emergency provisions has. Throughout the book, we refer to these provisions simply as "emergency constitutions." These are, in other words, not separate documents but simply those parts of the constitution that refer to emergencies. First, they are particularly important parts of the constitution because they typically outline which other parts of the constitution – including human rights, democratic institutions, and due process – the executive branch is allowed to ignore during an emergency. While emergencies – which different constitutions refer to using different vocabulary, such as emergency, state of siege, extraordinary conditions, and so forth – can provide governments with the necessary room for maneuver and much reduced reaction times, they are therefore also highly prone to political misuse. Second, we explicitly focus on constitutions and constitutional provisions throughout the book and not on statutory law or unwritten judicial norms. We do so because statutory law can change rapidly and easily, not least when a real or potential emergency arises, which means that such law does not provide de facto binding constraints for political actors. Constitutional provisions cannot be changed whenever the political situation changes, although it remains an open question whether they work as intended.

States of emergency can indeed be crucial moments in the development of countries. Referring to nineteenth-century Latin America, Loveman (1993) argues that emergency constitutions made the region's numerous populist and military governments of the twentieth century possible. Events in 1930, when Rafael Trujillo became president of the Dominican Republic, provide a pertinent example. Shortly after his rise to power, the country was struck by a hurricane, which Trujillo used as a pretext to seize bank accounts, levy emergency taxes, and impose martial law on all citizens. This was instrumental in firmly establishing his autocratic rule over the country, which was to last decades.

Yet the (mis-)use of emergency declarations is not a thing of the past. Following the failed coup of July 2016, Turkish president Erdogan declared an SOE, which enabled him not only to detain thousands of citizens without trial and dismiss more than 100,000 employees from public service but also to change the constitution such that it now gives even more powers to the president. It seems that no world region is exempt from the misuse of emergency provisions against its citizens, which became evident across locked-down Western societies in 2020 and 2021.

Amnesty International (2017, [6]) calls the years following the Bataclan terrorist attacks in Paris and elsewhere "a profound shift in paradigm across Europe ... Individual EU states and regional bodies have responded to the attacks by proposing, adopting and implementing wave after wave of counter-terrorism measures that have eroded the rule of law, enhanced executive powers, peeled away judicial controls, restricted freedom of expression and exposed everyone to government surveillance." Although not all European governments resorted to states of emergency, as Belgium and France did, the report lists no less than 12 problematic measures taken by many European countries. We document in this book that these measures were not isolated events but reflections of a larger and more general pattern of political behavior.

However, taking these examples – and many more could be named – as well as the frequency with which SOEs are invoked into account, it is amazing how little we know about constitutional emergency provisions, and particularly about the factors that cause societies to adopt them in the first place. Little is known about: (1) the amount of additional powers granted to governments acting under an SOE; (2) the trends in the evolution of emergency provisions over time; (3) the factors that cause societies to adopt them in the first place; and (4) their effects, that is, their effectiveness in achieving the goals stated in the underlying legislation.

Although the first known emergency provisions were part of the constitutional framework of the Roman Republic, and later the Roman Empire, and although the constitutionalization of emergencies is evidently the rule in modern constitution-making, this is the first comprehensive and systematic exploration of the topic, based on empirical evidence as well as case studies.

The book is the result of a research project which we undertook at the University of Hamburg and Aarhus University between 2015 and 2023. Most of the chapters in this book first appeared as journal articles. But for this book, they have been significantly rewritten and updated.

1.1 Outline

Chapter 2 is entitled The Architecture of Emergency Constitutions and first appeared under the same title in the *International Journal of Constitutional Law*, volume 16 (1), 101–127. It provides answers to two of the questions just mentioned, namely the amount of additional powers granted in emergency constitutions to governments acting under an SOE and describes trends in the evolution of emergency provisions over time. Chapter 3 was exclusively written for this book and is entitled The Determinants of Emergency Constitutions. As the headline indicates, it deals with the factors that lead countries to adopt different types of emergency constitutions. However, having an emergency constitution does not imply its actual use. In Chapter 4 – Why do Governments Call a State of Emergency? – we therefore inquire into the conditions that make the declaration of an SOE by governments more likely. The chapter first appeared in the *European Journal of Political Economy*, volume 54, 110–123.

Chapters 5 through 7 all deal with the consequences of SOEs. Now, not all SOEs are created equal, which is why we devote three chapters to the issue, differentiating between different causes underlying an emergency declaration: In Chapter 5, we analyze the effects that such declarations have subsequent to natural disasters, in Chapter 6 subsequent to terrorist events, and in Chapter 7 subsequent to domestic turmoil such as assassination attempts, insurgencies, and coups.

We propose to distinguish between these events as natural disasters are exogenous to government policies whereas terrorist events and domestic turmoil appear to be highly endogenous to government behavior. Chapter 5 first appeared under the heading "Emergencies: on the misuse of government powers" in *Public Choice*, volume 190(1–2), 1–32, while Chapter 6 emerged out of two papers, namely "When does terror induce a state of emergency? And what are the effects?" in *Journal of Conflict Resolution*, volume 64 (4), 579–613 and "Terrorism and emergency constitutions in the Muslim world" in *Journal of Peace Research*, volume 59 (3), 305–318.

Chapters 8 and 9 focus on the particular challenges that federally constituted countries face with regard to SOEs. It is well known that keeping a sustainable balance between the powers of the states on the one hand and those of the center on the other is no mean feat. In India, the federal government has the so-called "President's rule" at its disposal: If it believes that any state government is unfit for the job, it can substitute it for another. This is a far-ranging power that has been subject to frequent misuse. But balancing the powers between the states and the center is a recurring question for all federally constituted states, which is why numerous other cases are alluded to in Chapter 9. In a sense, Chapter 8 can be read as a prelude to Chapter 9. In it, we compare the emergency constitutions that all the US states have given themselves. It turns out they are very different from each other, with some states granting the executive substantial power while the Texan constitution grants no additional powers during an emergency. Chapter 8 first appeared as "Dealing with Disaster: Analyzing the Emergency Constitutions of the US States" in *Arizona State Law Journal*, volume 49, 883–906.

As other elements of civil liberties, media freedom is important in many respects. It has, for example, been shown that no country with a high degree of realized media freedom has ever suffered from a famine. More generally speaking, media freedom has an important function in making governments accountable to the general population. But how does media freedom perform in the wake of an SOE even if it is constitutionalized? Do governments seize the opportunity to reduce it in order to be less tightly controlled? Unfortunately, the answer we provide to this question in Chapter 10 is a clear yes. Chapter 10 first appeared as "Is constitutionalized media freedom only window dressing? Evidence from terrorist attacks" in *Public Choice*, volume 187 (3–4), 321–348.

A low degree of actually realized media freedom, even when the constitution solemnly promises it, is only one dimension in which governments may create a de jure/de facto gap in the sense that constitutional reality does not accord well with constitutional text. We pick up the possibility of unconstitutional SOEs in Chapter 11. We define SOEs as unconstitutional if their declaration does not follow the rules spelled out in the constitution, if government behavior during an SOE is not constrained by the respective emergency provisions, or if the SOE does not end after the maximum term accorded to SOEs in the constitution. After having identified these unconstitutional events, we inquire into the factors that make their occurrence more likely. The original paper was written together with Mahdi Khesali and it first appeared under the title "Unconstitutional states of emergency" in *The Journal of Legal Studies*, volume 51 (2), 455–481.

The recent pandemic was accompanied by the declaration of an SOE in every second country of the world – a number previously perceived as highly unlikely. In our analysis of these SOEs, we ask if it was different on this occasion in the sense that it was not the self-serving arguments of politicians that prevailed but rather concerns for public health. We also use this event to study the use of executive decrees which, strangely enough, has rarely been analyzed in a large N comparative setting. A possible reason for this lacuna may be the very different concrete meaning that executive decrees take on in different legal orders. In Chapter 12, we ask if SOEs and executive decrees can be thought of as substitutes and answer the question in the affirmative. A previous version of this paper entitled "This time is different? – on the use of emergency measures during the corona pandemic" first appeared in the *European Journal of Law and Economics*, volume 54, 63–81.

Many, if not most, scholars of emergency politics claim that the ultimate political aim is to reestablish the status quo ante. But then again, SOEs may be (mis-)used to bring about permanent change such as to reduce media freedom or civil liberties more broadly. In Chapter 13, we analyze the question of whether the status quo ante is ever reached again after an SOE and if yes, how long it takes to get there. Also, we ask whether democracies are more likely to return to pre-SOE levels than autocracies. Unfortunately, we find that in situations where the executive can gain substantially more power by declaring an SOE, reestablishing the status quo ante takes longer than when there is less additional power to grab.

Until here, our analyses are almost entirely positive: We are interested in describing trends, uncovering cause–effect relationships, and understanding how emergencies affect political incentives. But how, if at all, could one legitimize emergency constitutions? This is the question dealt with in Chapter 14. It is located at the end of this book to make our approach transparent: Normative questions are best answered taking all the available knowledge explicitly into account. Here, all the results presented in Chapters 2 through 13 serve as a background for our attempt to legitimize emergency constitutions. The paper was originally single authored by Stefan and appeared as "Contracting for catastrophe: Legitimizing emergency constitutions by drawing on social contract theory" in *Res Publica*, volume 28 (1), 149–172.

Chapter 15 spells out a number of important questions that have not received much attention in the book and thus serves as a sort of outlook chapter. One pertinent question is what sort of consequences we can draw from the recent experiences with regard to the COVID-19 pandemic. Should resilience be increased and if so how? Does that imply any modification for the underlying emergency constitutions? Given that the European Union has become a central actor for its 27 member states, should the EU also get an emergency constitution? These are only two of the questions touched upon in Chapter 15.

2 The Architecture of Emergency Constitutions

2.1 Introduction

As already mentioned in Chapter 1, some 90 percent of all constitutions worldwide contain explicit provisions for how to deal with states of emergency (Elkins et al. 2009). The inclusion of emergency provisions – those legal rules specifying who can declare a state of emergency (SOE), when they can do so, and what actors have what powers once it has been declared – into constitutions has become the norm. In this book, we refer to these provisions simply as "emergency constitutions." These are, in other words, not separate documents but simply those parts of the constitution that refer to emergencies. And these provisions are used quite frequently and their use is often far from innocuous. Between 1985 and 2014, at least 137 countries declared an SOE at least once. During the COVID pandemic alone, at least 125 nation-state governments declared an SOE emergency due to health concerns.

Under an SOE, some individual rights and liberties are usually suspended and the separation of powers is curtailed in favor of the executive or even a single person such as the head of state or government and, by implication, to the detriment of parliament and the courts. Assuming that states of emergency can be crucial moments for the development of entire countries and taking into consideration how frequently they are used, it is amazing how little we know about constitutional emergency provisions. Little is known about: (1) the amount of additional powers granted to governments acting under an SOE, (2) the trends in the evolution of emergency provisions over time, (3) the factors that cause societies to adopt them in the first place, and (4) their effects, that is, their effectiveness in reaching the goals stated in the underlying legislation. In this chapter, we focus exclusively on the first two questions. We discuss the third question in Chapter 3 and the fourth question throughout the book; Chapters 4 through 6 in particular are devoted to exploring the fourth question.

International studies analyzing the additional powers that emergency provisions grant to respective governments as well as the development of emergency provisions over time are extremely scarce. There is one important exception though: Loveman (1993) is a very thorough analysis of the genesis of the emergency constitutions of many Latin American countries in the nineteenth century. The existing international studies rather focus on their consequences.

Because of this gap in the literature, we describe the main components of emergency constitutions as well as how they have changed over time. To make the powers that emergency constitutions allocate to governments comparable over time and between countries, we develop an additive Index of Emergency Powers (INEP) that consists of six separate subindices, which we employ throughout the book. Quite often, legal scholars assert that emergency constitutions do not lend themselves to meaningful comparison. If this were true, questions dealing with the effectiveness of emergency constitutions would be almost impossible to answer. In this chapter, we therefore try to prove these scholars wrong by empirically exploring the general architecture of emergency constitutions. We use the indices that we develop in cluster analysis to see whether we can find a limited number of clusters or "families" of constitutions that share a number of traits.

Drawing on 351 constitutions (both current and defunct) for which we have sufficient information available and relying on thirty-one different variables capturing the most important features of emergency constitutions, we identify six such clusters and, hence, show that emergency constitutions often share many features. We find preliminary evidence that the consequences of emergency constitutions differ along the lines of these clusters.

The rest of this chapter is structured as follow. Section 2.2 names the main features of emergency constitutions and identifies time trends in their evolution. Section 2.3 briefly describes the main features of cluster analysis while Section 2.4 reports the results of the cluster analysis and a set of simple descriptive statistics. In Section 2.5, we apply a different approach to analyze emergency constitutions. There, the length in words of emergency constitutions is used to inquire whether longer emergency constitutions create additional restrictions on governments or inversely more additional powers under states of emergency. Section 2.6 concludes and spells out a number of follow-up questions that can be tackled with the INEP and the clusters proposed here.

2.2 Defining Constitutional Emergency Provisions

It is necessary first to define emergency provisions, and thus what an "emergency constitution" is. Our definition of an emergency constitution is that it is the set of formal legal provisions encoded in the constitution that specify who can declare an SOE, under which conditions an SOE can be declared, who needs to approve the declaration, and which actors have which special powers once it has been declared. What we refer to as the "emergency constitution" here and throughout the book is, hence, not a document separate from the ordinary constitution but those formal provisions of it that explicitly deal with emergencies. We therefore do not capture decrees promulgated by governments during an SOE, the conferral of emergency powers in statute, or any informal constitutional conventions or political traditions as they are not part of what we define here as a country's emergency constitution. Consequently, we consider the formal provisions written in the constitution to be the strict outline of a legal maximum of government actions that are constitutionally permitted.

As such, emergency constitutions are paradoxical documents: Their declared goal is to reestablish constitutional order by temporarily suspending it. They are also paradoxical in the sense that a constitution that includes emergency provisions spells out in these provisions the conditions under which its regular application may be suspended. As such, emergency constitutions deal with the delicate balance between suspending individual rights by temporarily reducing the separation of powers, while also typically providing monitoring mechanisms intended to reduce the likelihood of the SOE being misused by power-maximizing politicians.

There are large differences in the additional powers available to the executive during emergencies. Most emergency constitutions give the executive the right to derogate a number of basic rights, including the right to move freely, the right to assemble and to demonstrate or strike; they also give the executive the right to censor the press. They often give the police the right to search private homes without a warrant and allow the executive to use military forces in domestic settings.

But there is more to emergency constitutions. Quite a large number of emergency constitutions give the head of state the authority to issue decrees during an SOE. Such authority is given to heads of government only rarely, but this does occur as, for example, in the

Hungarian constitution. Other provisions deal with the military (the government can be granted, e.g. the authority to enlarge the standing army or to deploy soldiers domestically), public finance (many constitutions enable governments to levy forced loans or to collect taxes prior to their regular due date), measures to keep government in power (the 1995 constitution of Armenia, e.g. excluded the possibility of a vote of no confidence under an SOE), and many others.

2.3 Trends in Emergency Powers

In this section, we give a general overview of constitutional emergency provisions. We first look at their emergence and diffusion over time. We then deal with six central components of emergency provisions in detail.

2.3.1 On the Diffusion of Emergency Constitutions

Constitutional emergency provisions make little sense under absolute monarchy or totalitarian regimes. If the head of the executive is unconstrained, why should there be special provisions giving him (or her) powers he (or she) already enjoys? This is why the history of constitutional emergency provisions is closely linked with the advent of constitutional monarchy and with restricted government more generally.

France was the first modern nation state to introduce constitutional emergency provisions in 1795. Emergency constitutions have since spread to those countries whose legal development was heavily influenced by France. In 1808, Joseph Bonaparte became king of Spain and the corresponding constitution – named after the French city of Bayonne because it was negotiated there – included explicit emergency provisions similar to those of the French model. The provisions contained in the Bayonne constitution, as well as the 1812 Constitution of Cádiz, in turn served as a model for the first constitutions of many Latin American countries emerging out of the Spanish Empire. In fact, with the exception of Portugal (1826), all of the subsequent countries to create emergency constitutions in the following decades were Latin American. In chronological order, these were Argentina (1819), Chile (1822), Brazil (1824), the United Provinces of the Rio de la Plata (1824), Bolivia (1826), Peru (1826), Ecuador (1830), Uruguay (1830), and Venezuela (1830). Two observations are noteworthy: First, in all

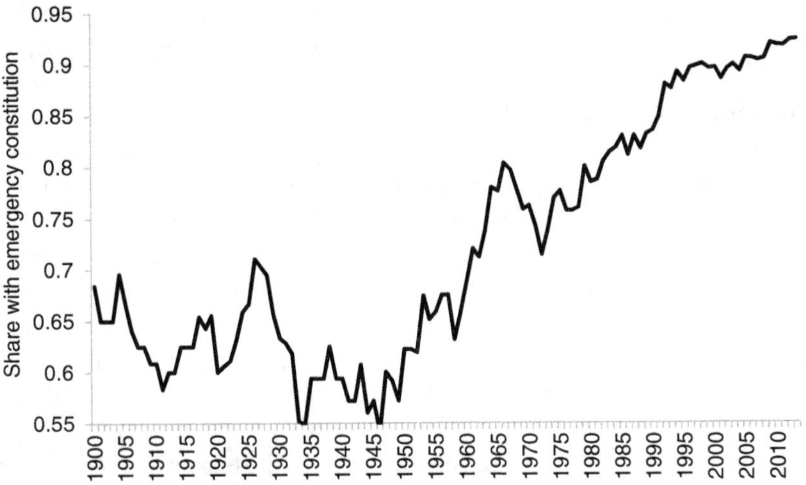

Figure 2.1 Share of constitutions with emergency provisions, 1900–2013

of the cases mentioned, the inclusion of emergency provisions in the constitution was part of an entirely new constitution and hence not part of constitutional amendment; second, all of these countries belong to the French legal family. By 1850, twenty countries had an emergency constitution; today, all of them are coded as "French legal origin."

But the spread of emergency constitutions did not stop in Latin America or countries of French legal origin. Using the extensive information contained in the Comparative Constitutions Project (CCP), we find that by 2013, 171 countries had in fact adopted emergency constitutions. The number of states also increased over this period. Expressed as a proportion, less than 60 percent of all sovereign states had an emergency constitution in 1850 whereas today, some 90 percent of all countries do. This development is clearly illustrated in Figure 2.1, where we plot the share of independent countries with an emergency constitution, starting in 1900. The figure shows relative stability before 1950. After 1950, two developments have clearly affected the share: the independence of former colonies, starting in the late 1950s; and the de facto independence of countries formerly part of or controlled by the Soviet Union.

The data show that once a country has included emergency provisions in its constitution, it is unlikely ever to get rid of them. According to the CCP, only seventeen countries have discarded constitutional emergency provisions. Most countries that did get rid of their emergency constitution – often as a consequence of abolishing the constitution altogether – introduced a new one after a short interval. The only exception is Austria, which abolished its 1934 emergency constitution and has not reintroduced another to date. In all other cases, the abolition was the consequence of a military or communist takeover that eventually resulted in the reintroduction of emergency provisions.

As described earlier, the first constitutional emergency provisions in the nineteenth century were all part of entirely new constitutions. Virtually all of today's emergency constitutions were already included in the last "new" constitution of a country. The 2002 amendment to the constitution of the Czech Republic is a notable exception in which emergency provisions were included later on. Hence, having an emergency constitution is now the rule rather than the exception. Yet as we outline next, there is considerable variation with regards to specific details and the scope of the provisions.

2.3.2 *Single Components of Emergency Provisions*

We suggest that every emergency constitution must, at least implicitly, deal with six different questions:

1. What are the necessary conditions for an SOE?
2. Who has the power to declare an SOE?
3. Who has the power to declare the end of an SOE?
4. Who has the power to monitor the legality of the means used during an SOE?
5. Who exercises emergency powers?
6. What (additional) competences does an SOE confer on the emergency government?

(1) Necessary Conditions

Concerning the first question, the preconditions necessary for an SOE to be declared, two trends are noteworthy. First, emergency constitutions have become broader in the enumeration of events that can justify the declaration of an SOE. We rely on the variable in the CCP that lists six possible preconditions for declaration (Elkins et al. 2009): (1) war/aggression, (2) internal security, (3) national disaster, (4) general danger, (5) economic emergency, and (6) threat to constitutional system. Any of these aspects might be found in a given proportion of

Table 2.1 ***Percent of all emergency constitutions that name the respective topic as a possible reason for declaring an SOE***

Topic	1950	2017
War/aggression	31.9	48.6
Internal security	31.9	38.8
National disaster	6.9	37.6
General danger	16.7	25.7
Economic emergency	5.6	7.7
Threat to constitutional system	0.0	4.1

constitutions, that is, the share of constitutions that include them can assume a value between 0 and 100 percent in any year. Adding up the resulting proportions for each of the six categories can, hence, yield a theoretical maximum of 600 (six categories of 100 percent). Although this is a crude measure, it does give an impression of how the preconditions for declaring an SOE evolved over time: For 1950, the actual sum was 97.14, whereas the same exercise for 2011 yields a sum of 167.53. This implies that the possible causes for declaring an SOE have been considerably broadened and the typical, modern emergency constitution mentions two such conditions.

Second, Table 2.1 shows that some preconditions have become more widely included than others. In 1950, 6.9 percent of all constitutions named any kind of "national disaster" as a potential justification for declaring an SOE; this proportion had grown to slightly above one third by 2017. "Economic emergencies," on the other hand, were explicitly mentioned in 5.6 percent of all constitutions with emergency provisions in 1950. By 2017, this proportion had increased to only 7.7 percent. The sixth precondition in the list given above, "threat to the constitutional system," did not exist in 1950, but by 2017 it was included in 4.1 percent of all constitutions with emergency provisions.

(2) Power to Declare

The second component of emergency constitutions deals with the question of who has the power to declare an SOE. No matter how precisely the necessary preconditions are defined, some actors need to decide whether the conditions mentioned in the constitution are present or not. On the one hand, one can imagine a constitution that allocates the power to declare an SOE to the head of the executive without any other political actor or authority needing to approve this decision. This would be equivalent to very few checks on executive power. On the other hand, an alternative scenario would be that more than one constitutional actor must be involved in the declaration and more than one actor must approve it. A third scenario, located somewhere between the two more extreme approaches just mentioned, could be that some other branch needs to be consulted; if its advice is not followed, this might increase the political costs of declaring an SOE in terms of reduced government legitimacy. Ideally, the necessary parliamentary majorities should also be taken into account.

Emergency constitutions typically reduce the degree of the separation of powers for a limited period of time. Yet regarding nonemergency periods, there has been a secular trend toward a stricter separation of powers. The variable CHECKS, which serves as a proxy for the degree of checks and balances and is part of the Database of Political Institutions (Beck et al. 2001), had a mean score of 1.7 in 1975 which had risen to 3.1 by 2020 (around a stable median of 2). Likewise, the mean score of a measure of political veto player power approximately doubled from 0.16 in 1950 to 0.33 in 2016, the latest year for which data are available. It seems possible then, that even emergency constitutions might place more checks on the government operating under an SOE than they used to, if they follow the general constitutional trend. In the following we document that, in fact, the opposite has in general happened.

Regarding the competence to declare an SOE, we observe two somewhat contradictory trends. In 1950, 59 percent of countries (22/37) with an emergency constitution gave the head of state the right to declare an SOE. By 2017, this proportion had increased to 81 percent (129/159) as most constitutions in the countries that achieved independence in the decolonization wave of the 1950s and 1960s gave declaration rights to the head of state. This indicates the overwhelming importance of a single person, namely the head of state. On the other hand, around ten percent (16/159) of all constitutions currently containing an emergency constitution allocate that competence to the entire cabinet. This does not represent an increase in the separation of powers between legislature and executive, but it is at least an increase in the number of actors involved in the decision. Keith (2012) goes one step further and asks whether the responsibility for declaring an SOE is given explicitly to the legislature. In 1979, the first year of her dataset, this was the case in 4.2 percent of all countries. By 2010, this proportion had increased to 10 percent. If legislatures declare an SOE and executives are in charge during emergencies, then this change denotes an increase in the separation of powers.

Another way to implement checks in emergency constitutions is to require the declaration of an SOE to be approved by an actor other than the one declaring it. In 1950, 44 percent of all emergency constitutions contained such a provision. By 2017 this proportion had increased to 56 percent, again indicating some increase in the level of checks. Today, the consent of the following organs is most frequently required: (1) the first (or only) chamber of the legislature (39 percent); (2) both chambers of the legislature (19 percent); and (3) the government/cabinet (14 percent). Approval provisions are important because SOEs have often been misused by self-serving politicians. In particular, some of them have simply dissolved the legislature to eliminate a watchdog. As of 2017, 15 percent of all emergency provisions explicitly excluded the possibility of dissolving the legislature during an SOE. In 1979, the respective number was only 3.9 percent. According to the CCP, no emergency constitution implemented before 1950 included an explicit ban on dissolving the legislature.

(3) Power to End

The third important component of emergency constitutions is the power to end an SOE. One possibility – famously used by the Romans – is to have it expire automatically (after six months in Republican Rome). Here, too, the separation of powers is central. Acknowledging that every SOE entails the danger of misuse and the possibility of descending into permanent autocracy, it seems reasonable to allocate the power to end an SOE to an actor other than the one endowed with the exercise of emergency powers. Ackerman (2004) proposes a "supermajoritarian escalator": the longer the SOE lasts, the more inclusive the parliamentary majority necessary to sustain it. In other words, over time, ever smaller factions of parliament can end the SOE.

Keith (2012) asks whether the SOE is constrained to a set time period and whether an extension is subject to legislative approval. In 1979, a little less than 19 percent of the 153 surveyed constitutions had such provisions; in 2017 the proportion had increased to 35.9 percent. At least de jure, many emergency constitutions thus try to sustain a high degree in their separation of powers by making extensions dependent on the consent of the legislature.

(4) Power to Monitor Legality of Means Used under an SOE

Fourth, regarding actors who could monitor the legality of the means used under SOEs, both the legislature and the judiciary seem natural candidates. Ferejohn and Pasquino (2004, 216ff.) identify a "legislative model" of emergency powers, which they distinguish from the (neo) Roman model. In the legislative model, the legislature "is expected to monitor the use of emergency powers, to investigate abuses, to extend these powers if necessary, and perhaps to suspend them if the emergency ends." They quote France as an example of a presidential system in which the legislature can impeach the president if it believes he has overstepped his powers (Art. 16 of the French Constitution). As an example of legislative monitoring under a parliamentary system, they mention independent commissions in the United Kingdom installed to monitor the executive in the way it implements anti-terror legislation.

Independent courts are a possible ex post monitoring device. The US Supreme Court decisions *ex parte* Milligan (1866) and Korematsu v United States (1944) are two (in)famous examples. Yet many scholars traditionally believe that speed is of the essence in emergency situations and that judicial review should be postponed. Contemporaneous scholars, such as Ackerman (2004) or Dyzenhaus (2006), point to the dismal record of the judiciary in constraining government action under SOEs. Unfortunately, we are not aware of any dataset that would allow us to identify any time trend regarding this aspect.

(5) Who Exercises Emergency Powers?

It seems natural to think of the head of the executive as the actor exercising emergency powers. Other provisions are, however, possible, such as, for example, the head of the military or technocrats. The French version of an SOE, the *état de siège*, implies an expansive delegation of powers to the military (Rossiter 2009, chapter VI gives an excellent account of that concept). Again, we are not aware of any dataset that would allow us to identify any change in this aspect over time.

(6) What Additional Competences Des the SOE Confer on the Emergency Government?

Finally, one must ask what competences are conferred on the emergency government. First, emergency governments frequently entail the competence to suspend a number of basic rights. The proportion of countries whose constitutions provide for the suspension of rights during an SOE has remained virtually unchanged: 70 percent (30/43) in 1950 and 69 percent (118/172) in 2017. The dataset compiled by Keith (2012) analyzes the same issue from the opposite angle: according to her, the proportion of countries that do give a list of nonderogable rights or include a statement that certain rights cannot be infringed changed from 5.2 percent in 1979 to almost 26 percent in 2010.

Beyond the suspension of rights, there is a vast heterogeneity in the competences conferred on emergency governments. Everything from "all powers necessary" to very detailed enumerations exists. Provisions frequently found include: (a) measures to keep all government organs broadly conceived in office (vote of no confidence impossible; all elections suspended; terms of constitutional court judges extended), (b) increasing the size of the army (including the use of national guards for military purposes), and (c) measures to keep the country solvent (introducing new taxes, levying payment of existing taxes in advance) but also more dubious measures such as exempting state servants from all legal liability of state acts committed under martial law or enabling forced labor. Of course, there are also constitutions that expressly limit the competence of governments under SOEs, for example, spelling out that no constitutional amendment can be passed under an SOE or that all decrees issued are only valid until the end of the SOE.

2.3.3 *Our Workhorse: An INEP*

In order to synthesize these different aspects into a single dimension, we develop a measure that can be thought of as capturing the difficulty – or political cost – of calling and maintaining an SOE as well as its potential benefits. The simplest way to create an Index of Emergency Powers (INEP) is to rely on variables that serve as proxies for the most important aspects just described and add them up. Using the extensive information available from the CCP, this is exactly what we do. In the following, we therefore employ information covering up to 351 current as well as defunct constitutions for which we have been able to obtain sufficient information. Although the CCP naturally covers many more constitutions, central information of specific features in many now defunct constitutions is simply missing, which limits our sample to 351 examples.

The INEP takes into account: (1) the degree to which the right to declare an SOE is concentrated in a single person – or very few people – or limited by multiple veto players; (2) the need to and the degree to which the right to approve or disapprove the declaration is concentrated; (3) how many different situations are explicitly mentioned in the constitution and can be used to justify the declaration of an SOE; (4) whether fundamental civil and political rights can be suspended during an SOE; (5) whether parliament can be dissolved during an SOE; and (6) whether the government can introduce censorship of the media and expropriate property during an SOE. The first three variables are, hence, concerned with the rules for declaring an SOE, whereas the last three are concerned with the powers that governments enjoy under an SOE. The first three can also be thought of as "the cost element" of declaring an SOE, while the last three cover "the benefits element" of running an SOE from the point of view of the incumbent government. In the cases where the constitution refers to different types and degrees of emergencies and thus allows government a political choice, we code the type that provides government with the most comprehensive power. Throughout the rest of the book, we therefore refer to the two halves of the index as the Cost INEP and the Benefit INEP.

In the INEP, higher codings imply more power to the executive. For the first three components (the cost part of the INEP), high codings imply relative ease in declaring an SOE. Framed differently: higher codings are equivalent to a lower degree in the separation of powers. For the last three components (that is, the benefit part of the INEP), higher codings imply more benefits and discretionary powers allocated to the sitting government. For all elements of the index, no limits on the respective aspect is coded 3, some as 2, uncertainty as 1, and tight limits as 0. As we scale each of the six separate components on a 0–1 scale and subsequently scale the entire INEP as well as the Cost and Benefit INEPs on the same 0–1 scale, a coding of 1 would imply that there are no effective limits to the powers of the executive during SOEs and a coding of 0 that limits are maximally tight. The entire INEP is an additive index of the six separate components, as the different parts all represent different mechanisms allowed by the emergency constitution through which governments and leading political actors can directly affect decisions during emergencies. As such, a given level of checks and balances can, for example, be achieved by either limiting declaration power, limiting approval power, or perhaps including a sunset clause or a substantial limit on the powers given to the executive during an SOE. In other words, there is no clear progression

Table 2.2 *Constructing the INEP*

Component	Additive coding based on:
Declaration power	2 if declaration rights rest with the head of government or the incumbent government; 1 if they are vaguely defined; 0 if they rest with the legislature or other (mainly courts)
Approval power	3 if emergencies need no approval; 2 if approval rights rest with the head of government or the incumbent government; 1 if they are vaguely defined; 0 if they rest with the legislature or other (mainly courts)
Conditions	3 if conditioned on "internal security" or "general danger"; 2 if they include "economic emergency" or "constitutional threat"; 1 if they include "other" or are vaguely defined; 0 if conditions are only "war" and "natural disasters"
Dissolution power	1 if parliament can be dissolved during emergencies; 0 otherwise
Rights suspension	3 if all rights can be suspended during emergencies; 2 if some can be suspended; 1 if the provisions are vague; 0 if no rights can be suspended
Censorship and expropriation	1 if censorship can either be introduced during emergencies or is constitutionally allowed; 2 if authorities can expropriate without due compensation during emergencies

across the six components, which would have necessitated a nonadditive construction of an INEP. As such, due to the lack of a fine-grained (and broadly accepted) theory that would inform us about the relative importance of each of those six components and their interplay, it seems straightforward to simply add the components up.

In Table 2.2, we summarize the construction of the six components of the INEP. The components capture: the power to declare an SOE and how concentrated it is; approval powers; conditions that are progressively more inclusive or vaguely defined; whether or not the legislature can be dissolved during emergencies; whether or not basic rights can be suspended during emergencies; and whether or not the constitution allows for censorship and expropriation of property. The INEP thus broadly consists of two main dimensions: (1) a cost dimension consisting of the first three components that outline the political costs and the difficulty of declaring an SOE; and (2) a benefit dimension that outlines the particular, discretionary powers that are allocated to the executive (or other government actors) during an SOE. These include the possibility of derogating basic rights, introducing censorship and expropriation without due compensation, and – for the executive – dissolving parliament.

Aggregating such issues into one index shows that emergency powers were quite limited in most constitutions for which we have information that were introduced before the Great Depression. A number of constitutions implemented in the 1930s, conversely, gave substantial powers to the executive, for instance those of Yugoslavia (1931, INEP = 0.50), Poland (1935, INEP = 0.53) and Brazil (1937, INEP = 0.55). During the post–World War II period, as we illustrate in Figure 2, one can also observe clear developments. Several newly independent countries, for example, introduced emergency constitutions with strongly limited discretionary rights, but rapidly increased those rights in amendments and new constitutions. Ghana's 1957 constitution, with an INEP of 0.14, did not leave any declaration rights with the executive alone and clearly delimited both approval rights and the conditions under which SOEs could be declared. Based on its 1969 constitution, Ghana's INEP score increased to 0.51. The new constitution allocated all declaration powers to the head of government, allowed quite a few conditions under which an SOE could be declared, and allowed basic rights to be suspended during SOEs. The evolution of Ghana's constitution is overall representative of the general development of former colonies as they became independent and implemented constitutions of their own.

While there was a slight tendency for emergency constitutions to be more delimiting during the late 1980s and 1990s, in more recent years a number of new constitutions give the executives substantial unchecked emergency powers. New constitutions in Kenya (2010, INEP = 0.55), Guinea (2010, INEP = 0.66) and Hungary (2011, INEP = 0.71) all leave significant discretionary power to the executive during broadly defined SOEs. In Figure 2.2, these developments can be clearly seen as an uptick. Although they seem to coincide with the time after the 9/11 attacks, it is unclear whether the attacks caused the uptick in the figure as it is driven by constitutional changes in countries not directly affected by terrorist threats. The world map in Figure 2.3 displayed here shows the differences in permissiveness (measured by the overall INEP) that the various emergency constitutions allow for.

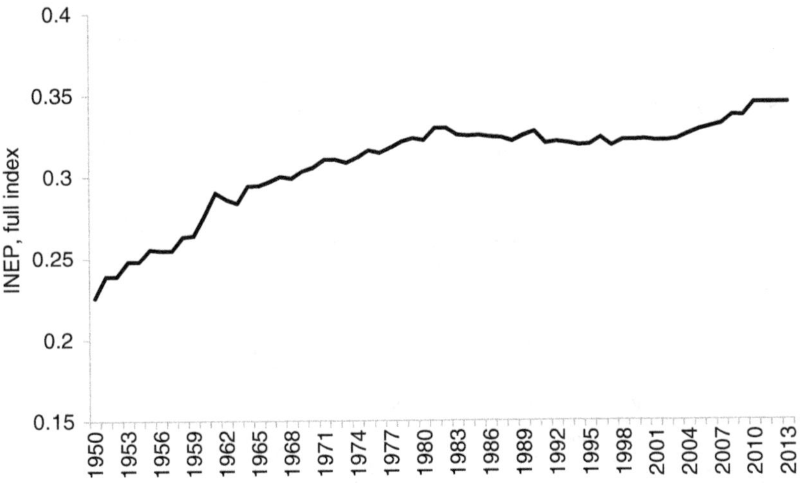

Figure 2.2 Average INEP, 1950–2013

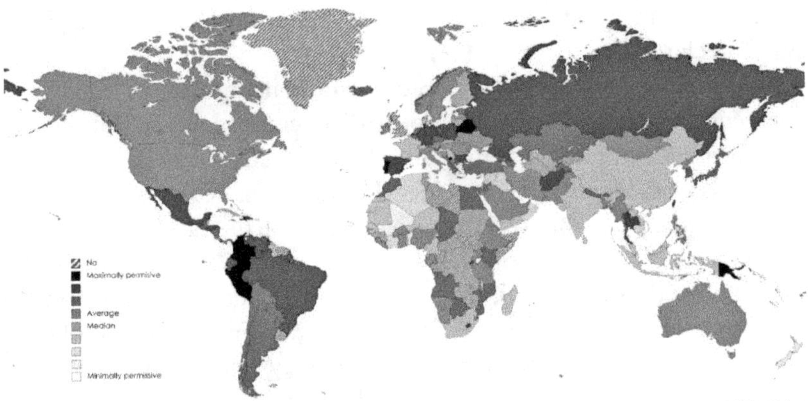

Figure 2.3 Map indicating permissiveness of emergency constitutions
Note: permissiveness is here measured as the overall INEP.

Separating the six components of the INEP, as we do in Figure 2.4, reveals that the main development in the early years after World War II is a concentration of declaration rights. Similarly, the figure shows that the new constitutions, implemented in former colonies between 1960 and the late 1970s, were also more likely to allow for the dissolution of the legislature. Conversely, constitutions implemented after the

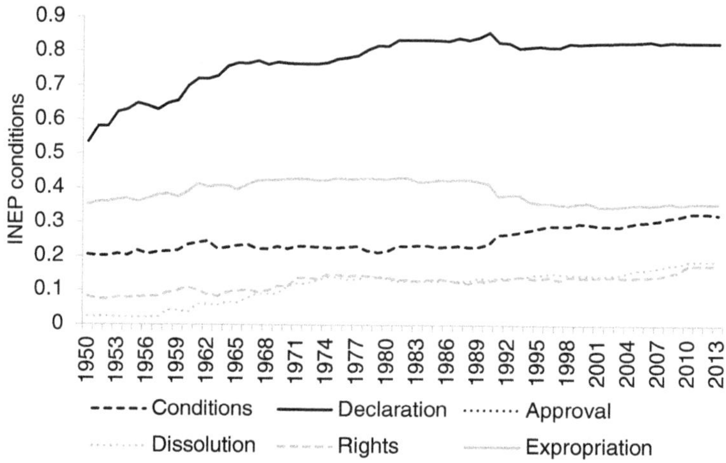

Figure 2.4 Six separate indices, INEP, 1950–2010

collapse of communism clearly tend to be less likely to allow expropriation and censorship but include more conditions under which an SOE can be declared.

Distinguishing between democracies and nondemocracies regarding emergency powers, one could expect democratic governments to be more constrained under emergencies than autocracies. If this expectation holds true, then the INEP values should be smaller for democracies than for autocracies. But this does not seem to be the case. Relying on a democracy indicator developed by Cheibub et al. (2010) and updated in Bjørnskov and Rode (2020), the average INEP value is 0.31 for democracies as well as for autocracies. The democracy indicator also allows for the separation of three types of democracy (parliamentary, presidential, and mixed) and three types of dictatorship (civil, military, and royal). In the data, only royal dictatorships in our sample have much stronger declaration rights – other autocracies do not – while presidential democracies tend to include more conditions under which an SOE can be declared. Historically mixed democracies, that is, democracies with mostly ceremonial presidents without actual powers, have been less prone to allow expropriation, censorship, and the suspension of rights. But in the contemporaneous emergency constitutions, all types of democracies now appear similar on average.

How would one make sense of the counterintuitive finding that democracies and autocracies are apparently quite similar? Three possible

Table 2.3 *Characteristics of emergency constitutions, regime types*

	Parliamentary	Democracy mixed	Presidential	Civilian	Autocracy military	Royal
Overall INEP	0.32	0.26	0.33	0.29	0.33	0.30
Declaration power	0.66	0.71	0.69	0.71	0.78	0.85
Approval power	0.21	0.18	0.19	0.21	0.23	0.17
Conditions	0.29	0.24	0.44	0.23	0.30	0.21
Dissolution power	0.18	0.13	0.08	0.09	0.09	0.03
Rights suspension	0.19	0.08	0.25	0.15	0.18	0.08
Exprop. and censorship	0.39	0.25	0.32	0.36	0.43	0.46

reasons come to mind: Firstly, it could be that autocrats are given more powers than governments of democratic countries to begin with. In case of extreme situations, there would then be less need to rely on emergency provisions. Previewing Chapter 3, this does not seem to be the case. Secondly, it could be that on paper both autocratic and democratic governments enjoy similar additional powers under an SOE but that, in reality, autocratic governments are simply able to overstep constitutional constraints without political repercussions. The question, therefore, centers on the degree to which emergency constitutions are being complied with by different types of government, a topic we will take up again in Chapter 11. Thirdly, it could be that some general standards of emergency constitutions have evolved over the last couple of decades. This seems to have happened to other parts of the constitution – no country today can do without an elaborate rights section. So it may also have happened with regard to emergency constitutions. We will look into this possibility in the next section, asking whether a limited number of "typical" emergency constitutions can be identified (Table 2.3).

Tracing the development of emergency constitutions over time, we thus find both general patterns and substantial differences across countries. Emergency constitutions have become more prevalent while the discretionary powers that they confer on the executive continue to vary.

2.4 Cluster Analysis

In the previous section, we mentioned that emergency constitutions first evolved in France and then spread across the countries belonging to the French legal family. Some scholars propose that the type of emergency constitution brought about within the French legal family is different from that brought about within the Common law legal family. The French approach is referred to as the state of siege (état de siège) whereas the British one would originate from martial law (e.g. Rossiter 2009, in particular chapter X). Two aspects in particular make them distinct from each other, namely: (1) the identity of the actor authorized to monitor the SOE, and (2) the degree of judicialization. Under a state of siege, monitoring would primarily fall to the legislature whereas it would fall on the judiciary, and more precisely the regular courts, under martial law. An important consequence of this difference is that monitoring by the legislature can take place during an SOE while monitoring by the courts will only take place after the SOE has been ended. Other than for the state of siege, martial law could be characterized by "the absence of statutory foresight for its initiation and use" (ibid., 141). This last trait makes the identification of martial law via the analysis of formal constitutions somewhat difficult. We now ask whether this dichotomy regarding types of emergency constitutions is reflected in the data, that is, whether there are clear "families" of emergency constitutions.

In order to assess whether one can identify families of emergency constitutions, we employ cluster analysis. To generate clusters, we rely on exactly the same variables used for creating the INEP. Cluster analysis is a set of methods that, at its most basic, aims at minimizing the distance in n-dimensional space between member observations within a cluster while maximizing the distance between clusters. In other words, cluster analysis is a way to identify families of observations that are as similar as possible while being distinctly different form other families.

As we do not have strong priors about the correct or merely reasonable number of clusters, we perform a set of analyses defining between two and ten clusters. Based on this set of analyses, we select what we believe to be the number of clusters that best fits the data. Our criteria are: that intra-cluster distances ought to be relatively small, that is, we require clusters to be fairly coherent; that distances between clusters ought to be comparatively large; and finally, that no single cluster has disproportionately high intra-cluster distances or large outlier members. This last criterion ensures that we do not obtain clusters that are "residual" clusters only containing observations that do not fit into any other cluster but also do not fit together in any meaningful way. We employ these criteria using graphs similar to standard screen plots in which the gain in identification can be easily observed. We outline later the details of these analyses before describing our preferred solution.

2.5 Are There Typical Emergency Constitutions?

We run the analysis on the basis of six clusters. Our criteria for choosing this number are described in detail in the appendix. Table 2.4 reports the full cluster membership of this solution for all 351 constitutions in the dataset.

Table 2.4 *Cluster memberships, preferred six-cluster solution*

Cluster	Members
1. Domestic security	Afghanistan (2004), Albania (1918, 1998), Angola (2010), Antigua and Barbuda (1981), Argentina (1853), Azerbaijan (1995), Barbados (1966), Belarus (1994), Bolivia (1938, 1947, 1961, 1967, 2009), Brazil (1967), Cambodia (1971), Chile (1833, 1980), Congo (1991, 2001), DR Congo (1964), Costa Rica (1917), Cyprus (1960), Ecuador (1869, 1897, 1946, 1967, 1978, 1984, 1998), Eritrea (1997), Estonia (1991), Ethiopia (1994), Ghana (1979, 1991), Guatemala (1945, 1965), Haiti (1889, 1950, 1964, 1983, 1987), Honduras (1965, 1981), Iran (1979), Kenya (2010), Kosovo (2008), Kyrgyzstan (2010), Liberia (1986), Lithuania (1921), Macedonia (1991), Madagascar (1991), Malawi (1994), Maldives (2008), Mexico (1857, 1917), Mongolia (1991), Mozambique (2004), Myanmar (2008), Namibia (1990), Nepal (1990), Nicaragua (1987), Niger (1960), Nigeria (1989, 1999), Panama (1971), Paraguay (1991), Peru (1979), Philippines (1973), Poland (1921, 1935, 1997), Portugal (1976), Samoa (1961), Saudi Arabia (1991), Seychelles (1993), Spain(1931), St. Kitts and Nevis (1983), St. Vincent and The Grenadines (1979), Swaziland (2005), Syria (1953), Tajikistan (1994), Thailand (1968, 1997, 2007), Turkey (1924, 1945, 1961, 1981), Uganda (1995), Uruguay (1918), Uzbekistan (1991), Vanuatu (1980), Venezuela (1999)

Table 2.4 (*cont.*)

Cluster	Members
2. Middle of the road	Afghanistan (1964), Albania (1915), Benin (1964), Bolivia (1851), Bulgaria (1991), Burundi (1981, 1991, 2005), Cameroon (1961), Central African Republic (1981, 2004), China (1913, 1954), Colombia (1886), Comoros (1978), Congo (1963), Cote D'Ivoire (2000), East Timor (2001), Egypt (1971), Estonia (1937), Ethiopia (1955, 1987), Fiji (1970, 1990, 1997), Finland (1999), France (1851), Gabon (1961, 1975), Gambia (1970), Greece (1951), Guatemala (1879), Guinea (1981), Haiti (1843, 1946), Kazakhstan (1995), Kenya (1963), Kiribati (1979), Kuwait (1961), Kyrgyzstan (1993), Latvia (1921), Lithuania (1918, 1938), Madagascar (1998), Maldives (1998), Mali (1974), Mauritania (1991), Mongolia (1960), Morocco (1961), Mozambique (1990), Myanmar (1974), Nauru (1968), Nepal (1948, 1959, 1961), Niger (1996, 1999), Pakistan (1961), Peru (1818), Philippines (1987), Poland (1951, 1991), Qatar (2003), Senegal (2001), Sierra Leone (1978), Solomon Islands (1978), Spain (1978), Togo (1963, 1991), Tuvalu (1986), Venezuela (1961), South Vietnam (1956), Zimbabwe (1979)
3. Serious on rights	Albania (1976), Andorra (1993), Bolivia (1816), Bulgaria (1947, 1971), Burkina Faso (1960), Burundi (1974), Central African Republic (1994), Chad (1961), Denmark (1953), Dominican Republic (1947), Equatorial Guinea (1981), Germany (1871), Ghana (1957), Guinea (1990), Honduras (1936), Japan (1889), Jordan (1946), Laos (1991), Madagascar (1975), Mali (1991), Mauritania (1961), Moldova (1994), Mozambique (1975), Nicaragua (1905, 1948, 1950, 1974), Niger (1991), Peru (1867), Somalia (1979), South Africa (1961, 1983), Syria (1950, 1973), Thailand (1949), Togo (1979), Trinidad and Tobago (1961), United States of America (1789), Venezuela (1904, 1947,1953), Vietnam (1980, 1991), Yugoslavia (1953)
4. Current design	Afghanistan (1977, 1990), Albania (1924), Bahamas (1973), Bahrain (2001), Benin (1990), Botswana (1966), Cambodia (1989), Chile (1811), China (1981), Congo (1979), DR Congo (2003), Costa Rica (1949), Djibouti (1991), Egypt (1923, 2011), Equatorial Guinea (1991), Estonia (1920),

Table 2.4 (*cont.*)

Cluster	Members
	Fiji (2013), Gambia (1996), Guinea (2010), Guyana (1970), Indonesia (1945), Iraq (2005), Jordan (1951), Kyrgyzstan (2007), Lesotho (1966), Libya (1951), Malawi (1964), Poland (1947), Russia (1993), Rwanda (1961), Senegal (1960, 1963), Seychelles (1979), Soviet Union (1977), Sri Lanka (1978), Sudan (1973, 1998), Surinam (1987), Thailand (1974), Uganda (1967), Ukraine (1996), North Vietnam (1960), Arab Republic of Yemen (1970), Zambia (1964, 1973, 1991), Zimbabwe (1969, 2013)
5. Strong legislature	Argentina (1819, 1826), Austria (1934), Brazil (1891, 1946), Chile (1925), Costa Rica (1869), Cuba (1935, 1940), Dominican Republic (1896, 1908, 1914, 1917, 1955, 1961a, 1961b, 1963, 1966, 1994, 2001), El Salvador (1886, 1939, 1950, 1983), France (1946), West Germany (1949), Haiti (1807), Honduras (1880, 1904, 1914, 1957), Hungary (2011), Lithuania (1991), Montenegro (2007), Nicaragua (1893, 1911), Nigeria (1960, 1963), Panama (1904, 1946), Paraguay (1870), Peru (1860, 1910), Portugal (1933), Serbia and Montenegro (2003, 2006), Sierra Leone (1961), South Africa (1993, 1996), Venezuela (1874, 1881, 1891), Yugoslavia (1921)
6. Rights suspenders	Armenia (1995), Belize (1981); Bhutan (2008), Bolivia (1878, 1880), Brazil (1937), Burkina Faso (1991), Cameroon (1971), Central African Republic (1964, 1976), Chad (1960, 1996), Comoros (1996), DR Congo (1978, 2005), Cuba (1959), Ecuador (1884, 1906, 1993, 1996, 2008), France (1848, 1958), Ghana (1969), Jamaica (1961), Lesotho (1993), Mauritania (1978), Morocco (1970, 2011), Niger (1989), Oman (1996), Paraguay (1940), Rwanda (2003), Sri Lanka (1971), Yugoslavia (1931, 1974)

2.5.1 The Cluster Solution

Although cluster analysis can at times yield solutions that are difficult to interpret, the present six-cluster solution in the table indicates that the clusters are all defined by traits common to their specific member constitutions. Cluster 1 thus appears to be defined by a concern for domestic security, cluster 3 by having particularly well-defined rights protections, while cluster 4 contains many relatively recent constitutions and thus represents what may be termed a current consensus on constitutional design. Cluster 2, on the other hand, is characterized by emergency constitutions that on most counts represent an average constitutional design. Finally, the average within-country distances indicate that clusters 5 and 6 may be less clearly defined than the first four clusters (based on information contained in Table 2.4). We nevertheless find that constitutions allocated to clusters 5 and 6 share particular identifiable features.

Overall, it turns out that most of the differences in the various types of emergency constitutions can be traced back to four variables: (1) legislative declaration, that is, the role of the legislature in declaring an SOE; (2) the specific approval powers; (3) the specific conditions that allow declaration of an SOE; and (4) which rights, if any, can be suspended during emergencies. We therefore interpret these final clusters as defined by having strong legislatures and easy rights suspension, respectively. We proceed with a number of noteworthy observations summarized in Table 2.5.

Let us begin with those constitutions not grouped in any of the six clusters because they do not have emergency constitutions. We identify fifty-eight such constitutions from twenty-one countries. On average, these constitutions are older, shorter, and less likely to belong to a civil law country. Of the twelve constitutions without emergency provisions that remain in use today, five belong to systems coded as democratic according to Bjørnskov and Rode (2020). These democracies are in no way clearly different from democracies in which the constitutions include emergency provisions. The second noteworthy observation is that the mean INEP for clusters 1, 2, and 4 is fairly similar at around 0.35 whereas it is substantially lower in clusters 3 and 5 (around 0.25) and much larger in cluster 6 at 0.49. However, as is evident in Table 2.6, the regular constitutions in countries in cluster 6 also have the strongest veto player institutions, as measured by Henisz's (2012) PolConIII index. As such, regardless of the mix of characteristics, cluster 6 seems to be characterized by a substantially larger difference between the separation of powers in ordinary versus emergency times than other clusters.

We also note that constitutions in cluster 1 are, in general, substantially longer and thus more detailed than in other clusters whereas constitutions in cluster 3 are shorter. Conversely, comparing legal

Table 2.5 *Cluster characteristics*

	1	2	3	4	5	6
	Domestic security	Middle of the road	Serious on rights	Current design	Strong legislature	Easy rights suspenders
Centroid	Guatemala 1945	Congo 1963	Bulgaria 1947	Zimbabwe 1969	Paraguay 1870	Ecuador 1906
Av. distance	2.81	2.37	2.31	2.11	3.19	3.49
Members	94	73	45	50	53	36
INEP	0.36	0.33	0.26	0.34	0.23	0.49
Declaration power	0.94	0.92	0.64	0.95	0.07 Legislative declaration	0.94
Approval power	0.13 Legislative approval	0.29	0.24 Vague approval prov.	0.21	0.38	0.29 Other approval
Conditions	0.50 Internal security	0.23 Nat. disasters not mentioned	0.15 War, nat. disasters not mentioned	0.13 Vague conditions	0.39	0.39
Dissolution power	0.07	0.08	0.04	0.20	0.06	0.31
Rights suspension	0.21 Rights suspension	0.07	0.06	0.12	0.23 Rights suspension	0.56 Some rights suspension

Table 2.5 (*cont.*)

	1	2	3	4	5	6
	Domestic security	Middle of the road	Serious on rights	Current design	Strong legislature	Easy rights suspenders
Expropriation and censorship	0.32	0.40 Censorship	0.40 Censorship	0.44	0.27	0.44 Censorship
Age	45	51	62	42	84	48
Length	18,706	13,138	8,727	15,800	13,466	15,226
Legal origin	83% civil	79% civil	67% civil	60% civil	91% civil	81% civil
Democracy	37%	25%	20%	14%	38%	33%
PolConIII	0.10	0.098	0.063	0.065	0.12	0.19
GDP at birth	2905	2565	2062	2443	2361	2268
Still in use	18	6	6	22	8	13
Post-cold war	39%	29%	18%	34%	17%	36%

Table 2.6 ***Determinants of cluster placement, constitutional characteristics***

Cluster	2	3	4	5	6
Declaration power	−0.506	−2.682***	0.402	−7.835***	−0.156
	(0.796)	(0.789)	(0.992)	(1.159)	(0.979)
Approval power	2.329***	2.156**	1.329	5.632***	2.515***
	(0.745)	(0.912)	(0.880)	(1.326)	(0.853)
Conditions	−6.874***	−10.903***	−12.848***	0.528	−2.999***
	(1.169)	(1.716)	(1.774)	(1.682)	(1.131)
Dissolution power	−0.427	−1.668*	0.508	−1.366	0.929
	(0.655)	(0.993)	(0.666)	(1.019)	(0.643)
Rights suspension	2.958***	−4.279***	−1.099	−2.547	3.267***
	(1.058)	(1.545)	(1.045)	(1.617)	(.745)
Expropriation and censorship	1.633*	2.292**	2.697**	2.234*	1.964*
	(0.863)	(1.115)	(1.118)	(1.263)	(1.085)
Observations	351				
LR Chi squared	490.76				
Pseudo R squared	0.402				

origins and national income per inhabitant (PPP-adjusted GDP) at the time when the constitution was introduced, we find no discernible differences in legal origins or GDP, while constitutions in cluster 3 tend to be older and very few constitutions in cluster 4 were written when the country was democratic. This is a rather unexpected finding given the history of emergency powers described in Section 2.2.

Table 2.6 depicts the particular mix of powers in an alternative way by being based on a multinomial logistic regression. In the table, clusters 2 to 6 are compared with cluster 1, which forms the baseline. Emergency provisions grouped in both clusters 3 and 5 make the declaration of an SOE relatively difficult. Regarding approval powers, all depicted clusters – except cluster 4 – show highly significant positive coefficients, implying that clusters 1 and 4 are characterized by weaker approval powers than the rest, although it is also clear that cluster 1 is characterized by having legislative approval while approval in cluster

6 is left to "other," meaning nonpolitical actors. Regarding the possibility of suspending basic rights, this is strongly circumscribed in cluster 3 and broadly allowed in constitutions in clusters 2 and 6. Finally, clusters 3, 4, and 6 are characterized by allowing censorship and expropriation without ordinary compensation during emergencies.

In this way, a simple cluster analysis reveals that a limited number of "typical" emergency constitutions can be identified. As such, although we do not want to overstate the degree of familiarity within each cluster, the standard claim that each emergency constitution is a unique document that does not lend itself to easy comparison seems at least questionable. To sum up, we observe that emergency constitutions can be separated into six clusters with relative precision. These clusters differ not only in the make-up of the emergency provisions and the specific degree of powers given to the executive, but also in their likelihood of declaring an SOE if an actual emergency arises. It is on this background that we now turn to our theoretical considerations and an intuitive test of whether the distribution of countries within the cluster families is stable over time.

2.5.2 *How Stable Are Countries' Cluster Assignments?*

As a final element in describing the six types of emergency constitution, we provide information on how stable a country's placement in a particular cluster (or constitutional family) is. This exercise requires that we can observe constitutional changes in the emergency provisions within countries. The data include 284 constitutions from eighty-one countries on which we have sufficient information.

The data show, first of all, that eight countries represented by more than one emergency constitution in the data have not changed clusters and therefore constitutional families: El Salvador (4 emergency constitutions), Fiji (3), Gabon (2), Mexico (2), Russia and the Soviet Union (2), Sudan (2), Turkey (4), and Zambia (3). Their constitutional choices of emergency provisions have remained quite consistent over the years due to either political tradition, geographical circumstance, or mere coincidence. In many cases, this is entirely predictable as the emergency constitution remains unchanged even though parts of the rest of the constitution have been substantially rewritten. Emergency constitutions within new constitutions can therefore at times contain language and remnants of political preferences from more than a century of constitution making.

Conversely, of the fifty-three countries with at least three constitutions in the dataset, twenty-three had emergency constitutions represented in three different families. Moreover, Albania, Bolivia, Niger, Peru, and Venezuela have all had emergency constitutions belonging to four different families.

However, many of these constitutional changes occur between families that are not particularly different. We therefore further note that comparing the Euclidean distance between cluster centroids, the largest relative changes occur between clusters 1 and 3, and clusters 4 and 5. Conversely, clusters 1 and 2, and clusters 2 and 6 are more similar than other cluster pairs. One should therefore not overestimate the importance of emergency constitutions changing constitutional types.

The countries with the relatively largest changes are: Albania in clusters 1 (1918 and 1998) and cluster 3 (1976), Bolivia in clusters 3 (1816) and cluster 1 (all twentieth-century constitutions); Chile in clusters 4 (1811) and 5 (1925); Costa Rica in clusters 4 (1949) and 5 (1869); Ghana in clusters 3 (1957) and 1 (subsequent constitutions); Honduras in clusters 3 (1936) and 1 (1965 and 1981); Madagascar in clusters 3 (1975) and 1 (1991); and Mozambique in clusters 1 (2004) and 3 (1975); Nicaragua, whose 1987 constitution in cluster 1 was also substantially different from its other emergency constitutions (all in cluster 3); Niger in clusters 1 (1960) and 3 (1991); Peru in clusters 3 (1867) and 1 (1979); Thailand whose 1949 constitution in cluster 3 was substantially different from its subsequent emergency constitutions; and Venezuela in which Hugo Chavez's 1999 socialist constitution in cluster 1 had very different emergency provisions than previous constitutions (all in cluster 3).

We do not want to delve deeper into the reasons for these changes except to note two regularities. First, in the cases of the 1991 Bulgarian and the 2003 Serbian emergency constitutions, it is evident that they both represented a return to the constitutional family that their constitutions prior to communism had belonged to. The second regularity is that Latin American countries are substantially more likely to have experienced larger changes to their emergency constitutions. While these countries have also had the most constitutional changes, 47 of the 100 emergency constitutions in the 20 Latin American countries with recorded changes have occurred in countries that have changed constitutional family. 11 of the 20 countries have even had constitutions in at least three clusters, thereby confirming the usual assertion that Latin America for some reason is less institutionally stable than the rest of the world.

To summarize, identifying a limited number of "typical" emergency constitutions seems realistically possible via cluster analysis. Generally, the content of many constitutions changes only marginally even after regime changes (Elkins et al. 2009). This is different with regard to emergency constitutions. Here, shifts between clusters are not at all uncommon.

2.6 Conclusions and Outlook of the Chapter

Given that nine out of ten constitutions contain emergency provisions, it is amazing how little we know about them. This chapter is foundational for the rest of the book in trying to reduce our ignorance by doing two things. First, it documents the development of an Index of Emergency Powers (INEP) that measures the degree of discretionary power constitutionally allocated to the executive during emergencies. We have already mentioned that the overall degree in the separation of powers outlined by constitutions has increased over recent decades. Relying on the INEP, we find that this is emphatically not true for emergency constitutions. On the contrary, we observe a clear long-run trend to allocate more, rather than fewer, powers to the executive during times of emergency. Our data suggest that this trend has been a consequence of the relatively weak separation of powers in the constitutions of newly independent countries since the late 1950s, and the particular features of constitutions in the countries that became de facto independent after the collapse of the communist bloc in the early 1990s.

Second, this chapter deals with the frequently read presumption that emergency constitutions are unique and do not lend themselves to meaningful comparisons with other emergency constitutions. Drawing on 31 different variables and employing cluster analysis, we are able to identify six clusters in which we group 351 different constitutions for which we have sufficient information. These clusters each define what can be thought of as a "family" of emergency constitutions that are sufficiently similar to be characterized by very comparable constitutional traits. The main features that separate these families of emergency constitutions from each other are: choices regarding the role of the legislature in declaring an SOE; the specific approval powers; the constitutional conditions that allow an SOE to be declared; and which basic individual rights, if any, can be suspended during an SOE.

Our main interest in this chapter is to pave the way for the rest of the book – and hopefully for future research – by making emergency constitutions empirically comparable. The indicator of emergency powers (the INEP) introduced here is used in subsequent chapters to deal with a number of highly topical follow-up questions. Firstly, what are the factors that determine what kind of emergency constitution a country adopts, given that it adopts one? Is being prone to natural disasters as prominent a factor as one might expect or are other, less salient ones, even more important? This question is taken up in Chapter 3.

Secondly, having an emergency constitution does not imply its use. Can one show that where emergency constitutions make it easy to declare an SOE, governments will tend to do so more frequently? And that emergency constitutions granting more additional powers to the executive are an incentive to make use of those powers more frequently? What about the use of SOEs in countries without explicit emergency provisions or the systematic nonuse of emergency constitutions in countries that have them? Some of these questions are taken up in Chapter 4.

Thirdly, what are the effects of emergency constitutions? Given that we have identified six different components of emergency powers, can one identify one as particularly apt in reestablishing the status quo ante? Or as apt in minimizing the number of dead when a natural disaster occurs? Or as inadequate in reestablishing ex ante levels of civil rights? How do countries without an explicit emergency constitution fare in comparison? Chapters 5 and 13 deal with these questions.

Fourthly, emergency constitutions are but one tool that can serve the interests of power-maximizing politicians. Other tools include, but are not restricted to, the frequent use of executive decrees, the creation of special courts, and use of the military. It appears worthwhile to look at the relationship between these tools on both the institutional and behavioral levels. Reliance on executive decrees as a substitute for SOEs will be dealt with Chapter 12.

Finally, it is generally accepted that, in many countries, constitutional text diverges widely from constitutional reality. It is, therefore, unlikely that politicians always stick meticulously to the constraints laid down in the respective emergency provisions and it would be interesting to analyze more systematically differences between the de jure and the de facto emergency constitution. Such an analysis would begin by analyzing to what degree the de jure provisions have been implemented in practice. Chapter 11 will shed some light on the conditions under which politicians are unlikely to stick to the constraints spelt out in the respective emergency constitution.

Generally valid answers to all these questions must rely on some form of comparable operationalization of the features of emergency constitutions. This is why this chapter has laid the groundwork for much of the analysis to be developed in the rest of this book.

Appendix

Data Description

Table A2.1 *Variables and sources*

Type of explanation	Variables	Source
Regime types	Parliamentary, mixed, presidential, civil autocracy, military autocracy, royal autocracy, democracy, monarchy, Post-Cold War	Cheibub et al. (2010)*, CIA (2014)
	PolConIII, no constraints	Henisz (2012)
	Log GDP per capita	
Frequency of disasters	Low elevation, log latitude, coastline, volcano area	CIA (2020)
	Log coups (10 yrs)	*
Legal history	Common law, civil law, Islamic law, communist law	CIA (2020)
Composition of constitutional assembly	Constituent assembly, legislative decision, executive decision, constituent legislature, length, age, still in use	Ginsburg et al. (2009)
Economic factors	Log GDP per capita, log population size	Heston et al. (2012), Maddison (2008)

Note: * refers to the recent update and expansion by Bjørnskov and Rode (2020) of the database developed by Cheibub et al. These data are available on request from the authors.

Table A2.2 ***Descriptive statistics, data used in Tables 4a, b, and 8a, b***

Variable	Mean	Standard deviation	Observations
INEP	0.307	0.138	411
Declaration power	0.729	0.392	411
Approval power	0.206	0.279	411
Conditions	0.272	0.245	411
Dissolution power	0.095	0.293	411
Rights suspension	0.162	0.255	411
Expropriation and censorship	0.377	0.232	411
Mixed	0.058	0.235	411
Presidential	0.088	0.283	411
Civil auto.	0.421	0.494	411
Military auto.	0.226	0.419	411
Royal auto.	0.083	0.276	411
Monarchy	0.165	0.372	411
PolConIII	0.097	0.257	402
No constraints	0.766	0.604	402
Log GDP per capita	7.356	0.846	372
Log population size	8.459	1.710	402
Post–Cold War	0.260	0.439	411
Log coups (10 yrs)	0.423	0.552	386
Common law	0.118	0.322	407
Civil law	0.747	0.435	407
Islamic law	0.027	0.162	407
Communist law	0.074	0.262	407
Age	59.871	46.609	411
Low elevation	0.791	0.407	411
Log latitude	2.798	0.960	411
Coastline	0.162	0.986	409
Volcano area	0.299	0.458	411
Constituent assembly	0.165	0.372	411
Legislative decision	0.253	0.435	411
Executive decision	0.391	0.489	411
Constituent legislature	0.044	0.205	411
Length	13,485	12,115	409
Democracy	0.270	0.445	411
Still in use	0.314	0.465	411

Table A2.3 *Descriptive statistics, data used in Tables 6–7*

Variable	Mean	Standard deviation	Observations
Introduction of EC	0.106	0.307	2084
Reintroduction	0.042	0.200	2085
First constitution	0.039	0.193	2085
Mixed	0.108	0.309	2044
Presidential	0.143	0.350	2044
Civil auto.	0.321	0.467	2044
Military auto.	0.129	0.335	2044
Royal auto.	0.042	0.201	2044
No constraints	0.401	0.490	2001
Log GDP per capita	8.430	1.304	1935
Log population size	8.957	1.827	2085
Postcommunist	0.058	0.252	2085
Common law	0.284	0.451	2084
Civil law	0.538	0.499	2084
Islamic law	0.012	0.111	2084
Communist law	0.103	0.304	2084

Table A2.4 *Variable definitions*

Variable	Description
INEP	Defined in text
Declaration power	Defined in text
Approval power	Defined in text
Conditions	Defined in text
Dissolution power	Defined in text
Rights suspension	Defined in text
Expropriation and censorship	Defined in text
Mixed	Democracy with weak / ceremonial president
Presidential	Presidential democracy
Civil auto.	Civilian autocracy, defined as a having a government leader without a military rank
Military auto.	Military dictatorship, defined as a having a government leader with a military rank
Royal auto.	Absolutist monarchy

Table A2.4 *(cont.)*

Variable	Description
Monarchy	Monarchy, including constitutional monarchies
PolConIII	Measure of veto player strength, defined 0–1
No constraints	Dummy for situations with no veto players
Log GDP per capita	Purchasing-power adjusted GDP per capita in logarithms
Log population size	Logarithm to population size
Post-Cold War	Dummy for the period after 1990
Log coups (10 yrs)	Logarithm to the number of coups the preceding ten years
Common law	Common law legal origins
Civil law	Civil law legal origins
Islamic law	Islamic law
Communist law	Communist law, that is communist regimes
Age	Age of the present constitution
Low elevation	Height above sea level of the lowest point in the country
Log latitude	Logarithm to latitude of country capital
Coastline	Length of coastline relative to country area
Volcano area	Dummy for countries in volcano areas
Constituent assembly	Constitution created by constituent assembly
Legislative decision	Constitution created legislative decision
Executive decision	Constitution created executive decision
Constituent legislature	Constitution created constituent legislature
Length	Length of constitution in English translation
Democracy	Dummy for democracy of any kind
Still in use	Dummy if the constitution is still in use

Choosing the Number of Constitutional Clusters

In Table A2.5, we outline some pertinent features of each of the first nine cluster solutions we obtain. The results, for example, show that the two clusters in a two-cluster solution have intra-cluster distances of 3.05 and 3.33 (in 31-dimensional space), respectively. The average distance is therefore 3.19 with the largest outlier being the 2007 Montenegrin constitution, which was 8 points from its cluster centroid (the central or most typical constitution in a cluster).

Following the results in the table towards the right, it is easy to see that the intra-cluster distance across the solutions decreases until the six-cluster solution, to the right of which it increases again. The minimum distance – indicating the coherence of a cluster – also decreases until the six-cluster solution. Likewise, the largest outlier in the six-cluster solution, that is, the constitution placed the furthest away from other cluster members in 31-dimensional space, is relatively small. Moving beyond a solution with six clusters entails a deterioration in at least one of our goodness of fit measures and in particular leaves larger outliers and, in all cases, at least one comparatively poorly defined cluster, as captured by the average distance. In all cases, we find that three particular constitutions fit any family of constitutions poorly: emergency provisions of the present constitutions of Germany (the 1949 constitution as amended in 1968), Hungary, and Montenegro are structurally different from most other emergency constitutions. The overall intra-cluster coherence on the basis of six clusters is also fairly good in comparison to alternative cluster numbers. This is a final reason for choosing six clusters. Based on the proposed criteria, a solution with six clusters best fits the present data.[1]

[1] Countries without emergency constitutions are left out of this assignment.

Table A2.5 *Cluster solution specifics*

	Average intra-cluster distance							
No. of clusters	2	3	4	5	6	7	8	9
Cluster 1	3.05	2.92	3.31	3.05	2.81	2.22	2.09	2.58
Cluster 2	3.33	3.11	2.88	2.88	2.37	2.53	2.74	1.89
Cluster 3		3.18	2.69	2.24	2.31	3.27	2.29	2.69
Cluster 4			2.92	2.92	2.11	2.39	2.62	2.65
Cluster 5				2.97	3.19	3.44	2.22	2.95
Cluster 6					3.49	2.25	3.46	4.91
Cluster 7						3.09	2.44	2.11
Cluster 8							3.05	2.43
Cluster 9								3.56
	'Goodness of fit' measures							
Av. distance	3.19	3.07	2.96	2.81	2.72	2.74	2.61	2.83
Min. distance	3.05	2.92	2.69	2.24	2.11	2.22	2.09	1.89
Max distance	3.33	3.18	3.31	3.06	3.49	3.44	3.46	4.91
Largest outlier	8.012 Montenegro (2007)	8.34 Germany (1949)	7.72 Hungary (2011)	7.35 Germany (1949)	7.13 Germany (1949)	7.25 Germany (1949)	7.54 Hungary (2011)	7.36 Montenegro (2007)

Note: average, minimum, and maximum distances reported in the lower panel are inter-cluster distances. The largest outlier is the distance of the given country to the centroid of the cluster in which it is placed.

Table A2.5a *Countries with more than one nonbenevolent emergency provision in 2010*

Country	Emergency provision	Country	Emergency provision
Samoa	Int. security, general danger, ec. emergency	Bolivia	Int. security, general danger
Chad	Int. security, const. threat, nonconst. law	Tajikistan	Int. security, general danger
Cuba	Int. security, general danger, ec. emergency	Chile	Int. security, general danger
Bangladesh	Int. security, general danger, ec. emergency	El Salvador	Int. security, general danger
Uganda	Int. security, general danger, ec. emergency	Guatemala	Int. security, general danger
Ecuador	Int. security, general danger, const. threat	Honduras	Int. security, general danger
Venezuela	Int. security, general danger, ec. emergency	Kenya	Int. security, general danger
Bhutan	Int. security, general danger, const. threat	Korea, Rep.	Int. security, general danger
Thailand	Int. security, general danger, ec. emergency	Mexico	Int. security, general danger
Turkey	Int. security, general danger, const. threat	Peru	Int. security, general danger
Qatar	General danger, nonconst. law	France	Int. security, general danger
Congo, Rep.	Int. security, general danger	Portugal	Int. security, general danger
Tanzania	Int. security, general danger	Lithuania	General danger, const. threat
Cameroon	General danger, const. threat	Taiwan	General danger, const. threat
Eritrea	Int. security, general danger	Albania	Int. security, general danger
Montenegro	General danger, const. threat	Dominican Rep.	Int. security, general danger
Namibia	Int. security, general danger	Estonia	Int. security, general danger
Seychelles	Int. security, general danger	Malta	General danger, const. threat
South Africa	Int. security, general danger	Nepal	Int. security, ec. emergency

Table A2.5b ***Countries with one nonbenevolent emergency provision in 2010***

Country	Emergency provision	Country	Emergency provision
Jordan	General danger	Sierra Leone	General danger
Kuwait	Nonconst. law	Uruguay	Int. security
Oman	Nonconst. law	Armenia	Const. threat
Morocco	Int. security	Finland	Nonconst. law
Swaziland	General danger	Kyrgyzstan	General danger
Cen. African Rep.	Int. security	Mali	Nonconst. law
Egypt	Nonconst. law	Mongolia	Int. security
Libya	Int. security	Poland	Int. security
Mauritania	Int. security	Senegal	Nonconst. law
Syria	Nonconst. law	Serbia	General danger
Yemen	Int. security	Antigua	General danger
Afghanistan	Int. security	Barbados	General danger
Angola	Int. security	Greece	Int. security
Azerbaijan	Int. security	Jamaica	General danger
Belarus	Int. security	Latvia	Int. security
Cambodia	General danger	Netherlands	Int. security
Congo, Dem. Rep.	Const. threat	Pakistan	Int. security
Ethiopia	Int. security	Slovenia	General danger
Haiti	Int. security	Spain	Nonconst. law
Mozambique	Const. threat	St. Kitts	General danger
Togo	Nonconst. law	St. Lucia	Int. security
Burundi	Int. security	St. Vincent	General danger
Comoros	Const. threat	Trinidad	General danger
Costa Rica	General danger	Vanuatu	Int. security
Cyprus	General danger	Bosnia	*Uncertain status*
Ghana	General danger	Somalia	*Uncertain status*
Indonesia	Nonconst. law	United States	*Uncertain status*
Liberia	Int. security	Iceland	*Uncertain status*
Micronesia	Int. security	Ireland	*Uncertain status*
Palau	Int. security	Australia	*Uncertain status*
Panama	Int. security	Canada	*Uncertain status*
Paraguay	Int. security	Japan	*Uncertain status*
Philippines	Int. security	Marshall Islands	*Uncertain status*

3 *The Determinants of Emergency Constitutions*

3.1 Introduction

In the last chapter, we introduced the Index of Emergency Powers (INEP) which allows us to compare emergency constitutions across countries and over time. There, we used it to take stock of various types of emergency constitution. Emergency constitutions, however, do not appear from nowhere but are deliberately introduced and phrased by constitution writers. In this chapter, we inquire into the factors behind the introduction of constitutionalized emergency provisions. We do so in two steps: We first ask what factors lead to the explicit inclusion of emergency provisions in a country's constitution. Given that the emergency provisions are constitutionalized, we then ask what the determinants are of the specific provisions allocating much or little discretion to the executive.

Our strongest result is that once they have introduced it, countries are extremely unlikely ever to get rid of an emergency constitution. This is not only true with regard to constitutional amendments but also with regard to entirely new constitutions. In other words: Emergency constitutions are here to stay. Further, the way in which a constitution is produced has an important impact on the kind of emergency provisions promulgated: More legislative control over the constitutional process is associated with more control by the legislature before the executive can call a state of emergency (SOE) and with fewer benefits to the executive after an SOE has been declared. Interestingly, disaster-prone countries are not more likely to grant their executives more powers under an SOE, a fact that we return to in Chapter 5.

The rest of the chapter is structured as follows. In the theory section (Section 3.2), we present a number of hypotheses regarding the likely content of emergency provisions. Section 3.3 answers our first question (When are emergency provisions likely to be constitutionalized?) and

Section 3.4 our second question (Which factors determine the amount of power delegated to the executive under an SOE?). In Section 3.5, we approach the content of emergency constitutions from a different angle, namely by asking whether their length (clearly a quantitative measure) is systematically correlated with their content, while Section 3.6 concludes.

3.2 Conjectures

In this section, we present a number of straightforward conjectures referring both to the (first-time) introduction of emergency constitutions as well as their content.

(1) Legal History

In the last chapter we saw that the constitutionalization of emergency provisions began in revolutionary France, which first introduced them in her 1795 constitution. Emergency constitutions took off from there to Latin America via the Iberian Peninsula. We illustrate this development, as a background for the following discussion, in Figure 3.1 where the earliest adopters are white and the most recent black.

Historians of emergency constitutions such as Rossiter (2009) or Friedrich (1968) have stressed the differences between the (French) *état de siège* and the (British) martial law traditions. This ties in well with the legal origins literature that separates three civil law origins (French,

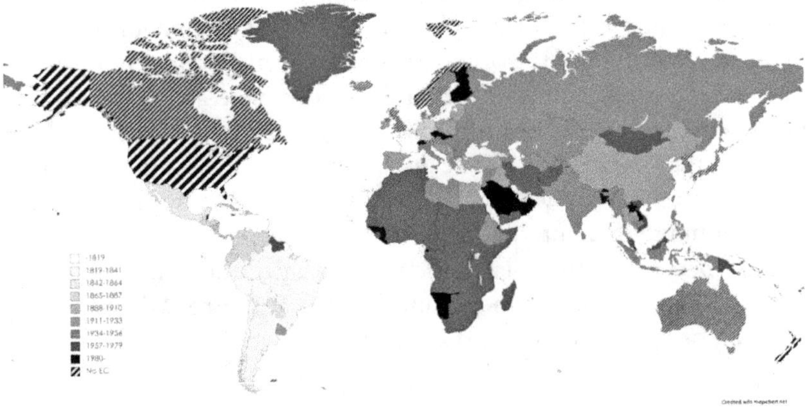

Figure 3.1 The expansion of emergency constitutions over time

German, and Scandinavian) from the common law tradition.[1] Were we to analyze the determinants of the introduction of emergency constitutions in the middle of the nineteenth century, belonging to the French legal family would definitely show up as a highly significant predictor. We include legal origins here to see if they still play a role in both introducing an emergency constitution and in the provisions it contains.

Under the British parliamentary sovereignty tradition, parliament has always been authorized to legislate on any matter without any formal constraints. Also under that tradition, specific liberties or rights were only suspended after parliament had voted on the respective legislation. If we assume that the way the British handled emergencies carried over to nation states that were once British colonies, then we expect: (1) a limited number of rights that can be derogated; and (2) high parliamentary influence on SOEs. In terms of the INEP introduced in the last chapter, we would, hence, expect common law countries to score low values, indicating an important role for the legislature.

In addition, Loveman (1993, 23) points out that post-emergency, it fell to the judiciary to decide whether government action had been legal during the SOE in countries belonging to the common law tradition. The judiciary is, hence, expected to play an important role in these countries, at least post-emergency. Friedrich (1968, 562) interprets this as the main difference between the two models: Under the state of siege, the executive and (or) the legislature has the ultimate word, whereas under military rule it is the judiciary.

In the legal origins literature, not only Spain and Portugal, but also the Netherlands and Italy as well as almost all of Latin America are coded as having French legal origin. An explicit distinction between colonizing powers and the originators of the legal system is not usually made. We propose to make such a distinction here as marked differences between some of the respective emergency constitutions can be observed that might have been caused by the specific colonization history of a country. Loveman (1993, 28) observes: "With this tradition of a militarized internal administration and special privileges for military personnel, the role of the military institutions in Spain, and later in Latin America, came to differ significantly from their French, German, or Italian counterparts."

[1] The codification of legal traditions remains a knotty issue of which La Porta et al. (2008) is an excellent summary.

Some of the more recent literature on legal origins adds two types: Islamic law (e.g. Rosen 2000) and communist legal systems. Islamic law rests on Shari'a that provides a constitutional context that need not be included in the constitution per se, which then leaves both details and central rules unmentioned. Conversely, communist traditions often provide detailed constitutions with substantial rules such as the 1936 Soviet constitution, which included meticulous protection of human rights and democratic institutions. The Soviet sphere was nevertheless a particularly clear example of the divide between de jure rights and de facto enforcement.

(2) Composition of Constitutional Assembly

As we show in Chapter 2, SOEs regularly imply a broadening of the power of the executive to the detriment of parliamentary and (or) judicial powers. Assuming that all actors are power maximizing, we would expect a constitutional assembly dominated by representatives of the executive to propose emergency articles transferring relatively more competences to the executive and correspondingly allocating the legislature relatively little monitoring or control rights.[2]

(3) Frequency of Disasters: Both Natural and Man-Made

We hypothesize that a pragmatic response to experiencing frequent natural disasters, such as droughts, floods, earthquakes, or volcanic eruptions, would be the constitutionalization of provisions enabling the government to deal with such emergencies. In parallel, we also expect that the constitutionalization of provisions may be more likely when man-made events such as coup attempts, domestic turmoil, or terrorism appear more likely.

(4) Economic and Institutional Capacity

Further, we need to stress that emergency constitutions may arguably reflect the economic and institutional capacity of a country at a given point in time. Wealthier countries are, all other things being equal, more likely to have a standing capacity for handling natural disasters as well as countering external and internal threats to both the populace and the incumbent government (cf. Andersen and Aslaksen 2013). Likewise, countries with relatively better judicial and bureaucratic institutions are

[2] Ginsburg et al. (2009) is an excellent survey analyzing the effects different ways of constitution-making have on the content of the constitution.

also more likely to handle risks and hold threats in check. We therefore proxy for such factors in the analyses that follow.

(5) Controls: Regime Type and Spatial Proximity
In the last chapter, we saw that emergency constitutions of democratic countries on average are not systematically different from those of autocratic states. Nevertheless, we include the various regime types here to be sure not to overlook a potentially important determinant. We also control for spatial proximity because neighboring states often share many of the general living conditions, such as the climate (a potential source for natural disasters) but also the state of development, history, and cultural similarity. In addition, citizens are often more familiar with the institutions of a neighboring than of a distant country. Similarity of living conditions combined with familiarity with the valid institutions of neighboring countries could make the spread of emergency constitutions via contagion of this kind more likely. We thus propose to take the geographical diffusion of constitutional emergency provisions explicitly into account.

3.3 When Are Emergency Constitutions Introduced?

Based on these considerations, we now ask which factors affect the likelihood that a country introduces an emergency constitution. Section 3.4 then examines the determinants of the particular traits of the emergency constitutions as captured by the INEP and its six components. All data used in this section are summarized in Tables A3.1 to A3.3 in the appendix.

We report the results of estimating the determinants of introducing (or reintroducing) an emergency constitution in Table 3.1. All estimates are obtained by a random effects panel logit estimator including regional fixed effects (for Latin America and the Caribbean, Sub-Saharan Africa, the Middle East and North Africa region, the Pacific, and Asia).[3] We only include country observations in years in which

[3] While the data are in principle categorical and therefore call for the use of a dichotomous estimator such as ordered probit, we report GLS estimates. The reason is that the results of using either a probit or a continuous GLS estimator are very similar. We therefore report the GLS results as they, contrary to probit, are directly interpretable.

the constitution was either amended or a new constitution was introduced. Without this sample restriction, we would face two problems. First, we would be estimating the determinants of the existence rather than the introduction of emergency constitutions. Second, our estimates would be confounding the introduction of emergency provisions with the introduction or amendment of the entire constitution. All data used in Table 3.1 are summarized in the appendix. In columns 1 and 2, we include all countries while we exclude Western countries in columns 3 and 4. We do this to test if our findings are universally valid and not simply driven by rich Western countries. Further, in columns 2 and 4, we include regional fixed effects in order not to merely pick up purely geographical variation.

Six insights from the estimates depicted in Table 3.1 are noteworthy: First, the results clearly show that countries with constitutions that historically have included emergency provisions are substantially more likely to reintroduce them after a period of either not having an emergency constitution or during which the constitution was suspended.

Second, we find no evidence that any regime type, no matter whether democratic (mixed and presidential) or autocratic (civil, military, and royal autocracies) is more (or less) likely to introduce emergency provisions than parliamentary systems. This complements our insight from Chapter 2 that there are no significant differences between the emergency constitutions relied upon by different regime types.

Table 3.1 ***Determinants of introducing emergency constitutions (given constitutional change), 1950–2010***

	1	2	3	4
Reintroduction	6.024***	6.042***	6.473***	6.442***
	(0.549)	(0.549)	(0.649)	(0.648)
First constitution	2.922***	2.988***	2.938***	2.949***
	(0.413)	(0.420)	(0.412)	(0.419)
Mixed	0.137	0.119	0.795	0.788
	(0.464)	(0.459)	(0.528)	(0.535)
Presidential	−0.286	−0.446	−0.719	−0.527
	(0.594)	(0.562)	(0.685)	(0.715)

Table 3.1 (*cont.*)

	1	2	3	4
Civil auto.	0.133	0.247	0.324	0.275
	(0.444)	(0.433)	(0.477)	(0.483)
Military auto.	0.131	0.116	0.209	0.276
	(0.588)	(0.583)	(0.622)	(0.622)
Royal auto.	−0.194	0.039	0.152	−0.003
	(0.699)	(0.641)	(0.763)	(0.804)
Monarchy	0.334	0.227	0.081	0.229
	(0.449)	(0.434)	(0.584)	(0.617)
Coup government	0.826**	0.818**	0.796**	0.807**
	(0.391)	(0.388)	(0.393)	(0.396)
PolConIII	1.026	0.672	0.845	1.302
	(1.384)	(1.323)	(1.539)	(1.584)
No constraints	0.685	0.633	0.699	0.799
	(0.561)	(0.544)	(0.602)	(0.616)
Log GDP per capita	0.002	−0.119	−0.074	0.016
	(0.141)	(0.113)	(0.125)	(0.147)
Log population size	−0.207***	−0.192***	−0.213***	−0.241***
	(0.080)	(0.071)	(0.076)	(0.088)
Postcommunist	1.388***	1.136***	0.855*	1.414**
	(0.479)	(0.384)	(0.444)	(0.710)
Common law	−0.208	−0.114	−1.085	−1.305
	(0.562)	(0.542)	(0.796)	(0.836)
French civil law	−0.234	−0.083	−1.067	−1.395
	(0.562)	(0.527)	(0.768)	(0.847)
Islamic law	1.657**	1.904***	0.922	0.573
	(0.786)	(0.738)	(0.931)	(0.993)
Communist law	−0.105	−0.170	−1.024	−0.916
	(0.659)	(0.655)	(0.836)	(0.843)
Regional controls	No	Yes	No	Yes
Observations	1834	1834	1385	1385
Countries	175	175	149	149
Log likelihood	−332.834	−335.136	−277.300	−275.296
Wald Chi squared	214.31	213.56	172.40	173.50

Note: *** (**) [*] denote significance at $p < 0.01$, ($p < 0.05$), and [$p < 0.10$]. With legal origins, the omitted category is German/Scandinavian legal systems; with form of government, the omitted category is parliamentary democracy. Western countries are excluded from columns 3 and 4.

When It Takes Two Decades to Agree on an Emergency Constitution: The Case of Germany

The current constitution of Germany – the *Grundgesetz* – has been in place since 1949. It took until 1968 to amend the constitution to include emergency provisions. But eventually such provisions were included and Germany thus fits our general insight: "once an emergency constitution always an emergency constitution."

Among scholars, there is almost unanimous agreement that the emergency provisions contained in the Weimar constitution – and their use by German president Hindenburg – facilitated Hitler's ascent to power. Still, the framers of the *Grundgesetz* were convinced that West Germany needed an emergency constitution. East Germany was part of the Soviet bloc and there were fears both of military attacks from the east and of Moscow-paid agents causing trouble from within the West German state. Therefore, the original draft (the so-called *Herrenchiemsee Entwurf*) contained an article dealing with emergencies. Had it been included in the *Grundgesetz*, it would have enabled the government to curtail press freedom, freedom of expression, freedom of assembly, freedom of association, and the privacy of communications and telecommunications. It also included a provision for the issuance of decrees. Although direct evidence is still unavailable, it is likely that this paragraph did not find its way into the *Grundgesetz* because it was opposed by the Allies.

After the original noninclusion of emergency provisions in West Germany's 1949 constitution, it took two decades until emergency provisions were finally included. Over these two decades, there was a continuous struggle between those who put more emphasis on the stability of the state and those who gave individual rights higher priority. Although the governments of the day continuously tried to find enough support to amend the constitution, this only became possible under the first "grand coalition" in Germany which was formed by the two largest factions in parliament, namely the Christian Democrats and the Social Democrats. The 1968 amendments were met with powerful "nonparliamentary" protests, enabling the protestors to claim credit for another amendment to the constitution which gives "all Germans" the right to act against any government attempt to eliminate Germany's basic democratic order.

A very detailed description of the many attempts to include emergency provisions in the German constitutions is Diebel (2019).

Third, we find clear evidence that formerly communist countries are substantially more likely to introduce emergency constitutions in the constitutions they introduced after communism collapsed. As most of these constitutions were written in the early 1990s, this variable might, however, also be thought of as a proxy for the 1990s. Yet as almost all of these constitutions were passed in postcommunist societies, this particular aspect is picked up by the postcommunism dummy. A fourth regime characteristic that turns out to be significantly associated with the introduction of emergency provisions is if the government introducing emergency provisions came to power through a coup. We find that such governments are twice as likely to introduce emergency provisions in new or amended constitutions as governments coming to power through regular means.

Fifth, more populous countries have been less likely to introduce emergency constitutions. At least three possible explanations come to mind: (1) Disasters, whether natural or man-made, are less likely to threaten the existence of large countries than small ones, making the constitutionalization of emergency provisions less objectively necessary; and (2) countries with large populations are likely to be organized as federations and the constitutionalization of emergency provisions might, hence, take place on the state level and not the federal one.[4]

Finally, while neither veto-player institutions nor any regular legal origins tend to matter significantly, we find that countries with Islamic legal systems are substantially more likely to include emergency provisions. Yet as is evident in columns 3 and 4, this result is driven by the comparison of relatively rich Islamic oil nations with rich Western countries. As we delete the latter, Islamic law ceases to be significant.

3.4 Determinants of the Characteristics of Emergency Provisions

We now move on to ask what factors lead to an extensive transfer of competences to the executive and what factors inhibit such transfers, given that an emergency constitution exists in the first place. Hence,

[4] The US being a good example where the contents of the 50 state constitutions differ widely. Both the contents of US state emergency constitutions as well as their effects are analyzed in Chapter 8.

we are interested in the determinants of the INEP values identified for different constitutions. We confine the analysis to those emergency provisions that were introduced between 1950 and 2010, as background data for earlier periods is too scarce. Tables 3.2a and 3.2b report our estimates. Column 1 in both tables reports the results of using the full index while the following columns report the results with the indices of declaration power, approval power and conditions (i.e. the variables we refer to as the Cost INEP, Table 3.2a), and dissolution power, rights suspension, and expropriation and censorship (i.e. the variables we refer to as the Benefit INEP, Table 3.2b). As in Table 3.1, all estimates result from applying a random effects estimator including regional fixed effects (for Latin America and the Caribbean, Sub-Saharan Africa, the Middle East and North Africa region, the Pacific, and Asia).

Starting with regime characteristics, we find that the constitutions of countries with a mixed presidential political system, that is, a democratic system with a weak president, tend to allow significantly less discretionary power to the executive during emergencies. This effect appears driven by mixed democracies listing fewer conditions under which emergencies can be called, and emergency constitutions that are substantially less likely to allow the suspension of any basic rights. The latter characteristic also tends to be shared by monarchies (but not royal dictatorships) in which a hereditary constitutional monarch may share similar features as a weak president.[5]

We next find that countries with stronger veto institutions (as measured by Henisz's [2012] PolConIII index) tend to have a higher INEP, indicating the granting of significantly stronger emergency powers to the executive. In other words, constitutions creating strong veto players in nonemergency times tend to make both the declaration of an emergency as well as its management relatively easy for the sitting government. This effect is caused by veto strength affecting the power to approve SOEs, to dissolve the parliament during emergencies, and to suspend basic rights. The result could reflect the constitution writers' beliefs that government should be constrained in normal times but

[5] In Tables 3.2a and 3.2b, the institutional category "monarchy" refers to all monarchies whether they are democratic constitutional monarchies in Western Europe or absolutist monarchies in the Middle East. The difference between royal autocracy and monarchy thus is the effect that only pertains to democratic constitutional monarchies but not to absolutist regimes.

Table 3.2a *Determinants of constitutional characteristics*

			INEP	Declaration power	Approval power	Conditions
Regime characteristics	________	Mixed	−0.119***	0.055	−0.063	−0.158**
			(0.042)	(0.124)	(0.079)	(0.073)
	________	Presidential	−0.044	0.088	−0.122	−0.039
			(0.040)	(0.119)	(0.077)	(0.077)
	________	Civil auto.	−0.017	0.122	−0.009	−0.059
			(0.033)	(0.102)	(0.060)	(0.056)
	________	Military auto.	−0.001	0.093	0.015	−0.056
			(0.035)	(0.104)	(0.064)	(0.061)
	________	Royal auto.	−0.005	0.076	0.067	−0.044
			(0.045)	(0.094)	(0.085)	(0.078)
	________	Monarchy	−0.021	0.113	−0.046	−0.042
			(0.036)	(0.103)	(0.064)	(0.060)
	________	PolConIII	0.072***	0.049	0.094**	−0.004
			(0.028)	(0.049)	(0.040)	(0.029)
	________	No constraints	0.002	0.027	−0.001	0.009
			(0.009)	(0.022)	(0.018)	(0.014)
	________	Log coups (10 yrs)	0.025*	0.089**	−0.023	0.064***
			(0.014)	(0.044)	(0.033)	(0.024)

Development factors	Log GDP per capita	0.032***	0.066**	0.011	0.054***
		(0.010)	(0.027)	(0.021)	(0.019)
	Log population size	0.014***	0.013	0.017	0.023***
		(0.004)	(0.014)	(0.011)	(0.009)
	Post–Cold War	0.034**	0.016	0.018	0.101***
		(0.017)	(0.044)	(0.039)	(0.034)
Legal origins	Common law	0.085**	0.061	0.038	0.152***
		(0.038)	(0.102)	(0.080)	(0.053)
	French civil law	0.076**	–0.001	0.030	0.148***
		(0.034)	(0.083)	(0.067)	(0.041)
	Islamic law	0.046	–0.004	–0.129	–0.063
		(0.045)	(0.107)	(0.0924)	(0.092)
	Communist law	0.043	0.023	0.044	–0.042
		(0.039)	(0.109)	(0.079)	(0.049)
Type of introduction	Constituent assembly	–0.001	0.003	–0.093**	0.138***
		(0.022)	(0.061)	(0.038)	(0.046)
	Legislative decision	–0.067***	–0.081*	–0.111***	–0.046
		(0.017)	(0.049)	(0.035)	(0.031)
	Executive decision	0.016	0.065	0.035	0.008
		(0.015)	(0.042)	(0.033)	(0.026)
	Constituent legislature	–0.074***	–0.119	–0.097	0.030
		(0.028)	(0.097)	(0.069)	(0.063)

Table 3.2a (*cont.*)

		INEP	Declaration power	Approval power	Conditions
Environmental characteristics	Low elevation	−0.069***	−0.068	−0.013	−0.069*
		(0.020)	(0.049)	(0.044)	(0.036)
———	Log latitude	−0.036***	−0.083***	−0.043*	−0.018
		(0.008)	(0.024)	(0.023)	(0.018)
———	Coastline	0.016*	0.015	0.004	0.009
		(0.009)	(0.019)	(0.008)	(0.011)
———	Volcano area	−0.014	0.048	−0.103***	−0.004
		(0.016)	(0.052)	(0.037)	(0.029)
	Regional controls	Yes	Yes	Yes	Yes
	Observations	360	360	360	360
	R squared	0.271	0.212	0.125	0.278
	F statistic	5.76	4.33	2.75	6.73
	RMSE	0.123	0.352	0.271	0.223

Note: *** (**) [*] denote significance at $p < 0.01$, ($p < 0.05$), and [$p < 0.10$]. With legal origins, the omitted category is German/Scandinavian legal systems; with form of government, the omitted category is parliamentary democracy. Distance from the equator (here entered as log latitude) has been shown to be highly correlated with institutional quality. We here rely on it as a proxy for institutional quality as there are no other measures available that stretch that far back in time.

Table 3.2b *Determinants of constitutional characteristics*

		INEP	Dissolution power	Rights suspension	Expropriation and censorship
Regime characteristics	Mixed	–0.119***	–0.158	–0.273***	–0.115
		(0.042)	(0.116)	(0.077)	(0.071)
	Presidential	–0.044	–0.102	–0.089	0.002
		(0.040)	(0.097)	(0.082)	(0.065)
	Civil auto.	–0.017	–0.003	–0.089	–0.064
		(0.033)	(0.088)	(0.071)	(0.049)
	Military auto.	–0.001	–0.020	–0.041	0.002
		(0.035)	(0.088)	(0.080)	(0.053)
	Royal auto.	–0.005	–0.098	–0.011	–0.022
		(0.045)	(0.081)	(0.072)	(0.063)
	Monarchy	–0.021	0.008	–0.137**	–0.019
		(0.036)	(0.079)	(0.054)	(0.049)
	PolConIII	0.072***	0.218***	0.132*	–0.054
		(0.028)	(0.049)	(0.072)	(0.036)
	No constraints	0.002	0.004	–0.010	–0.011
		(0.009)	(0.020)	(0.022)	(0.019)
	Log coups (10 yrs)	0.025*	0.017	0.005	0.000
		(0.014)	(0.033)	(0.024)	(0.026)
Development factors	Log GDP per capita	0.032***	0.035	0.039**	–0.014
		(0.010)	(0.025)	(0.019)	(0.016)
	Log population size	0.014***	0.017	0.021***	–0.006
		(0.004)	(0.009)	(0.008)	(0.007)

Table 3.2b *(cont.)*

		INEP	Dissolution power	Rights suspension	Expropriation and censorship
	Post–Cold War	0.034**	0.084*	0.038	–0.052*
		(0.017)	(0.049)	(0.036)	(0.028)
Legal origins	Common law	0.085**	0.103*	0.033	0.119
		(0.038)	(0.058)	(0.049)	(0.087)
	French civil law	0.076**	0.104**	0.127***	0.048
		(0.034)	(0.043)	(0.042)	(0.084)
	Islamic law	0.046	0.126	0.219*	0.126
		(0.045)	(0.118)	(0.119)	(0.095)
	Communist law	0.043	0.070	0.000	0.162*
		(0.039)	(0.046)	(0.046)	(0.088)
Type of introduction	Constituent assembly	–0.001	0.046	–0.029	–0.072*
		(0.022)	(0.050)	(0.042)	(0.041)
	Legislative decision	–0.067***	–0.070**	–0.030	–0.066**
		(0.017)	(0.035)	(0.032)	(0.030)
	Executive decision	0.016	0.029	–0.018	–0.021
		(0.015)	(0.035)	(0.030)	(0.027)
	Constituent legislature	–0.074***	–0.095**	–0.139***	–0.021
		(0.028)	(0.042)	(0.054)	(0.053)
Environmental characteristics	Low elevation	–0.069***	–0.146***	–0.094**	–0.024
		(0.020)	(0.053)	(0.043)	(0.029)

Log latitude	−0.036***	−0.031	−0.006	−0.034**
	(0.008)	(0.022)	(0.019)	(0.017)
Coastline	0.016*	0.019	0.036*	0.015***
	(0.009)	(0.022)	(0.020)	(0.005)
Volcano area	−0.014	−0.041	0.007	0.009
	(0.016)	(0.033)	(0.035)	(0.028)
Regional controls	Yes	Yes	Yes	Yes
Observations	360	360	360	360
R squared	0.271	0.212	0.125	0.278
F statistic	5.76	4.33	2.75	6.73
RMSE	0.123	0.352	0.271	0.223

Note: *** (**) [*] denote significance at $p < 0.01$, ($p < 0.05$), and [$p < 0.10$]. With legal origins, the omitted category is German/Scandinavian legal systems; with form of government, the omitted category is parliamentary democracy.

should be able objectively to get around such constraints and needs substantial additional powers during SOEs.

Likewise, countries with a recent history of *coups d'état* allocate more emergency powers to the executive. The specific areas affected by coups are declaration powers and a longer list of conditions under which SOEs can be declared. One way to interpret this finding is to think of emergency constitutions as an insurance device for the military: If it is challenged by domestic opponents, it will declare an SOE, thereby increasing its chances of surviving the challenge and to remain in power. When coup governments draft new constitutions, they therefore tend to use the emergency powers as a "coup-proofing" tool.[6]

Turning to development-related factors, richer countries share the same constitutional characteristics, but are also more likely to allow the suspension of rights during emergencies. However, as richer countries tend to have substantially stronger and more independent judiciaries, rights suspension is likely to be subject to statutory law that has a high probability of being impartially enforced. Larger countries, that is, countries with larger populations, also tend to include more conditions and allow the suspension of rights. The former feature is shared by countries with a communist past.

We also find some evidence of differences across legal origins. French civil and common law countries both allow emergencies under more conditions and are more likely to allow the dissolution of parliament relative to Islamic law and communist law origins, as well as the baseline category (German and Scandinavian origins). In addition, both French civil and Islamic law countries are more likely to include provisions allowing the suspension of basic rights during emergencies. Notice that common law countries are closer to the baseline German and Scandinavian countries in not allowing significantly more rights to be suspended under an emergency.

In addition, we find substantial evidence that the particular way the constitution was negotiated and which political actors were involved in the process is reflected in the emergency constitution. Those constitutions created by a constituent assembly or by legislative decision in an ordinary parliament allocate fewer approval powers to the executive and are less likely to allow censorship and expropriation during

[6] As Bjørnskov and Rode (2020) show, almost half of all governments coming to power through a coup since 1950 have implemented new constitutions.

emergencies. Constituent assemblies include significantly more conditions, while those created by legislative decision or by a constituent legislature – that is, by elected politicians in a regular or special parliament – are substantially less likely to allow for the dissolution of parliament. We also find robust evidence that emergencies negotiated and drafted by a constituent legislature are more likely to protect against rights suspension during emergencies. These results are perfectly in line with the assumption that politicians are utility maximizers: If members of the legislature dominate the constitution-making process, they tend to allocate more approval powers to themselves and make it impossible for the executive to dissolve parliament.

Finally, we turn to environmental factors that could influence constitutional design. Low elevation and the relative coastline capture the risk of floods, the log to latitude captures draught risk, while we also include a dummy for countries that encompass areas with volcanic activity. We find that countries that are more flood prone (with areas at very low elevations) list fewer emergency conditions and tend to ban the dissolution of parliament and the suspension of basic rights. Frequent experiences with floods are, hence, correlated with more checks and balances. In other words, frequent experience with disasters for which there are low-tech solutions – dikes, overflow basins, zoning restrictions, and architectural design – appears to make the allocation of additional powers to the executive superfluous. Surprisingly, those with long coastlines tend to be more likely to allow for censorship and expropriation. Likewise, it seems difficult to explain why countries in volcano areas have weaker executive approval powers. A final and less surprising finding is that countries further away from the equator tend to grant weaker powers of declaration and approval to the executive and be substantially less likely to allow expropriation and censorship during emergencies. While there are no good geographical reasons, latitude is known to correlate significantly with the de facto quality of judicial and bureaucratic institutions. As such, it appears that emergency constitutions tend to grant more power to the executive when institutions are weak.

The remaining question is what to make of these differences – what do they tell us about the political process of drafting and implementing emergency constitutions? Before taking up these questions in the final section, we now turn to a completely different way of analyzing the content of emergency constitutions – and the underlying factors determining the respective contents.

3.5 Verbosity in Emergency Constitutions

A completely different approach toward analyzing emergency constitutions is to study their length. The number of words spent on dealing with emergency situations in constitutions does vary enormously from a mere 47 words and less than 0.3 percent of the constitution in Australia to 4,293 words in India or 19 percent of the current Thai constitution. Ex ante, it is unclear what it means if a country has a particularly long – or short – emergency constitution.[7] In principle, longer emergency constitutions can be used to constrain the executive in very specific ways. But the exact opposite is just as plausible: Many words can also be used to describe the additional competences that government enjoys under an SOE.

Focusing on the conditions around the time of constitution writing, we conjecture that older emergency constitutions will – on average – be shorter as emergency constitutions seem to have become ever more detailed and elaborate over time. And indeed, we find that older constitutions tend to have much shorter emergency constitutions, which is consistent with the fact that relatively few constitutions included emergency provisions prior to the 1930s. Second, we find that governments that came to power through a coup apparently try to coup-proof the regime by writing substantially longer emergency constitutions.[8] To prevent this, they could spill additional ink enabling them to declare an SOE in case there are rumors of yet another coup. The results do, indeed, show that constitutions written under coup governments use relatively more words to pin down the emergency provisions.

Interestingly, we find much the same pattern for constitutions written around the time of independence with the collaboration of colonial

[7] When assessing the length of an emergency constitution, we do not include Organic Law or other statutory law, which can have the effect of interpreting or implementing constitutional provisions. We refrain from doing so because these laws can be changed more easily by the incumbent government. This was for example the case in Denmark in March 2020 when the government pushed through a new epidemic law the day before locking down the country.

[8] This is far from a negligible observation, as about 45 percent of all governments that came to power through a coup since 1950 have implemented a new constitution within three years (Bjørnskov and Rode 2020). These regimes evidently prioritize being constitutionally able to act in the face of threats to their survival. The factors inducing coup governments to initiate the writing of a new constitution are analyzed in Bjørnskov and Voigt (2022).

authorities, which tend to have longer emergency provisions, and for constitutions that the legislature wrote itself. All the results reported here refer to the length of the emergency constitution relative to the length of the entire constitution. This seems the best way to reveal the relative importance attributed to emergency constitutions by the framers.

Apart from the question of length, another question is whether more words spent on the emergency provisions of a constitution imply more competences given to the government or more constraints put on government. We first find a significant negative association between the Cost INEP and social trust, indicating that constitutions in high-trust countries make it substantially more difficult to call an SOE. This finding is not surprising since high-trust societies tend to have substantially stronger civil society organizations that are arguably better able than government to handle local emergencies. It is also consistent with Aghion et al. (2010) who find that citizens in high-trust societies tend to demand (and get) less formal government regulation of markets. When analyzing the length of the emergency constitution, we find a strong positive correlation between its length and the Benefit INEP, implying that longer emergency constitutions allocate more additional powers to the executive under an SOE. Hence, it seems fair overall to conclude that longer emergency constitutions are likely to confer more benefits on the executive, rather than constraining the executive in such situations. In other words, the more political actors add to the emergency constitution, the more power they allocate to themselves.

3.6 Conclusions and Outlook

This chapter aims to identify the reasons that lead to the constitutionalization of emergency provisions. This is an important question because – as we noted in the introduction – 90 percent of all current constitutions contain emergency provisions. In our analysis of emergency constitutions introduced by constitutional change or amendment since 1950, we identify a small number of significant factors.

Firstly, countries which formerly included emergency provisions in a constitution are much more likely to do so in future constitutions, the constitutions of newly independent countries after 1950 were more likely to include an emergency constitution while smaller, formerly communist countries and countries in which the government came to power through a coup are also more likely. With the possible exception of the first result, these findings are difficult to reconcile with purely benevolent or pragmatic motives behind constitutional design.

Secondly, relying on the INEP, it turns out that democratic countries with a weak president assign fewer powers to the executive during emergencies. Further, countries with stronger veto institutions tend to allocate substantially more power to circumvent regular democratic rights during emergencies. This characteristic is shared by civil law countries while common law countries allow SOEs under significantly more conditions, as do countries that are more prone to experience coups. We also show that the negotiation forum for new constitutions – if the constitution is introduced by constituent assemblies, legislative decision, executive decision, or by a constituent legislature – clearly shapes the design of emergency constitutions. Conversely, being prone to a high risk of suffering from a natural disaster is not a reliable predictor regarding the contents of the respective emergency constitution.

We believe these findings hold lessons for constitution makers. If the misuse of emergency constitutions by power-maximizing politicians is perceived as a threat, the relevant actors should aim to create a constitutional assembly dominated by the legislature. Our results show that this increases the likelihood that the powers of the executive will be limited. We must also ask about the alternative of simply not including any emergency provisions in a country's constitutions at all. We suspect that this option is likely to be worse for safeguarding the rights of individual citizens, as governments can infringe upon these rights more easily. Specifically, the problem is that statutory law passed during an emergency is likely to become permanent and may have detrimental effects on individual rights even after the emergency is over. These issues will be taken up again in Chapter 14.

However, this chapter focuses on the determinants of emergency constitutions. At least three follow-up questions come to mind. Emergency provisions do not only exist on paper but are used quite frequently. What are the determinants of actually declaring an SOE? Can one show that emergency constitutions entailing more separation of powers are used less frequently? And how are SOEs used in countries without explicit emergency provisions? This is the topic of the next chapter.

Appendix

Table A3.1 *Variables and sources*

Type of explanation	Variables	Source
Regime types	Parliamentary, mixed, presidential, civil autocracy, military autocracy, royal autocracy, monarchy, Post–Cold War	Cheibub et al. (2010)
	PolConIII, no constraints	Henisz (2012)
	Log GDP per capita	
Frequency of disasters	Low elevation, log latitude, coastline, volcano area	CIA (2020)
	Log coups (10 yrs)	*
Legal history	Common law, civil law, Islamic law, communist law	CIA (2020)
Composition of constitutional assembly	Constituent assembly, legislative decision, executive decision, constituent legislature	Ginsburg et al. (2009)
Economic factors	Log GDP per capita, log population size	Heston et al. (2012)

Table A3.2 *Descriptive statistics, data used in Tables 4a, b, and 8a, b*

Variable	Mean	Standard deviation	Observations
INEP	0.307	0.138	411
Declaration power	0.729	0.392	411
Approval power	0.206	0.279	411
Conditions	0.272	0.245	411
Dissolution power	0.095	0.293	411
Rights suspension	0.162	0.255	411
Expropriation and censorship	0.377	0.232	411
Mixed	0.058	0.235	411
Presidential	0.088	0.283	411
Civil auto.	0.421	0.494	411
Military auto.	0.226	0.419	411
Royal auto.	0.083	0.276	411
Monarchy	0.165	0.372	411
PolConIII	0.097	0.257	402
No constraints	0.766	0.604	402
Log GDP per capita	7.356	0.846	372

Table A3.2 *(cont.)*

Variable	Mean	Standard deviation	Observations
Log population size	8.459	1.710	402
Post–Cold War	0.260	0.439	411
Log coups (10 yrs)	0.423	0.552	386
Common law	0.118	0.322	407
Civil law	0.747	0.435	407
Islamic law	0.027	0.162	407
Communist law	0.074	0.262	407
Age	59.871	46.609	411
Low elevation	0.791	0.407	411
Log latitude	2.798	0.960	411
Coastline	0.162	0.986	409
Volcano area	0.299	0.458	411
Constituent assembly	0.165	0.372	411
Legislative decision	0.253	0.435	411
Executive decision	0.391	0.489	411
Constituent legislature	0.044	0.205	411
Length	13,485	12,115	409
Democracy	0.270	0.445	411
Still in use	0.314	0.465	411

Table A3.3 ***Descriptive statistics, data used in Tables 3.6 and 3.7***

Variable	Mean	Standard deviation	Observations
Introduction of EC	0.106	0.307	2084
Reintroduction	0.042	0.200	2085
First constitution	0.039	0.193	2085
Mixed	0.108	0.309	2044
Presidential	0.143	0.350	2044
Civil auto.	0.321	0.467	2044
Military auto.	0.129	0.335	2044
Royal auto.	0.042	0.201	2044
No constraints	0.401	0.490	2001
Log GDP per capita	8.430	1.304	1935
Log population size	8.957	1.827	2085
Postcommunist	0.058	0.252	2085
Common law	0.284	0.451	2084
Civil law	0.538	0.499	2084
Islamic law	0.012	0.111	2084
Communist law	0.103	0.304	2084

4 *Why Do Governments Call a State of Emergency?*

4.1 Introduction

As you know by now, nine out of ten countries have constitutionalized their emergency provisions and they are used quite frequently: Between 1985 and 2014, 137 countries declared a state of emergency (SOE) at least once. This implies that roughly two-thirds of all sovereign nations declared an SOE during that period. Due to the COVID-19 pandemic alone, at least 125 countries declared an SOE. In this chapter, we seek to identify the factors that make governments declare an SOE. Declaring an SOE has far-reaching consequences for all citizens – not least because basic rights are frequently suspended under emergencies. But declaring an SOE also has far-reaching consequences for the balance of powers within government: The power of both the legislature and the judiciary are usually curtailed to the advantage of the executive.

At least two intuitive reasons for declaring an SOE come to mind: The government identifies an "exceptional and imminent danger to the life of the nation,"[1] which could be caused by natural disasters, but also by man-made dangers such as terrorist attacks. A charitable interpretation of why governments call SOEs would therefore be that the additional emergency powers granted by the constitution are necessary for them to act with speed and due diligence to save people and alleviate the social and economic consequences of emergencies.

[1] Quote from the Siracusa Principles on the Limitations and Derogations Provisions in the International Convention on Civil and Political Rights (ICCPR). In section II.A39(a)(b) of the Principles, such a threat is defined as one that "affects the whole of the population and either the whole or part of the territory of the State and threatens the physical integrity of the population, the political independence or the territorial integrity of the State or the basic functioning of institutions indispensable to ensure and project the rights recognized in the Covenant."

But a government might also declare an SOE because it is eager to use the additional powers connected to an SOE in its own favor, for example, to weaken its political opposition. As such, SOEs may be called for reasons not associated with actual emergencies, but as a tool to improve the chances of remaining in office or to implement policies that would otherwise be blocked.

States of emergency following natural disasters are not limited to earthquakes, volcanic eruptions, tsunamis, droughts, and floods as triggers but include many other causes. Here is a random list of causes that have been given over the last couple of years only: a cholera outbreak, the zika virus, a massive infestation of rats, and a locust plague. Beyond natural disasters, there are many additional reasons for declaring an SOE: an increase in homelessness, a high homicide rate, the number of heroin addicts, a warehouse fire, and an exploded freight train. But there are also some politically very sensitive reasons for declaring an SOE, such as: conflicts between government and indigenous communities; losing election (and declaring the SOE before the opponent has been sworn in, as happened in the Gambia); or against migration (as happened, e.g. in Hungary); and many more.

Other examples can easily be found. Many governments have declared an SOE to weaken the opposition. Two recent examples of such behavior occurred in Ethiopia and Honduras. According to human rights activists, the Ethiopian government used a ten-month SOE that lasted from the fall of 2016 until the summer of 2017 to kick off politically motivated criminal charges against key opposition leaders and journalists (Horne 2017). In December 2017, the Honduran government declared an SOE after disputed presidential elections. Jesús Garza, a political analyst, claims that "the government is provoking the chaos in order to justify the state of emergency." (http://progressive.org/dispatches/honduras-political-crisis-following-election-171204/).

But there are other ways in which disasters – natural or man-made – can be used politically. In 2015, the government of Nigeria postponed national elections in response to the activities of Boko Haram in the Northeast of the country. With regard to the US, it has been shown that emergency declarations are heavily influenced by political considerations. There, financial support from the federal government to the affected state seems to be driven by how important a state is for the US president and less by the severity of the disaster (Garrett and Sobel 2003).[2]

We are not aware of any previous study that has analyzed the factors that lead governments to declare an SOE.[3] Comparing cases in which governments did declare an emergency with those in which they did not but could have because the preconditions were given, we find that it is crucial to distinguish whether an SOE is declared as a consequence of a natural disaster or of political unrest. Relying on a sample of up to 116 countries, we find that states of emergency based on natural events are declared significantly more often when declaring them is possible without the explicit consent of other political actors such as the legislature or the judiciary: in other words, when declaration has low direct political costs. Declarations referring to domestic turmoil are more likely when an economic crisis is hitting the country and political unrest (measured by the number of anti-government demonstrations, general strikes, politically motivated assassinations, and the like) is high. We find that overall, democracies and autocracies behave remarkably similarly although declarations of SOEs based on political events are more frequent among democracies.

Yet we also find that the likelihood that a large natural disaster makes a government call an SOE increases the more powers are allocated to the legislature. Around domestic turmoil, conversely, we do not find that the ease of declaring an SOE affects the probability of doing so. We also observe that even military coup governments react to constitutional incentives by calling an SOE when the emergency

[2] Sobel and Leeson (2006) analyze the consequences of the way in which agencies such as the Federal Emergency Management Agency (FEMA) are organized on their incentives to help fast and effectively. With regard to disaster relief in India, Cole et al. (2012) find that voters punish incumbent governments for events beyond their control (such as rainfall). But voters reward the ruling party if it responds vigorously to such events. Cohen et al. also find that voters have a short memory: Disastrous events – and government reactions to them – only influence voting decisions if they occurred no more than a year ago.

[3] There are, however, two studies that are interested in the effectiveness of international law as that provides the possibility to derogate from a number of basic rights under specified conditions. Hafner-Burton et al. (2011, 703) find that governments of stable democracies and with strong courts are most likely to derogate "to provide themselves breathing space to respond to domestic crises by suspending individual liberties without breaching their treaty obligations." Richards and Clay (2012) ask whether the legal prohibition to violate nonderogable rights during SOEs works and answer that it does not.

constitution provides particular benefits and when they do not face a formally independent judiciary or other veto players.

The rest of the chapter is structured as follows. In Section 4.2, we discuss a number of potentially relevant factors for declaring an SOE. In Section 4.3, we describe the data on which our empirical estimates are built and offer some descriptive statistics. Section 4.4 contains a number of stylized facts as well as bivariate correlations between declarations of emergencies and country characteristics. Section 4.5 provides the regression results and their interpretation. A brief Section 4.6 subsequently explores the relatively few countries that never use their emergency provisions. Section 4.7 concludes.

4.2 Theory

We follow established tradition in public choice and political economy by assuming all actors to be individual utility maximizers (Buchanan and Tullock 1962). Here, we analyze the behavior of politicians who are in government and assume that their overarching goal is to remain in office, that is, that they strive for a positional good. This seems reasonable as remaining in office is usually the only way to keep on enjoying political rents.[4] We propose to distinguish two approaches to remaining in office: (1) to "play by the rules" and try to stay (or become) sufficiently popular to be reelected;[5] or (2) to misuse the emergency laws to postpone an election, weaken the opposition, or signal competence when a situation arises.

At base, the switch from not having declared an emergency to declaring one implies that some parameters must have changed. These might be exogenous events, such as natural disasters, but also upcoming events, such as national elections. Before these events, it must have been in the interest of the government and government actors not to declare an SOE. After their occurrence, this must have changed, implying that all possible alternative options were attributed lower net

[4] Note that our assumption regarding the goals of government does not restrict the analysis to democracies as autocratic governments also act under the threat of losing office.

[5] Then chancellor of Germany, Gerhard Schröder, was able to turn an almost certain defeat into a win at the national elections on September 22, 2002. The flood of the river Elbe had allowed him to send a strong signal of competence to voters and thereby position himself as a strong leader.

utility by those in a political position to declare the SOE. We propose to discuss a number of potential benefits resulting from the declaration of an SOE, and subsequently turn to possible cost components.

The use of any measure that increases the probability of staying in office is considered a benefit here. We assume that politicians not only prefer to remain in office, but also prefer to have more competences rather than fewer.[6] To ascertain the benefits that declaring an SOE confers on governing politicians we need, hence, to compare the (additional) powers that politicians have at their command under an SOE with those powers the government commands during nonemergency times. We refer to this as the power differential. We therefore hypothesize that:

Hypothesis 1: *The larger the power differential, that is, the difference in powers that a government enjoys under an SOE compared to a nonemergency, the higher the probability that it will declare an SOE.*

The power differential is likely to be a function of the form of government. Governments in parliamentary systems are permanently subject to the threat of a no-confidence vote, which governments in presidential systems are not. Prima facie, we would expect governments in presidential systems to have more power under their command in normal times, implying that, ceteris paribus, the power differential to states of emergency is smaller than in parliamentary systems. This would imply a complementary hypothesis, which reads:

Hypothesis 1a: *All other things being equal, governments in parliamentary systems are more likely to declare an SOE than governments in presidential ones.*

But all other things might never be equal. Political scientists employ the concept of "disciplined party" to describe situations in which all legislators belonging to one party vote together in highly contentious votes in parliament (see, e.g. Mainwaring and Liñán 1997). It is well known that parties are systematically more disciplined under parliamentary than under presidential systems (see, e.g. Shugart 1998).

[6] Notice that this is not universally true as refraining from certain competences is often the only way for politicians to make their promises credible (cf. Keefer and Stasavage 2002).

On average, parties can be expected to have a longer time horizon than individual politicians. If that is the case and the median party member expects democracy to perpetuate for the foreseeable future, then this is likely to considerably increase the costs of declaring an emergency, which provides one reason that the credibility problem every government needs to deal with will be more severe after an emergency.[7] We hence conjecture that:

Hypothesis 1b: *Countries with more disciplined parties have a lower likelihood of declaring emergencies under otherwise identical conditions.*

Now, hypotheses 1a and 1b are in conflict with each other. Which of the two prevails will only be revealed by an empirical test. Since the form of government is highly correlated with disciplined parties, a refutation of hypothesis 1a can be interpreted as a confirmation of hypothesis 1b and vice versa.

The power differential will not be determined by a simple comparison of the executive's competences in normal times with those in emergency times. Many governments also have the option to choose extraordinary policy measures that are below the threshold of an emergency. If these can also be used to keep the current government in office, they should be taken into account as explicitly as possible. Measures that come to mind include but are not limited to the use of executive decrees, the use of noncivil courts (usually military ones) to hear civil cases, and so forth. The more such options are available, and the easier it is to rely on them, the lower the power differential and the lower, hence, the likelihood of an SOE being declared. These alternatives need, hence, to be taken into account explicitly when calculating the power differential. From the previous chapter we know that countries with a high degree in the separation of powers in normal times allocate substantial power to the executive under emergencies. The question here is whether this power differential is, indeed, activated by declaring emergencies.

[7] By a credibility problem, we refer to the difficulty that all governments have in making their promises credible. They may promise many things, but when they have the last word on everything and command a strong military, they may sometimes "forget" some of their promises. Standard ways to mitigate that problem are the separation of powers or the ratification of international conventions.

Declaring an SOE also entails costs. The higher these are, the lower the likelihood of declaring an emergency. We propose to distinguish between two cost categories, namely direct and indirect costs. The direct costs of declaring an emergency are the costs of organizing the majorities that need to consent to it, whereas indirect costs refer to the loss of popularity that government suffers as a consequence of declaring an SOE among members of the legislature, the judiciary, and citizens at large.

The higher the number of veto players and the more heterogeneous their preferences, the more difficult it will be to declare an SOE and the higher, hence, the direct costs. One factor determining the willingness of legislators to consent to their own – if temporary – disempowerment is the degree of competences they forego under an emergency. But we do not need to include this negative power differential as it can be thought of as the flipside of the (positive) power differential just described with regard to the executive.

Hypothesis 2: *The more difficult it is to secure consent to declaring an emergency, the lower the probability of its declaration.*

Direct costs are unlikely to cover all costs that accrue to government by declaring an emergency. Since states of emergency usually entail a substantial shift in the balance of powers in favor of the executive and to the detriment of both the legislature and the judiciary, these branches are likely to give government a more difficult time after a declaration. Since SOEs usually also entail a containment of some basic rights, they might be unpopular among the population at large. A very general third hypothesis hence reads:

Hypothesis 3: *The higher the indirect costs of declaring an emergency, the less likely its declaration.*

This hypothesis is only testable after "indirect costs" have been broken down into their most important components and after they have been made measurable. We argue that indirect costs are determined by at least six factors, namely exogeneity of the event, regime type, relative strength of the judiciary, relative strength of the military, overall strength of institutions, and international commitments. We suggest ways to measure these as we go along.

It is also necessary to consider the event that formally triggers the SOE as causes for calling an emergency can be more or less exogenous.

In general, natural disasters are more exogenous than man-made disasters. These, in turn, tend to be more exogenous than domestic political causes and turmoil. We hypothesize that the higher the (perceived) degree of exogeneity of the event that is used to justify the declaration of an SOE, the lower the indirect costs (as well as the direct ones). After a natural disaster, most members of the other branches of government as well as the citizens at large are expected to comprehend that government may need extra powers to save lives. On the other hand, declaring an SOE to oppress political opposition will almost by definition be met with higher criticism and hence entail higher indirect costs. Expressed in terms of a testable hypothesis, we expect that:

Hypothesis 3a: *The higher the exogeneity of the underlying cause for declaring a state of emergency, the higher the probability of it being called.*

To test this hypothesis empirically, we simply assert that natural disasters are more exogenous than political turmoil.

Next, countries differ in the degree to which citizens who are unhappy with government decisions can inflict (indirect) costs on government. Democracies enable voters to get rid of their governments in more or less fixed intervals. Emergency declarations that are vastly unpopular among the population are, hence, less likely in democracies as opposed to nondemocracies (see Chapter 5). Combining this argument with hypothesis 3a leads us to expect that:

Hypothesis 3b: *Democracies are more likely to call an SOE based on exogenous events whereas autocracies are more likely to call an SOE based on endogenous events.*

We note that this hypothesis is in conflict with hypothesis 1, according to which the power differential is decisive for calling an SOE. As the power differential is likely to be higher in democracies, one would expect democracies to make more frequent use of constitutionalized emergency provisions. We need empirical analysis to ascertain which of the possible effects prevails.

Indirect costs might not all accrue immediately, but stretch into the future. The (future) behavior of political actors partially disempowered as a consequence of an SOE can also represent a separate aspect of indirect costs. Under some emergency constitutions, government decisions carried out under the emergency regime are subject to ex post judicial review, which is administered by the regular courts. This is true, in particular, for countries following the British approach of martial law (see, e.g. Rossiter 2009, chapter X). If judicial review can inflict costs upon the current government in the future, this is likely to have an effect on the government's current behavior, hence:

Hypothesis 3c: *If ex post judicial review exists, the probability of declaring an SOE is lower.*[8]

Time and again, scholars of emergency regimes have nevertheless evaluated ex post judicial review as a rather toothless instrument to constrain government (see, e.g. Ackerman 2004; or Dyzenhaus 2006, 17). A more general take on the shift of powers toward the executive – and away from both the legislature and the judiciary – is instead to inquire into the general strength of the judiciary. The higher the actual degree of independence that the judiciary enjoys, the higher is the likelihood that it will be able to give government a hard time under an SOE. This is, hence, another type of indirect cost.

In many countries, actors beyond the three branches of government, narrowly conceived, have substantial influence on government decisions. No government anywhere in the world can afford to alienate the military. Assuming that representatives of the military have a strong preference for "law and order," we conjecture that:

Hypothesis 3d: *The stronger the military, the higher the likelihood of calling an SOE, under otherwise identical conditions.*

According to Acemoglu et al. (2013), there can be settings under which voters have an interest in dismantling checks and balances. Their model assumes that there are two groups in society, namely the rich and the poor, and that there are more poor people than rich. If checks and balances function well, the executive's discretion is low, as is its overall income. This enables the rich who as a group are assumed

[8] In addition, we also expect a lower likelihood that government oversteps its competences during an SOE. Now, these effects will be more pronounced the longer the current government expects to stay in office or – in other words – the lower its discount rate. In addition to being a determinant of the decision to call an SOE, it could also have an effect on the length of time that the state of emergency is upheld. If judicial review only sets in once the SOE has ended and government expects negative effects of the review, it has incentives to prolong the SOE. Framed as a hypothesis: *if ex post judicial review exists, average spells of emergencies are expected to last longer.*

to have solved their collective action problem, and are therefore politically organized as a group, to bribe government into policies furthering their own interests. In such circumstances, the poor might prefer fewer checks and balances; although the overall income of the executive will increase, bribing it will be more difficult implying that policies are closer to the preferences of the poor. Acemoglu et al. (2013, 859) point out that this result is likely in "weakly institutionalized states" that are described as states in which "the rich lobby can successfully bribe politicians or influence policies using non-electoral means."

Assuming that the separation of powers is higher in normal times than in times of emergency, it follows that the poor may prefer an SOE over a "normal" state of affairs. There would, hence, be some "demand" for an SOE and the corresponding indirect costs for government would be low, although mainly in "weakly institutionalized states." The corresponding hypothesis thus reads:

Hypothesis 3e: *All other things being equal, more emergency declarations will be observed in weakly institutionalized states.*

We propose to test this argument empirically by relying on a measure of the (perceived) quality of judicial and bureaucratic institutions as proxy for the de facto weakness of institutions. This approach is based on a theory of institutions as equilibria; as soon as some institutions, such as those making up checks and balances, are not in equilibrium any more, there will be forces to establish a different one. In this particular case, the new equilibrium entails fewer checks and balances than the previous one. Interpreted like this, emergency constitutions can be seen as low-cost devices to switch equilibria.

In addition to indirect costs caused domestically, there might also be an international source for them: If a country has ratified the International Covenant on Civil and Political Rights (ICCPR) and its government has pledged not to derogate on a number of basic rights, then the emergency also needs to be declared to the international community. This might entail political as well as economic costs that might, in turn, make government less popular at home. We hence propose to control for ratification of the ICCPR. The corresponding final political hypothesis thus reads:

Hypothesis 3f: *Countries that have ratified the ICCPR are less likely to declare an SOE, under otherwise identical conditions.*

There are a number of choices that are very expensive when made for the first time. These high initial costs function as a kind of threshold that keeps many actors from ever making such a choice. But once the particular choice has been made, subsequent choices become less costly and the threshold vanishes. This refers to some kind of habituation and might also be true with regard to declaring emergencies, because such declarations become part of the regular "menu" of political options.[9] Loveman (1993, 26) goes even further and suspects that "... the use of regimes of exception becomes addicting. In most of Spanish America it became routine." Loveman (1993, 383) deals with nineteenth-century Latin America and concludes that "constitutional dictatorship became the rule rather than the exception." We, hence, conjecture that:

Hypothesis 4: *The more frequently emergencies have been called in the past, the more likely they are called today.*

In Chapter 3, we dealt with the determinants of both the inclusion of emergency provisions in constitutions and the degree of powers transferred to the executive in case an SOE is declared. We believe it is interesting to see whether some of the determinants driving the introduction of emergency provisions into constitutions also determine the likelihood of actually making use of these provisions. We also showed that governments that have assumed office in a coup are substantially more likely to introduce emergency provisions into the constitution and that the powers conferred on the executive are more pronounced. Both the inclusion of emergency provisions in the constitution and the powers transferred to the executive can be interpreted as a threat such that, if the country develops in a way disliked by the military, it will be ready to call an emergency and use the respective powers. If such threats are credible, then governments that have come to power in military coups should <u>not</u> be more likely to actually call SOEs. We will test whether this is, indeed, the case.

Note that the implicit assumption identifying these hypotheses is that governments strive to remain within the boundaries defined by the constitution. Alternatively, a government might, of course, decide

[9] In their influential paper on the effects of *coups d'état*, Londregan and Poole (1990) talk of a "coup trap." Once a country has experienced a coup, it is more difficult avoiding future ones.

that it is politically expedient not to comply with the constitution at all. In a sense, we therefore assume that intra-constitutional means are always less costly than extra-constitutional ones. The question of whether this is actually the case will be dealt with in Chapter 11.

This concludes our theory section and we now move on to present a number of stylized facts on the number of emergency declarations and some correlations.

4.3 Data Sources and Descriptive Statistics

4.3.1 The Dependent Variable

To identify the factors that determine whether a government calls an SOE or not, we need a sample that includes cases in which government could have declared an SOE but decided not to. The dataset created by Hafner-Burton et al. (2011) does just that. Relying on US Department of State Country Reports on Human Rights Practices, it covers the period from 1976 to 2007 for up to 193 countries. Interestingly, it covers not only states of emergency that were actually declared but also "undeclared domestic emergencies," that is, domestic events that might have justified the declaration of an SOE but where none was actually declared.

Since their coding regarding "nondeclared" emergencies is opaque, we decided to take a different route to identify situations in which an SOE could have been declared, but was, in fact, not. For natural disasters, we turn to the Emergency Events Database (EM-DAT; Guha-Sapir et al. 2014) which lists disasters based on their effects on humans (such as the number of casualties or the number of people affected).[10] When testing whether an SOE is called based on natural events, we therefore only include country-year observations in which such an event was actually present.

Regarding domestic turmoil, we first draw on the weighted conflict index as provided by Banks (2004) which takes into account assassinations, general strikes, guerrilla warfare, government crises, purges,

[10] Since counting all disasters regardless of how small they were would give us a rather inclusive list, we effectively require that the disaster is of a size such that it affects at least one in every thousand citizens in the country, or about 1000 people in the average country. We note that our results pertaining to natural disasters in the following are quite robust to changing this threshold.

riots, revolutions, and anti-government demonstrations. In addition, we ask whether there was a successful coup or a coup attempt in a given year which would have justified declaring an SOE (Bjørnskov and Rode 2020). We code a country as being able to declare an SOE: if any emergency is reported for a given country year in the EM-DAT; if the country receives a positive score by Banks; or if there was a coup or coup attempt.

In the following, we rely on an updated version of the Hafner-Burton dataset that allows us to estimate events up to 2010, and in subsequent chapters up to 2017. Since various hypotheses posit that the reasons for calling an SOE subsequent to a natural disaster might significantly differ from those subsequent to domestic political turmoil, we separate these two classes of potentially triggering events from each other and estimate their determinants separately. We also take care of the potential influence of repeat or perpetual SOEs by providing a set of estimates in which we exclude observations in which an SOE had also been in effect in the previous year.

4.3.2 Independent Variables

Our theory section focuses on both the costs and benefits of declaring an SOE. The Index of Emergency Powers (INEP) that we introduced at length in Chapter 2 will serve as one of our workhorses again.

The first hypothesis does not deal with the absolute powers a government enjoys after having declared an SOE – that is, the benefits tout court – but with the degree to which it enjoys powers beyond and above those it enjoys anyway. Fish and Kroenig (2009) have proposed a Parliamentary Powers Index (PPI) that is based on up to 32 criteria to estimate the power of the legislature relative to the other branches of government. To identify the power differential, it would have been a natural choice to draw on the difference between the INEP and the (inverse of the) PPI. Unfortunately, however, the PPI only exists for a cross section. This is why we construct our own Index of Parliamentary Legislative Influence (IPLI), which follows Fish and Kroenig (2009) as much as possible.

More specifically, we rely on 15 variables from Ginsburg et al. (2009) in order to calculate an index that varies over time. The elements capture: (1) whether the parliament can dismiss the head of government; (2) how broad are the conditions that allow parliament to do so; (3) whether ministers must be members of parliament; (4) whether the legislature has the power to investigate the executive; (5) whether it can initiate an election; (6) whether it can nominate ministers; (7) whether it needs to approve ministers; (8) whether it is wholly or partially responsible for the interpretation of the constitution; (9) whether members of parliament have immunity from prosecution; (10) whether the legislature is elected by citizens; (11) whether it can propose amendments to the constitution; (12) whether it can declare war; (13) whether it can sign treaties with foreign powers; (14) whether it has the power to dismiss judges; and (15) whether the constitution places limits on the eligibility to serve in parliament. All elements are coded on a 0–1 scale with constitutional uncertainty coded 0.5 and larger powers or lower limits coded with increasing scores. The total index is therefore scaled from 0–1. Inclusion of the IPLI allows us to test hypothesis 1. Our source for form of government is Cheibub et al. (2010) as updated by Bjørnskov and Rode (2020). A particularly attractive feature of their data is that they not only distinguish between democracies and autocracies but group democracies into parliamentary, mixed, and presidential and autocracies into civilian, military, and royal.

Hypothesis 2 states that the costlier it is to declare an emergency, the less likely this is to occur. To test this hypothesis, we propose to distinguish between the constitutional number of veto players and their actual number. As long as the constitution remains unchanged, the constitutional number of veto players will remain unchanged. However, the actual number of veto players is subject to change over time. It depends on whether, for example, the majorities of the two houses in a bicameral system are held by the same party or different ones. For data regarding the actual number of veto players, we rely on the most recent version of the PolCon III dataset by Henisz (2012). Inclusion of both the INEP as well as PolCon III allows us to test hypothesis 2.

On the one hand, we expect the indirect costs of declaring an SOE to be higher in democracies (hypothesis 3b). On the other, autocrats might enjoy more powers to start with so they might have fewer incentives to declare an SOE. The extra benefits an SOE conveys on the executive are determined not only by the (relative) power of parliament but also by the power of the judiciary (hypothesis 3c). While it would be ideal to have a measure for the competences the judiciary enjoys in reviewing legislation and decrees that have been passed while the SOE was in force, such an indicator is unfortunately not available. We hence propose to use the de facto degree of judicial independence as a proxy for the (relative) power of the judiciary; data are from Linzer and Staton (2015). We also add a measure of international legal obligations by capturing whether the country has ratified the United Nations ICCPR. Data on ICCPR ratifiers come from the UN Treaty Collection and we use the year in which the respective country ratified the ICCPR.[11] This allows us to test hypothesis 3f.

With respect to the factors that may trigger an SOE, we first include the weighted conflict index as provided by Banks (2004) that captures domestic turmoil. We secondly also include a set of four dummies capturing the presence of successful and failed coups. Following the distinction in Cheibub et al. (2010) and resting on the new database presented by Bjørnskov and Rode (2020), we separate coups driven by primarily military or civilian interests. We thereby include variables for failed military, failed civilian, successful military, and successful civilian coups.

For the natural events, we employ information on how many people are affected by either natural or man-made environmental disasters. The main idea is that the more people are affected by a natural disaster, the higher is the probability of an SOE being called on that rationale. We rely on the variable "Disaster affected" from the EM-DAT already mentioned above, effectively capturing how large a share of the population is affected by any given disaster.

4.3.3 Control Variables

In Chapter 2, we saw that almost all countries that adopted an emergency constitution before 1850 belong to the French or Iberian civil law traditions. In Chapter 3, we found that legal families can explain

[11] In additional tests not reported in the following, we also included a proxy for the strength to which states are institutionalized along the lines of hypothesis 3e. In a first set of tests, we employ a variable, which is a composite of the corruption and bureaucratic quality variables from the International Country Risk Guide (ICRG). In further tests, we employ measures of corruption and judicial accountability from the V-Dem project. These measures are occasionally significant, but are never close to significance when we exclude repeat declarations. As their inclusion further reduces our sample size, we prefer to report the more robust estimates obtained without direct institutional measures.

some of the differences in the emergency constitutions across countries. Since we cannot exclude that the likelihood of calling an emergency is also influenced by legal families, we control for them.

We include population size as, ceteris paribus, more people are likely to be affected in more populous countries. As a consequence, declaring an SOE could be more likely. To control for this possibility, we include the (log of) population size from the Penn World Tables, mark 7.1 (Heston et al. 2012).

Next, we include the (log to) per capita real income, as higher income is likely to be correlated with safer housing and a more resilient infrastructure. Natural disasters could have fewer effects on richer countries, which might therefore experience fewer states of emergency. We also control for events of negative growth. The rationale is that government popularity is, to a large extent, determined by how the economy develops. Periods of negative growth are likely to make government highly unpopular. In such periods, governments could be more willing to declare an SOE, simply to secure their survival in office. These variables are also based on the Penn World Tables.

We need to take into account that global politics and attitudes may have changed over the years. We therefore add a dummy variable capturing the period after the (official) end of the Cold War. This variable accounts for the possibility that governments were more (or less) likely to declare an SOE before the end of the Cold War. We refrain from including more fine-grained time variables to save degrees of freedom. For similar reasons, we control for postcommunist status by including a dummy variable indicating whether a country used to be communist. Inclusion of this variable allows us to disentangle the time effect (captured with the Cold War variable) from the effect of having a communist past, as well as the constitutional changes that these countries implemented when effectively regaining their independence.

4.3.4 Descriptive Statistics

To get an impression of the development of emergencies that have been called since 1980, Figure 4.1 simply indicates the number of emergencies called annually. We only begin the analysis in 1980 because, before this date, our data are relatively scarce and heavily unbalanced. The countries that have used their emergency provisions most frequently over the 31-year period from 1980 until 2010 are

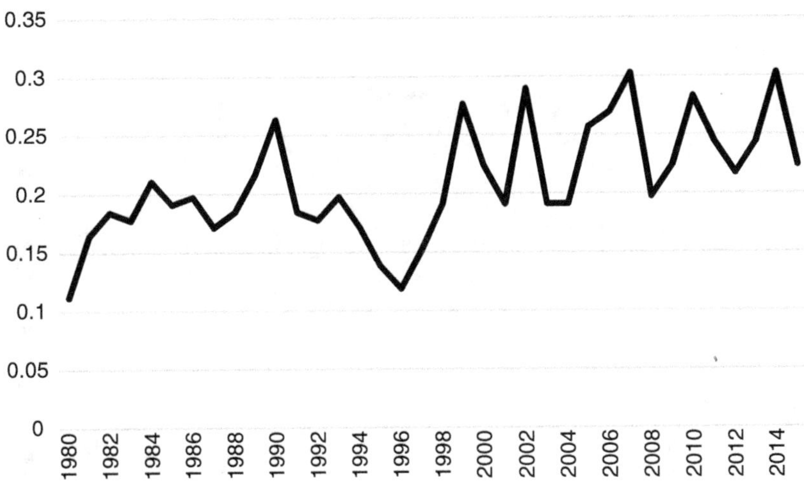

Figure 4.1 Probability of calling a state of emergency, 1980–2010

Egypt, Israel, Peru, and Syria. These have all had either a perpetual SOE or constantly repeated events. Outside of these countries, both Sri Lanka (29 times) and the United Kingdom (27 times) are frequent users of emergency powers. Conversely, out of a total of 191 societies across the world, a group of 42 countries ranging from the poorest to the richest had called no SOEs between 1980 and 2022. Of these, 16 countries decided not to call an SOE during the COVID-19 pandemic and have therefore still not declared. We provide an overview of these countries at the end of the chapter.

Figure 4.1 is based on the Hafner-Burton et al. (2011) coding of 1,835 events of which 945 resulted in an officially declared SOE. Of these, 1,458 are classified as domestic turmoil while 234 are natural disasters; the small remainder consists primarily of extraterritorial events such as wars and cross-border civil unrest. Yet the data also reveal the probability of a government calling an emergency given that there is an event that justifies the action. Resting on our alternative identification of events, we observe 705 situations in which an SOE was called (out of a total of 2,546) and where some political event allowed the call, and 701 situations in which an SOE was called and where a natural disaster was present (out of a total of 3,858).

The data behind the figure also illustrate that the share of all potential states of emergency resulting from national-political events that

Table 4.1 *Descriptive statistics*

	Mean	Std. deviation	Observations	Mean democracies	Mean autocracies
All declared SOEs	0.201	0.401	2968	0.207	0.193
Log population	8.953	1.852	2968	8.888	9.018
Log GDP per capita	8.171	1.292	2985	8.800	7.514
Negative growth	0.315	0.465	2965	0.254	0.378
Failed civilian coup	0.007	0.081	2968	0.004	0.010
Failed military coup	0.026	0.159	2968	0.013	0.039
Successful civilian coup	0.004	0.066	2968	0.001	0.007
Successful military coup	0.015	0.122	2968	0.003	0.028
Conflict index*1000	0.908	1.627	2954	0.785	1.032
After Cold War	0.546	0.497	2968	0.592	0.499
Postcommunist	0.069	0.254	2968	0.083	0.055
Disaster affected per 1000	0.042	0.110	1649	0.032	0.121
Cost INEP	0.421	0.193	2968	0.414	0.454
Benefit INEP	0.223	0.175	2968	0.209	0.236
Common law	0.235	0.424	2968	0.292	0.176
Civil law	0.593	0.491	2968	0.605	0.580
Islamic law	0.046	0.211	2968	0.003	0.091
Mixed presidential	0.110	0.313	2965	0.219	0
Presidential	0.176	0.380	2965	0.349	0
Civil autocracy	0.288	0.453	2965	0	0.580
Military dictatorship	0.168	0.374	2965	0	0.338
IPLI	0.403	0.118	2397	0.414	0.391
Judicial independence	0.474	0.309	2965	0.691	0.261
ICCPR ratified	0.646	0.478	2968	0.693	0.597
Political constraints	0.237	0.211	2855	0.392	0.080

were actually called decreased after the end of the Cold War but has increased again since the mid-2000s. The sharp uptick visible in the figure is driven by national-political responses to domestic turmoil in the form of SOEs in the most recent years that seem to have been caused by the financial crisis of 2007–2009. In addition, the political responses to the COVID pandemic in 2020–2022 resulted in a sharp increase in emergencies declared specifically for health reasons. We discuss this uptick as a separate and unique phenomenon in Chapter 12.

The data presented in Hafner-Burton et al. (2011) also show that while 47 percent of events of domestic turmoil resulted in a declaration of an SOE in the period from 1980 to 2010, natural disasters are significantly more likely to be followed by an emergency declaration; on average, 87 percent of all natural disasters that could constitutionally cause an SOE led to one being called. This is in line with hypothesis 3a which states that calling an SOE as a consequence of more exogenous events is connected with lower indirect costs and is, hence, more likely.

Our data, which we summarize in Table 4.1, also show that democracies tend to be more likely to call SOEs. The data reveal that 69 percent of all events resulted in an SOE while the corresponding likelihood for autocracies was only 43 percent. While democracies called an SOE in 92 percent of all natural disasters and 62 percent in all domestic turmoil events that qualified calling an SOE, the corresponding likelihoods in autocracies were 73 percent and 43 percent, respectively. This is, hence, in line with hypothesis 3b. In addition, we observe substantial differences across political institutions. Countries without constitutionalized emergency provisions are substantially more likely to call states of emergency when given the chance. Among the few countries without constitutional emergency provisions, 73 percent of all potential states of emergencies were called without a constitutional definition of emergency.

4.4 Stylized Facts and Bivariate Correlations

In this section, we start by presenting a number of simple, bivariate correlations. The figures that follow will hopefully help the reader to develop a sense of potentially interesting associations. Figures 4.2 and 4.3 depict the unconditional probability of observing an SOE in equally sized groups below (striped columns) and above (black columns) the median value of any of the eight variables, given that there

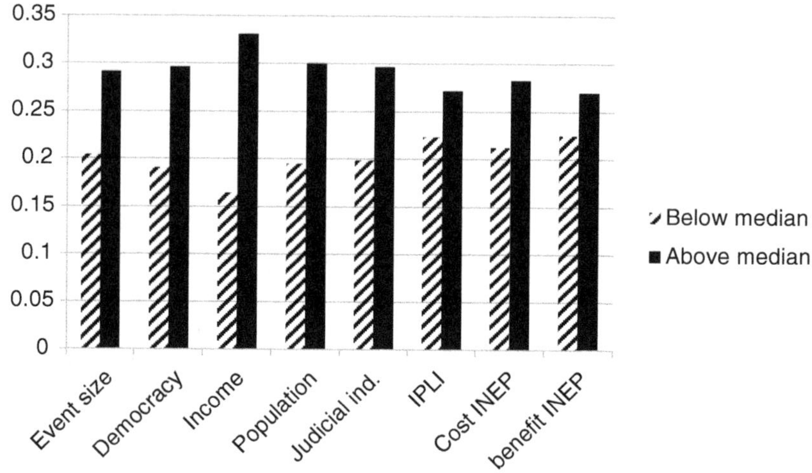

Figure 4.2 Natural SOEs and main characteristics

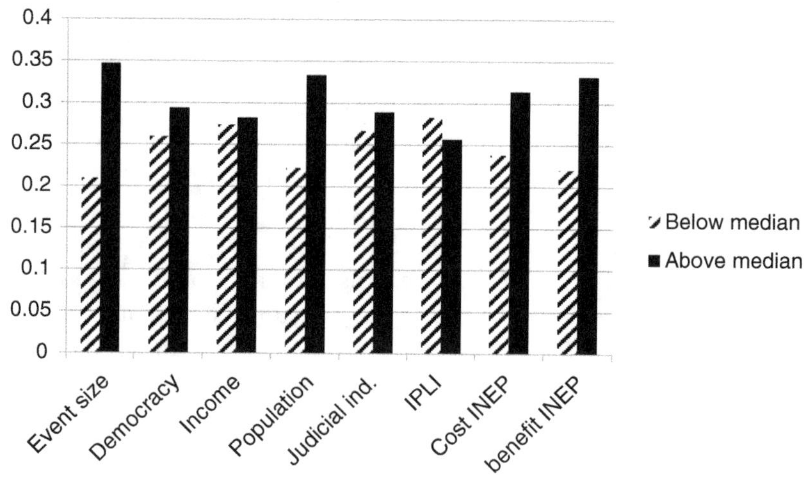

Figure 4.3 National-political SOEs and main characteristics

is a potential reason for calling an SOE based on either a natural disaster (Figure 4.2) or a political event (Figure 4.3).

In both cases, the figures illustrate that larger events – disasters affecting a larger part of the population in Figure 4.2 and larger conflicts in Figure 4.3 – are associated with a higher probability of calling an SOE: In both cases, the probability in the half-sample with larger events is significantly higher than in the half of the sample with smaller events. Similarly, the simple comparison indicates that more SOEs in situations with natural disasters are called in democratic, richer, more populous countries with stronger legislatures, more independent judiciaries, and emergency constitutions that yield more power to the executive (a higher Benefit INEP).

Likewise, in cases with larger social conflicts, SOEs called in response to domestic turmoil appear more likely in more populous countries with stronger emergency constitutions. However, the simple illustration does not exhibit any significant differences between democracies and autocracies, rich and poor countries, or more or less independent or strong judiciaries and legislatures. As such, a first look at the data clearly indicates that the determinants of calling SOEs are likely to differ substantially between the two main types of emergencies.

4.5 Regression Results and Their Interpretation

4.5.1 Main Effects

In Table 4.2, we report the results of estimating our baseline specification. We estimate the determinants employing a random effects logit estimator with regional fixed effect (Asia, Latin America and the Caribbean, the Middle East and North Africa, and Sub-Saharan Africa) and legal origins fixed effects (common, civil, and Islamic law). While we believe that the effects of natural disasters can be interpreted as direct, causal consequences, we note that care must be taken in the following as causality is only inferred from the temporal structure of any domestic turmoil.[12] We thus do not make any strong claims about the causality of these events.

We report results of using the full sample in columns 1 and 2; we restrict the sample in columns 1, 3, and 5 to countries in which at

[12] Natural disasters are obviously exogenous by their nature. However, our estimates could suffer from simultaneity bias for two reasons: (1) if emergency provisions are changed immediately following natural disasters; and (2) if the structure of the emergency provisions, as measured by the INEP, reflects the threat environment, that is, the likelihood of observing natural disasters of some size. However, in Chapters 2 and 3 we saw that either situation is quite far from being the case. Emergency provisions in general do not reflect the natural threat environment, and they are more stable over time than many other parts of the constitution.

Table 4.2 *Determinants of SOEs*

	1	2	3	4	5	6
	All	All	No Western	No Western	No repeat declaration	No repeat declaration
	Natural	Domestic	Natural	Domestic	Natural	Domestic
Log population	0.378***	0.625***	0.354***	0.593***	0.293***	0.312**
	(0.125)	(0.167)	(0.125)	(165)	(0.100)	(0.124)
Log GDP per capita	0.419*	0.165	0.459**	0.249	−0.049	0.048
	(0.225)	(0.274)	(0.229)	(0.282)	(0.204)	(0.274)
Negative growth	0.244	0.213	0.199	0.229	0.131	−0.097
	(0.225)	(0.237)	(0.228)	(0.241)	(0.263)	(0.290)
Disaster affected per 1000	0.630	0.534	0.901	0.587	0.401	2.259
	(0.869)	(1.246)	(0.884)	(1.249)	(0.912)	(1.431)
Conflict index*1000	0.198***	0.152**	0.194***	0.149**	0.049	0.078
	(0.068)	(0.064)	(0.068)	(0.064)	(0.071)	(0.076)
Benefit INEP	0.067	0.173	0.518	0.626	−0.172	−0.378
	(0.925)	(1.124)	(0.968)	(1.183)	(0.771)	(0.917)
Cost INEP	1.086	−0.547	0.939	−0.335	1.756**	−0.001
	(0.920)	(1.173)	(0.932)	(1.162)	(0.738)	(0.989)
IPLI	−2.023	1.531	−2.861*	0.452	−1.639	1.512
	(1.503)	(1.743)	(1.537)	(1.755)	(1.377)	(1.759)
Mixed democracy	1.596***	2.081***	1.261*	1.653**	0.754	1.776**
	(0.619)	(0.754)	(0.679)	(0.839)	(0.604)	(0.737)

Presidential democracy	1.790***	2.358***	1.344**	1.724**	1.052**	1.891***
	(0.567)	(0.764)	(0.611)	(0.801)	(0.522)	(0.729)
Civilian autocracy	0.194	1.224	−0.069	0.842	−0.261	0.977
	(0.566)	(0.749)	(0.602)	(0.796)	(0.586)	(0.758)
Military dictatorship	0.467	1.805*	0.127	1.328	−1.019	0.639
	(0.697)	(0.848)	(0.709)	(0.859)	(0.839)	(0.963)
Political constraints	−0.542	0.406	−0.492	0.328	−0.540	0.092
	(0.738)	(0.781)	(0.730)	(0.776)	(0.776)	(0.876)
Judicial independence	−2.232**	−1.737	−1.801*	−1.063	−0.614	−0.916
	(1.079)	(1.384)	(1.066)	(1.359)	(0.884)	(1.335)
Failed civilian coup	–	–	–	–	–	–
Failed military coup	1.175*	0.963	1.199**	0.931*	1.431*	1.541**
	(0.602)	(0.524)	(0.596)	(0.515)	(0.749)	(0.594)
Successful civilian coup	0.293	0.232	0.225	0.2014	–	0.468
	(1.412)	(1.100)	(1.426)	(1.076)		(1.336)
Successful military coup	1.473*	1.889**	1.541*	1.802**	1.956*	1.955**
	(0.889)	(0.908)	(0.875)	(0.881)	(1.031)	(0.913)
ICCPR ratified	−0.285	−0.441	−0.182	−0.323	−0.389	−0.212
	(0.359)	(0.402)	(0.362)	(0.399)	(0.372)	(0.439)
After Cold War	0.860	−0.049	0.759	−0.185	1.380	0.581
	(0.641)	(0.494)	(0.646)	(0.502)	(1.100)	(0.749)
Postcommunist	−0.227	0.128	−0.958	−0.481	−0.184	0.199
	(0.739)	(0.868)	(1.018)	(1.202)	(0.671)	(0.762)
Legal origins FE	Yes	Yes	Yes	Yes	Yes	Yes
Regional FE	Yes	Yes	Yes	Yes	Yes	Yes

Table 4.2 (*cont.*)

	1	2	3	4	5	6
	All	All	No Western	No Western	No repeat declaration	No repeat declaration
	Natural	Domestic	Natural	Domestic	Natural	Domestic
Observations	975	847	887	739	767	630
Countries	113	111	100	98	110	108
Wald Chi squared	70.09	52.55	62.82	43.73	73.88	37.10
Log likelihood	–405.478	–360.978	–380.767	–340.486	–261.854	–214.163

Note: ***(**) [*] denote significance at $p < 0.01$, ($p < 0.05$), and [$p < 0.10$]. Regime types include parliamentary, mixed presidential and presidential democracy, civil autocracy, military dictatorship, and absolutist monarchy; legal origins include common law, civil law, Islamic law, and German/Scandinavian law; and regions include Asia, Latin America and the Caribbean, the Middle East and North Africa, the Pacific and Sub-Saharan Africa.

least one in a thousand was affected in a given year by a natural disaster; and in columns 2, 4, and 6, we restrict the sample to countries in which there was at least one coup or conflict in a given year. In columns 3 and 4, we exclude all Western countries while in columns 5 and 6 we exclude all country observations in which the country also registered an SOE in the previous year. While we are aware that we are therefore likely to throw out a number of SOEs called in close sequence, the purpose in columns 5 and 6 is to focus on new SOEs only and not those either spanning more than one year or becoming permanent, as in Israel and Egypt. Requiring that all control variables are available reduces our sample to a maximum of 975 observations from 113 countries for the natural disasters and 847 observations from 111 countries for the disasters related to domestic turmoil.

We first have a look at the controls reported at the top of Table 4.2 and note that more populous countries are more likely to call SOEs under comparable conditions. While we also find what appears to be evidence of rich countries calling more natural SOEs, the results in columns 5 and 6 where we exclude all repeat or permanent SOEs show that the apparent result is driven by countries that declare emergencies permanently or extremely frequently. We find no evidence that natural disasters affecting a larger share of the population are more likely to lead to an official SOE than smaller disasters. GDP, whether in terms of the level or crises and recessions in which GDP growth turns negative, has only very limited effects. Its level is only significant regarding the declaration of an SOE subsequent to a natural disaster after the Western countries have been excluded (depicted in column 3).

However, the conflict index is significantly correlated with the likelihood of calling an SOE throughout. As such, governments are more likely to call an SOE referring to natural disasters when they are confronted with political opposition (see also Chapter 7). Natural disasters might, hence, be welcome pretexts for using the extra powers contained in emergency constitutions. One should nevertheless note that the association is not significant after excluding the countries under quasi-permanent SOEs, potentially implying that those governments are particularly likely to misuse emergency provisions.[13]

[13] We nevertheless refrain from drawing any strong conclusions here, as the fact that some countries are particularly prone to declaring SOEs also implies that natural disasters will *automatically* be highly correlated with declarations

Regarding the specific form of government, we first note that the comparison category is parliamentary democracy (monarchies are missing simply because we do not have an absolutist monarchy in our sample). Comparing regime types, we find that presidential democracies are more likely than either parliamentary democracies or autocracies to call an SOE. This is, hence, not in line with hypothesis 1a (according to which, governments of parliamentary systems are more likely to declare an SOE than governments of presidential systems) but – at least indirectly – consistent with hypothesis 1b (according to which countries with more disciplined parties have a lower likelihood of declaring SOEs). However, party discipline is far from the only characteristic that differs between types of democracy and we consequently can only interpret differences as preliminary indications. We also observe some evidence that even democracies with a weak president are more likely to call SOEs although this finding is only robust for SOEs around domestic turmoil.

Analyzing potential institutional determinants further, we find that the cost elements of the INEP, that is, how easy it is for the executive to call an SOE, strongly affect how likely it is that a new SOE is actually called when a natural disaster is evolving but not following domestic turmoil (in columns 5 and 6). This is indicative evidence in support of hypothesis 2 (which predicts that the higher the cost of declaring an SOE, the lower the likelihood of one being declared). We find no robust evidence of any direct effects of either judicial independence, the strength of the legislature, or whether countries have ratified the ICCPR (thus refuting hypotheses 3c and 3f). However, we find clear evidence that military coups (both failed and successful) are associated with substantially higher probabilities of calling an SOE (hence supporting hypothesis 3d) – an association, which we revisit in Chapter 7. Both civil and military autocracies are more likely to call an SOE on the basis of political turmoil than parliamentary democracies, which is perfectly in line with our theoretical expectations (hypothesis 3b). Within the three types of democracies, presidential systems seem significantly more likely to declare a natural disaster–based SOE than

in these countries. Another potential explanation for our observation may therefore be that the significant correlation in the full sample is a statistical fluke created by the purely mechanic correlation between natural disasters and SOEs in countries that are permanently or extremely often in an SOE.

parliamentary ones. Although this result is not robust to the exclusion of Western countries, it nevertheless contradicts our expectations as governments of presidential systems are likely to experience fewer power gains than those of parliamentary systems (and can, hence, be considered a tentative falsification of hypothesis 1a). Interestingly, governments of mixed democracies are more likely to declare political unrest–based SOEs than parliamentary ones.

Finally, neither of the two dummies (after Cold War, postcommunist constitution) turn out to be a significant determinant. An analysis of the legal origin fixed effect conversely reveals that common, French civil law as well as Islamic law systems are all more likely to declare a political SOE than the benchmark German/Scandinavian civil law system.

4.5.2 Conditional Effects

The main estimates in Table 4.2 assume that all effects are homogenous. In Tables 4.3 and 4.4, we relax this assumption by allowing the effects of the size of the events – the number of people affected by a natural disaster and the size of the conflict index, coups, and economic crises – to vary with political characteristics. Specifically, we estimate whether the sensitivity of governments to the size of events varies with five political factors that affect their objective ability to react by calling an SOE.

For natural disasters, we find a single important effect: the higher the IPLI, that is, the more powers are allocated to the legislature, the more likely it is that a larger natural disaster causes the government to call an SOE. We essentially find that with legislatures that are virtually lame ducks, the government is not sensitive to the size of the disaster. Conversely, in countries with strong parliaments, larger natural disasters are substantially more likely to cause the government to call an SOE.

Focusing instead on SOEs related to domestic turmoil, we first find that governments are much more likely to react to general social conflict by calling an SOE when the emergency constitution makes it substantially more difficult to do so. While this is certainly not in line with our theoretical expectations, it may not be entirely surprising. One way of interpreting what is otherwise a counterintuitive result is that the signal value of calling an SOE – that is, the implicit threat of

Table 4.3 *Determinants of SOE with interactions, disasters, and conflicts*

	Disaster affected per 1000					Conflict index*1000				
	Natural					Political				
Interacting var	Cost INEP	Benefit INEP	IPLI	JI	Pol. Con.	Cost INEP	Benefit INEP	IPLI	JI	Pol. Con.
0	−0.296	−0.894	−5.007*	3.505*	2.149	0.583**	0.176	−0.164	0.071	0.169
	(2.076)	(1.451)	(2.964)	(2.045)	(1.436)	(0.243)	(0.109)	(0.393)	(0.189)	(0.149)
0.25	0.096	1.208	−1.143	1.509	0.613	0.366**	−0.013	−0.022	0.075	0.099
	(1.239)	(1.094)	(1.389)	(1.105)	(0.936)	(0.149)	(0.105)	(0.178)	(0.103)	(0.079)
0.5	0.489	3.310	2.720**	−0.486	−0.923	0.149*	−0.202	0.119	0.079	0.028
	(0.931)	(2.478)	(1.239)	(1.288)	(1.388)	(0.087)	(0.232)	(0.099)	(0.083)	(0.109)
0.75	0.881	5.412	6.584**	−2.481	−2.458	−0.069	−0.391	0.262	0.084	−0.042
	(1.518)	(4.116)	(2.757)	(2.344)	(2.283)	(0.118)	(0.374)	(0.299)	(0.159)	(0.198)
1	1.274	7.515		−4.476		−0.286	−0.579		0.089	
	(2.418)	(5.796)		(3.567)		(0.205)	(0.519)		(0.255)	

Note: ***(**) [*] denote significance at $p < 0.01$, $(p < 0.05)$, and $[p < 0.10]$.

Table 4.4 ***Determinants of SOE with interactions, coups, and negative growth***

	Military coups Political					Negative growth Political				
Interacting var	Cost INEP	Benefit INEP	IPLI	JI	Pol. Con.	Cost INEP	Benefit INEP	IPLI	JI	Pol. Con.
0	1.011	0.712	−0.152	2.186**	1.957***	0.491	−0.415	0.255	−0.205	−0.269
	(1.297)	(0.817)	(2.232)	(1.026)	(0.711)	(0.772)	(0.455)	(1.131)	(0.565)	(0.466)
0.25	1.344*	1.823***	0.899	1.653***	1.479***	0.175	−0.029	0.045	−0.139	−0.096
	(0.736)	(0.576)	(1.019)	(0.553)	(0.565)	(0.439)	(0.299)	(0.527)	(0.348)	(0.288)
0.5	1.677***	2.934***	1.952***	1.119	1.002	−0.140	0.357	−0.165	−0.074	0.076
	(0.579)	(1.117)	(0.708)	(0.859)	(0.904)	(0.296)	(0.565)	(0.360)	(0.306)	(0.416)
0.75	2.010*	4.045**	3.004	0.585	0.524	−0.455	0.743	−0.375	−0.008	0.249
	(1.032)	(1.848)	(1.837)	(1.533)	(1.414)	(0.528)	(0.947)	(0.914)	(0.488)	(0.698)
1	2.343	5.156**	4.056	0.051		−0.771	1.128	−0.585	0.058	
	(1.653)	(2.614)	(3.107)	(2.268)		(0.877)	(1.349)	(1.548)	(0.744)	

Note: ***(**) [*] denote significance at $p < 0.01$, ($p < 0.05$), and [$p < 0.10$].

doing so – to an opposition or other political forces creating the turmoil is much stronger when the constitution makes it difficult to do so.

In contrast, we find that governments are more likely to react to military coups – which in the case of successful coups means the new government – by calling an SOE, the more benefits the emergency constitution provides them with. Finally, in the same situation, we note that military coups only tend to cause government to call an SOE when the judiciary is not independent and when government does not face substantial other veto players. In other words, even military coup governments are constrained by the political institutions they enter and the constitutional incentives they face.

As such, the more detailed estimates in which we allow effects to be heterogeneous provide three eminently intuitive results: stronger legislatures are more likely to call an SOE when they face larger natural disasters; and governments tend to react to military coups by calling an SOE either when they face no or very limited veto players and control the judiciary, or when the emergency constitution provides them with more influence during the emergency. However, the estimates also show the perhaps puzzling result that when facing a social conflict, governments in countries in which the emergency constitution makes it more difficult to call an SOE, are more likely to do so when facing more conflict. Yet before considering how to interpret this particular result, we briefly explore the robustness of our main findings.

4.5.3 Robustness Checks

We test the robustness in several different ways. We have first changed the cutoffs at which we define a potential SOE. In Tables 4.2–4.4, we apply a cutoff for natural disasters of events that affect at least one in every thousand inhabitants of the country. In separate tests, we have experimented with either lowering it to any inhabitants (1,128 observations) or increasing it five-fold (824 observations). Yet in general, the effects remain unchanged. Applying the same cutoff changes to events of domestic turmoil, leaves the results unchanged with two exceptions: while successful military coups lose significance, higher cutoffs yield military regimes significantly associated with more SOEs. In general, however, most results appear robust to intuitive changes of the sample. Likewise, we have added several additional variables capturing the geographical size of the country, military size, a dummy for federal states, colonial origins, a measure of the de facto quality of judicial and bureaucratic institutions from the International Country Risk Guide, constitutional monarchies, and decade fixed effects. None of these variables turned out to be significant and none affected the main findings. With this set of robustness tests supporting the main results, we therefore proceed to describing countries that never declare an SOE before discussing how to interpret the overall patterns.

4.6 Nondeclaring Countries

A particular problem when assessing why governments call an SOE is that a relatively small number of countries across the world appear *never* to use their emergency provisions. Prior to the COVID pandemic, which we cover in Chapter 12, a group of 42 countries had declared no SOE since 1980 – and a careful search for additional information revealed that only one of these countries (Bermuda) had called an SOE since 1970. 16 of these countries remain without an SOE in recent decades while 25 of them eventually declared an emergency as the pandemic of 2020–2022 hit their societies.

While a full analysis of why some countries never choose to use their emergency provisions is a topic that ideally requires much more attention than we give it here, we believe it is an interesting and potentially important topic. We therefore provide a brief exploration in the following, beginning with a list of countries for which we could find no declarations between 1970 and 2019, and another list of countries without any SOE since 1970; the countries are listed in Table 4.5.[14] We compare a set of indicators that might, a priori, distinguish the group of nondeclarers in Figure 4.4; all data in the figure are scaled between 0 and 1, and from the data already described.

The figure illustrates quite clearly that the nondeclarers are neither less likely to have an emergency constitution, nor do their constitutions make it any more difficult to declare an SOE. We also find that although it appears that countries with declarations prior to 2020

[14] Although it has been claimed that Switzerland did not declare an SOE in 2020, we believe these claims are due to purely semantic differences. The 1999 constitution distinguishes between states of emergency and states of extraordinary situations. The former allow the executive branch to take on substantial powers as those covered by constitutionalized states of emergency in most other countries. We therefore code Switzerland as in an SOE in 2020.

Table 4.5 *Nondeclaring countries*

No SOE prior to 2020		No declaration since 1970	
Antigua and Barbuda	Iran	Belarus	Singapore
The Bahamas	Laos	Belgium	South Korea
Belize	Luxembourg	Bhutan	Sweden
Cabo Verde	Malta	Cuba	Tanzania
China	Morocco	Denmark	Turkmenistan
Cyprus	Netherlands	Djibouti	
Dominica	Switzerland	Eritrea	
Equatorial Guinea	Togo	Norway	
Estonia	United Arab Emirates	Qatar	
Finland	United States	St. Vincent and the Gren.	
Germany	Vietnam	Saudi Arabia	
Guinea-Bissau			

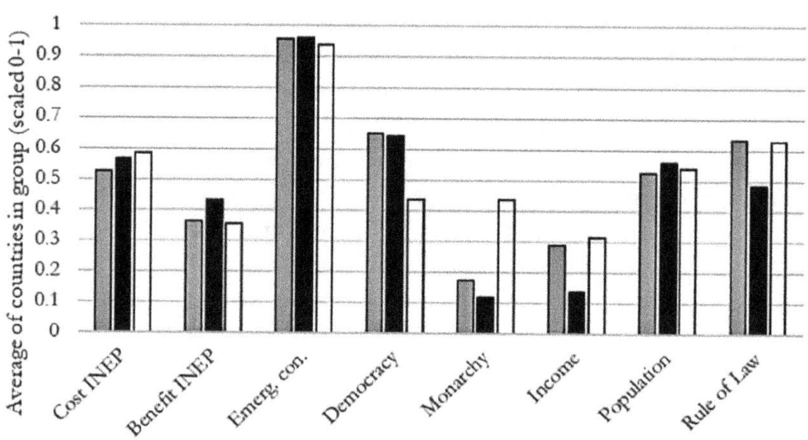

Figure 4.4 Characteristics of nondeclaring countries

tend to have more permissive emergency provisions, as measured by the Benefit INEP, the differences are not statistically significant; neither are they less populous. The group of nondeclaring of countries appears to be less likely to be democratic: the group includes

44 percent democracies versus 65 percent in the rest of the sample. However, while the group actually includes some of the least democratic countries in the world – for example Belarus, Saudi Arabia, and Turkmenistan – it also includes some of arguably the most democratic, not least the three Scandinavian countries.

Conversely, three characteristics distinguish nondeclarers from regular declarers. First, countries that either did not declare an SOE until 2020, or never did, have on average approximately twice the GDP per capita as regular declarers; while there is no clear difference between the two former groups, the GDP difference to the latter is significant at any level. Second, those in the nondeclaring group also tend to have substantially better institutions, as measured by the World Bank's Rule of Law index. Finally, countries that never declared an emergency are much more likely to be monarchies than both regular declarers and those that only declared an SOE in 2020.

Overall, even though larger countries are more likely to declare an SOE, we find that at the extensive margin – whether they ever declare – size is irrelevant. Instead, we find that better institutions, in the form of the rule of law and the particular veto players that monarchs are, appear most likely to affect whether a country has a tradition of using its emergency provisions or not.

4.7 Conclusions and Outlook

In this chapter, we have explored the factors that enable us to predict under which conditions an SOE will be called, and under which conditions it will not be called. Relying on a dataset comprising more than 2,000 events that might have triggered the declaration of an SOE and systematically separating SOEs potentially justified with natural disasters from SOEs justified with domestic turmoil, we find that it is, indeed, crucial to distinguish between natural and political disasters as the reasons for calling an SOE systematically differ between the two events.

Quite generally, we find that the less costly it is for governments to declare an SOE for natural disaster reasons, the more likely they are to do so. Regarding domestic turmoil, higher benefits as a consequence of calling an SOE are only significantly associated with a higher likelihood of calling an SOE in the context of coups – both successful and failed. However, we return to further exploring these aspects in

Chapter 7. Overall, democratic governments are more likely to call an emergency than autocratic ones. Yet this difference is driven by specific types of democracy: Within the group of democracies, parliamentary governments are substantially less likely to rely on emergency measures than both presidential and mixed governments. We also find evidence that in some contexts, for example, having strong veto institutions, legislatures with particular powers and independent judiciaries can effectively block governments' ability to call SOEs and also appear to affect whether a country ever employs its emergency constitution.

That being said, we are unable to deal with a number of potentially important questions here. From a political economy point of view, that is, relying on the assumption that all actors – politicians included – first try to maximize their own utility, we suspect that some emergencies are declared primarily to strengthen the position of the current executive and not to enhance the survival of the nation or its citizens. If the executive is motivated by such concerns, some natural disasters might be a very welcome pretext for being able to call an SOE regardless of their type or severity. Untangling cases in which a government was interested in the best reply to a natural disaster from those in which the natural disaster simply served as a welcome pretext, however, represents a substantial methodological challenge. As so often in political economy, we are unable to observe the actual motivations of the government. We can only infer them indirectly based on whether or not the patterns we observe are consistent with a particular type of motivation.

There is, however, quite some anecdotal evidence that this does occur frequently. The hurricane that swept over the Dominican Republic in 1931 is considered by some to be the initiation of the Trujillo dictatorship. The 1954 hurricane over the same island was used by the would-be dictator of Haiti, Paul Magloire, to more firmly establish himself. These – and more – examples are documented in Drury and Olson (1998). The possibility of misuse as well as the actual misuse of emergency constitutions will be discussed in Chapter 11.

Before getting there, however, we will deal with another question, namely whether emergency constitutions are effective. Do they help governments to reach the goals in the way they purport to do? Or do they simply imply a shift in the balance of powers toward the executive and less civil and political rights for the citizens at large?

This chapter has shown that it is important to distinguish between natural disasters and domestic turmoil when trying to identify the factors that lead to an emergency declaration. We assume that this distinction may be equally important when ascertaining the effectiveness of SOEs. In Chapter 5, we therefore analyze the effectiveness of emergency constitutions with regard to natural disasters, in Chapter 6, we focus on terror events, while Chapter 7 deals with other domestic turmoil events such as general strikes, mass demonstrations, and assassination attempts.

5 *The Effectiveness of Emergency Constitutions after Natural Disasters*

5.1 Introduction

As repeatedly pointed out in the previous chapters, nine out of ten national constitutions contain explicit emergency provisions and states of emergency (SOEs) are invoked frequently. Calling an SOE usually has two implications: (1) a shift in the balance of power away from both the legislative and the judicial branches of government toward the executive branch; and (2) a reduction in citizens' civil and political rights. Although using emergency provisions is common, it is amazing how little we know about the effectiveness of emergency constitutions in dealing with the consequences of natural disasters.

This chapter is a first attempt to analyze their effectiveness. Our analysis here is confined to the effectiveness of emergency constitutions enacted to deal with natural disasters such as earthquakes, floods, or pandemics. Chapter 6 will deal with the effectiveness of emergency constitutions subsequent to terror events and Chapter 7 with other democratic events such as coups, mass demonstrations, and general strikes. We begin our analysis regarding the effectiveness of emergency constitutions with natural disasters because they are truly exogenous events, yet their direct consequences and side effects depend on government policies and reactions. In the next two chapters, we will need to take the endogeneity of the studied events explicitly into account. In this chapter, we ask whether differences found in various emergency constitutions have clearly discernible effects on the number of people killed, relative to the number of people affected, as a direct consequence of a natural disaster. Because individual rights are likely to suffer under an SOE, we also ask whether the maintenance of individual rights, policies, and democracy differs based on the specific wording of emergency constitutions.

We are therefore concerned with the functionality of emergency constitutions: Do certain aspects of emergency constitutions work as officially intended, in the sense that fewer people are killed in disasters?

Or is there a trade-off in the sense that some aspects are associated with efficient disaster relief but simultaneously with a deterioration in the level to which individual rights are being protected?

The worst SOE scenario is that the executive is not only unable to curtail the loss of life in the wake of a natural disaster, but also effectively dams up individual rights. Although such a possibility might appear unlikely, numerous examples attest to this outcome being a real possibility. For example, as we discuss elsewhere, when a hurricane battered the Dominican Republic in 1931, Rafael Trujillo not only declared martial law and imposed "emergency taxes" on all citizens, he also used this natural disaster to turn his regime into one of the longest-lasting dictatorships in the history of Central America (Crassweller 1966). Trujillo's example is far from unique; any number of Latin American presidents have used emergency provisions in comparable ways. For example, Wright (2014) counts 292 decrees issued under SOEs by the presidents of Bolivia, Ecuador, and Peru between 2000 and 2010.

The behavior of governments during the COVID-19 pandemic offers a plethora of examples of misused emergency provisions, a topic we return to in Chapter 12. Censoring freedom of expression is probably the most frequently reported misuse of power; beyond that, a number of countries barred legislative assemblies (e.g. Mauritius, Thailand, and Serbia). Other countries suspended court operations (e.g. Bangladesh and Nigeria). When legislatures and/or judiciaries are prevented from monitoring the executive, the separation and balance of powers is threatened. In a number of countries, even the military has been used to enforce government measures (e.g. Iran, Malaysia, and Denmark).[1]

The perspective of political economy may help us make sense of this type of behavior, as disasters might allow self-serving governments to expand their power.[2] Rather than using the additional powers granted to them under an SOE to save lives, the powers are used to censor critical citizens.

[1] These examples are described in more detail in Chapter 12.

[2] Leeson and Sobel (2008) show that natural disasters in the US trigger federal natural disaster relief creating resource windfalls for the affected states. This federal relief creates incentives for fraudulent appropriation at the state level. Leeson and Sobel (ibid.) also find that disaster-prone states receive more disaster relief and in turn become more corrupt. The ratchet effect describes a scenario where government involvement provoked by a crisis does not return to the pre-crisis level. Robert Higgs (1987) describes and analyzes this effect in detail for the US.

In one of the very few studies that examine the effects of emergency constitutions, Davenport (1996) asks if the level of political repression exercised by a government can be predicted by the explicit mentioning of either martial law or SOE in a country's constitution. He finds that the existence of what we term an "emergency constitution" significantly lowers a government's willingness to resort to political repression and constrains governments even when they are under domestic pressure. Keith and Poe (2004) build on Davenport's (1996) analysis and focus on how domestic turmoil impacts respect for physical integrity rights. Contrary to Davenport (1996), they find that emergency provisions that place tighter constraints on the executive are associated with more human rights abuses. As with other questions about emergencies, the very limited empirical literature offers contradictory evidence.

Because we focus on SOEs instigated in response to natural disasters, and because one purpose of an emergency constitution is to empower the executive to save human lives, we explore whether the varying details of emergency constitutions are systematically correlated with the number of people who are killed by a natural disaster. We control for the severity of the disaster by taking the number of people affected explicitly into account. We find that the more benefits an executive enjoys after having called an SOE, the *higher* the number of people killed. This finding is definitely not what we expected and will, thus, be discussed in some detail later. Further, we find that basic human rights are likely to suffer more the easier it is for government to call an SOE, and that this effect is more pronounced the larger the disaster is. Finally, any type of autocracy is significantly more likely to impinge on empowerment rights (i.e. the freedom of movement, speech, religion, and political participation) compared to parliamentary democracies. There is an interesting correlation between our results and the results of a recent study that examines the relationship between the violation of democratic standards during the COVID-19 pandemic and a country's public health record. Maerz et al. (2020, 11) find that "pandemic-driven violations of democratic standards in the name of human life are unjustified and lack empirical merit."

Section 5.2 lays a foundation for the issue at hand and offers two hypotheses dealing with possible effects of declaring an SOE: one focusing on constraining the direct effects of the respective natural disaster, the other dealing with potential repercussions on human rights. Our data and descriptive statistics are presented in Section 5.3 and our estimation approach is discussed in Section 5.4. The actual estimates are presented in Section 5.5 and Section 5.6 concludes.

5.2 Hypotheses

We propose to think of emergency constitutions as having two overarching goals: to minimize the negative effects of events that caused the declaration of an emergency, and to reestablish the status quo ante in the medium to long run. This is the standard justification for the inclusion of emergency provisions in a country's constitution. When analyzing the effectiveness of emergency constitutions, both goals should, hence, be taken into account. From among the possible long-term goals, we explicitly focus on the protection of basic human rights here because they often seem to suffer in the aftermath of an SOE; reestablishing the status quo ante is the topic for Chapter 13.

It is conceivable that some short-term effects need to be traded off against long-term effects. For example, a justification for the temporary derogation from civil and political rights might be that doing so will enable government to deal more effectively with the emergency. If a trade-off exists, short-term derogations should lessen the time needed to return to pre-event levels and to lower casualty rates during natural disasters (cf. Ignatieff 2013). Regardless of the normative considerations, which are beyond the scope of our analysis in this chapter (but see Chapter 14), any emergency constitution is implicitly based on two conjectures. The writers of constitutions posit that constitutionalizing emergency provisions is better than not constitutionalizing them.[3] The fact that most national constitutions contain emergency provisions (Elkins et al. 2009) gives this conjecture some traction. The second implicit conjecture is that a temporary concentration of powers in the executive, and the limitation or derogation of some individual rights, increases the probability of the state's survival. The fact that most of the countries without constitutionalized emergency provisions have passed statutory law dealing with emergency provisions shows that this conjecture is shared widely. Before generating hypotheses on the possible effectiveness of different types of emergency constitutions, we want to

[3] The increased predictability of government behavior under a state of emergency might be an additional consideration.

be as precise as possible about the problem, which we structure based on the relationship between three factors: events, institutions, and actors.

5.2.1 Events

To justify the declaration of an SOE, an event must be far reaching for the people directly affected as well as for society as a whole. Although there are any number of event types, we focus on natural disasters as they are the most exogenous event type. Yet this does not imply that the consequences of a natural disaster are determined exogenously. For example, the thoroughness and enforcement of a country's construction regulations will likely impact both the number of people affected and the death toll of an earthquake (Escaleras et al. 2007).

Although declaring an SOE in response to an exogenous natural disaster may be less contentious than declarations following other event types,[4] such declarations may trigger consequences not necessarily intended by the writers of a constitution. If it is easier to declare an SOE in response to a natural disaster because it appears more innocuous, then governments that desire the discretionary executive powers offered during an SOE may use the disaster as a pretext to gain such powers. On the other hand, the repercussions (e.g. abuse of basic rights) of declaring an SOE in response to endogenous event types may be more pronounced because the government has more preemptive control.

We follow a conventional delineation and distinguish between four types of natural disaster: geophysical, hydrological, climatological, and biological.[5] Even after distinguishing between types of disaster, other variables must be considered, such as: areas most likely to be affected, the ability to anticipate and adjust to a disaster, the speed a

[4] Because terrorist incidents can be viewed as a reaction to government policies, voters might interpret the declaration of an SOE as an indication that government policies have been unsuccessful. Conversely, natural disasters are exogenous events even though their severity may not be perfectly exogenous. Floods and earthquakes are, for example, less likely to be severe events where governments or private initiatives have built dikes and reinforced buildings. However, we show that the design of emergency constitutions is generally not associated with the likelihood of a specific event.

[5] Biological disasters include epidemics such as malaria, Ebola, or COVID-19; geophysical ones (sometimes also called geological ones) include earthquakes and volcanic activity; hydrological ones include floods and landslides; while climatological events include droughts and glacial lake outbursts.

disaster develops, and the ratio between the number of people killed and the number affected in other ways by the disaster.

Disaster Types: A Brief Overview

We here follow the classification proposed by the International Disaster Database, which is hosted by the Centre for Research on the Epidemiology of Disasters (CRED) at Louvain University in Belgium. The two most important disaster types classified as geophysical are volcanic eruptions and earthquakes. Earthquakes, in turn, can be divided into those happening on land on the one hand and those happening under the ocean and causing tsunamis on the other.

Some *volcanic eruptions* have changed the course of mankind. The eruption of the Tambora volcano on the Indonesian island of Sumbawa in April 1815 is considered to be the largest and most deadly eruption in recorded history. As a direct consequence, more than 70,000 are said to have died on Sumbawa and the surrounding islands. There is evidence that the eruption is responsible for a temporary change in climate, which is why 1816 is called "the year without summer." Not only was there a noticeable drop in average temperatures, but the lack of sun and heat caused crop failures and famines.

Earthquakes have had similar far-reaching effects. Lisbon was hit by an earthquake on November 1, 1755. The earthquake triggered a tsunami and widespread fires that caused between 30,000 and 100,000 deaths (out of a population of 275,000). The earthquake had a profound impact on contemporary philosophy. The text of Voltaire's *Poème sur le désastre de Lisbonne* argues against Leibniz's belief that we live in the best of all possible worlds. In the twentieth century, Adorno created an analogy between the earthquake and the Holocaust, claiming that both were large enough to transform European philosophy and culture.

The *tsunami* that occurred in the Indian Ocean in December 2004 killed some 200,000 people. Just a couple of years later – in 2011 – another tsunami hit Japan and caused a major atomic disaster there.

Regarding hydrological disasters, the International Disaster Database includes floods and landslides. In the summer of 2022, torrential monsoon rains led to the most severe *floods* in Pakistan's recent history with hundreds of thousands of homes damaged or completely destroyed (www.unicef.org/emergencies/devastating-floods-pakistan-2022). However, floods are disasters with multiple consequences. While they are often deadly events, regular floods in Bangladesh and Pakistan also make large parts of the countries remarkably fertile.

5.2.2 Institutions

We are primarily interested in the effectiveness of emergency constitutions, that is, the degree to which these de jure judicial institutions enable governments to achieve the goals mentioned earlier. The basic notion behind emergency constitutions is that extraordinary events require the use of extraordinary measures not at the disposal of the executive in normal times. Since most emergency constitutions contain at least one of four extraordinary measures intended to mitigate the effects of natural disasters, we assume that the constitutional assemblies believe these measures will allow the government to more effectively deal with a natural disaster.

1. Swift action is usually of the essence, which is why some constitutions enable the executive to dissolve parliament.
2. It has been argued that certain basic rights make swift government action more difficult, which is why many emergency constitutions enable the government to derogate them under an SOE.[6]
3. It has been argued that to save lives during and after a natural disaster, government should have the right to infringe on private property. This includes trespassing on privately owned land and expropriating privately owned goods such as boats or trucks.
4. Some emergency constitutions allow the government to censor the media, based on the assumption that uncensored media reporting could impede fast and effective rescue missions.

These four measures can be thought of as the benefits an executive enjoys after an SOE is declared. But before the benefits can be enjoyed, an SOE needs to be declared and emergency constitutions contain a number of rules that must be met for the declaration of an SOE to be constitutional. Emergency constitutions can, first of all, make it more or less easy to declare an SOE. When an SOE that can only be declared by one actor but requires the approval of others (such as the legislature, possibly even from its two houses), the declaration is "costly" and we expect fewer declarations. If the high costs are accepted and there is widespread agreement in favor of an SOE, we also expect the chances of effective government response to be high. But the consent

[6] International law places a number of constraints on derogation, and a number of core basic rights cannot be derogated, even under an SOE.

of veto players may not be the only requirement a government must meet, as many constitutions enumerate the events that justify declaring an SOE. In the empirical section, we analyze these dimensions both as single aspects as well as in the aggregate.

5.2.3 Actors

The outcomes that we explore are determined not only by the specific event and emergency constitution, but also by two concrete policy choices. First, the executive needs to decide whether to declare an SOE.[7] Second, the executive must respond to the emergency, whether it declares an SOE or not.

The effects that we are interested in (from the number of people killed to the effects on basic human rights) are impacted by the interplay of three components: the type and size of the natural disaster, the content of extant constitutional emergency provisions, and the government's policy choices based on the emergency provisions, including the decision of whether or not to declare an SOE.

Figure 5.1 illustrates the interplay between events, institutions, policy choices, and outcomes. Obviously, the type and scope of a natural disaster will impact our two outcomes of interest. Both outcomes, however, will also be impacted by government behavior, that is, policy choices, which, in turn, are bounded by the institutional constraints embedded in emergency provisions and democratic veto institutions, be they constitutionalized or not.

Although we only focus on natural disasters, a large number of trajectories is possible, making the choice of an appropriate estimation

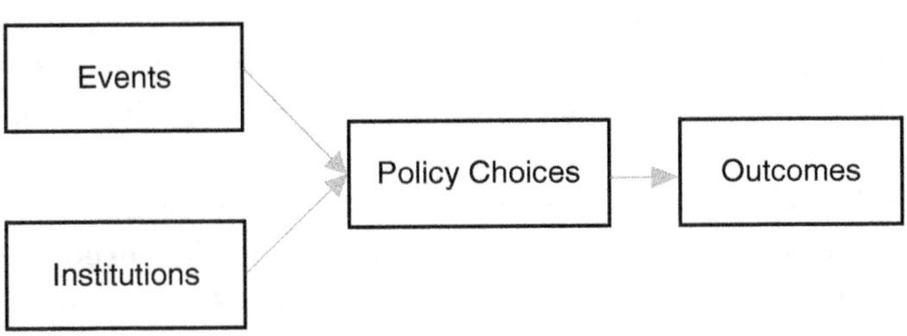

Figure 5.1 Events, institutions, policy choices, and outcomes

[7] The determinants of declaring a SOE are analyzed in Chapter 4.

approach critical. But first, we present two hypotheses on the effects of emergency constitutions. We begin with the obvious hypothesis that emergency constitutions work as intended:

Hypothesis 1: *The more benefits an emergency constitution gives the executive, the more effectively it will be able to deal with the disaster, implying fewer fatalities.*

After an earthquake or a flood, it is essential that rescue operations start as quickly as possible. If government can temporarily ignore private property rights (trespassing privately held land, forcing owners to support rescue operations with privately owned boats etc. and expropriation) this might increase the effectiveness of its operations. The same might be true if the executive branch of government has the competence to order medical personnel to support the rescue efforts, or to reallocate substantial budget means to the efforts without having to secure the consent of the legislature, as the US emergency constitution allows. But we are not only interested in the effectiveness of rescue operations but also in their possible side effects, and particularly in the effects of government behavior on the degree to which basic human rights suffer.

Hypothesis 2: *The easier it is for the executive to suspend basic human rights under an SOE, the more basic human rights are likely to suffer once an SOE has been declared.*

The downside of granting government additional competences under an SOE might be that basic human rights suffer *without* aiding the rescue efforts. Democratic and autocratic governments alike may prefer as wide executive powers as possible and thus have a vested interest in calling an SOE and using its emergency powers. A disaster may thus be a serendipitous event for such executives by opening a constitutional door to additional powers that they can misuse for other purposes.

These hypotheses rest on the assumption that the emergency provisions are de facto respected and used for their intended purposes. Hence, if the different branches and actors of a government are united in trying to limit the negative consequences of natural disasters, we do not expect the costliness of declaring an SOE to negatively impact the response to natural disasters. As already spelled out earlier, political reactions to natural disasters are regularly uncontroversial and reaching consensus across the political spectrum can therefore be assumed.[8] The benefit aspects, on the other hand, may be associated with weaker respect for human rights during emergencies. Yet to the extent that the provisions are merely used as a pretext for political action, we expect that stronger emergency provisions could even be associated with worse disaster consequences.

5.3 Data and Descriptive Statistics

In order to test the effectiveness and potential side effects of emergency constitutions following disasters, we draw data from a diverse set of sources.

5.3.1 Dependent Variables of Interest

For information on natural disasters and their severity, we use the Emergency Events Database (EM-DAT; Guha-Sapir et al. 2014). We limit our identification of a disaster by selecting only those disasters that affect at least one in every thousand citizens in the country (on average 1,000 people).[9] We use the total number of affected people to determine event size, and include country observations only in years when EM-DAT records at least one natural disaster in that country. This avoids censoring problems caused by comparisons to country-years without any disasters and ensures that our results are not influenced by the declaration of "fake" SOEs declared without any actual natural disaster occurring.

Our main dependent variable is the (log) number of people killed per year by natural disasters. Our descriptive statistics are presented in Table 5.1, which shows that the means across disaster types are remarkably similar, with biological disasters the only slight "outlier."

To assess the effects of emergency constitutions on human rights scores, we rely on two indicators developed by Cingranelli and Richards (2004). Their two indicators, a Physical Integrity Index and an Empowerment Index, are an aggregate of 16 categories that cover

[8] It is worth noting that the necessity of reaching consensus gives opposition parties the opportunity to hijack the situation by forcing acceptance of their policies in exchange for consent to emergency measures.

[9] Our results are quite robust, even when changing this threshold.

Table 5.1 *Descriptive statistics*

Variable	Mean	Standard deviation	Observations
Log killed, all disasters	3.120	2.381	2,582
Log killed, Biological	3.555	4.589	2,582
Log killed, Geophysical	2.991	2.416	2,582
Log killed, Hydrological	3.129	2.383	2,582
Log killed, Climatic	3.575	2.414	2,582
Log affected, all disasters	9.067	4.589	2,582
Log affected, Biological	8.792	4.732	2,582
Log affected, Geophysical	8.693	4.847	2,582
Log affected, Hydrological	9.105	4.569	2,582
Log affected, Climatic	8.233	5.187	2,582
Emergency constitution	0.733	0.442	2,559
Physical Integrity rights	4.514	2.286	2,395
Empowerment rights	8.523	3.923	2,394
SOE called	0.229	0.453	2,507
Log population	9.348	1.717	2,440
Log area	12.210	2.085	2,575
Log latitude	2.928	0.896	2,561
Log GDP per capita	8.276	1.318	2,376
Log openness	4.165	0.604	2,395
Log gov. expenditures	2.2598	0.557	2,395
Relative investment price	1.104	0.570	2,395
Federal	0.126	0.332	2,562
Mixed democracy	0.128	0.334	2,480
Presidential democracy	0.223	0.416	2,480
Civilian autocracy	0.269	0.444	2,480
Military dictatorship	0.127	0.334	2,480
Royal dictatorship	0.029	0.167	2,480
Cost INEP	0.431	0.195	1,593
Benefit INEP	0.224	0.183	1,593
Democratic, 1950–60	3.265	4.689	2,582
Predom. Protestant	0.072	0.258	2,424
Predom. Muslim	0.218	0.413	2,424
Common law	0.219	0.414	2,562
Civil law	0.751	0.433	2,562
Log coast line	5331.861	19961.830	2,582
Low elevation	42.128	176.431	2,582
High elevation	3319.296	2064.619	2,582
Landlocked	0.229	0.419	2,582

basic human, political and civil rights.[10] Further, we explore the consequences of emergency constitutions on policies by using four variables from the Heritage Foundation (2016)'s Index of Economic Freedom: government size, rule of law, market openness and regulation. We also control for the degree of democracy, for which we employ Vreeland's (2008) correction of the Polity IV Index, denoted "xpolity," which avoids the direct inclusion of social unrest through coding rules of violence and nondemocratic changes.

5.3.2 Explanatory Variables

To determine effectiveness of emergency constitutions in handling natural disasters, we rely on the dimensions included in the Index of Emergency Powers (INEP) introduced in Chapter 2. The INEP consists of six dimensions. As a reminder: Three of them represent the cost side of declaring an SOE and three of them capture the benefits government enjoys after having declared an SOE. From a legal perspective, the first three cover procedural aspects, and the latter three deal with substantive provisions. The INEP is coded between 0 and 1, higher codings indicate lower costs and higher benefits from the point of view of the executive.

5.3.3 Covariates

Following Kahn (2005)'s approach, we gather covariates on economic, geographic, and political factors. Our economic covariates include: real income per capita in log form, openness, investment price (the price level of capital goods relative to the general price level), and government expenditures (as percent of GDP) as a measure of general government activity. Our assumption is that richer countries are better equipped to deal with disasters. Openness might affect the diversity of a country's economy, and also captures established trade routes that facilitate aid flows following a disaster. We also add the relative

[10] The 16 categories are: occurrence of a coup, state of emergency or martial law, political or extrajudicial killing, disappearances, torture, people imprisoned due to political, religious or other beliefs, judiciary independent, government censorship of the media, official state religion, restrictions on religious practices, domestic and foreign travel, political participation, union activities, women's political rights, women's economic rights, and social equality of women.

investment price, captured as the price level of capital goods (relative to the general price level) as a measure of the structure of the economy. Specifically, if capital equipment is important in dealing with natural disasters and their immediate consequences, countries with a high capital price are likely to have more state and private capacity. All of these covariates are based on Heston et al. (2012).

Our political covariate is form of government. We assume that democratic and autocratic governments will react differently to disasters and the latter will more frequently abuse emergency constitutions. If these suppositions are correct, autocratic countries dealing with a natural disaster will experience more death and more severe infringements on human rights. To make precise inferences, we distinguish democracies as parliamentary, mixed and presidential, and autocracies as civilian, military and royal. Our source for these fine-grained delineations is Cheibub et al. (2010), updated by Bjørnskov and Rode (2020).[11]

Our geographic covariates include: population in log form, the log area of the country, and the log to the latitude of the country. Latitude is considered to be a good proxy for state capacity. The population data are from Heston et al. (2012), and area and latitude data are from CIA (2020). Our dataset panel and the period of our analysis (1990 to 2011) gives us a maximum of 1,511 observations from 122 countries where an SOE was declared in 23 percent of all cases. The period is capped by the end of the Cold War in 1990 and the availability of data on SOE declarations and human rights by 2011. In all cases, we use OLS with random effects and a lagged dependent variable to estimate the effects of characteristics of emergency constitutions in natural disasters, which we include to make sure that fatalities are not wrongly attributed when, for example, disasters either last more than one year or extend across January 1. Simultaneously, this variable also serves as a control for a country's

[11] In other contexts, this fine-grained delineation has proved important. When comparing presidential and parliamentary democracies, presidential systems seem to generate lower government revenue, have lower central government expenditure and suffer from higher corruption levels (Appendix 2 in Voigt 2020 is a synopsis of these findings). The distinction might also be relevant in this context because presidents cannot be forced out of office via a no-confidence vote and might, therefore, act more rigorously than prime ministers.

proneness to disasters, such that we cannot directly interpret the estimate, as it picks up two different factors.

5.4 Our Estimation Approach

In order to obtain a clean estimate of the effects of emergency constitutions on disaster outcomes, we add year fixed effects to our specification to control for joint global developments, dummies for legal origins (civil and common law) that might have an impact above and beyond the variables explicitly taken into account, and region fixed effects (Asia, Latin America and the Caribbean, the Middle East and North Africa, the Pacific Rim, and the post-communist countries) to control for the possibility that our estimates are tainted by region-specific differences. As such, we estimate Equation (5.1) where *INEP* refers to our two indicators, *X* is a vector of all control variables and *D* is a matrix of fixed effects. When exploring side effects, we use one of the measures of human rights, democracy or economic freedom as a left-hand side variable instead of the logarithm to the number of people killed.

$$\ln killed = \alpha + \beta \ln affected + \gamma\, INEP + \delta X + \upsilon D + \varepsilon \quad (5.1)$$

Our estimation strategy rests on the assumption that two countries treated with an identical event have or could have declared an SOE. The question is whether a particular type of emergency constitution clearly outperforms the other based on the goals introduced earlier. Relying on these characteristics captured by the INEP allows us to answer the question whether a particular constellation of competences outperforms others that are also empirically realized. In the next section, we estimate their effects using OLS with annual fixed effects. As a consequence of our dependent variable being entered in logarithmic form, the results pertaining to all other logged variables can be interpreted as elasticities, while the log to the affected population normalizes all effects relative to the size of the disaster.

While causality can never be perfectly established, we include a lagged dependent variable to rule out the possibility that constitutional characteristics are simply a reflection of the immediate changes to the threat environment. In addition, the inclusion of the lagged dependent variable ensures that our estimates cannot simply reflect that past repression of human rights creates more deaths during natural

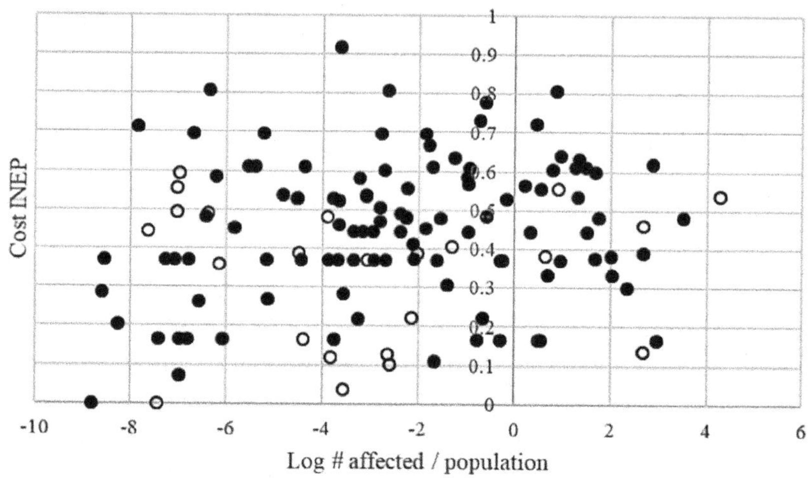

Figure 5.2 Average number of affected individuals, share of total population, versus Cost INEP
Note: Solid circles are democracies, and open circles are autocracies

disasters.[12] However, including lagged dependent variables does not fully alleviate our concern of simultaneity bias, which would arise if the design of emergency constitutions *reflects* the natural threat environment. In other words, if the constitutional drafters took explicitly into account the risk and/or type of disasters naturally occurring in their territory, and did so in an effective way, neither the risk of observing an event nor the number of affected individuals would be exogenous to the event.[13]

Figures 5.2 and 5.3 plot the average number of affected individuals (as a share of the total population) between 1990 and 2011, against

[12] While we are aware that the inclusion of a lagged dependent variable gives rise to Nickell bias, we believe it is relatively unimportant. As the size of the bias is approximately 1/T, where T is the length of the panel, the actual bias is about 5 percent, which does not warrant suffering the alternative problems yielded by estimators that can alleviate the Nickell bias.

[13] In Chapter 3, we report our finding that the specific characteristics of the emergency constitution are not affected by the frequency of natural disasters. The same holds for the probability to introduce an emergency constitution per se. We provide empirical evidence in an online appendix that strongly suggests that the emergency provisions are not affected by the threat environment. Specifically, we capture the severity of the threat environment through the average number of citizens affected by natural disasters in the period between

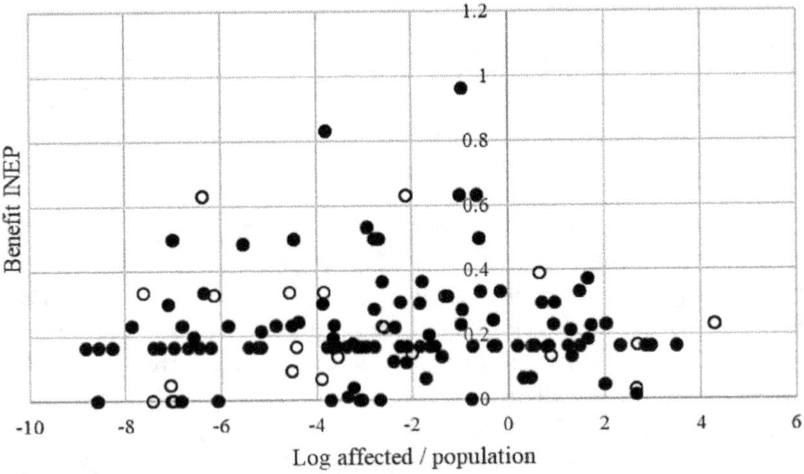

Figure 5.3 Average number of affected individuals, share of total population, versus Benefit INEP
Note: Solid circles are democracies, and open circles are autocracies

the cost and benefit INEP, respectively. If a general feature of emergency constitutions reflects the natural disaster risk, high-risk environments should invariably have more permissive provisions. We observe no such association and note, as is evident in both figures, that the correlations are close to zero. As such, our data do not exhibit any clear signs of associations that would induce simultaneity bias in our subsequent estimates. Our additional tests in Appendix Tables A5.1 also suggest that the risk environment does not affect the design of the emergency constitution, and that reverse causality is not a likely issue. We therefore interpret the events as approximately exogenous and the estimates as evidence of causal effects.

5.5 Estimation Results

Table 5.2 presents the main results of our analysis to determine whether the specific characteristics of an emergency constitution affect the number of people killed when a natural disaster motivates the

1960 and 1980, if the country is in a volcano zone, has a long coastline and is particularly low or mountainous. We subsequently show that these factors are not significantly associated with any of the INEP measures.

declaration of an SOE. Subsequent tables present the results of an expanded set of dependent variables.

5.5.1 Main Results – Casualties during Natural Disasters

Column 1 of Table 5.2 contains all observations, that is, all cases found in the data where a significant natural disaster occurred, where the country had an emergency constitution, and where an emergency might be declared. Yet it is well known that constitutional reality does not always perfectly reflect constitutional text. To exclude the possibility that results are driven by countries that are supposedly more constitution-abiding than others, all OECD member states are excluded in Column 2. Based on the full sample, Columns 3–6 focus on particular disasters: biological (Column 3), geophysical (Column 4), hydrological (Column 5) and climatic (Column 6).

Surmising an emergency constitution's effectiveness in limiting the number of people killed during a natural disaster must explicitly account for the severity of the disaster. Incorporating the log of the number of people *affected* by a disaster seems a straightforward measure of the disaster's severity. As expected, the number of people affected is highly correlated with the number of deaths. The coefficients indicate that on average, biological disasters are the least deadly and hydrological disasters the deadliest.

Ceteris paribus, the number of people killed is directly related to the size of a country's population, while its area is insignificant. Similarly, although previous studies have found latitude to be highly correlated with, for example, income, democracy, and respect for basic rights, we find that latitude is never significant for explaining the variation in the number of people killed. If latitude does have an effect, it is likely to be completely channeled via income.[14]

[14] Latitude is also used as a proxy for institutional quality or state capacity when more direct measures are unavailable. We do not use direct measures, as these would be 'bad controls' when the emergency constitution either affects or reflects state capacity or overall institutional quality. However, in an additional set of tests (not reported but available upon request) we add economic freedom to the specification, treating rule of law as a direct measure of institutional quality and government size as a proxy for state capacity. We find no robust evidence for direct effects of institutions as measured by the Heritage Foundation (2016).

Table 5.2 *Main effects*

	1	2	3	4	5	6
Dependent variable	No. killed	No. killed	No. killed	No. killed	No. killed	No. killed
Disaster type	All	All	Bio	Geo	Hydro	Climate
Lagged dependent	0.174***	0.167***	0.135***	0.165***	0.175***	0.136***
	(0.024)	(0.026)	(0.025)	(0.027)	(0.031)	(0.022)
Log affected	0.083***	0.079***	0.029***	0.078***	0.091***	0.035***
	(0.013)	(0.015)	(0.010)	(0.015)	(0.018)	(0.012)
Log population	0.545***	0.608***	0.704***	0.614***	0.586***	0.698***
	(0.058)	(0.065)	(0.058)	(0.065)	(0.075)	(0.058)
Log area	−0.042	0.004	0.002	0.006	0.020	0.002
	(0.038)	(0.046)	(0.040)	(0.046)	(0.054)	(0.039)
Log latitude	−0.049	−0.071	−0.089	−0.072	0.013	−0.086
	(0.080)	(0.084)	(0.073)	(0.084)	(0.094)	(0.072)
Log GDP per capita	−0.222***	−0.316***	−0.197***	−0.322***	−0.357***	−0.196***
	(0.065)	(0.078)	(0.068)	(0.079)	(0.088)	(0.068)
Log openness	−0.092	−0.068	−0.173**	−0.064	−0.018	−0.170**
	(0.091)	(0.098)	(0.086)	(0.098)	(0.106)	(0.086)
Log gov. expenditures	−0.149	−0.128	−0.135	−0.123	−0.218*	−0.136
	(0.106)	(0.113)	(0.099)	(0.113)	(0.126)	(0.099)
Capital price level	−0.273***	−0.255***	−0.173***	−0.254***	−0.219***	−0.173***
	(0.077)	(0.079)	(0.067)	(0.079)	(0.084)	(0.067)
Federal	0.159	−0.139	−0.063	−0.147	−0.293	−0.049
	(0.164)	(0.206)	(0.183)	(0.207)	(0.221)	(0.183)
Mixed democracy	0.404**	0.113	−0.120	0.108	0.277	−0.042
	(0.194)	(0.281)	(0.239)	(0.281)	(0.341)	(0.246)

Table 5.2 (*cont.*)

	1	2	3	4	5	6
Dependent variable	No. killed	No. killed	No. killed	No. killed	No. killed	No. killed
Disaster type	All	All	Bio	Geo	Hydro	Climate
Presidential democracy	−0.037	−0.496**	−0.386*	−0.496*	−0.323	−0.334
	(0.192)	(0.254)	(0.223)	(0.254)	(0.295)	(0.225)
Civilian autocracy	0.183	−0.198	−0.205	−0.199	−0.064	−0.141
	(0.184)	(0.238)	(0.205)	(0.238)	(0.279)	(0.209)
Military dictatorship	0.284	−0.011	−0.109	−0.016	0.159	−0.045
	(0.225)	(0.266)	(0.229)	(0.266)	(0.312)	(0.233)
Royal dictatorship	0.742**	0.662	0.151	0.668	0.751	0.221
	(0.356)	(0.416)	(0.354)	(0.416)	(0.534)	(0.355)
Cost INEP	−0.115	−0.395	−0.215	−0.372	−0.315	−0.279
	(0.286)	(0.333)	(0.291)	(0.333)	(0.389)	(0.292)
Benefit INEP	0.807***	1.024***	0.619**	1.036***	1.259***	0.652**
	(0.296)	(0.346)	(0.302)	(0.346)	(0.397)	(0.302)
Annual FE	Yes	Yes	Yes	Yes	Yes	Yes
Legal origins FE	Yes	Yes	Yes	Yes	Yes	Yes
Regional FE	Yes	Yes	Yes	Yes	Yes	Yes
Observations	1,511	1,254	1,377	1,253	1,001	1,372
Countries	122	99	99	99	95	100
R squared between	0.794	0.814	0.790	0.812	0.757	0.788
R squared within	0.039	0.046	0.021	0.046	0.047	0.022
Wald Chi squared	1101.10	933.04	1232.36	933.24	4640.34	1240.12

Note: *** (**) [*] denote significance at $p < 0.01$, ($p < 0.05$), and [$p < 0.10$]. Column 2 excludes all OECD member states.

The fact that openness to trade is only correlated with biological and climatic disasters (typically slowly evolving disasters) demonstrates the importance of differentiating between different disaster types. In general, we find the size of government is insignificant, while the relative investment price, our measure of economic distortions associated with government regulations, is associated with substantially fewer deaths.[15] We also find that while a country's specific organizational structure has no clear impact on the number of people killed, some forms of government do. Even when excluding OECD countries, presidential democracies are better at saving their citizens from being killed as a consequence of a natural disaster while the apparently lower effectiveness of royal dictatorships is spuriously driven by a few oil-rich monarchies.

When analyzing the effects of emergency constitutions, the cost INEP (how difficult it is to call a state of emergency) never reaches conventional significance levels, despite our findings reported in Chapter 4 that lower costs of calling an SOE lead to more declarations. Remarkably, the benefit INEP (the powers granted exceptionally to government during an SOE) is highly *positively* correlated with the number of people killed, implying that the more attractive it is for government to declare an SOE, the more people die. Our results indicate that the government's special privileges (such as seizing property, censoring the press or dissolving parliament) make it less, rather than more, effective in dealing with natural disasters. To alleviate concerns that these results might be driven by Latin American countries, we run a robustness test distinguishing between democracies and autocracies, and including separate estimates for both Sub-Saharan Africa and Latin America. It turns out that the results are mainly driven by autocracies.[16]

Observing that the benefit INEP is significantly correlated with the number of people killed in a natural disaster, we isolate the single INEP variables to see which specific constitutional element is likely to

[15] Our interpretation the impact of the relative investment price is based on the idea that countries with low investment prices have government regulations and price controls (including legislation against price gouging) that can limit the prevalence of capital equipment necessary to deal with emergencies, and that can constrain the ability of the private sector to help during disasters.

[16] The results are reported in more detail in the Appendix in Table A5.5.

drive this result. The first three rows in Table 5.3 are the cost components and the last three are the benefit components. Among the benefit components, it is the possibility to temporarily suspend rights that drives the results across disaster types. Although the overall cost INEP is not significant in our previous estimations, two of the underlying variables show significance in some settings.

Our results show that emergency constitutions explicitly mentioning a broad range of conditions justifying the declaration of an SOE (for geophysical disasters), as well as granting government the power to derogate from basic rights are associated with more fatalities.[17] In estimates presented in the appendix, we interact the cost and benefit INEP indicators with a dummy capturing if an SOE is declared to test whether it matters if the government actually calls an SOE in response to a natural disaster. None of our results indicate a significant difference in the consequences of the constitutional characteristics when an SOE is called, or any effects of calling an SOE per se. Yet while none of the interactions are significant, the effects of declaring an SOE in response to a natural disaster are estimated much less precisely, which may indicate that at least some governments make effective use of SOEs, while others abuse it. As such, the purely formal procedural aspects of calling an SOE are evidently not important while some aspects of an emergency constitution affect political behavior if a de facto SOE exists, that is, the country has experienced a natural disaster without its government having formally declared an SOE.

We extend our analysis by interacting the cost and benefit INEP measures with the logarithm to the number of people affected (per 1,000 inhabitants) to determine if the effects of emergency constitutions *mediate* the effects of natural disasters. While confirming previous results, the estimates indicate that, for geophysical and hydrological disasters (e.g. earthquakes, volcanic eruptions, floods and tsunamis that pose particularly immediate threats), more people are killed in countries in which the emergency constitution makes it relatively *easy* to call an SOE. When calling an SOE is particularly easy, the estimates suggest that 15 percent of the affected people are killed. Conversely,

[17] Although we observe indications that approval rights are negatively associated with the death toll, an association that is significant at the 5% level for geophysical and hydrological disasters (when OECD member countries are not included), we must warn that applying a Bonferoni correction for multiple test bias leaves these estimates only weakly significant.

Table 5.3 *Main effects, INEP unbundled into single variables*

	1	2	3	4	5	6
Dependent variable	No. killed	No. killed	No. killed	No. killed	No. killed	No. killed
Disaster type	All	All	Bio	Geo	Hydro	Climate
			Full baseline included			
Declaration rights	−0.030	−0.221	−0.147	−0.213	−0.089	−0.189
	(0.153)	(0.173)	(0.151)	(0.173)	(0.200)	(0.152)
Approval rights	−0.296	−0.370*	−0.216	−0.363*	−0.388*	−0.199
	(0.188)	(0.201)	(0.175)	(0.202)	(0.233)	(0.175)
Conditions	0.406**	0.426**	0.298	0.434**	0.387	0.278
	(0.191)	(0.216)	(0.191)	(0.217)	(0.243)	(0.192)
Dissolution	0.221	0.243	0.066	0.246	0.452**	0.081
	(0.147)	(0.167)	(0.145)	(0.167)	(0.196)	(0.145)
Rights suspension	0.519***	0.613***	0.485**	0.612***	0.539**	0.450**
	(0.197)	(0.227)	(0.201)	(0.227)	(0.253)	(0.201)
Expropriation and censorship	0.223	0.291	0.250	0.309	0.298	0.306
	(0.228)	(0.265)	(0.230)	(0.266)	(0.303)	(0.230)

Note: *** (**) [*] denote significance at $p < 0.01$, ($p < 0.05$), and [$p < 0.10$]. Each column reports the main result of six different regressions. All goodness of fit statistics are similar to those reported in Table 2. Column 2 excludes OECD member states.

although the point estimates differ, there is no significant association between the number killed and the number affected in countries hit by a climate or biological event, if the emergency constitution's INEP cost indicators are very restrictive.

5.5.2 Side Effects

Because these results are counterintuitive, and suggest the abuse of emergency provisions by political actors during natural disasters, we explore the effects of emergency constitutions on the respect for human rights, democracy and policies during disasters. Table 5.4 presents the results of adding an interaction between the cost INEP indicator and the logarithm of the number of affected, allowing us to assess the conditional effects of the size of disasters. In a lower panel, we provide conditional estimates by including an interaction with the benefit INEP indicator.

Focusing on the effects of natural disasters on economic policies and institutions, we use the Heritage Foundation's Index of Economic Freedom (IEF), where values range from 0 to 100 with higher values indicating higher levels of economic freedom. In Column 1, we report the results drawing on the entire Index, subsequent columns report estimates using the subindices rule of law (RoL), government size (Gov), regulatory activity (Reg) and market openness (Mar). The control variables exhibit substantial persistence over time, consistent with previous evidence (cf., Sobel and Coyne 2011). Also consistent with previous studies, we find that the rule of law is significantly associated with latitude, that richer countries tend to develop larger government sectors (the negative estimate in Column 3), and more openness toward international markets (Column 5), and that autocracies tend to be more regulated.

The results in the first columns of Table 5.4 show that as the size of the disaster increases, and when the cost INEP measure is high, more protection is granted to citizens. The opposite is the case for the benefit INEP measure for both regulatory activity and government size, suggesting that the more benefits granted to the executive by the emergency constitution, the more regulatory activity and spending increase.

Focusing on conflicts and human rights, we again observe substantial persistence over time. Conflicts are more frequent in poorer

Table 5.4 *Side effects, policies, human rights, and democracy*

	1	2	3	4	5	6	7	8	9
Dependent variable	IEF	IEF RoL	IEF Gov	IEF Reg	IEF Mar	Ln conflict	CIRI Emp	CIRI phys	Xpolity
Disaster type	All	All	All	All	All	All	All	All	All
Lagged dependent	0.951***	0.891***	0.905***	0.865***	0.902***	0.384***	0.826***	0.680***	0.882***
	(0.011)	(0.012)	(0.013)	(0.015)	(0.015)	(0.025)	(0.017)	(0.020)	(0.016)
Log affected	−0.143***	−0.038	−0.159	−0.342***	−0.171	−0.214***	0.042	0.017	−0.008
	(0.058)	(0.093)	(0.113)	(0.107)	(0.112)	(0.067)	(0.031)	(0.026)	(0.016)
Log population	0.036	−0.042	0.051	0.065	0.167	0.404***	−0.049	−0.198***	0.024
	(0.078)	(0.123)	(0.152)	(0.143)	(0.149)	(0.087)	(0.041)	(0.036)	(0.037)
Log area	−0.032	−0.016	0.116	−0.022	−0.114	0.000	0.002	0.027	−0.038
	(0.057)	(0.090)	(0.112)	(0.105)	(0.109)	(0.064)	(0.031)	(0.025)	(0.027)
Log latitude	0.136	0.497***	0.059	0.001	0.185	−0.485***	0.157**	0.151***	0.163***
	(0.112)	(0.179)	(0.219)	(0.206)	(0.216)	(0.132)	(0.063)	(0.052)	(0.059)
Log GDP per capita	0.079	0.899***	−0.409**	0.164	0.553***	−0.325***	0.164***	0.136***	0.089*
	(0.109)	(0.199)	(0.199)	(0.201)	(0.201)	(0.107)	(0.053)	(0.044)	(0.050)
Federal	−0.209	−0.051	0.146	−0.503	−1.138**	0.993***	−0.285**	−0.365***	−0.176
	(0.250)	(0.394)	(0.484)	(0.457)	(0.485)	(0.283)	(0.134)	(0.111)	(0.113)
Mixed democracy	−0.028	−0.491	−0.307	−0.759	0.213	−0.305	−0.089	0.094	0.106
	(0.308)	(0.485)	(0.598)	(0.561)	(0.589)	(0.349)	(0.167)	(0.136)	(0.134)
Presidential democracy	0.070	−0.314	−0.515	−0.601	0.572	−0.414	−0.136	0.027	0.122
	(0.283)	(0.452)	(0.551)	(0.531)	(0.544)	(0.321)	(0.155)	(0.126)	(0.139)
Civilian autocracy	0.023	−1.100**	−0.681	−0.989*	0.046	−0.074	−0.601***	−0.232*	−0.413**
	(0.286)	(0.456)	(0.532)	(0.512)	(0.541)	(0.306)	(0.163)	(0.123)	(0.163)
Military dictatorship	0.248	−1.029*	0.631	−1.251**	0.139	−0.392	−0.447**	−0.216	−0.345
	(0.348)	(0.559)	(0.655)	(0.629)	(0.666)	(0.374)	(0.199)	(0.148)	(0.202)

Table 5.4 (*cont.*)

	1	2	3	4	5	6	7	8	9
Dependent variable	IEF	IEF RoL	IEF Gov	IEF Reg	IEF Mar	Ln conflict	CIRI Emp	CIRI phys	Xpolity
Disaster type	All	All	All	All	All	All	All	All	All
Royal dictatorship	0.187	−0.162	−0.961	0.753	1.329	−0.436	−0.308	0.012	−0.431
	(0.549)	(0.869)	(1.074)	(1.011)	(1.055)	(0.632)	(0.312)	(0.250)	(0.308)
Cost INEP	−2.284*	−0.971	−2.319	−5.558**	−2.940	−3.178**	0.799	−0.314	−0.089
	(1.250)	(1.993)	(2.433)	(2.295)	(2.411)	(1.477)	(0.699)	(0.575)	(0.199)
Benefit INEP	−0.041	0.448	−0.851	−0.184	−0.595	1.619***	0.007	−0.261	0.068
	(0.429)	(0.682)	(0.835)	(0.791)	(0.823)	(0.497)	(0.233)	(0.192)	(0.203)
Affected * Cost INEP	0.232**	0.112	0.324	0.522**	0.284	0.443***	−0.084	−0.035	0.082**
	(0.115)	(0.184)	(0.223)	(0.211)	(0.221)	(0.135)	(0.064)	(0.052)	(0.040)
Annual FE	Yes	Yes	Yes	Yes	Yes	Yes	Yes	Yes	Yes
Legal origins FE	Yes	Yes	Yes	Yes	Yes	Yes	Yes	Yes	Yes
Regional FE	Yes	Yes	Yes	Yes	Yes	Yes	Yes	Yes	Yes
Observations	1033	1033	1033	1033	1033	1354	1288	1288	1349
Countries	109	109	109	109	109	119	118	118	110
R squared between	0.676	0.609	0.488	0.637	0.564	0.074	0.402	0.226	0.585
R squared within	0.992	0.996	0.983	0.972	0.989	0.796	0.983	0.955	0.985
Wald Chi squared	19578.71	31551.80	10737.67	7748.82	9990.41	751.63	9966.64	3755.20	15742.23
Conditional estimates									
Benefit INEP	2.992**	2.276	4.269	5.049**	1.106	0.185	−0.147	−0.138	0.001
	(1.349)	(2.140)	(2.633)	(2.489)	(2.601)	(1.589)	(0.743)	(0.611)	(0.208)
Affected * Benefit INEP	−0.311**	−0.187	−0.526**	−0.538**	−0.175	0.143	0.016	−0.012	−0.037
	(0.131)	(0.208)	(0.256)	(0.243)	(0.253)	(0.153)	(0.071)	(0.058)	(0.044)

Note: *** (**) [*] denote significance at $p < 0.01$, ($p < 0.05$), and [$p < 0.10$].

countries closer to the equator, while we observe significant evidence for the exact opposite pattern for both types of human rights and democracy. We also see more conflicts and less respect for physical integrity rights in more populous countries, and in federal states and civilian autocracies. Consistent with previous studies, we find less repression in countries further from the equator. We also find that countries with larger government sectors suspend or suppress empowerment rights substantially more.

Most pertinently, we find that the more power is allocated to the executive during emergencies (i.e. a higher benefit INEP), the more social and political conflicts are created by disasters.[18] While the ease with which an SOE can be declared is negatively associated with conflict, the opposite association with the benefit INEP may shed light on the finding that more people are killed when the emergency constitution allows basic rights to be derogated. The conditional effects of the size of disasters given the benefit INEP in the bottom panel show that physical integrity rights are substantially more repressed in larger disasters in countries where SOEs offer more benefits to the executive. We consider this to be confirmation of our counterintuitive result that political actors in certain countries abuse emergency provisions during natural disasters.

All our findings are unaffected by whether or not a country actually declares an SOE in response to a natural disaster, indicating that emergency constitutions do not offer positive effects that contribute to saving lives in natural disasters. We do, however, find evidence that a government's reaction is affected by the emergency provisions they are de jure subject to. The existence of an emergency constitution seems to have significant consequences, although perhaps not the officially intended ones. Our evidence on side effects of emergency constitutions indicates that rather than enabling governments to deal effectively with disasters, and in particular limiting the number of fatalities, most governments use them for other purposes. What those purposes are, and more generally how to interpret our findings, is the topic of our final section.

[18] The results also indicate that democratization is more likely during larger disasters when the cost INEP is higher. We have, however, been unable to replicate this result with other indicators of democracy such as the original Polity IV index, or the dichotomous DD indicator from Cheibub et al. (2010).

5.6 Conclusions and Open Questions

Emergency constitutions have been used since ancient Rome with the normative justification that it is necessary to allow the executive to bypass the separation of powers and provide it with additional powers in order to counter the consequences of emergencies. While some emergencies are a consequence of government action, natural disasters (floods, earthquakes, epidemics, and extreme weather conditions) are random acts of nature, making them exogenous and a natural experiment to test whether emergency constitutions deliver on their implicit promise.

We ask whether the characteristics of an emergency constitution impact its effectiveness in minimizing the casualties caused by a natural disaster, and explore its side effects. Using a panel of up to 1,511 observations from 122 countries where at least one natural disaster occurred that affected part of the population, we estimate how many people are killed in natural disasters relative to how many are affected, and how two separable components of emergency constitutions affect the death toll. We rely on the same set of natural disasters to estimate the effects of a given emergency constitution on respect for human rights, democracy, conflict intensity using a set of indicators for economic policy and institutions.

We find that when emergency constitutions allocate more powers to the executive, more people are killed during natural disasters. This empirical finding clearly suggests that granting additional powers to the executive is not only ineffective, but can have unintended consequences. Our finding that the ease with which an SOE can be called results in more intense conflict caused by larger disasters lends credibility to this interpretation. We also observe that when the emergency constitution allocates more power to the executive, governments use natural disasters as a pretext to increase market regulations and spending. Allocating more discretionary power to the executive may thus undermine private disaster relief (cf. Skarbek 2014).

Given our analysis, one may ask why emergency constitutions that do not fulfill their intended purpose, and have a deplorable impact on human rights, are not redesigned or abandoned entirely. A simple answer is that permissive emergency constitutions are politically attractive. For example, the ability to censor media may be a way to remain in power, despite objective shortcomings (Leeson 2008; see also Chapter 10). In very few cases (e.g. Austria following WW II), these shortcomings were sufficient to compel the constitutional assembly not to preserve the emergency provisions of the previously valid constitution. Our analysis also suggests a concrete way to redesign emergency constitutions. Specifically, limit the power of a government that has declared an SOE to suspend property and basic human rights, even if this constraint is inconsistent with the incentives of most political actors. In other words, an accurate description of the reality of emergency constitutions is inconsistent with much legal work in the area and more likely to be explained by public choice theory.

The question whether – given the dismal performance of emergency constitutions – their inclusion into a country's constitution can be justified at all, will be taken up in Chapter 14. Taking a social contract theory perspective, it suggests that emergency provisions could protect politicians and citizens from the urge "to do something" after a natural disaster (or terrorist event), saving them from action bias and succumbing to time-inconsistent preferences. In principle, emergency constitutions also make government behavior under emergencies more predictable. Using statutory law to enact emergency provisions tends to make these measures permanent, whereas emergency constitutions give the assurance that the provisions are temporary.

Once a decision in favor of an emergency constitution has been made, its main traits need to be chosen. Given the results reported in this paper, limiting the benefits allocated to governments under SOEs seems warranted. This refers, in particular, to the possibility to suspend rights, which should ideally be kept to a minimum. However, we must also note that such constitutional restraint is likely inconsistent with the incentives of most political actors.

This chapter is only a first step in ascertaining the effectiveness of emergency constitutions. The content of emergency constitutions may impact the survival of a country's constitutional order tout court, although the evidence remains disputed. Lührmann and Rooney (2021) argue that an SOE declaration is frequently the starting point of democratic decline and interpret their finding in a way completely consistent with our findings. Peltz (2020) conversely argues that these findings are the result of selection, and that democratic decline might have happened without an emergency. Both interpretations are in line with what we have already emphasized: that disasters can be pretexts for politicians to more easily pursue their own agenda because of reduced constraints. But not all SOEs incentivize democratic decline, and another issue that deserves attention is the number of years it takes to return to the status quo ante.

Appendix

Table A5.1 *Predicting emergency provisions*

	INEP		Cost INEP		Benefit INEP	
Log latitude	-0.026	0.013	-0.067***	-0.016	0.014	0.042
	(0.017)	(0.021)	(0.019)	(0.027)	(0.023)	(0.030)
Log area	-0.006	-0.008	-0.007	-0.005	-0.005	-0.011
	(0.007)	(0.007)	(0.009)	(0.010)	(0.009)	(0.010)
Landlocked	-0.050	-0.048	-0.125**	-0.120**	0.025	0.025
	(0.039)	(0.041)	(0.050)	(0.052)	(0.057)	(0.061)
High elevation	0.000**	0.000**	0.000	0.000	0.000	0.000
	(0.000)	(0.000)	(0.000)	(0.000)	(0.000)	(0.000)
Low elevation	-0.000*	-0.000*	-0.000	-0.000	-0.000	-0.000
	(0.000)	(0.000)	(0.000)	(0.000)	(0.000)	(0.000)
Volcano zone	-0.006	-0.017	-0.039	-0.053	0.029	0.019
	(0.029)	(0.033)	(0.036)	(0.044)	(0.046)	(0.044)
Coastline	0.010	0.006	0.029	0.016	-0.008	-0.005
	(0.031)	(0.058)	(0.045)	(0.089)	(0.045)	(0.063)
Democracy 1950–60	-0.005*	-0.003	-0.009**	-0.005	-0.001	-0.000
	(0.003)	(0.005)	(0.004)	(0.007)	(0.004)	(0.005)
Coups 1950–60	0.011	0.008	0.016	0.004	0.006	0.012
	(0.012)	(0.011)	(0.018)	(0.020)	(0.017)	(0.019)
Average disaster affected 1960–80	0.000	0.000	0.001	0.000	0.000	0.000
	(0.001)	(0.001)	(0.001)	(0.001)	(0.001)	(0.001)
Legal origins FE	No	Yes	No	Yes	No	Yes
Region FE	No	Yes	No	Yes	No	Yes
Observations	115	115	115	115	115	115
R squared	0.122	0.208	0.219	0.291	0.048	0.110
F statistic	2.92	4.89	6.54	7.18	0.79	1.92
Root MSE	0.136	0.135	0.184	0.184	0.170	0.172

Note: *** (**) [*] denote significance at $p < 0.01$, ($p < 0.05$), and [$p < 0.10$]. Legal origins FE include dummies for civil, common and Scandinavian law; and region FE include dummies for Asia, Latin America and the Caribbean, the Middle East and North Africa, and Sub-Saharan Africa.

6 *When Does Terror Induce a State of Emergency? And What Are the Effects?*

6.1 Introduction

States of emergencies are declared frequently. Among the reasons for declaring a state of emergency (SOE), terrorist activities have become ever more important. In this chapter, we are interested in three questions: (1) What factors determine the declaration of an SOE subsequent to terrorist attacks? (2) Given that a terrorist act has occurred and an SOE been declared, what are the consequences on civil and political rights? (3) Coming full circle and given that terrorist acts are endogenous to government behavior, do changes in the degree to which civil and political rights are implemented as a consequence of an SOE impact the likelihood of experiencing further terrorist incidents? We deal with these three specific questions as a precondition for answering an overarching one, namely whether emergency provisions that allow governments to declare an SOE are effective in preventing future terrorist incidents from occurring.

A seasoned piece of advice from successful scholars is never to deal with more than one question in a single study. We explicitly violate that advice here because we argue that the three questions are intimately linked. In the theoretical section, we argue that they can be thought of as constituting a circular relationship: The government response to a terrorist incident might well result in a reduction of civil and political rights, which might, in turn, be the cause of additional terrorist events. Adequately dealing with endogeneity is thus key for reaching reliable results. We do so by estimating the determinants of having any terrorist attack and the subsequent probability that the government calls an SOE. We do so using Heckman's two-step estimator, which allows us to separately estimate the dynamics of the potential repression of citizens' rights around such events and thereby get around the problem that one often observes either no attacks or cascades of terrorism.

Now it seems likely that democratic governments will react differently to acts of terror than autocratic ones. To reveal whether this assumption is correct, we first analyze the behavior of seventy-nine countries with a Western-style constitution and then go on to compare their behavior with a group of countries largely composed of autocratic regimes, namely the forty-eight member states of the Organization of Islamic Cooperation (OIC). This is also interesting as the area covered by these countries is subject to frequent terrorist incidents relative to the more peaceful democracies in Europe and the Americas.

Based on up to seventy-nine countries with a Western-style constitution, the main findings with regard to the three questions just sketched are as follows. (1) The higher the number of terrorist events in a given country and a given year, the higher the probability that an SOE will be declared. SOEs are more likely to be declared when the emergency constitutions simultaneously make it easy to declare an SOE and allocate substantial additional powers to the executive. *Ceteris paribus*, right-of-center governments are more likely to declare an SOE, and they are less likely to be declared in election years. (2) Regarding the effects in terms of civil and political rights, more terrorist events go along with government being more repressive; governments that have called an SOE subsequent to a terrorist attack tend to increase repression levels. Compared to parliamentary systems, presidential democracies, civil autocracies, and military autocracies all repress significantly more following terrorist incidents. (3) Asking whether increases in repression levels cause additional terrorist incidents, we find evidence in support of that conjecture. We also find that countries already under an SOE are more likely to suffer from terrorist incidents at least casting doubt on the effectiveness of emergency declarations. Confining the models to democratic countries only, we find that a strong civil society is significantly correlated with fewer terrorist events.

With regard to the forty-eight member states of the OIC, we find that the reactions to terrorist events are also channeled by the contents of their emergency constitutions even though most of these countries are autocracies. First, if the constitution makes it easier and politically less costly to call an SOE, countries in the OIC are less likely to experience terrorist events. Second, if they do so, the regimes with constitutionally easier access to calling emergencies are also more likely to do so. Our estimates are thus consistent with the interpretation that the declaration of an SOE in countries where the constitutions make them relatively likely are indeed credible deterrents of terrorism. Unlike Western democracies, the likelihood of declaring does not depend systematically on the additional powers granted by the constitution.

Finally, we find that once events occur, it is the benefit side of the emergency constitution that affects the degree to which the predominantly autocratic governments within our forty-eight-country sample use repression. The more additional discretionary power is constitutionally allocated to the government in emergencies (in the form of the ability to suppress basic rights, censor the press, expropriate property etc.), the more governments actually increase repression after terrorist events. These reactions follow strongly from terrorist attacks on military and police facilities and, to a much smaller extent, when the targets of the attacks are government facilities or infrastructure. In addition, the size of the typical repressive reaction is far from negligible.

This chapter is a logical sequel to Chapter 5 in which we inquire into the effectiveness of emergency provisions with regard to natural disasters where endogeneity concerns are largely absent. As already alluded to, endogeneity is a central issue to take into account when trying to ascertain the effectiveness of emergency provisions with regard to terrorist activities.

The chapter is structured as follows. In Section 6.2, we propose a way to delineate terrorist events from other, no terrorist events. In Section 6.3, we present our theoretical approach. Section 6.4 compares the emergency constitutions of our Western sample with those of our OIC member country sample. Our data as well as our estimation approach are described in Section 6.5. We report our empirical findings in Section 6.6. Section 6.7 concludes and spells out a number of open questions.

6.2 Defining Our Key Terms

Terrorism has been defined as "the premeditated use or threat to use violence by individuals or subnational groups to obtain a political or social objective through the intimidation of a large audience beyond that of the immediate victims" (Enders and Sandler 2012). The definition refers to both the means and the goals of the relevant actors.

Two means need to be present, one direct, the other more indirect; use of violence is quite direct whereas the intimidation of a large audience is more indirect. Assassination of a leading politician is an act of violence – but as long as there is no intention to intimidate a large audience it would not count as a terrorist act.

National terrorism is often distinguished from transnational terrorism.[1] Among the many potential differences between domestic and international terrorism discussed in the literature, two are of particular relevance in the context of this chapter. Todd Sandler, one of the world's eminent experts on terrorism, conjectures that the effectiveness of counterterrorist policies may differ depending on whether we deal with domestic or international terrorism (Sandler 2014). Further, the costs of counterterrorist policies might also depend on the kind of terrorism one is dealing with. In other words, transnational terrorism and governments' responses to it are fraught with a number of border-crossing externalities that are largely absent with regard to domestic terror. Another reason not mentioned by Sandler but potentially relevant in our context is that declaring an SOE implies a shift of competences away from the legislature and the judiciary to the executive. It usually also implies that some civil and political rights are being suspended. We argue that the perceived legitimacy of an SOE might also be a function of whether terror is domestic or international.

In addition, we propose to analyze terrorism taking into account whether carrying out a terrorist attack is logistically demanding or not. The events around 9/11 were logistically demanding. Meticulous planning was necessary, substantial amounts of money were needed, many terrorists needed to coordinate their behavior. On the other hand, there are attacks that are carried out by only a handful of people or even single individuals. Using a car to run into a crowd or a knife to kill bystanders are examples of terrorism not implying any logistical challenge. We assume that counterterrorism policies – including all those made possible by calling an SOE – will affect these two kinds of terrorism very differently. In the following, we therefore try to separate types by whether or not the attacks were heavily armed and which types of institution they targeted.

[1] For example, Enders et al. (2011); Sandler (2014, 9) with a number of arguments in favor of such a distinction.

6.3 Theory

Our theory section consists of two main parts. In the first part, we develop a number of potential answers to the three questions formulated earlier and in the second part, we ask if – and if yes, why – autocratic governments behave differently than democratic ones in response to terrorist activities. We begin with the three questions raised in the introduction. As already suggested there, it might prove useful to think of the various cause–effect relationships as being in a circular relationship to each other: Terrorist activities might induce government to declare an SOE, which might lead to higher repression levels, which might, in turn, lead to a higher – or lower – number of terrorist incidents. Such a conceptualization constitutes a challenge for the empirical analysis, as terrorist activities are endogenous to government behavior. For the theoretical part, it implies that the causes underlying terrorist activities should be incorporated explicitly into the analysis.

6.3.1 The General Logic

Since terrorist activities are endogenous, it is important to take the factors driving them explicitly into account. Terrorists strive to reach some social or political change, and their behavior can thus be analyzed as a reaction to government behavior. It has been argued that no respect for physical integrity rights, such as being tortured or imprisoned for political beliefs, could lead to more terrorist activities because the communities from which (potential) terrorists are drawn will be alienated from the rest of society and will, in turn, be less likely to monitor potential terrorists and report suspicious activities to the police. Drawing on game theory, Dragu and Polborn (2014) present a model consisting of an interaction between a representative voter, an elected executive, and members of the community whose support can help prevent terrorist activities. If voters demand tougher counterterrorism policies, governments are likely to supply them because they want to be reelected. However, tougher policies can lead to additional alienation between a government and communities from which terrorists might emerge, making it more difficult to discover terrorist activities before the event.[2] Tough anti-terror policies could also

[2] Cf. the seminal analysis in Londregan and Poole (1990).

potentially curtail the ability of civil society to counteract terrorism and the attraction of joining terrorist organizations. Being tough on terrorists could therefore lead to more, rather than fewer, terrorist activities.

Walsh and Piazza (2010) discuss two other potential transmission channels that could lead to more terrorist incidents as a consequence of nonrespect for physical integrity rights. In addition to the channel just discussed, they hypothesize that nonrespect could cause conflicts with other political groups in the country and could also reduce other governments' willingness to cooperate. They find that improvements in government respect for physical integrity rights reduce the likelihood of terrorist attacks substantially (ibid., 566): "Raising respect for physical integrity rights from its lowest level of 0 by only one unit reduces the expected number of terrorist attacks by between 17 percent and 40 percent, depending on the measure of terrorism."[3]

Walsh and Piazza (2010) point out that their finding might be subject to reverse causality: It could be that it is not low levels of physical integrity rights that cause terrorist acts to be committed but that as a consequence of terrorist acts, physical integrity rights are curtailed. They admit not having found a convincing instrument to establish causality from the nonrespect of physical integrity rights to terrorist incidents but are fairly confident that the causation runs this way due to a number of plausibility tests. Gassebner and Lüchinger (2011) point at the same problem but are less confident regarding the direction of causality. In addition, there might even be something like a vicious cycle; a low level of civil and political rights induces some terrorist activities. As a consequence, civil and political rights are curtailed which induces still more terrorist activities and so forth.

We have presented a number of possible transmission channels according to which little respect for basic human rights could lead to more terrorist activities. These considerations point to a number of factors that may affect the probability of observing terrorist attacks, which we treat in the empirical section. We now move on to discuss

[3] Walsh and Piazza (2010) is a cross-country study. There are a number of country studies referring to France, India, Israel, Italy, Spain, and the UK finding that repressive politics can induce more, rather than fewer, terrorist incidents (Dragu and Polborn 2014, 513 with detailed references).

under what conditions we expect governments to declare an SOE given that a terrorist incident has occurred. We propose to distinguish between the direct and indirect costs of such a declaration.

Direct costs of declaring an SOE can be thought of as the difficulty of securing the consent of those actors whose consent is needed. The higher the number of veto players, the less likely it is that an SOE will be declared. If parliamentary consent is needed, then the fractionalization of parliament is one determinant of the declaration costs: Highly fractionalized legislatures are less likely to approve of an SOE simply because it is more difficult to secure their consent.

But there are also more indirect costs: Declaring an SOE implies a shift in competences from the legislature and (or) judiciary toward the executive but also a reduction in civil and political rights for everybody. Reductions in civil and political rights are generally unpopular but might be accepted by large parts of the population if the terrorist threat is perceived as real and emergency provisions are generally thought to be an effective means to deal with such threats. Formulated differently: the higher the number of incidents, the lower the indirect costs of declaring due to a loss in popularity.

If voters perceive a high threat level – and indirect costs of declaring an SOE are correspondingly low – governments might use the perceived threat level as a welcome pretext to declare an SOE if that increases their discretionary powers and allows them to bypass regular veto institutions. Governments could thus rationally use terrorist attacks as a pretext to implement policies that would either be unconstitutional or vetoed outside of an SOE. Notice that this argument also holds even if reductions in civil and political rights are ineffective means of combating terrorism but mere political signals. We thus have two separate reasons to hypothesize that the number of terrorist attacks as well as their severity in terms of number of people killed are two important factors determining this decision.[4]

[4] Yet another argument explaining why governments might display too tough a reaction subsequent to terror attacks has been developed by Dragu (2011) who shows that security agencies will always advise the government on reducing privacy in the name of additional security. Even after terrorist threats have become less acute, these agencies do not have any incentives to relinquish their added powers. In particular, the choice not to cancel an SOE would, hence, be determined by the influence the leaders of security agencies have on government.

Ideological preferences can also impact on the indirect costs the declaration of an SOE causes. *Prima facie*, one could expect right-of-center politicians of a "law & order" variety to experience lower costs by declaring an SOE than more liberal politicians. One would, accordingly, expect right-of-center majorities to declare more often than left-of-center majorities.

But this reasoning might well be shortsighted. Based on a game-theoretic model, Di Lonardo (2019) predicts that left-wing governments respond to terrorist attacks more aggressively than right-wing governments because they want to signal to the electorate their firm stance on fighting terrorism, which is taken for granted with right-wing governments. In his model, incumbents' responses to terror events are also a function of the perceived threat level (if it is low, then voters weigh liberty more heavily than security, while the inverse is true if the threat level is perceived as high). The entire model is, hence, based on the perceived trade-off between liberty and security, which might be empirically wrong but may well be right according to the perceptions of many voters. Transferring the results of that model to our question, one would, hence, expect left-wing governments to display a higher propensity to declare an SOE than right-wing governments.

Finally, the potential benefits accruing to the government are also expected to impact its decision. The more additional competences come with the declaration of an SOE, the more attractive is its declaration for government. We thus expect effects to be conditional on the contents of constitutional emergency provisions, given that politicians actually respect the constitution.

Declaring an SOE is not the only possible reaction of government to terrorist events. Governments might be convinced that to fight terrorism, they need some of the additional competences currently reserved to times of emergency or, as noted earlier, use terrorist threats as a pretext to gain more discretionary competences. To make these competences permanent, counterterror legislation might be passed. The more encompassing the counterterror legislation, the less likely calling an SOE will be in the future. In a sense, then, counterterror legislation is a substitute to declaring an SOE.

This leads us to the third and final cause–effect relationship. Once an SOE has been called subsequent to a terrorist attack, we are interested in its effects. We propose to distinguish immediate from intermediate effects. With regard to the former, we hypothesize that an

SOE will diminish the level to which civil and political rights are implemented. Intermediate effects of an SOE include changes in the behavior of terrorists. If, due to an SOE, supervision of some buildings is improved or public vigilance increases, terrorists are likely to change their behavior by, for example, attacking those buildings whose supervision has not been improved. In other words, terrorists may rationally change their targets instead of abandoning their plans when policies change.

The rational choice analysis of terrorist behavior implies that changes in the costs of certain terrorist activities need to be taken into account. If an SOE increases the costs of particular modes, other modes become (relatively) less costly and we would expect terrorists to resort to them. Sandler (2014, 6), for example, shows that the improved protection of one target group (say, officials) led terrorists to move on to another one (say, the military). With regard to the effects of retaliatory raids, Enders and Sandler (1993) found intertemporal substitution, that is, terrorists moved planned attacks to be executed in the future to the present in order to protest against the raid. Adding an international element, making terrorist activities more costly in one country might lead to increased activity elsewhere, hence inducing border-crossing externalities (Krieger and Meierrieks 2017).

We propose to ask whether these findings also apply to the use of SOEs. Declaring an SOE could provoke terrorists to protest against such measures by carrying out planned attacks sooner than originally planned. Regarding the potential substitution of specific attacks by alternative ones, we propose the following argument: SOEs shift competences to the executive, which implies that it can use the additional powers to survey and monitor potential perpetrators more closely which is likely to make large and complex terrorist attacks – such as 9/11 – more difficult and thus more costly for terrorists. We propose to call this kind of terrorism "logistically challenging." This implies, however, that very simple attacks, we propose to call them nonchallenging, become relatively cheaper.[5] Formulated as a hypothesis: *In the wake of SOEs declared subsequent to terrorist attacks, logistically challenging attacks will be substituted for nonchallenging ones.*

[5] Countries in which the possession of firearms is legal might suffer from low-tech terrorism in particular.

6.3.2 Differences Due to Regime Types

Theorizing about the use of emergency constitutions by autocrats, we suggest separating two distinct aspects, namely, the decision to declare an SOE and the concrete means used by governments while running a state of emergency. We develop our hypotheses in explicit contradistinction to democratic governments.

As just argued, every government will weigh the expected benefits of declaring an SOE with its expected costs. We continue to split the costs into direct and indirect ones while benefits here refer to the differences in competences government enjoys under an SOE compared to "normal," nonemergency times. If one assumes that autocratic governments are less tightly constrained by their constitutions than democracies, declaring an SOE would grant them fewer additional powers than (more tightly constrained) democracies, which would imply that, other things being equal, they have a lower propensity to declare an SOE.

Moving on to the cost side, it could be argued that both direct and indirect costs are lower in autocracies compared to democracies. If members of the legislature and (or) the judiciary are handpicked by and loyal to the autocratic executive, the costs of organizing the necessary majorities would be lower than in democracies. In addition, indirect costs can also be lower in autocracies. Declaring an SOE is generally unpopular and is likely to decrease government popularity which is, at least *ex ante*, more relevant in democratic than in autocratic regimes.

Autocratic governments need not be reelected fairly. The indirect costs of declaring an SOE are, hence, also expected to be lower for autocratic governments, which increases their propensity to declare. A similar argument holds with regard to the other indirect cost category – namely opposition by parliament and (or) the judiciary. As these are weaker in autocracies to begin with, their opposition could be less relevant in autocracies, which should, again, increase the propensity of autocratic governments to declare an SOE.

Yet the assumption that autocratic regimes are not concerned with perceived government legitimacy and hence their popularity has been challenged in recent years (see, e.g. the survey of the institutional turn in the study of autocracies in Pepinsky 2014). Most autocracies tend to hold regular elections in order to co-opt potential opposition, avoid coup attempts, and create a sheen of government legitimacy.[6] Williamson (2019) documents the specific efficacy of such strategies in the Arab world.

In several studies, Ron Wintrobe (1990, 2019) has argued that autocrats have two means to secure their survival in office: They can rely on buying loyalty or repressing opposition. A regime having at its disposal substantial amounts of resources can more easily choose to buy loyalty – and needs, correspondingly, to rely less on repression. If the declaration of an SOE is interpreted as increasing the level of repression, then we would expect resource-poor countries to be more likely to declare than resource-rich countries. This type of mechanism may be of particular concern to the oil-rich regimes in the OIC (Ishak 2019).

An even more fundamental take on the same issue could argue that autocrats can only remain in power because they have been able to secure some support of sufficiently powerful groups in society.[7] Many autocrats, for example, either use military spending as a way to appease the military elite and to prevent coups from occurring (Bove and Nisticò 2014a) or attempt to bring the military under civilian control (Besley and Robinson 2010; Leon 2014; Bjørnskov 2020). The argument is, hence, that unpopular autocrats will be unable to stay at the helm indefinitely.

In sum, a view of autocracy as a regime type which allows the incumbent government to take political decisions without constraints, political costs, or risks to the survival of the regime might be overly simplistic. However, spelling out a number of more fine-grained arguments does not help us to generate more clear-cut predictions regarding the decisions of autocratic regimes to declare an SOE. In brief, the costs of declaring an SOE might be lower in autocracies than in democracies but so might be its benefits. In other words, it is difficult to make predictions and we will need to let the data speak.

We now move on to analyze government behavior once an SOE has been declared. We are, hence, concerned with the means used by governments, their effects and, in turn, the effectiveness of emergency constitutions. The same theoretical ambiguity applies to the question of whether emergency constitutions in autocracies effectively constrain the actions taken by governments in response to terrorist attacks. Although many constitutions explicitly exclude the derogation from

[6] As argued by Gandhi (2008) or Krishnarajan and Rørbæk (2020).

[7] See, for example Acemoglu et al. (2010) and Bove and Nisticò (2014b).

a number of basic rights, autocratic governments might simply ignore these constraints. The danger that a government will misuse the additional powers it receives under an SOE has been recognized for a long time. It has been observed that democratic governments are significantly more likely than autocratic ones to respect constraints spelled out in a country's constitution. This is why we expect an increase in repression levels *a fortiori* among autocratic governments.

When evaluating the effectiveness of emergency constitutions with regard to terrorist activities, a central question is whether their use leads to fewer such incidents. As already described earlier in this chapter, Walsh and Piazza (2010) argue that infringements into basic human rights following terrorist attacks are likely to lead to more, rather than fewer terrorist incidents because such infringements reduce the loyalty to the regime of those who could serve as whistleblowers informing authorities of planned terrorist attacks. Expanding their argument, we conjecture that low levels – and not only changes in the levels – of respect for basic human rights would increase the probability of terrorist incidents occurring. Given that the level on which physical integrity rights are respected among OIC member countries and other autocracies is significantly lower than among their Western sample, one would – all other things being equal – expect more terrorist events to occur among OIC members. Yet since the (average) level is already low, we expect changes in these scores subsequent to the declaration of an SOE to be smaller than in the Western sample.

The hypotheses developed so far have all focused on a single aspect prevalent with almost all OIC governments, namely their being autocratic. But members of the OIC belong to an organization explicitly calling itself "Islamic," which is why we now ask which consequences this may have on the behavior of its member governments.[8] Supposing

[8] The focus in this chapter is *not* on "Islamic terror" but on terrorism in those countries of the world explicitly professing to foster Muslim values. We therefore do not provide any extensive treatment of the phenomenon of Jihad or groups such as Hezbollah or the so-called Islamic State. Neither do we analyze terrorist events originating in the member states of the OIC, but executed in the West, as we are primarily interested in terrorist events within the region. However, as we recognize that at least some terror occurring in the Muslim world is or could be motivated by religious concerns, we briefly deal with the possible connection between Islam and terror.

that terrorists explicitly acknowledge Islam as a motivation behind their terrorist attack, this situation may create a predicament for governments that acknowledge Islam as a motivation behind their policy decisions: Striking down hard on terrorist organizations would document conflicts within Islam, which is supposed to be comprised of a homogeneous *umma*. In addition, in such societies, the religious establishment may well act as a further veto player. We therefore expect more explicitly Islamic governments to be less likely to declare an SOE, all other things being equal.

"The Troubles" – The British Emergency

Until 1922, the entire island of Ireland was under the control of the United Kingdom. Then, the larger part of the island parted from the UK and formed the Irish Free State which became the Irish Republic in 1937. Six of the nine counties of Ulster in the north of the island decided, however, to remain within the UK. Inhabitants of these counties were primarily Protestants whereas Catholics formed the majority in the Irish Republic. In Northern Ireland today, Catholics outnumber Protestants. From its founding, the country was "in a state of incipient civil war" due to this religious division (Finn 1991, 53).

The so-called "Special Powers Act" passed in 1922 was an attempt to deal with the hatred between Protestants and Catholics in Northern Ireland. Not only did it specify a number of offenses, but it allowed the passing of regulations under the act. The act allowed the executive to delegate this power to any of its representatives "including any officer of the Royal Ulster Constabulary" (ibid., 54). It seems fair to say that under the Act, the government enjoyed powers akin to those enjoyed under an SOE. The Act remained in force until 1973 when it was replaced with the Emergency Provisions Act, following the reimposition by the United Kingdom of direct rule on Northern Ireland in 1972. This Act still provided for a number of extrajudicial powers such as arrest and detention for seventy-two hours (without a warrant, the detainees had no right to a preliminary hearing, no right to silence, and no formal right to a solicitor); interim custody for twenty-eight days; and detention allowing the security forces to detain suspected terrorists indefinitely without charge or trial (Finn 1991, 92). An interim order authorized detention for fourteen days but a study found that "many suspects were held on interim custody orders for periods of five or six months or longer pending the hearing of their cases" (Boyle as cited in Finn 1991, 93).

One of the reasons that led the British government to reinstate direct rule in Northern Ireland was the so-called internment operation implemented in the second half of 1971. Officially called "interrogation in depth," it included five techniques – wall-standing, hooding, subjection to noise, deprivation of sleep, and deprivation of food and drink – and was equivalent to torture. Finn (ibid., 69) refers to most observers agreeing that the internment operation "greatly increased the IRA's membership." This evaluation regarding Northern Ireland is, thus, completely in line with the argument by Walsh and Piazza (2010) that repression can breed terrorism, as described earlier. Later on (in *Ireland* v *the United Kingdom*), the European Court of Human Rights decided that the practice of "interrogation in depth" constituted "a practice of inhuman and degrading treatment" and that this practice was in breach of Article 3 of the European Convention on Human Rights though it did not judge the practice as amounting to outright torture.

Before turning violent, the Irish civil rights movement had demanded that all Irish people be given the same rights. The Cameron Commission, a body formed to report on a series of instances that had evolved in 1968 and 1969 reported that many of the grievances felt by the Catholics were well justified. It explicitly mentioned the allocation of houses, local authority appointments, and gerrymandering with the aim of discounting Catholic votes as compared to those of Protestants. It is, of course, speculation but a possibility that the worst part of "The Troubles" could have been prevented had the (justified) demands of the Catholic civil rights movement been satisfied.

It is usually maintained that it is the aim of SOEs to reinstate the status quo ante. In his take on the development of political terrorism in Northern Ireland, Finn (1991, 40f.) argues that in case of political violence, this might be a bad idea. Instead, "In crises that result from civil insurrection or domestic political terrorism ... the legitimacy of the preexisting constitutional order is often the most salient and troublesome of questions ... Constitutional maintenance in such cases requires not the restoration of a constitution in dispute but rather the restoration of conditions in which all parties can reason fairly and honestly about the proper reconstruction of the constitutional order."

6.4 Are the Emergency Constitutions of OIC Members Special?

Reactions to terrorist events may be influenced not only by whether the observed government is democratic or not but also by the explicit constraints laid down in the country's emergency constitution. This is, at least, what one would hope for. In the following paragraphs, we therefore describe the central traits of the emergency constitutions of OIC member states and compare them to the emergency constitutions of our Western sample.

The OIC currently counts fifty-seven members, that is, more than a quarter of all sovereign states of the world. On its webpage, it describes itself as "the collective voice of the Muslim world," representing some 1.5 billion Muslims the world over. The core of its member states is situated in the MENA region.[9] However, the OIC also has an important number of members in Asia and Africa, two South American members – Guyana and Suriname – and a single European member, namely Albania. In its Charter, member states declare their determination "to be guided by the noble Islamic values of unity and fraternity" and "to endeavor to work for revitalizing Islam's pioneering role in the world." So membership is clearly motivated by religious concerns, which provides a further reason to ask if the emergency constitutions passed in these countries differ systematically from those passed in the West.

Exploring the design of emergency constitutions in the OIC suggests that while there is substantial heterogeneity within the group of countries, they are fundamentally different from those of Western democracies in some respects but not in others. In recent years, the permissiveness of emergency constitutions, as measured by the index of emergency powers (INEP) scores in the OIC region, has varied between a low of 0.15 in Egypt and a high of 0.56 in Sierra Leone, as illustrated in Figure 6.1. The mean score for the Cost INEP among all forty-eight countries included in our OIC sample is 0.72, which compares to a mean score for the Western sample (based on seventy-six countries) of 0.43.[10] It is, in other words, much easier to declare an

[9] A list of all OIC member states is provided in the Appendix.

[10] While there are fifty-seven members of the OCI, as noted earlier, our sample is restricted to forty-eight countries due to the limited availability of constitutional data as well as other data from the remaining nine countries.

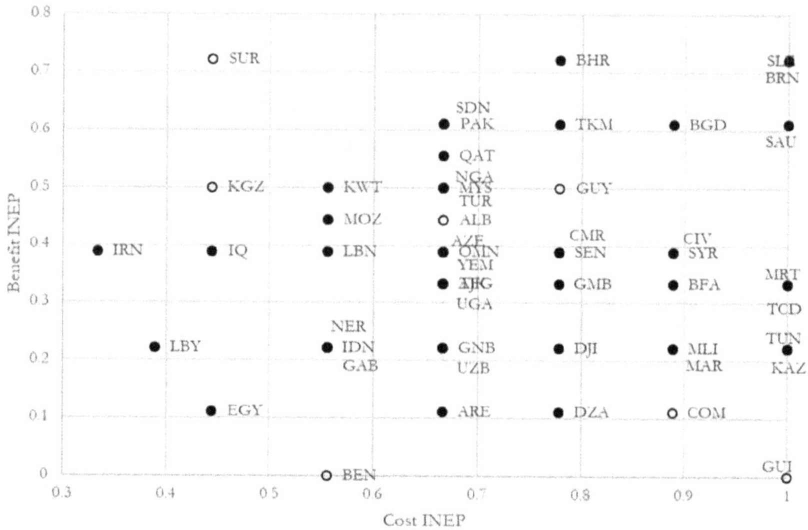

Figure 6.1 Structures of emergency constitutions in the OIC
Note: INEP scores as measured in 2015. The black markers denote autocratic countries while the white markers denote democracies.

SOE in the typical member state of the OIC. Interestingly, the means of the Benefit INEP are far more similar to Western ones, with the OIC countries having a slightly and insignificantly higher mean (0.39 vs. 0.33). Despite the predominance of autocracies in the OIC, their de jure provisions thus do not allow them more discretionary emergency powers than Western democracies.

However, these averages contain substantial structural differences, as the figure that plots the difficulty of declaring an emergency (the Cost INEP) and the political benefits of doing so (the Benefit INEP) also shows. In particular, the constitution of Iran (Cost INEP = 0.17) and the new constitutions of Egypt, Iraq, and Libya (0.25) make it substantially more difficult and politically costly to declare an SOE while it is comparatively easy in countries such as Jordan, Saudi Arabia, Sierra Leone, and Tunisia (0.67). At the same time, the emergency provisions in Benin and Guinea provide virtually no additional discretionary powers during emergencies (Benefit INEP = 0) while those of Bahrain, Brunei, Sierra Leone, and Suriname (0.46) are substantially more permissive by, for example, allowing the incumbent regime to derogate a number of rights as long as an emergency has been declared.

As such, the diversity of constitutional choices in this group of countries mirrors the substantial diversity across countries with Western political institutions. If any clear differences can be observed, they show that the cost components of the INEP are in general more permissive in the OIC than in democratic Western countries. However, given the diversity of OIC emergency constitutions, it is difficult to conclude that they are systematically different. We therefore next turn to exploring their use and effectiveness.

6.5 Data and Estimation Approach

6.5.1 Data

In the following, we focus on three specific outcomes: (1) whether any terrorist event occurred; (2) whether the event or events resulted in the government calling an SOE; and (3) whether the government changed its level of repression as a result of the event or events. For (1) and (2), we employ data from the Global Terrorism Database maintained at the University of Maryland (GTD 2018).

The GTD includes a very large number of events, starting in 1970 and ending in 2016. We include all events that satisfy the criteria and definition of a terrorist event as "the threatened or actual use of illegal force and violence by a nonstate actor to attain a political, economic, religious, or social goal through fear, coercion, or intimidation" (GTD 2018, (9) which covers more than 170,000 events). Within our Western sample, the GTD comprises a total of 60,649 episodes from eighty-two countries that satisfy a particular set of criteria outlined further below, while across the forty-eight countries in the OIC sample we have a total of approximately 76,000 events. We aggregate the data on a yearly basis because our control variables are only available on a yearly basis. This reduces the potential dataset to 3,585 country-year observations from the Western sample and to 2,311 country-year observations for the OIC sample in which an event took place in almost exactly half of the observations. Our first main dependent variable is a dummy that captures whether any such events occurred in a given calendar year. In addition, we include the logarithm to the number of events (plus 1) in a calendar year. For practical reasons of data availability, we cover all available years from 1970 to 2014 in the Western sample and 1970 to 2016 in the OIC sample.

Data from GTD also allow more precise analyses because they include measures of how many events targeted government functions, and how many targeted the military or police. In separate tests, we also use a dummy of whether any events targeted the government, the military, or the police, respectively, instead of the dummy for whether any events took place. In addition, we also create an alternative measure of the number of attacks with multiple targets ("multiple targets events"), which we think of as a proxy for logistically challenging events, versus nonchallenging with a single target. The online appendix provides two alternative ways of separating more from less challenging events relying on the type of weapons used and whether or not there were repeated attacks during more than one day.

Our second dependent variable captures whether the incumbent government officially declared an SOE or martial law as a result of any of these events. We introduced this dataset at length in Chapter 4 and there is, hence, no need to describe it in detail again.

Finally, our third dependent variable measures the degree to which governments repress the population by, for example, violating human rights. We use the indicator developed by Fariss (2014), which combines all available standards-based and events-based indicators available for many countries and several years since 1950. The index effectively captures the latent degree of absence of repression, that is, higher values indicate *less* repression.

Earlier, we argued that the likelihood of calling an SOE subsequent to a terrorist attack is mainly driven by the (direct or indirect) costs as well as the benefits connected to such a declaration. By now, you are familiar with our index of emergency powers (INEP) containing three cost elements and three benefit elements as described in considerable detail in Chapter 2 and used in the subsequent chapters. We use it again in this chapter.

One additional cost component – and one that has not been included in the Cost INEP as it is only very indirectly affected by constitutional provisions – refers to the fractionalization of parliament because it makes it more difficult to declare an SOE. In our Western sample, we include the Herfindahl-Hirschman index of the legislature, which captures the degree of fractionalization of the parliament. The Herfindahl-Hirschman index is coded between 0 and 1 such that higher values imply *less* fractionalization and 1 means that a single party holds all seats in parliament. Further, legislator ideology was hypothesized to influence the likelihood of agreeing to an SOE. We include a measure of the average political ideology of the legislature in the Western sample. This index is calculated by first placing all parties in parliament in five categories: –1 (unreformed communist or socialist); –0.5 (reformed or modern socialist); 0 (modern social democratic); 0.5 (conservative or moderate liberalist); and 1 (classical liberalist and libertarian). Next, we calculate an average of these positions weighted by the seat share in parliament. We get these data from an updated version of Berggren and Bjørnskov (2017). In the OIC sample, we do not include fractionalization or government ideology, but more simply control for differences between single-party regimes, multi-party autocracies, and full electoral democracies. We do so because most of the governments in the OIC countries are either nonprogrammatic or difficult to fit into a Western left–right distinction. Finally, we argue that more terrorist incidents would lower political opposition to declaring an SOE, which would make its declaration more likely. Data on the (logarithm to the) number of incidents in a given year are also from the GTD.

Regarding economic covariates, we include the income per capita in log form because we assume richer countries will be better equipped to deal with terrorist events. We further include a dummy capturing recessions – years in which GDP growth was negative – in our Western sample as terrorist attacks could be more likely when government is perceived to be weak and unpopular.[11] These data are all purchasing-power-adjusted and from the Penn World Tables, mark 9.0 (Feenstra et al. 2015).[12] From the same sources, we include the logarithm to the size of the population, as larger countries are more likely to experience terrorist attacks.

With regard to political covariates, we first include separate forms of political institutions. We do this based on the assumption that

[11] Although it may seem inconsistent, we choose not to include a recession dummy in our OIC sample. The reason is twofold. First, data quality is substantially lower in the OIC sample, which means that we have difficulty precisely identifying recessions. Second, many OIC countries are oil producers, which are subject to apparent recessions for the simple reason that the international oil price varies over time. Such recessions are not comparable to economic recessions in non–oil producers in which domestic factors are more typical reasons.

[12] There has been substantial discussion of the different GDP measures in the new Penn World Tables (cf. Pinkovskiy and Sala-i-Martin 2016). We use the rgdpna variable, as it is much more consistent with alternative sources than the GDP series in the new edition of Penn.

autocratic governments might react quite differently to terrorist events than democratic ones. To tease out the most of this distinction, we follow Cheibub et al. (2010), as updated in Bjørnskov and Rode (2020), and distinguish between parliamentary (our comparison category), mixed (i.e. systems with weak presidents), and presidential democracies on the one hand and civilian and military autocracies on the other.[13] The difference between civilian and military autocracies derives from whether or not the head of state or government has military status or not. As noted earlier, in the OIC sample we also distinguish between single-party and multi-party autocracies, which we do not do in the Western sample due to the lack of any single-party regimes. Throughout, we include a dummy for the occurrence of *coups d'état*, which we get from the same source. We also include a dummy for election years in the mostly democratic Western sample, based on the assumption that governments may have different incentives immediately before elections. All of these variables derive from the background data for Bjørnskov and Rode (2020), which in bi-cameral systems provide data on the lower house.

In further tests, we account for the de facto quality of formal institutions by using three variables from the V-Dem database (Coppedge et al. 2016). These variables capture civil society strength, judicial accountability, and judicial corruption; each variable is scored such that higher scores imply stronger civil society, and more accountable and less corrupt judicial institutions.[14]

To the extent that SOEs aim at reducing the likelihood of terrorist events occurring in the future, they can be interpreted as one type of counterterrorism measure. To be able to evaluate the effectiveness of SOE declarations, other policies should therefore be

[13] It should be noted that the update in Bjørnskov and Rode (2020) does not follow calendar years, but is effectively lagged half a year such that democracy and other features of political institutions up to July 1 in year X are counted as pertaining to year X while any changes after July 1 pertain to year X+1. This feature alleviates most endogeneity concerns if terrorist attacks could cause changes to political institutions.

[14] Seminar audiences have suggested that we add media coverage as an additional control based on the conjecture that more coverage could lead more people to execute terrorist acts. Beckmann et al. (2017) find that media coverage does indeed cause more terrorist incidents. However, their study is confined to three countries only (namely Germany, the UK, and the US) and complete data for additional countries are extremely difficult to get.

controlled for. To do so, we draw on Shor (2011) who has produced a dataset covering up to 219 countries and territories spanning the period between 1850 and 2014.[15] Since we cannot exclude that an SOE was declared due to some other event such as a natural disaster, we always include a variable "log affected by natural disasters." In addition, as Berrebi and Ostwald (2011) claim that natural disasters are occasionally accompanied by terrorist attacks, including natural disasters implies that our first-step estimates are likely to be conservative if disasters incentivize terrorist attacks. Although it may seem counterintuitive to include the Cost and Benefit INEPs, that is, controlling for the specific emergency provisions in the first stage, we nevertheless do so as it also helps us to alleviate most endogeneity concerns. Terrorist attacks may, for example, be more likely when the constitution prevents governments from reacting resolutely, and the emergency constitution could in principle also reflect the historical threat level.

As a final consideration, we address two problems specific to our sample of OIC countries by including the Islamic State Index (ISI) developed by Voigt et al. (2015), which varies from 0 – a situation in which Islam has no formal role at all – to 4 where the law essentially *is* Shari'a. The inclusion of this index captures the complex role that Islam may play for both politics and civil society in these countries. We furthermore include the per capita revenue from oil and gas, which derives from the Ross and Mahdavi (2015) dataset. We believe this is necessary in this specific sample as many OIC member states are resource economies, which are known to exhibit weaker institutions

[15] Epifanio (2011) published a dataset covering twenty liberal western countries and the years between 2001 and 2008. She is interested in the regulations covering citizens, suspects, and immigrants and finds that there are important differences in the legislative responses: whereas some countries such as the US and UK implement all possible regulations identified by Epifanio, others (namely the Scandinavian countries as well as Canada and Switzerland) are much more cautious. In trying to identify the determinants of legislative response, she finds that income (both in absolute size and per capita), involvement in Afghanistan and Iraq, the share of a country's population that is Muslim, and the ideological position of the cabinet are significant predictors. In our context, we propose to complement this list by the share of a country's population that are refugees – because parts of the citizenry might suspect refugees to be potential terrorists –, but also by the temporal distance to the next election, growth, unemployment – the last two indicate domestic problems, government could use SOE to detract attention from home-made problems.

and might be better able to buy loyalty from their subjects using revenue from, from example, oil sales.

Table 6.1 summarizes our data. The upper part of the table refers to the countries with a Western-style constitution and the lower part to the OIC sample. The "Western" sample consists of 2,925 observations

Table 6.1 *Descriptive statistics*

Variables, Western sample	Mean	Standard deviation	Observations
Declared SOE	0.179	0.383	3533
No. of events	1.099	1.509	3583
No. targeting government	0.536	0.924	3585
No. targeting military/ police	0.469	1.028	3585
Log GDP per capita	9.552	0.759	3330
Recession	0.207	0.405	3274
Log population size	1.738	1.899	3330
Log affected natural disasters	4.011	4.809	3582
Mixed democracy	0.176	0.380	3578
Presidential democracy	0.233	0.423	3578
Civilian autocracy	0.147	0.354	3578
Military dictatorship	0.065	0.246	3578
Herfindahl index, legislature	0.439	0.242	3204
Ideology, legislature	0.075	0.408	3204
Coup	0.009	0.106	3948
Election year	0.228	0.419	3780
Uncertain provisions	0.429	0.495	3565
Cost INEP	0.433	0.180	3565
Benefit INEP	0.333	0.206	3565
Civil society strength	0.741	0.283	2989
Judicial accountability	2.406	1.046	2989
Judicial corruption	2.784	0.894	2989
Spatial attacks	2.017	1.541	3948
Repression	0.824	1.399	3319
No. armed events	0.975	1.437	3585
No. killed	0.702	1.431	3585

Table 6.1 *(cont.)*

Variables, OIC sample	Mean	Standard deviation	Observations
SOE	0.197	0.429	1968
Any attack	0.420	0.494	2538
Any attack, military	0.265	0.441	2311
Any attack, gov. or infrastructure	0.343	0.475	2311
Average attack risk	0.188	0.228	2491
Log no. of events	1.075	1.619	2311
Log events against military	0.553	1.198	2311
Log events against government	0.545	1.041	2311
Log events against infrastructure	0.511	1.037	2311
Repression	-0.217	1.019	2187
Log GDP per capita	8.561	1.399	2156
Trade volume	0.402	0.303	2156
Log oil and gas revenue per capita	2.327	2.613	2230
Log population size	1.901	1.671	2156
Judicial accountability	0.144	0.989	2216
Civil society	0.439	0.267	2369
Single-party regime	0.204	0.403	2491
Multi-party autocracy	0.390	0.488	2491
Democracy	0.153	0.360	2491
Successful coup	0.029	0.169	2491
Log natural disaster, affected	3.988	5.258	2538
ISI	2.969	0.930	2491
Cost INEP	0.719	0.172	1237
Benefit INEP	0.397	0.181	1237

Note: the upper half of the table refers to the counties having a Western constitution whereas the lower half refers to the member states of the OIC.

from seventy-nine countries with full data between 1970 and 2014; when using the additional data from V-Dem, the dataset is reduced to 2,586 observations from seventy countries. The OIC sample consists of 948 observations from forty-eight countries with full data. Each of the seventy-nine countries from the "Western" sample has either democratic political institutions or formal constitutional institutions that resemble those of Western democracies. We thus ensure that the de jure political institutions are similar in all countries within the sample such that politics and political reactions are formally structured in similar ways. These seventy-nine countries cover Europe, the Americas, and Australasia. We include fixed effects for the regions in the data, as well as a set of decadal fixed effects. Finally, in the Western sample we also include dummies for whether countries were communist or post-communist as an effective way of handling any events around the transition away from communism in Central and Eastern Europe.

6.5.2 Estimation Strategy

Throughout, our estimation strategy is guided by the need to separate the extensive margin – whether any events occurred – from the intensive margin in the form of the number of events. We believe it is necessary to do so for three reasons. First, the data make it clear that terrorist attacks often come in "cascades" such that one is likely to observe either none or several attacks. This may be a major problem in countries such as the OIC group that have particularly high levels of terrorist activity, and where attacks are either coordinated or one successful attack incentivizes other terrorist groups to attempt attacks (however, see Conrad and Milton 2013). Empirically, this gives rise to a censored distribution of terrorist attacks with relatively many zero observations. Second, multiple attacks on the same or adjacent days may reflect the existence of terrorist organizations with advanced organizational skills that are structurally different from those perpetrated by simpler organizations. In the following, we therefore also create similar variables for three specific types of event: (1) events against the military or police; (2) events against the government and government installations; and (3) events against public infrastructure. Finally, politicians and governments are likely to react quite differently to a single attack than a string of attacks that raise the observable risk of experiencing more attacks in the near future.

The solution to separating the extensive and the intensive margins is to estimate all effects using Heckman's two-step estimator. In the first step, we estimate the likelihood of observing any potential terrorist event while in the second step we estimate the likelihood of calling an SOE or martial law, given that at least one event occurred. As such, we solve the selection bias that would be inherent in estimates in which we either used the entire sample or only focused on cases in which some event occurred. While the Heckman model is known to be sensitive to the specification of the first step and particularly how well it identifies the events (i.e. handles the selection bias), we argue that it effectively resolves the causality issue (Briggs 2004). Given that the first step is reasonably precisely identified, and where variables not included in the second step are similar to instrumental variables in other types of estimators, the second step estimates can be interpreted causally. As we include the lagged SOE variable, that is whether or not an SOE was called in the preceding year, we argue that our first-step estimates may also be interpreted causally, although with some care.[16]

Using the Heckman estimator thereby alleviates a number of endogeneity concerns in the second stage where we estimate whether government calls an SOE and thus invokes the set of constitutional provisions. In addition, as noted, we also include a dummy capturing whether or not the government called an SOE in the preceding year in the first step, as this both captures a general willingness to call an emergency and whether previous SOEs might help prevent future attacks.

In our second set of estimates, we are interested in assessing if and when governments react to potential terrorist events by increasing repression. We estimate these reactions using OLS with decadal fixed effects, and including a twice-lagged dependent variable, given that any event took place. As such, we only explore changes in repression *following* terrorist attacks, given the initial level of repression.

While causality can never be perfectly established, the inclusion of a twice-lagged dependent variable in these regressions implies that we can be reasonably certain that the characteristics of the emergency constitution do not simply reflect the repression environment and that

[16] We cannot directly establish causality in the first step of a Heckman estimator, and it is practically impossible to do so in a potential set of separate instrumental variables estimates of the first-step specification. The reason is that we were unable to find suitable instruments for the constitutional emergency provisions (the Cost and Benefit INEP measures). We note that it appears to be a general problem to predict which countries choose which types of provision. However, in a set of instrumental variables estimates reported in the appendix, we find no evidence of the *reverse* causal direction. As such, it appears very unlikely that our first-step estimates of effects of the INEP measures in the following suffer from endogeneity bias.

it cannot be repression of human rights that creates more events. The twice-lagged dependent variable should capture the initial repression level, and thereby reflect these characteristics, before the onset of any of our potential terrorist events. We also only include the observations with full data in which there was an event. The repression estimates can therefore also be interpreted as a quasi-second stage to the first-stage results using the Heckman estimator.

6.5.3 *Descriptive Statistics*

The data exhibit substantial variation across time and countries. While some countries have been very prone to declaring states of emergency, other countries have refrained from ever declaring an official emergency. Israel has been in a perpetual SOE for its entire existence and the United Kingdom has called emergencies in thirty-six years since 1970, most of which were related to attacks by the Irish Republican Army. Conversely, although Denmark has had a number of events, it has never declared an SOE since the current constitution was implemented in 1953, even though the option is formally available to government.

Figure 6.2 illustrates the development in our Western sample between 1970 and 2014 while Figure 6.3 illustrates the comparable development in the OIC sample between 1970 and 2016; one should note that the data prior to 1980 are from relatively fewer countries than the full 48-country sample. The figures first of all show that terrorist attacks were about as likely in Western countries at the beginning of the 1970s as they have been in the most recent years. The threat of terrorism peaked in the very early 1990s after having been at a high level all through the 1980s. Similarly, from the early 1970s until recent years, the likelihood that a government would call an SOE approximately doubled. These trends have been similar in the entire Western sample (the black lines) and a smaller subsample consisting of countries without any communist past (the gray lines). The decline after 1990 is therefore not a result of the new countries emerging out of the Soviet sphere being less prone to experiencing terrorism.[17]

[17] It should be noticed that part of the decline may be due to the GTD changing coding procedures after 1997. However, two factors speak against this interpretation. First, the decline in terrorism took place in the early 1990s, and therefore before the change in coding procedures. Second, alternative data from the Cline Center's (2017) SPEED dataset exhibits a very similar decline.

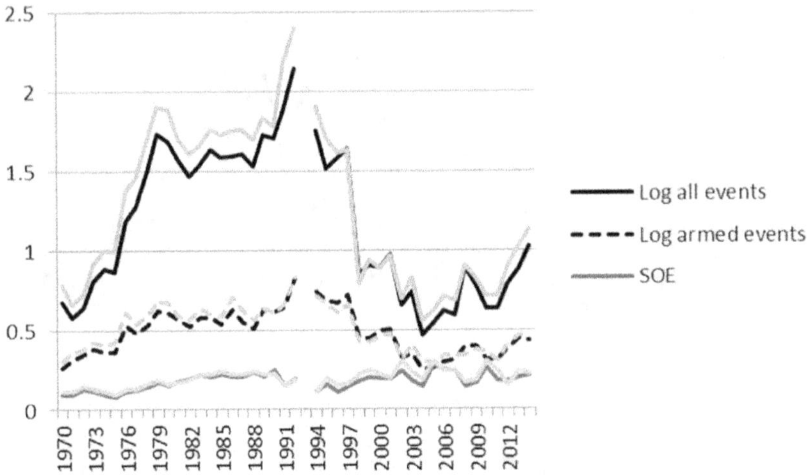

Figure 6.2 Terrorist attacks and states of emergency, 1970–2014, Western countries
Note: The curious gap around the year 1993 is because the GTD data for that year were lost.

Conversely, in the OIC we observe much the same peak around 1990, but an even steeper increase in more recent years as organizations such as *Islamic State* and *Boko Haram* have gained influence in the Middle East and North Africa.

These developments over time nonetheless hide that the likelihood of terrorist attacks varies across countries as well. We illustrate this point in the map in Figure 6.4, which both shows the number of terrorist attacks between 1990 and 2016 – from the lowest numbers in white to the highest numbers in black – as well as which countries are included in the empirics; nonincluded countries are striped. We observe extremely small numbers in both small countries such as Iceland (three events) as well as somewhat larger countries such as Romania (five events). Conversely, the highest numbers are in Pakistan and Iraq (both well over 10,000 events), but also in a medium-size country such as the United Kingdom, which saw 2,037 terrorist attacks in the 47 years we cover.

However, particularly in the Western countries, the character of the typical terrorist attack also changed over the years. In the 1970s and 1980s, the typical threat was often motivated by political

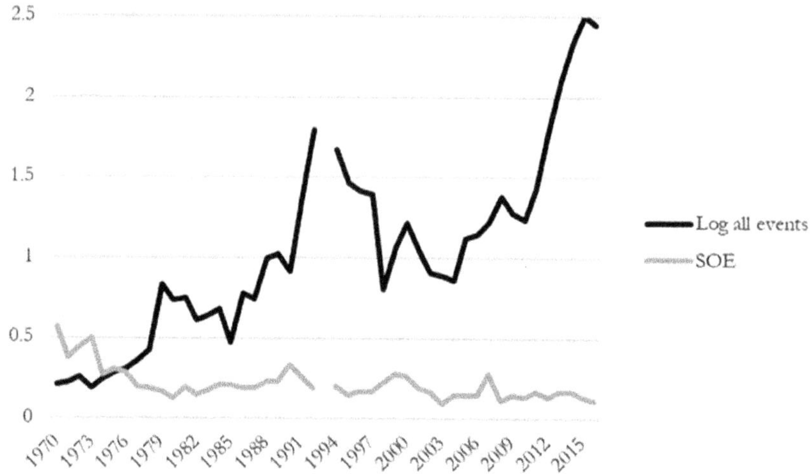

Figure 6.3 Terrorist attacks and states of emergency, 1970–2016, OIC countries

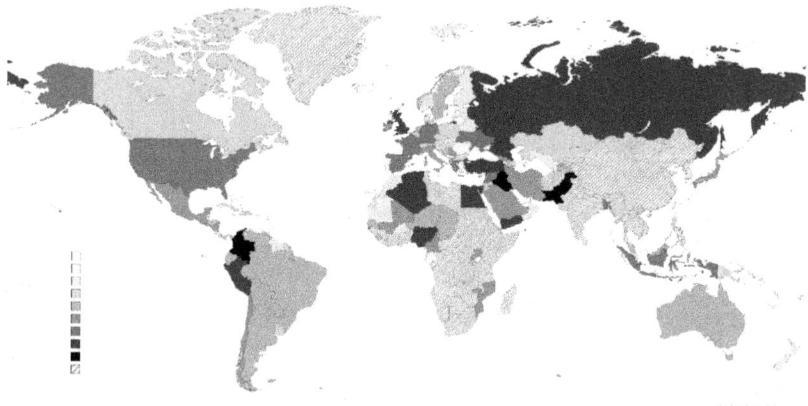

Figure 6.4 Terrorist attacks in sample countries, 1990–2016
Note: Countries marked by stripes are not included in either sample in this chapter.

ideology. Left-wing terrorist organizations, such as Rote Armee Fraktion (the Red Army Faction) that was active in Germany from 1970 to 1989, Brigate Rosse (the Red Brigades) in Italy, and Sendero Luminoso (the Shining Path) in Peru, all subscribed to some form of revolutionary Marxism. Conversely, in more recent years, the typical threat has been from organizations motivated by extreme forms of fundamentalist Islam. In addition, the share of attacks that have been committed by heavily armed groups has increased from about half in the 1970s to 60 percent in more recent years. These differences across countries, variation over time, and changes in event characteristics allow us to estimate the potential effects of emergency constitutions on terrorist events.

6.6 Estimation Results

6.6.1 Calling an SOE

We begin this section by outlining our main findings for the sample of Western countries in Table 6.2a, where column 1 reports the first step and column 2 the second step of the Heckman estimates. Column 1 provides the estimates of whether or not an event took place – that is, what we think of as an extensive margin – and shows substantial persistence in terrorist events. We find that larger countries are significantly more prone to experiencing terrorist attacks, whereas countries with a stronger presence of liberal parties in their legislatures experience fewer attacks. If these societies are more open and tolerant in general, fewer people might be tempted to resort to terrorism as a means of politics. We also observe weak evidence for positive effects of recessions, and some indications that terrorist attacks may be less likely at the time of natural disasters,[18] and in mixed democracies.

Most importantly, we find that countries that have either no or uncertain emergency provisions experience significantly fewer terrorist attacks, as do countries in which the emergency constitution allows the executive access to no or few additional benefits during emergencies. Yet we must emphasize that we cannot claim that these particular features of the emergency constitution are causally associated with the likelihood of terrorism. While elements of the emergency constitution

[18] This finding is opposite to the Berrebi and Ostwald (2011) finding that disaster-related deaths *increase* the likelihood of subsequent terrorist activities. Differences in findings might be due to the very different sample size: whereas Berrebi and Ostwald cover 167 countries, we only cover seventy-nine. Probably more importantly, they "found the effect to be concentrated in countries with low to middle GDP per capita" (ibid., 386). These countries are clearly underrepresented in our sample.

Table 6.2a *Main results, all observations*

	1	2	3	4	5	6	7	8
	Event	Calling SOE	Event	Calling SOE	Event	Calling SOE	Event	Calling SOE
Lagged SOE	0.812***		0.788***		0.801***		0.799***	
	(0.075)		(0.076)		(0.076)		(0.076)	
No. of events		0.105***		0.105***		0.102***		0.106***
		(0.019)		(0.020)		(0.020)		(0.020)
No. targeting government		−0.117***		−0.118***		−0.113***		−0.119***
		(0.018)		(0.019)		(0.019)		(0.019)
No. targeting military / police		0.024		0.026		0.027		0.027
		(0.017)		(0.017)		(0.017)		(0.017)
Log GDP per capita	−0.096	−0.090***	−0.038	−0.097***	−0.009	−0.124***	0.189**	−0.145***
	(0.063)	(0.018)	(0.071)	(0.020)	(0.072)	(0.021)	(0.082)	(0.024)
Recession	0.119*	0.026	0.119*	0.024	0.116*	0.026	0.120*	0.024
	(0.066)	(0.025)	(0.069)	(0.027)	(0.069)	(0.026)	(0.069)	(0.026)
Log population size	0.331***		0.295***		0.298***		0.266***	
	(0.024)		(0.028)		(0.027)		(0.028)	
Log affected natural disasters	−0.012*	0.011***	−0.012*		−0.013*		−0.014**	
	(0.007)	(0.002)	(0.007)		(0.007)		(0.007)	
Mixed democracy	−0.149*	0.056*	−0.168**	0.062*	−0.177**	0.073**	−0.218***	0.081**
	(0.079)	(0.031)	(0.082)	(0.033)	(0.082)	(0.033)	(0.082)	(0.033)
Presidential democracy	−0.001	0.049*	−0.005	0.053*	−0.024	0.067***	−0.097	0.076**
	(0.098)	(0.030)	(0.105)	(0.031)	(0.106)	(0.032)	(0.107)	(0.032)
Civilian autocracy	−0.043	−0.053	0.046	−0.051	0.063	−0.029	−0.159	0.003
	(0.131)	(0.049)	(0.159)	(0.055)	(0.152)	(0.053)	(0.158)	(0.055)
Military dictatorship	−0.122	0.057	−0.365*	0.086	−0.280	0.122*	−0.369**	0.109*
	(0.161)	(0.059)	(0.197)	(0.072)	(0.173)	(0.0654)	(0.174)	(0.063)

Herfindahl index, legislature	−0.468***	0.097	−0.324*	0.086	−0.248	0.056	−0.134	0.034
	(0.174)	(0.065)	(0.195)	(0.069)	(0.192)	(0.069)	(0.194)	(0.070)
Ideology, legislature	−0.304***	0.144***	−0.268**	0.139***	−0.231**	0.114***	−0.232**	0.119***
	(0.106)	(0.041)	(0.110)	(0.043)	(0.111)	(0.043)	(0.110)	(0.042)
Coup	0.235	0.128	0.232	0.130	0.177	0.133	0.262	0.119
	(0.327)	(0.105)	(0.331)	(0.107)	(0.331)	(0.106)	(0.338)	(0.107)
Election year	0.032	−0.068***	0.024	−0.066***	0.025	−0.067***	0.021	−0.067***
	(0.059)	(0.023)	(0.061)	(0.024)	(0.061)	(0.023)	(0.062)	(0.024)
Uncertain provisions	−0.435***	0.182***	−0.436***	0.186***	−0.429***	0.192***	−0.479***	0.201***
	(0.089)	(0.031)	(0.094)	(0.033)	(0.094)	(0.032)	(0.095)	(0.033)
Cost INEP	0.249	0.003	0.221	0.004	0.249	−0.014	0.087	0.023
	(0.162)	(0.063)	(0.167)	(0.065)	(0.167)	(0.064)	(0.168)	(0.065)
Benefit INEP	0.621***	−0.165**	0.638***	−0.161**	0.540**	−0.126*	0.797***	−0.197***
	(0.211)	(0.068)	(0.219)	(0.071)	(0.222)	(0.070)	(0.222)	(0.072)
Civil society strength			−0.399*	0.050				
			(0.222)	(0.077)				
Judicial accountability					−0.110***	0.045***		
					(0.040)	(0.015)		
Judicial corruption							−0.335***	0.071**
							(0.057)	(0.021)
Region FE	Yes	No	Yes	No	Yes	No	Yes	No
Decadal FE	Yes	Yes	Yes	Yes	Yes	Yes	Yes	Yes
Observations	2,924		2,586		2,586		2,586	
Censored	1385		1090		1090		1090	
Countries	79		70		70		70	
Wald Chi squared	291.96		287.11		301.31		300.60	
Log likelihood	−2197.657		−2088.188		−2083.156		−2070.551	

Note: ***(**) [*] denote significance at $p < .01$, ($p < 0.05$), and [$p < 0.10$].

Table 6.2b *Main results, OIC countries*

	All sample		Av. attacks<0.75		No military regimes	
	Selection	SOE	Selection	SOE	Selection	SOE
Lagged SOE	0.919**		0.803**		0.854**	
	(0.109)		(0.155)		(0.140)	
Log no. of events		0.033*		0.094**		0.025
		(0.014)		(0.019)		(0.019)
Log GDP per capita	0.071	−0.023	−0.140	0.066	0.078	0.037
	(0.114)	(0.035)	(0.143)	(0.044)	(0.177)	(0.047)
Trade volume	−0.089		−0.171		0.007	
	(0.208)		(0.244)		(0.283)	
Log oil and gas revenue	−0.071†	0.014	0.038	0.012	−0.124†	−038†
	(042)	(0.015)	(0.059)	(0.023)	(0.066)	(0.021)
Log population size	0.311**		0.314**		0.284**	
	(0.039)		(0.049)		(0.050)	
Judicial accountability	−0.269**	0.098**	−0.221**	−0.002	−0.252**	0.134**
	(0.061)	(0.025)	(0.069)	(0.026)	(0.098)	(0.035)
Civil society	1.289**	−0.401**	0.833*	0.229	1.853**	−0.833**
	(0.289)	(125)	(0.332)	(0.140)	(0.456)	(0.171)
Single-party regime	−0.256	0.129	−0.269	0.149	−0.638	0.215
	(0.232)	(0.109)	(0.270)	(0.119)	(0.444)	(0.145)
Multi-party autocracy	−0.287†	0.179*	−0.357	0.172*	−0.836*	0.307*
	(0.159)	(0.068)	(0.187)	(0.073)	(0.404)	(0.121)

Democracy	−0.408*	0.396**	0.197	0.184**	−1.079**	0.613**
	(0.199)	(0.082)	(0.242)	(0.093)	(0.390)	(0.124)
Successful coup	1.490**	0.455**	1.274*	0.473**	0.062	0.845**
	(0.442)	(0.141)	(0.444)	(0.129)	(0.659)	(0.335)
Natural disaster	0.022*	−0.005	0.036**	−0.005	0.036*	−0.005
	(0.011)	(0.005)	(0.013)	(0.005)	(0.014)	(0.006)
ISI		−0.081**		−0.062*		−0.150**
		(0.029)		(0.031)		(0.037)
Cost INEP	−0.695*	0.611**	−0.619	0.436**	−0.701	0.947**
	(0.342)	(0.148)	(0.385)	(0.164)	(0.445)	(0.185)
Benefit INEP	1.102**	−0.324*	1.175**	−0.419**	0.454	−0.090
	(0.294)	(0.141)	(0.330)	(0.134)	(0.381)	(0.181)
Period FE	Yes	No	Yes	No	Yes	No
Region FE	Yes	No	Yes	No	Yes	No
Observations		948		752		592
Censored		520		334		344
Countries		48		42		33
Wald Chi squared		83.52		63.98		106.44
Log likelihood		−770.726		−548.649		−479.278

Note: **(*) [†] denote significance at $p < 0.01$, ($p < 0.05$), and [$p < 0.10$]. All regressions include a constant term.

may deter attacks, it also reflects the historical threat environment, not least as the estimates clearly show that the likelihood of terrorist attacks is substantially persistent over time.[19]

However, in the second step in column 2, we can establish causality. We observe throughout Table 6.2a that more events make it more likely that an SOE is called as a reaction to terrorist events. As the estimates on the number of events targeting the government and the military or police, respectively, should be interpreted as an *additional* effect of attacks on these specific targets, it occurs that attacks on the government are not associated with the likelihood of calling an SOE.[20] In addition, poorer countries and countries with right-wing legislatures are more likely to call an SOE while election years seem often to prevent governments from calling an SOE.[21] This last finding might come as a surprise as one might expect that a majority of voters would be in favor of reacting swiftly against terrorist attacks. Previous research has nevertheless shown that one (terrorist) strike is often sufficient to prevent the reelection of government (Gassebner et al. 2008). The nondeclaration subsequent to

[19] In order to know whether terrorist activities in our country sample deviate from more general samples, we compare our results regarding factors determining terrorist events with the results of an extreme bounds analysis reported by Gassebner and Lüchinger (2011). Covering forty-three studies that take sixty-five potential determinants into account, they find that eighteen variables survive their extreme bounds analysis. By and large, our results echo theirs. In addition, entering a lagged dependent variable in the first step instead of the lagged SOE variable reconfirms the persistence of attacks, but affects the remaining results to a negligible degree.

[20] In addition, we also more precisely test whether having called an SOE the previous year affects the likelihood of observing events this year. If calling an SOE has a preventative effect, we would expect to observe a weaker link between the number of events in year t−1 and the likelihood of events in year t. Yet when including the lagged number of events as well as an interaction between lagged events and a lagged SOE, we find no significant difference between the persistence of events whether or not an SOE was called. We thus find no clear evidence that calling an SOE has such preventative effects.

[21] Our findings do, hence, not support Di Lonardo's (2019) prediction that left-wing governments are more likely to call an SOE. Note, however, that our analysis focuses on a single counterterrorist measure, namely the declaration of an SOE. Our result should, hence, not be interpreted as a refutation of Di Lonardo's more general claim.

a terrorist attack but during an election year therefore appears perfectly rational: By declaring an SOE government would signal that the attack was a grave incident. By not declaring, in turn, it might want to downplay the relevance of the event to maintain its reelection chances.

We also observe the opposite association as the likelihood of observing terrorist events when it comes to the emergency constitution: Countries with uncertain emergency provisions and provisions that provide more benefits to the executive are significantly more prone to calling an SOE when an event happens.

In the rest of the table, we test the potential effects of a set of institutional characteristics in Western countries: the strength of civil society, judicial accountability, and judicial corruption. We find clear support for effects of judicial corruption, as more corruption is associated with more terrorist attacks, and also weakly with more SOEs.[22] We also confirm in Table 6.3, which repeats the estimates in Table 6.2a but excluding all country-years without full democracy, that no finding is driven by autocracies. In addition, we find only minor differences across types of events. In Table 6.4, we repeat our main estimates in columns 1 and 2, and focus in subsequent columns on attacks with multiple targets – and thus logistically more complicated – attacks against the government, and attacks against the military or police. We find three clear, significant differences. The estimates exhibit less persistence in terrorist attacks against the government, and the benefit components of the emergency constitution are more important to whether or not an SOE is called after attacks on the military or the police. Finally, we see clear indications in column 4 that SOE declarations are predominantly driven by the logistically more challenging terrorist attacks with multiple targets instead of simpler events.

These findings pertain to our sample of "Western" countries, but it remains an open question if they generalize to other types of societies and political regimes. The main findings for our other group of countries – the OIC sample – are documented in Table 6.2b. As we rely on the same estimation approach with regard to our OIC

22 While judicial accountability is also significant in Table 6.2a, further tests suggest that this particular association is driven entirely by the inclusion of Israel in the sample.

Table 6.3 *Main results, only democracies*

	1	2	3	4	5	6	7	8
	Event	Calling SOE	Event	Calling SOE	Event	Calling SOE	Event	Calling SOE
Lagged SOE	0.689***		0.639***		0.678***		0.691***	
	(0.088)		(0.093)		(0.089)		(0.089)	
No. of events		0.114***		0.115***		0.109***		0.131***
		(0.021)		(0.022)		(0.021)		(0.021)
No. targeting government		−0.131***		−0.132***		−0.124***		−0.132***
		(0.019)		(0.020)		(0.020)		(0.019)
No. targeting military / police		0.023		0.022		0.024		0.025
		(0.018)		(0.019)		(0.018)		(0.018)
Log GDP per capita	−0.177**	−0.083***	−0.124	−0.078**	−0.162*	−0.122***	0.065	−0.131***
	(0.073)	(0.019)	(0.083)	(0.022)	(0.083)	(0.022)	(0.096)	(0.026)
Recession	0.109	0.030	0.105	0.029	0.100	0.031	0.101	0.029
	(0.072)	(0.027)	(0.075)	(0.028)	(0.074)	(0.028)	(0.075)	(0.028)
Log population size	0.359***		0.331***		0.342***		0.302***	
	(0.027)		(0.031)		(0.031)		(0.032)	
Log affected natural disasters	−0.017**	0.011***	−0.016**	0.011***	−0.019**	0.012	−0.019**	0.012***
	(0.008)	(0.002)	(0.008)	(0.002)	(0.008)	(0.002)	(0.008)	(0.002)
Mixed democracy	−0.121	0.045	−0.152*	0.047	−0.148*	0.066**	−0.192**	0.069**
	(0.081)	(0.031)	(0.083)	(0.033)	(0.083)	(0.033)	(0.084)	(0.033)
Presidential democracy	0.232**	0.048	0.189	0.052	0.191	0.072***	0.076	0.073**
	(0.111)	(0.031)	(0.119)	(0.032)	(0.119)	(0.032)	(0.121)	(0.032)
Herfindahl index, legislature	0.129	−0.035	0.041	−0.032	0.145	−0.071	0.172	−0.070
	(0.228)	(0.079)	(0.239)	(0.083)	(0.237)	(0.083)	(0.237)	(0.083)

Ideology, legislature	−0.313**	0.069	−0.322**	0.059	−0.297**	0.024	−0.277**	0.044
	(0.122)	(0.047)	(0.129)	(0.049)	(0.129)	(0.049)	(0.129)	(0.049)
Coup	0.211	0.046	−0.063	0.059	0.176	0.025	0.149	0.035
	(0.684)	(0.234)	(0.685)	(0.236)	(0.677)	(0.235)	(0.656)	(0.236)
Election year	0.014	−0.065***	0.014	−0.065***	0.018	−0.065**	0.015	−0.065**
	(0.063)	(0.024)	(0.0656	(0.025)	(0.065)	(0.024)	(0.065)	(0.025)
Uncertain provisions	−0.257***	0.171***	−0.266***	0.172***	−0.255**	0.188***	−0.308***	0.192***
	(0.099)	(0.033)	(0.103)	(0.034)	(0.103)	(0.034)	(0.104)	(0.034)
Cost INEP	0.096	0.069	0.054	0.069	0.074	0.049	−0.065	0.091
	(0.173)	(0.066)	(0.179)	(0.068)	(0.178)	(0.068)	(0.179)	(0.068)
Benefit INEP	0.635***	−0.193***	0.706***	−0.179**	0.627***	−0.152**	0.879***	−0.239***
	(0.227)	(0.071)	(0.235)	(0.073)	(0.238)	(0.073)	(0.239)	(0.075)
Civil society strength			−0.879***	−0.024				
			(0.276)	(0.089)				
Judicial accountability					−0.066	0.057**		
					(0.043)	(0.015)		
Judicial corruption							−0.325***	0.066**
							(0.064)	(0.022)
Region FE	Yes	No	Yes	No	Yes	No	Yes	No
Decadal FE	Yes	Yes	Yes	Yes	Yes	Yes	Yes	Yes
Observations	2500		2207		2207		2207	
Censored	1163		907		907		907	
Countries	75		67		67		67	
Wald Chi squared	207.53		200.45		224.02		216.78	
Log likelihood	−1880.432		−1788.168		−1786.822		−1779.322	

Note: ***(**) [*] denote significance at p < .01, (p < 0.05), and [p < 0.10].

Table 6.4 *Main results, only democracies with different events*

	1	2	3	4	5	6	7	8
	Any event	Calling SOE	Multiple targets	Calling SOE	Gov. event	Calling SOE	Mil. Event	Calling SOE
Lagged SOE	0.689***		0.695***		0.457***		0.800***	
	(0.088)		(0.089)		(0.101)		(0.077)	
No. of events		0.114***		-0.004		0.116***		0.111***
		(0.021)		(0.011)		(0.028)		(0.033)
No. of events, multiple targets				0.141***				
				(0.020)				
No. targeting government		-0.131***				-0.145***		-0.169***
		(0.019)				(0.027)		(0.028)
No. targeting military / police		0.023				0.032		0.044
		(0.018)				(0.022)		(0.028)
Log GDP per capita	-0.177**	-0.083***	-0.178**	-0.090***	-0.316***	-0.053**	-0.434***	-0.058*
	(0.073)	(0.019)	(0.073)	(0.019)	(0.078)	(0.024)	(0.083)	(0.033)
Recession	0.109	0.030	0.113	0.026	0.016	0.033	0.095	0.019
	(0.072)	(0.027)	(0.072)	(0.027)	(0.074)	(0.033)	(0.078)	(0.043)
Log population size	0.359***		0.359***		0.394***		0.322***	
	(0.027)		(0.027)		(0.029)		(0.031)	
Log affected natural disasters	-0.017**	0.011***	-0.016**	0.011***	-0.020***	0.009***	-0.006	0.002
	(0.008)	(0.002)	(0.008)	(0.002)	(0.008)	(0.003)	(0.008)	(0.004)
Mixed democracy	-0.121	0.045	-0.122	0.055*	-0.122	0.027	0.074	0.089*
	(0.081)	(0.031)	(0.081)	(0.031)	(0.087)	(0.040)	(0.095)	(0.052)

Presidential democracy	0.232**	0.048	0.217*	0.074**	0.331***	0.044	0.181	0.034
	(0.111)	(0.031)	(0.111)	(0.031)	(0.113)	(0.038)	(0.119)	(0.052)
Herfindahl index,	0.129	−0.035	0.138	−0.109	0.496**	−0.022	0.975***	−0.193
legislature	(0.228)	(0.079)	(0.229)	(0.079)	(0.230)	(0.096)	(0.237)	(0.127)
Ideology, legislature	−0.313**	0.069	−0.316**	0.081*	−0.044	0.099*	−0.227*	0.026
	(0.122)	(0.047)	(0.122)	(0.047)	(0.127)	(0.059)	(0.133)	(0.078)
Coup	0.211	0.046	0.414	−0.168	0.531	0.027	0.035	−0.290
	(0.684)	(0.234)	(0.641)	(183)	(0.663)	(0.237)	(0.633)	(0.318)
Election year	0.014	−0.065***	0.014	−0.062***	0.007	−0.068**	0.067	−0.064*
	(0.063)	(0.024)	(0.063)	(0.024)	(0.065)	(0.029)	(0.069)	(0.038)
Uncertain provisions	−0.257***	0.171***	−0.257***	0.174***	−0.225**	0.141***	−0.185*	0.234***
	(0.099)	(0.033)	(0.098)	(0.032)	(0.096)	(0.039)	(0.099)	(0.048)
Cost INEP	0.096	0.069	0.097	0.010	0.381**	0.173**	−0.347*	0.124
	(0.173)	(0.066)	(0.173)	(0.066)	(0.182)	(0.083)	(0.195)	(0.110)
Benefit INEP	0.635***	−0.193***	0.635	−0.168**	0.692***	−0.252***	1.098***	−0.526***
	(0.227)	(0.071)	(0.225)	(0.071)	(0.217)	(0.086)	(0.222)	(0.111)
Region FE	Yes	No	Yes	No	Yes	No	Yes	No
Decadal FE	Yes	Yes	Yes	Yes	Yes	Yes	Yes	Yes
Observations	2500		2508		2500		2500	
Censored	1163		1345		1568		1846	
Countries	75		75		67		67	
Wald Chi squared	207.53		218.99		143.91		122.27	
Log likelihood	−1880.432		−1883.131		−1670.219		−1356.547	

Note: ***(**) [*] denote significance at p < .01, (p < 0.05), and [p < 0.10].

sample, we can easily compare the findings. Notice though that we employ the full sample in columns 1 and 2 while columns 3 and 4 exclude countries that have had SOEs in more than 25 percent of all possible years (that is, 11 of the 45 years) our sample covers and columns 5 and 6 exclude all military dictatorships.

As in the Western sample, emergencies are persistent, as indicated by the large coefficient on the lagged dependent variable: If the government called an SOE in year *t–1* – potentially due to terrorist attacks – it is highly likely to observe events in year *t*. We further find that more populous countries are more likely to experience terrorism, as we do in the Western sample. Revenues from the export of oil and gas imply a slightly lower chance of being subject to a terrorist attack but once we exclude the most terror-prone countries, this relationship loses its significance. Coups, on the other hand, are highly correlated with terrorist events only as long as military regimes are not excluded from the sample.

Turning to the robust relationships, we find that higher levels of judicial accountability (here used as a proxy for overall institutional quality) are always associated with fewer terrorist events, lending support to hypotheses claiming that higher quality institutions make terrorist incidents less likely (Dragu 2011). Interestingly, countries with more active civil societies are more likely to experience terrorist events although we can claim neither causality nor a specific mechanism. It may, for example, be the case that civil society organizations are stronger because of a need to handle consequences of terrorism through private organizations as well as political action. It also remains an option that strong civil society organizations in OIC countries reflect a weak state or that they lobby against policies that may be repressive but are effective deterrents against terrorism. Finally, we find that natural disasters are positively correlated with terrorist events. This is in line with previous analyses that found the increased vulnerability of a government subsequent to a natural disaster to be employed to instigate additional terrorist attacks (Berrebi and Ostwald 2011).

Focusing on the determinants of emergency declarations, we do not find that richer countries in the OIC are more likely to declare an SOE when hit by terrorism. This is markedly different from our analysis of the Western sample where we found that richer countries are significantly less likely to declare an SOE subsequent to a terrorist event. Democracies and, to a somewhat lesser extent, autocracies with multi-party elections are more likely to declare an SOE as are countries in which government changed through a successful *coup d'état* (however, see also Chapter 7). A strong civil society is associated with a lower propensity to declare an SOE, yet this association seems to be driven by the most terror-prone countries as the insignificant relationship displayed in column 4 suggests. Finally, oil and gas revenues are not significantly correlated with the likelihood of declaring an SOE. The data thus do not support the conjecture that oil-rich countries might buy the loyalty of their citizens instead of increasing repression levels.

Focusing next on the constitutional differences, the results show that when countries with higher Cost INEP scores experience terrorist events, they are also more likely to declare an emergency. This is, hence, in line with our theoretical priors. Countries with higher values in the Islamic State Index, that is, countries giving pride of place to principles of Islam in their public policies, are less prone to declaring emergencies, also in line with our theoretical priors. Conversely, although the Benefit INEP is strongly significant in columns 2 and 4 (as in columns 1 and 3), the identification here derives almost exclusively from military dictatorships. Overall, our findings indicate that constitutions affect both terrorism and autocratic governments' reactions to terrorism. These findings are confirmed in Table 6.5 where we distinguish between all attacks (repeating our results from columns 1 and 2 in Table 6.2b), terrorist attacks on military installations or the police in columns 3 and 4, and government installations and infrastructure in columns 5 and 6. Although the political nature of these terrorist events may arguably be quite different, we find no significant differences between their determinants.[23]

[23] When estimating the specifications in columns 3 to 6 in Table 6.5 with the sample restrictions as in Table 6.2b (not shown), we find a few noteworthy differences. When excluding either highly terrorism-prone countries or military regimes, only the Cost INEP is significant, and only in the second-step estimates, while judicial accountability becomes insignificant in the selection step. These additional results thus correspond to those in Table 6.2b.

Table 6.5 *Specific results, types of attack*

	All attacks		Only military		Only gov./infra.	
	Selection	SOE	Selection	SOE	Selection	SOE
Lagged SOE	0.905**		0.820**		0.739**	
	(0.109)		(0.098)		(0.109)	
Log events against military		0.068**		0.025		
		(0.022)		(0.021)		
Log events against government		−0.051				−0.088
		(0.070)				(0.080)
Log events against infrastructure		0.019				0.083
		(0.071)				(0.075)
Log GDP per capita	0.069	−0.019	0.166	−0.044	0.118	−0.052
	(0.114)	(0.035)	(0.114)	(0.046)	(0.126)	(0.043)
Trade volume	−0.107		−0.378†		−0.384†	
	(0.209)		(0.214)		(0.229)	
Log oil and gas revenue	−0.067	0.013	−0.112**	0.034†	−1.04*	0.033†*
	(0.042)	(0.015)	(0.040)	(0.019)	(0.045)	(0.018)
Log population size	0.316**		0.300**		0.379**	
	(0.039)		(0.041)		(0.042)	
Judicial accountability	−0.269**	0.097**	−0.326**	0.105**	−0.409**	0.134**
	(0.061)	(0.024)	(0.066)	(0.032)	(0.068)	(0.031)
Civil society	1.304**	−0.399**	0.779**	−0.432**	1.339**	−0.389**
	(0.290)	(0.124)	(0.303)	(0.156)	(0.317)	(0.148)

Single-party regime	−0.237	0.113	0.039	−0.015	0.212	−0.026
	(0.222)	(0.109)	(0.238)	(0.139)	(0.250)	(0.132)
Multi-party autocracy	−0.279†	0.166*	−0.290†	0.152	−0.118	0.094
	(0.159)	(0.068)	(0.159)	(0.088)	(0.168)	(0.081)
Democracy	−0.395*	0.386**	−0.156	0.397**	−0.097	0.350**
	(0.199)	(0.081)	(0.189)	(0.107)	(0.204)	(0.096)
Successful coup	1.490**	0.449**	−0.068	0.341†	0.433	0.516**
	(0.445)	(0.141)	(0.333)	(0.204)	(0.343)	(0.184)
Natural disaster	−0.021†	−0.004	0.013	−0.003	0.014	−0.006
	(0.011)	(0.005)	(0.012)	(0.007)	(0.012)	(0.006)
ISI		−0.078**		-106*		−0.075†
		(0.029)		(0.038)		(039)
Cost INEP	−0.689*	0.562**	−0.517	0.743**	−0.626†	0.825**
	(0.343)	(0.149)	(0.349)	(0.196)	(0.364)	(0.189)
Benefit INEP	1.085**	−0.265†	1.298**	−0.514**	0.934**	−0.404*
	(0.294)	(0.142)	(0.314)	(0.189)	(0.313)	(0.178)
Period FE	Yes	No	Yes	No	Yes	No
Region FE	Yes	No	Yes	No	Yes	No
Observations		948		925		925
Censored		520		338		396
Countries		48		48		48
Wald Chi squared		91.26		70.67		95.69
Log likelihood		−794.292		−645.971		−656.671

Note: **(*) [†] denote significance at $p < 0.01$, $(p < 0.05)$, and $[p < 0.10]$. All regressions include a constant term.

The results indicate that when the constitution makes it easier to declare an SOE following events such as terrorist attacks, countries are less likely to experience such attacks. The specific results in Table 6.5 nevertheless indicate that this does not hold for attacks against the military, but only for attacks on other targets. Conversely, once attacks occur, the same countries are indeed more likely to declare an emergency. Making it easy for governments to declare an SOE is thus an effective deterrent in the form of a credible threat in the typical OIC member state. It is therefore interesting to note that the ease with which an SOE can be called is not systematically important in Western countries per se where it is the Benefit INEP that appears important to declaring an SOE. Yet whether countries that actually declare an SOE do so within the limits of the constitution and without violating human rights is an open question to which we now turn.

Returning to the Western sample, we test whether elements of the emergency constitution exhibit heterogeneous effects. In Table 6.6a, we find only minor differences except two: Interacting with judicial corruption, we find significant negative effects on the likelihood of calling an SOE of having uncertain emergency provisions and significant positive effects of having high Cost and Benefit INEP in societies with relatively substantial corruption. Second, we find that the two elements of the emergency constitution are substitutes. The more substantial the benefits the constitution confers on the executive once an SOE is called, the stronger and more significant is the association between the Cost INEP and the likelihood of calling an SOE.

In Tables 6.6a, 6.6b, we test further interactions with judicial accountability, civil society strength, and social trust, which in general yield similar heterogeneity as in Table 6.5. Finally, we add a spatial measure of terrorist attacks, which captures the potential association with terrorist attacks in neighboring countries. If, for example, terrorists choose to attack a neighboring country if policies make attacks on a given country particularly difficult, we would expect to see a negative association. We nevertheless find a significantly positive association with the likelihood of experiencing terrorist attacks, and a significant but small negative effect on the likelihood of calling an SOE.

Table 6.6a *Only democracies, interactions*

	1	2	3	4	5	6	7	8
	Event	Calling SOE	Event	Calling SOE	Event	Calling SOE	Event	Calling SOE
Herfindahl index, legislature	0.333	−0.016	0.132	−0.041	0.089	0.054	0.110	−0.072
	(0.574)	(0.238)	(0.230)	(0.080)	(0.229)	(0.081)	(0.239)	(0.082)
Ideology, legislature	−0.273**	0.064	−0.103	0.074	−0.292**	0.054	−0.242*	0.011
	(0.124)	(0.048)	(0.323)	(0.127)	(0.123)	(0.048)	(0.130)	(0.049)
Uncertain provisions	−0.824***	0.232***	−0.256**	0.198***	−0.249**	0.155***	0.949**	−0.481***
	(0.228)	(0.085)	(0.106)	(0.037)	(0.099)	(0.033)	(0.376)	(0.132)
Cost INEP	−0.119	−0.041	0.156	0.062	0.448	−0.194*	−0.583	0.575***
	(0.465)	(0.194)	(0.189)	(0.073)	(0.301)	(0.109)	(0.644)	(0.239)
Benefit INEP	1.955***	−0.110	0.659***	−0.177**	1.229***	−0.625***	−1.076	0.492*
	(0.554)	(0.209)	(0.238)	(0.073)	(0.537)	(0.170)	(0.803)	(0.282)
Judicial corruption							−0.462***	0.143***
							(0.116)	(0.041)
Uncertain * Herfindahl	1.455***	−0.168						
	(0.529)	(0.216)						
Cost * Herfindahl	0.737	0.277						
	(1.159)	(0.479)						
Benefit * Herfindahl	−3.508**	−0.272						
	(1.385)	(0.559)						
Uncertain * ideology			0.000	−0.164				
			(0.354)	(0.126)				
Cost * ideology			−0.512	0.198				
			(0.619)	(0.247)				

Table 6.6a (*cont.*)

	1	2	3	4	5	6	7	8
	Event	Calling SOE	Event	Calling SOE	Event	Calling SOE	Event	Calling SOE
Benefit * ideology			0.032	−0.116				
			(0.828)	(0.292)				
Cost * Benefit					−1.557	1.081***		
					(1.118)	(0.374)		
Uncertain * corruption							−0.433***	0.233***
							(0.125)	(0.043)
Cost * corruption							0.191	−0.195***
							(0.218)	(0.081)
Benefit * corruption							0.669**	−0.222***
								(0.089)
							(0.269)	
Region FE	Yes	No	Yes	No	Yes	No	Yes	No
Decadal FE	Yes	Yes	Yes	Yes	Yes	Yes	Yes	Yes
Observations	2500		2500		2500		2207	
Censored	1163		1163		1163		907	
Countries	75		75		75		67	
Wald Chi squared	210.71		212.37		194.42		256.85	
Log likelihood	−1874.668		−1877.897		−1885.529		−1760.421	

Note: ***(**) [*] denote significance at $p < .01$, ($p < 0.05$), and [$p < 0.10$].

Table 6.6b *Only democracies, interactions*

	1	2	3	4	5	6	7	8
	Event	Calling SOE	Event	Calling SOE	Event	Calling SOE	Event	Calling SOE
Herfindahl index, legislature	0.203	−0.045	0.176	−0.042	−0.003	−0.011	0.137	−0.049
	(0.247)	(0.086)	(0.247)	(0.085)	(0.247)	(0.084)	(0.247)	(0.083)
Ideology, legislature	−0.318**	0.031	−0.260*	0.036	−0.257*	0.105**	−0.346***	0.077
	(0.133)	(0.051)	(0.134)	(0.051)	(0.136)	(0.052)	(0.130)	(0.049)
Uncertain provisions	0.188	−0.137	0.704*	−0.389***	0.274	−0.034	−0.168	0.136***
	(0.279)	(0.088)	(0.379)	(0.135)	(0.253)	(0.084)	(0.106)	(0.033)
Cost INEP	−0.675	0.411*	−0.530	0.570**	−0.573	0.373***	−0.216	0.116*
	(0.604)	(0.233)	(0.651)	(0.246)	(0.385)	(0.144)	(0.181)	(0.069)
Benefit INEP	−0.071	−0.035	−0.806	0.485*	−0.086	0.264	1.003***	−0.254***
	(0.642)	(0.205)	(0.813)	(0.293)	(0.579)	(0.202)	(0.244)	(0.075)
Judicial accountability	−0.179	0.076*						
	(0.114)	(0.043)						
Civil society			−0.384***	0.115***				
			(0.118)	(0.043)				
Social trust					−0.025***	0.004*		
					(0.006)	(0.002)		
Uncertain * accountability	−0.181*	0.122***						
	(0.107)	(0.033)						
Cost * accountability	0.248	−0.144*						
	(0.213)	(0.079)						
Benefit * accountability	0.320	−0.056						
	(0.248)	(0.077)						

Table 6.6b (*cont.*)

	1	2	3	4	5	6	7	8
	Event	Calling SOE	Event	Calling SOE	Event	Calling SOE	Event	Calling SOE
Uncertain * civil society			−0.348***	0.189***				
			(0.126)	(0.044)				
Cost * civil society			0.167	−0.199**				
			(0.221)	(0.083)				
Benefit * civil society			0.585**	−0.210**				
			(0.274)	(0.093)				
Uncertain * trust					−0.024**	0.008***		
					(0.011)	(0.003)		
Cost * trust					0.025*	−0.015***		
					(0.014)	(0.005)		
Benefit * trust					0.036	−0.019**		
					(0.022)	(0.007)		
Spatial attacks							0.328***	−0.049***
							(0.023)	(0.010)
Region FE	Yes	No	Yes	No	Yes	No	Yes	No
Decadal FE	Yes	Yes	Yes	Yes	Yes	Yes	Yes	Yes
Observations	2117		2117		2187		2360	
Censored	873		873		917		1079	
Countries	67		67		69		74	
Wald Chi squared	209.02		207.43		205.99		213.40	
Log likelihood	−1729.563		−1721.548		−1756.183		−1715.721	

Note: ***(**) [*] denote significance at $p < .01$, ($p < 0.05$), and [$p < 0.10$].

6.7 Consequences for Repressive Policy

Our final question is if terrorist attacks cause an increase in repressive policy, which we test in Table 6.7 for our Western sample and in Table 6.8 for our OIC sample. We here include lagged repression, such that we effectively identify the determinants of *changes* around terrorist attacks. The sample used in the tables therefore only includes years in which a country was subject to an attack.

With respect to the control variables, we first observe policy declines, that is, more repression, following years with more events and events in which more people were killed.[24] We also see more repression in smaller countries, yet must note that this may be spurious, as the control for population size effectively "scales" the number of events and number of people killed to the size of the country. Using the full sample in column 1, we also find indications that presidential democracies, civilian autocracies, and military dictatorships – that is, regimes in which the executive branch is particularly powerful – react to terrorist attacks with more repressive policy than parliamentary democracies. However, restricting the sample to include only democracies in columns 2 to 4, we find no indications that presidential democracies are different from other forms.

Turning to the emergency constitution, the results strongly suggest that the declaration of an SOE in a Western society is associated with significantly more repression as a result of terrorist attacks. In other words, in societies in which the government uses the emergency provisions actively, it is likely to react to terrorism with repression. Finally, we find that while attacks in which more people are killed are more likely to lead to repressive policy, this effect does not occur when the emergency constitution makes it very difficult to call an SOE (the Cost INEP). Larger events in which more people are killed only tend to lead to more repression when the constitution makes it relatively easy for the executive to call an SOE.

Overall, we thus find that while the emergency constitution may arguably reflect the historical threat level, uncertain emergency

[24] In addition to adding the numbers of events, armed events, and people killed, we have also experimented with focusing on attacks with multiple targets. We nevertheless do not find any different repression reactions to these attacks, despite that they appear more likely to result in an SOE. These results are available upon request.

Table 6.7 *Main repression results, all observations, Western sample*

	All	Democratic	Democratic	Democratic
	Repression	Repression	Repression	Repression
Lagged repression	0.858***	0.847***	0.845***	0.844***
	(0.011)	(0.012)	(0.012)	(0.012)
No. of events	−0.050***	−0.055***	−0.052***	−0.056***
	(0.018)	(0.019)	(0.019)	(0.019)
No. armed events	0.033*	0.035*	0.031*	0.038**
	(0.018)	(0.018)	(0.018)	(0.018)
No. killed	−0.026***	−0.025***	−0.024***	0.014
	(0.006)	(0.007)	(0.007)	(0.015)
SOE declared	−0.073***	−0.085***	−0.140***	−0.085***
	(0.017)	(0.018)	(0.051)	(0.018)
Log GDP per capita	0.045*	0.055*	0.054*	0.057*
	(0.024)	(0.031)	(0.032)	(0.032)
Recession	−0.013	0.001	0.001	0.003
	(0.014)	(0.015)	(0.015)	(0.015)
Log population size	−0.026***	−0.035***	−0.037***	−0.035***
	(0.009)	(0.011)	(0.012)	(0.012)
Mixed democracy	0.028	0.003	0.005	0.003
	(0.029)	(0.035)	(0.036)	(0.036)
Presidential democracy	−0.112***	−0.086	−0.082	−0.099*
	(0.036)	(0.055)	(0.057)	(0.057)
Civilian autocracy	−0.161***			
	(0.040)			
Military dictatorship	−0.313***			
	(0.049)			
Herfindahl index, legislature	−0.057	−0.044	−0.045	−0.036
	(0.042)	(0.059)	(0.059)	(0.059)
Ideology, legislature	0.053*	−0.006	−0.007	−0.010
	(0.029)	(0.037)	(0.037)	(0.037)
Coup	−0.095	−0.034	−0.044	−0.034
	(0.069)	(0.155)	(0.156)	(0.154)
Election year	0.005	0.002	0.002	0.000
	(0.013)	(0.013)	(0.013)	(0.013)
Uncertain provisions	0.045*	0.061	0.0590	0.061
	(0.028)	(0.035)	(0.038)	(0.039)
Cost INEP	−0.079	−0.118	−0.140*	−0.029
	(0.057)	(0.070)	(0.075)	(0.079)

Table 6.7 (*cont.*)

	All	Democratic	Democratic	Democratic
	Repression	Repression	Repression	Repression
Benefit INEP	-0.040	0.062	0.069	0.043
	(0.066)	(0.086)	(0.089)	(0.094)
Uncertain * declared			0.026	
			(0.045)	
Cost * declared			0.124	
			(0.105)	
Benefit * declared			-0.023	
			(0.116)	
Uncertain * killed				-0.003
				(0.012)
Cost * killed				-0.091***
				(0.029)
Benefit * killed				0.003
				(0.029)
Region FE	Yes	No	Yes	No
Decadal FE	Yes	Yes	Yes	Yes
Observations	1505	1308	1308	1308
Countries	76	72	72	72
Within R squared	0.846	0.818	819	819
Wald Chi squared	21914.47	–	–	–

Note: ***(**) [*] denote significance at p < .01, (p < 0.05), and [p < 0.10].

provisions make it more likely that governments call an SOE after terrorist attacks while emergency constitutions that confer larger benefits on the executive make it less likely, in particular when the constitution makes such calls more politically costly. When democratic governments do so, they tend to repress the population substantially more and, in particular, during larger attacks when the constitution makes declarations difficult.

As in the previous sections, we now turn to the results regarding the OIC sample as a comparison to the Western group. In Table 6.8, we hence explore the potential consequences of terrorist attacks for

Table 6.8 *Main repression effects, OIC sample*

	All attacks		Only military		Only gov./infra.	
	(1)	(2)	(3)	(4)	(5)	(6)
Lagged repression	0.826**	0.829**	0.829**	0.837**	0.804**	0.807**
	(0.031)	(0.034)	(0.053)	(0.049)	(0.047)	(0.049)
Log no. of events	−0.046**	−0.043				
	(0.017)	(0.051)				
Log events against military			−0.022	0.009		
			(0.030)	(0.071)		
Log events against gov / infra					−0.056**	−0.108†
					(0.019)	(0.058)
Log GDP per capita	0.015	0.005	0.026	0.002	−0.012	−0.018
	(0.029)	(0.028)	(0.036)	(0.033)	(0.035)	(0.036)
Recession	−0.098**	−0.095*	−0.062	−0.061	−0.112**	−0.113*
	(0.039)	(0.039)	(0.043)	(0.042)	(0.049)	(0.048)
Log oil and gas revenue	0.004	0.004	0.010	0.006	−0.005	−0.002
	(0.010)	(0.011)	(0.013)	(0.014)	(0.008)	(0.009)
Log population size	−0.064**	−0.068**	−0.079**	−0.085**	−0.078**	−0.081**
	(0.017)	(0.017)	(0.021)	(0.018)	(0.024)	(0.023)
Judicial accountability	0.020	0.032	0.029	0.054**	0.056*	0.064**
	(0.024)	(0.021)	(0.025)	(0.019)	(0.025)	(0.024)
Civil society	0.184	0.171	0.153	0.132	0.165	0.175
	(0.116)	(0.113)	(0.125)	(0.124)	(0.133)	(0.135)
Single-party regime	−0.152*	−0.171**	−0.087	−0.137	−0.169	−0.166
	(0.062)	(0.062)	(0.098)	(0.085)	(0.107)	(0.111)

Multi-party autocracy	0.011	–0.007	0.065	0.037	–0.009	0.001
	(0.053)	(0.048)	(0.065)	(0.057)	(0.069)	(0.072)
Democracy	0.069	0.028	0.069	0.033	–0.006	–0.011
	(0.064)	(0.058)	(0.078)	(0.066)	(0.085)	(0.083)
Successful coup	–0.076	–0.129	0.021	–0.046	–0.243†	–0.233†
	(0.098)	(0.093)	(0.156)	(0.134)	(0.132)	(0.135)
Natural disaster	0.002	0.003	0.002	0.004	0.001	0.001
	(0.003)	(0.003)	(0.003)	(0.003)	(0.003)	(0.003)
ISI	0.026	0.024	0.003	0.002	0.060**	0.059*
	(0.022)	(0.021)	(0.028)	(0.023)	(0.022)	(0.022)
Cost INEP	–0.011	–0.239	0.039	–0.385*	–0.078	–0.301†
	(0.136)	(0.155)	(0.152)	(0.182)	(129)	(0.165)
Benefit INEP	–0.355*	–0.022	–0.374*	0.291	–0.603**	–0.538†
	(0.149)	(0.184)	(0.155)	(0.247)	(0.169)	(0.298)
Cost INEP * log events		0.089		0.165		0.115
		(0.064)		(0.078)		(0.075)
Benefit INEP * log events		–0.144**		–0.335**		–0.036
		(0.051)		(0.093)		(0.093)
Period FE	Yes	Yes	Yes	Yes	Yes	Yes
Region FE	Yes	Yes	Yes	Yes	Yes	Yes
Observations	488	488	298	298	292	297
Countries	42	42	35	35	34	34
Within R squared	0.800	0.801	0.818	0.830	0.844	0.846
Wald Chi squared	–	–	–	–		–

Note: **(*) [†] denote significance at $p < 0.01$, ($p < 0.05$), and [$p < 0.10$]. All regressions include a constant term.

government repression, given the constitutional emergency provisions. In odd-numbered columns, we report results with a similar specification as in previous tables while even-numbered columns also include interaction terms between the Cost INEP and Benefit INEP and the logarithm to the number of terrorist events.

We first note that repression is as highly persistent as in Western countries, as indicated by the lagged dependent variable, which indicates that many events most probably do not lead to changes in repression. We also find significant evidence that larger countries tend to repress more, and that economic recessions typically lead to more repression. Most importantly, we find that *on average* – in columns 1 and 5 – terrorism leads to more repression. However, the size of the effect is limited and corresponds to an increase of about 8 percent of the within-country standard deviation.

Yet when we interact the Cost and Benefit INEPs with the number of events in columns 2, 4, and 6, we find that the repression reactions to terrorist events are mediated by the Benefit INEP, that is, the degree to which the constitution allows the government more discretionary power within an emergency. As is evident when comparing the large and significant interaction terms in columns 2 and 4 with the small insignificant estimate in 6, the effects are primarily driven by attacks on military or police targets, in which case the repression reactions can be substantial. While we find no effects when the constitution does not grant the government any additional powers (a Benefit INEP of zero as in Benin), the effect of *one* additional attack as evaluated with the most permissive emergency constitutions – for example Brunei and Sierra Leone – is about 20 percent of the within-country standard deviation.[25]

Noting that the median country is subject to four attacks on the military or police, once any attacks occur, this is a large effect with potentially important consequences. Overall, we thus find that terrorist attacks give rise to marked government reactions in both Western

[25] Our interpretation of the interaction terms follows the guidelines in Brambor et al. (2006). We find that the effects of terrorist attacks on repression remain insignificant at levels of the Benefit INEP below approximately 0.4. As indicated by the interaction term, the effects are strongly increasing in the Benefit INEP, and an assessment of the estimate at maximum levels is -0.043 - 0.144 = -0.187. The online appendix also shows that these and additional results are robust to controlling for societal inequality.

countries and the OIC countries in the form of both the declaration of an SOE and increased repression. These reactions are nevertheless clearly affected by the constitutional design of their emergency provisions, and in slightly different ways across political regimes, as we discuss in the concluding section.

6.8 Conclusions and Open Questions

This is an unusually long chapter explicitly analyzing the relationship between terrorist events and states of emergency. It deals both with the determinants that lead to the declaration of an SOE following a terrorist event and with one of the main consequences that follow such a declaration. It does so for two different samples, namely a group of countries with a Western-style constitution that are predominantly democratic, and another group of countries that are all members of the Organization of Islamic Cooperation and predominantly autocratic. Drawing on basically the same estimation approach to analyze the two samples allows us to compare the findings with each other.

We find that more terrorist events are correlated with a higher likelihood of an SOE being declared. Richer countries are less likely to declare whereas countries with a presidential form of government are more likely to declare. Interestingly – and in contrast to some theoretical arguments found in the literature – democratic governments soon facing an election are less likely to declare an SOE. When the emergency constitution makes it easy to declare (high value of Cost INEP) and allocates substantial additional powers to the executive (high values of Benefit INEP), governments are more likely to declare.

Our further results suggest that once a government calls an SOE, it strongly tends to implement more repressive policies, regardless of which types of country we focus on, potentially to counteract the consequences of terrorism. However, the specific provisions of the constitution do not matter, and we find the same repressive response regardless of whether or not the constitution yields larger discretionary power during emergencies. To some extent, it seems sufficient even for democratic governments to call an SOE to repress civil society and its citizens.

In this chapter, we have analyzed the effectiveness of SOEs from the point of view of those who suffer from terrorism. In principle, it is, of course, possible to analyze the effectiveness of emergency provisions from a different angle by asking to what degree terrorists have reached their goals. There are various possibilities to do so. One could, for instance, ask whether governments have given in to the demands of terrorists? Abrahams (2008, 83) claims that this has never occurred, whereas Jones and Libicki (2008) find 132 campaigns where terrorist groups renounced terrorism. These findings show how difficult it is to evaluate results: These events can be counted as successes for the terrorists, but on the other hand, one can also argue that they led to an end of terror, hence proving the effectiveness of anti-terror measures.

This chapter can also be read as contributing to a discussion on the foundations of the state that has been ongoing for centuries. Many thinkers have discussed a tension between security on the one hand and freedom on the other. Whereas for Hobbes, securing order over anarchy was of utmost importance – and for him the value of security clearly trumped the value of freedom –, Locke had already moved toward a trade-off attributing freedom relatively more weight. It was Spinoza (1670, 258f.) who wrote: "It follows, plainly, from the explanation given earlier, of the foundations of a state, that the ultimate aim of government is not to rule, or restrain, by fear, nor to exact obedience, but contrariwise, to free every man from fear, that he may live in all possible security; in other words, to strengthen his natural right to exist and work without injury to himself or others ... In fact, the true aim of government is liberty."

Our finding that respect for physical integrity rights is negatively correlated with terrorist incidents sheds new light on this debate. Higher levels of freedom (as proxied with both physical integrity rights as well as economic freedom rights) go hand in hand with *higher* levels of security (as expressed as the absence of terrorist incidents). In other words, freedom and security are not competing with each other. Quite to the contrary, they complement each other. This finding is directly policy relevant.

Finally, terrorist activities are only one type of event that challenge order and stability within the state. Others include mass demonstrations, general strikes, and civil war. Future studies should inquire into the effectiveness of emergency constitutions regarding these other events.

Appendix

Table A6.1 *Countries included in the sample*

Albania	Cyprus	Israel	Poland
Antigua and Barbuda	Czech Republic	Italy	Portugal
Argentina	Denmark	Jamaica	Romania
Armenia	Dominica	Japan	*Russia*
Australia	Dominican Republic	Korea (South)	Serbia
Austria	Ecuador	Latvia	*Singapore*
The Bahamas	El Salvador	Lithuania	Slovakia
Barbados	Estonia	Luxembourg	Slovenia
Belarus	Finland	Macedonia	Spain
Belgium	France	Malta	Suriname
Belize	Georgia	Mexico	Sweden
Bermuda	Germany	Moldova	Switzerland
Bolivia	Greece	*Montenegro*	Taiwan
Brazil	Grenada	The Netherlands	Trinidad and Tobago
Bulgaria	Guatemala	New Zealand	Turkey
Canada	Guyana	Nicaragua	Ukraine
Chile	Honduras	Norway	United Kingdom
Colombia	Hungary	Panama	United States
Costa Rica	Iceland	Paraguay	Uruguay
Croatia	Ireland	Peru	Venezuela

Note: countries in italics have not been democratic in any year in the sample period.

Table A6.2 *Definitions and sources of variables*

Variable	Source	Definition
Declared SOE	Update of Hafner-Burton et al. (2011)	Dummy for declared SOE
No. of events	GTD (2018)	No. of all terrorist events in a year
No. targeting government	GTD (2018)	No. of all events coded as targeting government and infrastructure

Table A6.2 *(cont.)*

Variable	Source	Definition
No. targeting military / police	GTD (2018)	No. of all events coded as targeting he military and police installations
Log GDP per capita	Feenstra et al. (2015)	Logarithm to purchasing-power-adjusted GDP per capita
Recession	Based on Feenstra et al. (2015)	Dummy for years with negative GDP growth
Log population size	Feenstra et al. (2015)	Logarithm to population size
Log affected natural disasters	EM-DAT (2019)	Logarithm to no. of affected citizens after natural disasters
Mixed democracy		Democracy with president not directly elected
Presidential democracy		Democracy with president directly elected and substantial powers
Civilian autocracy		Autocracy with head of government without military rank
Military dictatorship		Autocracy with head of government with military rank
Herfindahl index, legislature	Berggren and Bjørnskov (2017)	Herfindahl index of parties in parliament/lower chamber
Ideology, legislature	Berggren and Bjørnskov (2017)	Average ideological position of all parties in parliament/lower chamber
Coup		Dummy for whether *coup d'état* occurred
Election year	Berggren and Bjørnskov (2017)	Year with parliamentary election
Uncertain provisions		Dummy for uncertain constitutional status of emergency provisions

Table A6.2 *(cont.)*

Variable	Source	Definition
Cost INEP		Index of ease of calling a state of emergency
Benefit INEP		Index of additional discretionary powers of government during emergencies
Civil society strength	Coppedge et al. (2016)	Index of strength and independence of civil society organizations
Judicial accountability	Coppedge et al. (2016)	Index of accountability of judicial actors
Judicial corruption	Coppedge et al. (2016)	Index of likelihood of corruption in the judicial branch
Spatial attacks	Based on GTD (2018)	Average of no. of terrorist attacks in geographical neighbors
Repression	Fariss (2014)	Index of repressive policy
No. armed events	GTD (2018)	No. of terrorist events using heavy arms
No. killed	GTD (2018)	No. of citizens killed in terrorist events

7 States of Emergency after Domestic Turmoil

7.1 Introduction

In the preceding chapters, we showed that some types of emergency constitutions may have intended beneficial consequences following terrorist attacks, but also come with some problematic side effects. At the same time, these same emergency constitutions appear to have only negative consequences following natural disasters. In this chapter, we are interested in ascertaining the consequences of states of emergency (SOEs) following what we here refer to as domestic turmoil. Under this term, we summarize a number of different events such as mass demonstrations against government and general strikes, but also rarer events such as riots, insurgencies, and attempts to overthrow the governments, that is, *coups d'état*. All these events can lead governments to declare an SOE. Examples abound: A general strike in Guinea led the government to declare an SOE in 2007; the government of Nepal reacted to guerilla warfare by declaring SOEs in both 2001 and 2002; and after the assassination of Anwar El Sadat in Egypt in 1981, an SOE was declared that turned out to be long-lasting.

Most of these events occur in direct response to government behavior. In a sense, then, these events could also be the most dangerous for the survival of a sitting government as they are initiated to challenge it. In all likelihood, governments will try to react firmly against such events, including the possibility of declaring an SOE.

At the same time, precisely because most of these events are a direct response to government behavior, they are highly endogenous – they may sometimes be the end results of cycles of reactions to reactions – implying that endogeneity concerns loom large. Endogeneity was already a major concern with regard to terrorist events that we dealt with in the last chapter. This is why our approach to analyzing government reactions to domestic turmoil will be very similar to the approach in the last chapter in which we analyzed the use of emergency provisions subsequent to terrorist events.

In this chapter, we are interested in two questions: (1) What domestic events are most likely to trigger the declaration of an SOE? (2) Given that any kind of domestic turmoil is observed and an SOE has been declared, what are the consequences for civil and political rights?

We find that that a general conflict index is highly correlated with the declaration of an SOE. The events most likely to trigger an SOE are major government crises, riots, and revolutions. With regard to coups – both successful and unsuccessful – we find a significant correlation with SOEs in autocracies only. We do find that a coup followed by an SOE does lead to a (further) reduction in civil liberties.

The rest of the chapter is organized as follows. In Section 7.2, a number of hypotheses regarding the possible relationship between events of domestic turmoil and the declaration of SOEs are developed; Section 7.3 briefly presents the data and contains a description of our estimation approach; the results themselves are presented and discussed in Section 7.4; Section 7.5 concludes.

7.2 Theory

"Domestic turmoil" is a rather fuzzy term, which is why we explicitly list the events here taken into account before developing a number of conjectures. The events that could lead a government to declare an SOE and which we analyze here are anti-government demonstrations, assassinations and assassination attempts of political leaders, general strikes, guerilla warfare, government crises, riots, revolutions, and coups – both successful and unsuccessful attempts. Although this is a very heterogeneous group of events, they all have one thing in common: All of them can be interpreted as a reaction to government behavior and all of them aim at challenging government and changing government behavior, if not at even overthrowing it.

We assume that governments strive to remain in power, which leads to a very general conjecture: The more government actors and members of an incumbent political elite believe that a specific event endangers their remaining in power, the higher the likelihood that government will declare an SOE. Now, not all emergency constitutions are alike, which is why both the cost of declaring as well as the benefits after having declared need to be taken into account. We expect declarations to be more likely if the costs of declaring are low.

Similarly, we expect declarations to be more likely if the benefits to government after having declared are high.

Since the events taken into account here can all be thought of as reactions to previous government behavior, policies potentially triggering these events should be taken into account. Quite generally speaking, we assume that economic downturns are an important reason for being unhappy with one's government and that such downturns are likely to increase opposition against government.

In the last chapter, we showed that deteriorations in basic human rights as well as in civil and political liberties can cause people to become terrorists and commit terrorist acts. This is, of course, a very extreme type of behavior and other – less extreme – ones appear more likely. In essence, these less extreme reactions include all the events analyzed here. In the last chapter, we also saw that terrorists are most likely to emerge from groups that feel discriminated against. These can be ethnic minorities but also socially delineated groups.

We now briefly mention conjectures related to the specific events covered in this chapter.

- As long as anti-government demonstrations remain largely nonviolent, we do not expect them to trigger SOEs;
- As long as assassinations and assassination attempts remain singular events and are neither targeted at the head of state or the head of government, we do not expect them to trigger SOEs;
- General strikes that are "aimed at national government policies or authority" (Banks) are unlikely to lead to an SOE;
- Guerilla warfare "aimed at the overthrow of the present regime" (Banks) is expected to lead to the declaration of an SOE if the corresponding threat is perceived as sufficiently serious;
- Major government crises which are defined by the Banks dataset as "any rapidly developing situation that threatens to bring the downfall of the present regime" are likely to be accompanied by an SOE;
- Riots are expected to cause an SOE depending on the number of participants and the degree of violence used in them;
- Fully fledged revolutions are very likely to cause the declaration of an SOE; and
- Coups – which can be thought of as a particularly rapidly executed subcategory of revolutions – are also expected to trigger the declaration of an SOE with high probability.

It is, of course, desirable to make these conjectures more specific. To do so presupposes, however, two pieces of information, one objective, the other subjective: We would need to know not only if any kind of event occurred in a specific country in a specific year but also how many people participated in it, how much violence was used and so forth. Even having this information would not allow us to make very specific predictions as we would need to know the (subjective) evaluation of the ensuing threat to government survival by government officials. These depend on a host of factors – such as the attitude toward risk – but are not intersubjectively accessible.

At a more general level, we can nevertheless conjecture which types of government action might lead to domestic turmoil of a nature that would incentivize the government to call an SOE. Reviewing more than 400 domestic SOEs, we find a large number of reasons given for their declaration. In 2001, Argentina declared an SOE following major riots in Buenos Aires, which were themselves reactions to an economic collapse after years of economic mismanagement. In many cases, violent riots, demonstrations, and major strikes are reactions to economic decline. These events may be organized by civil society organizations including labor unions and opposition parties, thereby posing a very direct threat to the political survival of the incumbent government. Some of these events may also pose problems to society at large, such as the 2010 strike by Spanish air traffic controllers, which threatened to disable a major part of the country's infrastructure.

In these cases, an interesting complication arises when the emergency constitution requires that opposition parties – that may be in favor of anti-government demonstrations or against the government policies that cause domestic turmoil – must vote for declaring an SOE. In such cases, it is either highly unlikely that an SOE can be declared or likely that an SOE, if declared, will be unlawful. An exception may be when demonstrations, riots, or more severe types of resistance to government power get out of hand, such that even opposition factions that are *a priori* positive toward the cause of the turmoil nevertheless support an SOE in order to keep the public order.

However, another source of unrest is crises within government, which governments then attempt to resolve by declaring an SOE that allows the executive branch to govern without ordinary checks and balances that may appear to have contributed to the crisis. Examples of this type include the political deadlock in Lebanon in 2007, which the government attempted to bypass by declaring an SOE. Yet less questionable events also exist, not least several SOEs declared in Nauru, where the constitution requires that the executive declares an SOE in order to dissolve parliament in case an early election has to be called.

Finally, a set of rather obvious domestic events are likely to lead to the declaration of an SOE where the cost of declaration has little influence. These events include violence committed by drug cartels in Colombia and Guatemala, civil wars as in Sri Lanka, direct attempts to overturn the government through coups, and when political actors refuse to honor the constitution. A rare example of the latter occurred in the Gambia in 2017, when Yahya Jammeh – who had come to power in a military coup – first acknowledged the election outcome and then refused to accept losing a democratic election and handing power over to the winner, Adama Barrow.

As these examples show, it is therefore difficult to make more precise overall predictions because these events – even if we define them as a particular type – remain highly diverse. In addition, in many of the cases we describe, there was a large random element to the outcomes and actors in the midst of the events would have found it difficult to predict what would happen. Our empirical approach in the following is therefore structured around a set of basic expectations but remains exploratory.

7.3 Data and Estimation Approach

The data for most of the events included in our analysis are from the Cross-National Time-Series Data Archive (also known as the Banks dataset). It has the advantage of being available for many countries and a rather high number of years. We here analyze the period from 1970 to 2017. The Archive also contains a weighted conflict measure that is constructed by weighting all of the events included in the dataset according to the following scheme: Anti-Government Demonstrations (10), Assassinations (25), Strikes (20), Guerrilla Warfare (100), Government Crises (20), Purges (20), Riots (25), and Revolutions (150). We use it to ascertain whether conflict as such – no matter what specific type – is correlated with a higher likelihood of an SOE declaration. Since the Banks dataset does not include any information on coups but we do want to include coups, we rely on the data provided by Bjørnskov and Rode (2020).

Unfortunately, the information on the events is provided in the form of dummy variables. We do not know how many times a given event occurred in a given year, nor do we know how many people participated, how violent it became, and so forth. In other words: The coding is coarse and in the absence of any substantially richer sources of data, we can only offer a first take on the two questions we are discussing here.

We work with two different groups of dependent variables, depending on the specific question we are discussing. To ascertain the likelihood of an SOE being declared subsequent to any of the events just enumerated, we rely on the list of SOEs provided by Hafner-Burton et al. (2011) and complemented (and corrected) by ourselves as described in previous chapters. To see whether the events covered here in conjunction with an SOE have effects on civil liberties, we rely on the dataset on repression provided by Fariss (2014).

As mentioned in the theory section, the likelihood of an SOE being declared subsequent to one of these domestic events also depends on how difficult ("costly") it is to declare an SOE and the additional benefits such a declaration conveys upon the government. As in the preceding chapters, we control for these aspects by including our Cost INEP as well as our Benefit INEP.

Most of the other controls have been used already in previous chapters, which is why we only mention them very briefly. We include the form of government to tease out whether democracies behave differently than autocracies. Within these two major forms, additional distinctions are made: Among democracies, we distinguish between presidential, semi-presidential, and parliamentary democracies, whereas among autocracies, a distinction is made between military, civilian, and monarchic autocrats.

Parliaments can be more or less fractionalized. A given quorum necessary to declare an SOE is more likely to be reached in less fractionalized legislatures, which is why we control for it. The ideological leaning of parliamentarians might also influence their choice of political measures. We expect parties on the extreme ends of the one-dimensional ideology space to be more in favor of law and order than those parties in the middle.

Nonapproval of government is often triggered by unfavorable economic development (as the saying goes: "It's the economy, stupid!"). This is why we control for recessions. With regard to the likelihood of an SOE declared in the follow-up to terrorist events, we found that it is substantially lower in election years, supposedly because governments are afraid that they may lose office as a consequence (see Chapter 6). Something similar may play out here, which is why we explicitly control for election years. With regard to terrorist events, we also found that SOEs are significantly less likely if civil society was strong, supposedly because civil society organizations function as a channel through which groups that feel discriminated against can communicate with government. We therefore also include a variable indicating the strength of civil society.

Before presenting our results in detail, here is a look at our sample: Table 7.1 provides descriptive statistics. Figure 7.1 records the

Table 7.1 *Descriptive statistics*

Variable	Mean	Standard deviation	Observations
SOE declaration	0.044	0.205	9412
Log population	1.859	1.899	7887
Log GDP per capita	8.940	1.245	7887
Recession	0.269	2.443	7861
Trade	0.507	0.465	7887
Government spending	0.197	1.00	7887
Cost INEP	0.466	0.113	7222
Benefit INEP	0.355	0.226	7222
Causality problem	0.003	0.051	9412
Successful coup	0.018	0.136	9412
Failed coup	0.023	0.159	9412
Log conflict index	3.119	3.617	8344
Assassinations	0.180	0.944	8344
General strikes	0.136	0.667	8344
Guerrilla warfare	0.693	8.427	8344
Government crises	0.139	0.455	8344
Purges	0.069	0.395	8344
Riots	0.480	1.840	8344
Revolutions	1.53	0.458	8344
Anti-gov. demonstrations	0.875	4.019	8344
Parliamentary democracy	0.242	0.429	9412
Mixed presidential dem.	0.117	0.322	9412
Presidential dem.	0.143	0.351	9412
Civilian autocracy	0.258	0.437	9412
Military dictatorship	0.164	0.371	9412
Royal autocracy	0.075	0.263	9412

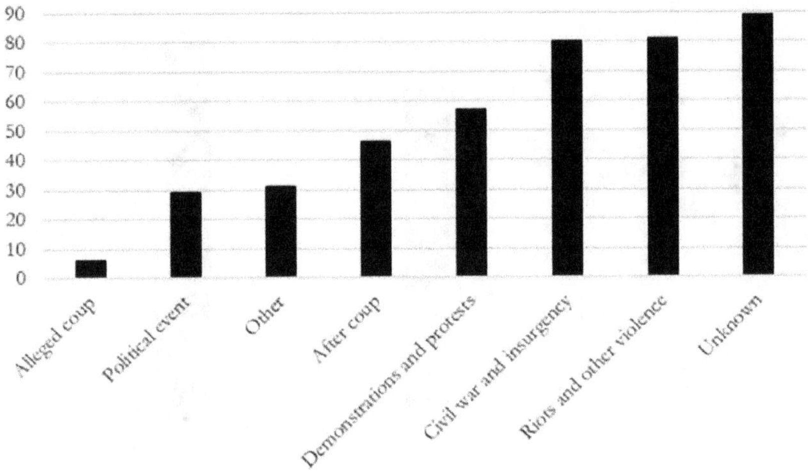

Figure 7.1 Reasons for declared SOEs

number of times a specific event led to the declaration of an SOE, based on our reading of each of the approximately 400 events. The figure displays absolute numbers and hence not the percentage of a specific event followed by an SOE. The category "unknown" which is connected with almost ninety SOEs, is a catch-all category. It indicates that there was an SOE but we were not able to identify the event triggering it.

The second figure does not report absolute numbers but the probability of an SOE taking the number of coups and recorded conflict level into account. We here illustrate the likelihood of declaring an SOE based on three criteria: whether there was no coup attempt, one coup attempt, or multiple coup attempts in a year (the black columns); whether the general conflict level was low, medium (i.e. the middle third of our observations), or high (the gray columns); and whether the year-to-year change in conflict level indicated reduced conflict, unchanged conflict, or increasing conflict levels (the white columns).

These figures can nevertheless only provide indications, and particularly Figure 7.2 hints at somewhat more complex conflict dynamics around SOEs. We therefore also provide a set of conditional fixed effects logit estimates, in which we test the effects both of coups (successful and failed) and the overall conflict index from Banks as well

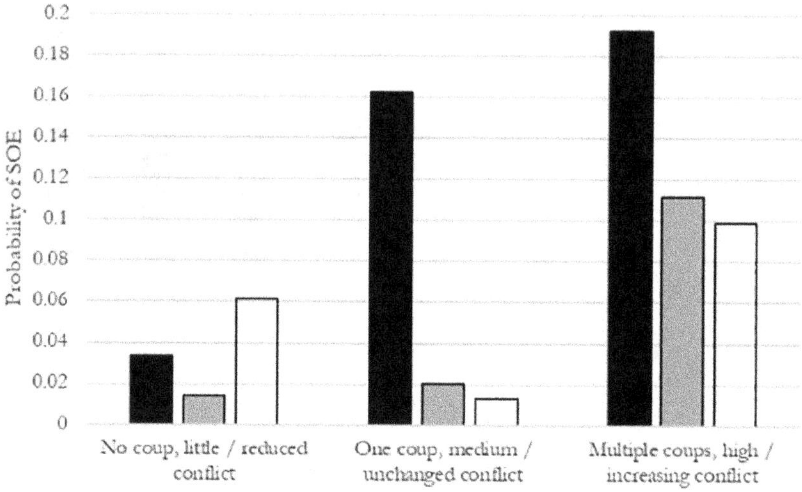

Figure 7.2 Probability of SOE, three sources

as the aggregated conflict indicators. While our choice of a fixed effects estimator means that we are effectively controlling for countries' conflict histories and "normal" levels of domestic turmoil, we must note that our data do not allow us to make any substantial causal claims.

7.4 Results

7.4.1 Calling an SOE

The basic results are reported in Table 7.2. The first column includes all 4,387 observations from ninety-nine countries and establishes the correlation between the (log of the) weighted conflict index and SOEs whereas the second column digs deeper by indicating the correlation between the different types of events and SOEs. Since coups are not directly part of the conflict index, they appear in both columns.

The takeaway from the first column is that there is a significant correlation between the conflict index and the likelihood that an SOE will be declared. From column 2, we learn that this result is driven by government crises, riots, and revolutions but not by anti-government demonstrations, assassinations, general strikes, or guerilla warfare. In

Table 7.2 *Main results*

	All	All	No causal problems	Only democracies	Only autocracies
Sample	1	2	3	4	5
Log population	2.16***	2.406***	2.461***	0.151	3.712**
	(0.843)	(0.835)	(0.852)	(1.470)	(1.760)
Log GDP per capita	0.501	0.295	0.213	−0.570	0.892
	(0.391)	(0.403)	(0.412)	(0.805)	(0.611)
Recession	0.388**	0.363**	0.369**	0.683**	0.101
	(0.179)	(0.178)	(0.187)	(0.283)	(0.232)
Trade	0.639	0.478	0.429	−0.239	1.116
	(0.595)	(0.614)	(0.632)	(0.974)	(0.954)
Government spending	2.859***	3.097***	2.770***	3.378	4.328***
	(1.089)	(1.127)	(1.047)	(2.347)	(1.612)
Successful coup	0.826***	0.791**	0.605	0.203	0.933**
	(0.315)	(0.358)	(0.381)	(1.438)	(0.395)
Failed coup	0.393*	0.420*	0.262	0.331	0.715**
	(0.236)	(0.252)	(0.276)	(0.644)	(0.311)
Log conflict index	0.257***				
	(0.038)				
Assassinations		0.003	0.003	0.004	0.016
		(0.030)	(0.029)	(0.032)	(0.073)
General strikes		−0.065	−0.063	−0.118	0.032
		(0.075)	(0.078)	(0.139)	(0.138)
Guerrilla warfare		0.001	0.001	0.003	−0.003
		(0.006)	(0.005)	(0.003)	(0.011)
Government crises		0.488***	0.516***	0.403***	0.550*
		(0.128)	(0.122)	(0.145)	(0.309)
Purges		0.026	−0.042	0.294	−0.201
		(0.153)	(0.196)	(0.289)	(0.399)
Riots		0.122***	0.134***	0.049	0.181***
		(0.031)	(0.033)	(0.049)	(0.056)
Revolutions		0.431***	0.435***	0.456***	0.400**
		(0.114)	(0.117)	(0.166)	(0.175)
Anti-gov. demonstrations		0.005	0.001	0.018	0.014
		(0.015)	(0.016)	(0.013)	(0.032)
Regime FE	Yes	Yes	Yes	Yes	Yes
Country FE	Yes	Yes	Yes	Yes	Yes

Table 7.2 (*cont.*)

	All	All	No causal problems	Only democracies	Only autocracies
Sample	1	2	3	4	5
Observations	4387	4387	4316	1723	2223
Countries	99	99	98	60	69
Pseudo R sq.	0.140	0.116	0.115	0.169	0.203
Wald Chi squared	843.63	677.01	1004.16	–	–
Log likelihood	-866.931	-891.329	-843.746	-350.336	-392.974

Note: all estimates are conditional fixed effects logit; ***(**) [*] denote significance at $p < 0.01$, ($p < 0.05$), and [$p < 0.10$].

other words, consistent with our earlier considerations, only domestic turmoil that clearly threatens the survival of the incumbent government is systematically associated with SOEs. Conversely, we cannot claim any effects induced by coups as the indicators fail significance in column 3, in which we remove seventy-one cases in which we know from our reading of the events that an SOE *preceded* a coup attempt or major domestic turmoil.

In columns 4 and 5, we separate democracies from autocracies. By and large, the general results are not sensitive to this sample split: Only riots occurring in democracies are not correlated with SOEs. There are, however, two interesting differences in the covariates: Whereas recessions are correlated with SOEs in democracies, but not in autocracies, the inverse holds for population size; larger populations are correlated with a higher likelihood of an SOE occurring in autocracies, but not in democracies.

In the theory section, we pointed out that the likelihood of declaring an SOE is likely to depend not only on the specific domestic event but also on the provisions of a country's emergency constitution. In Tables 7.3 and 7.4, the difficulty of declaring an SOE and the benefits offered during an SOE are explicitly taken into account. This is done by interacting the specific event with the Cost INEP in Table 7.3, and interacting the specific event with the Benefit INEP in Table 7.4.

Table 7.3 ***Results conditional on ease of declaring***

	All	All	No causal problems	Only democracies	Only autocracies
Sample	1	2	3	4	5
			Full baseline included		
Successful coup	0.019	0.778	0.732	−5.815	2.391
	(1.796)	(2.239)	(2.367)	(5.596)	(2.746)
Failed coup	−0.328	0.520	0.189	10.216**	2.287
	(1.115)	(1.109)	(1.271)	(4.054)	(2.719)
Log conflict index	0.379**				
	(0.173)				
Cost INEP	1.501	0.895	1.195	2.720	−3.266
	(2.707)	(1.913)	(1.673)	(5.349)	(2.428)
Benefit INEP	0.387	0.218	0.444	2.025	−0.747
	(0.874)	(0.887)	(0.883)	(1.588)	(1.059)
Succ. coup * Cost INEP	1.584	0.328	−0.574	11.760	−3.018
	(3.639)	(4.709)	(5.205)	(11.1586)	(5.912)
Fail. coup * Cost INEP	1.749	0.189	0.674	−20.559**	−2.500
	(2.293)	(2.337)	(2.674)	(8.868)	(5.485)
Conflict * Cost INEP	−0.249				
	(0.391)				
Assassinations		−0.084	−0.099	0.434	0.209
		(0.140)	(0.139)	(0.318)	(0.650)
General strikes		0.196	0.408	0.589	0.032
		(0.397)	(0.404)	(0.705)	(0.554)
Guerrilla warfare		0.026	0.019	0.054	−0.441
		(0.036)	(0.034)	(0.063)	(0.279)
Government crises		1.298	1.302**	−0.025	2.699
		(0.549)	(0.568)	(0.635)	(1.109)
Purges		−2.890**	−2.681**	−7.828**	−3.659
		(1.147)	(1.192)	(3.595)	(2.336)
Riots		0.352**	0.306*	0.312	0.685*
		(0.165)	(0.157)	(0.256)	(0.411)
Revolutions		0.248	0.215	1.159	−0.996
		(0.732)	(0.751)	(0.831)	(1.262)
Anti-gov. demonstrations		0.005	0.012	−0.013	−0.199
		(0.115)	(0.115)	(0.117)	(0.288)
Assassinations * Cost INEP		0.135	0.151	−0.738	−0.324
		(0.233)	(0.230)	(0.505)	(1.186)

Table 7.3 (*cont.*)

	All	All	No causal problems	Only democracies	Only autocracies
Sample	1	2	3	4	5
Strikes * Cost INEP		−0.452	−0.868	−1.238	0.259
		(0.822)	(0.840)	(1.419)	(1.096)
Guerrilla * Cost INEP		−0.069	−0.049	−0.129	1.168
		(0.092)	(0.085)	(0.158)	(0.742)
Gov. crises * Cost INEP		−1.547	−1.389	1.491	−4.629*
		(1.082)	(1.148)	(1.276)	(2.439)
Purges * Cost INEP		5.469***	5.071**	15.673**	6.798
		(2.118)	(2.292)	(7.024)	(4.935)
Riots * Cost INEP		−0.482	−0.367	−0.485	−1.274
		(0.342)	(0.326)	(0.480)	(0.934)
Revolutions * Cost INEP		0.551	0.661	−1.448	3.579
		(1.412)	(1.446)	(1.567)	(2.527)
Demonstrations * Cost INEP		−0.009	−0.032	0.048	0.562
		(0.225)	(0.223)	(0.245)	(0.648)
Regime FE	Yes	Yes	Yes	Yes	Yes
Country FE	Yes	Yes	Yes	Yes	Yes
Observations	3578	3578	3527	1569	1621
Countries	93	93	92	56	59
Pseudo R sq.	0.137	0.125	0.133	0.223	0.257
Wald Chi squared	679.33	1402.49	2407.52	–	–
Log likelihood	−701.564	−711.533	−675.651	−293.747	−272.095

Note: all estimates are conditional fixed effects logit; ***(**) [*] denote significance at $p < 0.01$, ($p < 0.05$), and [$p < 0.10$].

Remarkably, we find very little evidence that the way that domestic turmoil affects the probability of declaring an SOE varies with the costs of declaration in Table 7.3. In only one case – around failed coups – do we observe any systematically heterogeneous effect, and as the results in column 3 make clear, these estimates are unlikely to reflect a causal relation (SOEs often come before failed coups).

After having analyzed the costs of declaring an SOE, Table 7.4 offers a look at the effect of taking the benefits into account that a government enjoys after declaring an SOE. We first find that purges

Table 7.4 ***Results conditional on emergency powers***

	All	All	No causal problems	Only democracies	Only autocracies
Sample	1	2	3	4	5
			Full baseline included		
Successful coup	−0.055	−0.244	−0.509	−2.299	0.009
	(0.670)	(0.749)	(0.918)	(1.787)	(1.039)
Failed coup	0.027	0.091	−0.332	−6.744***	0.622
	(0.542)	(0.585)	(0.754)	(1.547)	(0.592)
Log conflict index	0.348***				
	(0.053)				
Cost INEP	0.760	0.657	1.019	3.883	−2.914
	(1.747)	(1.707)	(1.569)	(4.616)	(2.548)
Benefit INEP	1.387	0.129	0.288	2.255	−1.051
	(1.131)	(1.012)	(0.951)	(1.667)	(1.186)
Succ. coup *	2.549**	2.825**	3.122*	5.759*	2.569
Benefit INEP	(1.235)	(1.436)	(1.753)	(3.032)	(1.881)
Fail. coup *	1.208	1.089	1.904	15.160***	1.449
Benefit INEP	(1.426)	(1.419)	(1.682)	(3.116)	(1.499)
Conflict * Benefit	−0.234*				
INEP	(0.127)				
Assassinations		−0.171	−0.167	−0.079	−0.124
		(0.131)	(0.120)	(0.339)	(0.200)
General strikes		−0.114	−0.092	0.084	0.038
		(0.174)	(0.188)	(0.402)	(0.353)
Guerrilla warfare		−0.054	−0.051	0.034	−0.057
		(0.049)	(0.049)	(0.059)	(0.117)
Government crises		0.676*	0.848***	0.964**	0.607
		(0.402)	(0.319)	(0.474)	(0.385)
Purges		−0.621**	−0.812**	−1.664*	−1.797**
		(0.279)	(0.333)	(0.934)	(0.781)
Riots		0.212***	0.230**	0.004	0.222**
		(0.075)	(0.085)	(0.130)	(0.099)
Revolutions		0.913***	0.912***	1.512***	1.168***
		(0.294)	(0.269)	(0.514)	(0.414)
Anti-gov.		−0.003	−0.010	0.012	0.057
demonstrations		(0.033)	(0.039)	(0.049)	(0.045)
Assassinations *		0.313	0.304	0.131	0.314
Benefit INEP		(0.203)	(0.189)	(0.545)	(0.291)

Table 7.4 (*cont.*)

	All	All	No causal problems	Only democracies	Only autocracies
Sample	1	2	3	4	5
Strikes * Benefit INEP		0.212	0.147	−0.303	0.505
		(0.413)	(0.446)	(0.920)	(0.876)
Guerrilla * Benefit INEP		0.117	0.112	−0.067	0.174
		(0.099)	(0.099)	(0.119)	(0.178)
Gov. crises * Benefit INEP		−0.263	−0.432	−0.646	0.193
		(0.773)	(0.605)	(0.879)	(0.803)
Purges * Benefit INEP		1.384***	1.656***	5.689**	3.046***
		(0.513)	(0.592)	(2.454)	(1.112)
Riots * Benefit INEP		−0.257	−0.270	0.084	−0.174
		(0.158)	(0.174)	(0.271)	(0.242)
Revolutions * Benefit INEP		−0.916	−0.844	−2.111	−1.053
		(0.593)	(0.551)	(0.975)	(0.861)
Demonstrations * Benefit INEP		0.035	0.029	−0.024	−0.086
		(0.105)	(0.114)	(0.124)	(0.174)
Regime FE	Yes	Yes	Yes	Yes	Yes
Country FE	Yes	Yes	Yes	Yes	Yes
Observations	3578	3578	3527	1569	1621
Countries	93	93	92	56	59
Pseudo R sq.	0.141	0.129	0.140	0.230	0.263
Wald Chi squared	694.00	3199.78	2541.22	–	–
Log likelihood	-698.394	-708.819	-670.419	-290.856	-269.908

Note: all estimates are conditional fixed effects logit; ***(**) [*] denote significance at $p < 0.01$, ($p < 0.05$), and [$p < 0.10$].

are substantially more likely to be associated with an SOE when the Benefit INEP is higher, that is, when the emergency constitution allows substantial discretionary power during the emergency. Second, we find that governments coming to power through successful coups are somewhat more likely to declare an SOE after the coup if the emergency constitution provides them with more discretionary power.

To facilitate the interpretation of the results, a look at Figure 7.3 may be helpful. It depicts the likelihood of an SOE after a failed or a successful coup taking the Benefit INEP explicitly into account. It

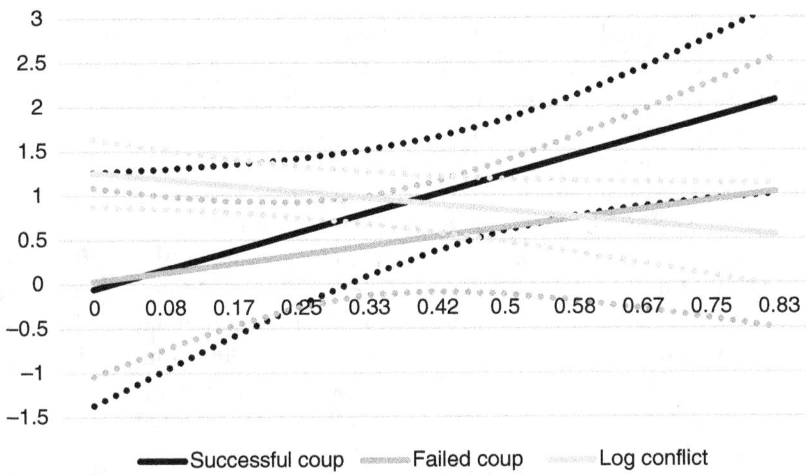

Figure 7.3 Marginal effects, conditional on benefits
Note: Dotted lines indicate 95 percent confidence intervals.

turns out that – while there is no significant correlation after a failed coup – the probability of an SOE after a successful coup increases with the benefits governments enjoy after such a declaration.

Turkey's State of Emergency after a Failed Coup in 2016

That we do not find a significant correlation between failed coups and SOEs does, of course, not mean that there are no such cases. The best known such case is probably the SOE that was declared in Turkey in July 2016 by President Erdogan after a coup attempt allegedly initiated by the so-called Gülen movement.

Turkey has a history of coups staged by the military whose representatives see themselves as guardians of secular Turkey as envisioned by Mustafa Kemal Atatürk. Such coups occurred in 1960 and 1980. In addition, in 1971, the military forced prime minister Suleyman Demirel to step down and, in 1997, prime minister Erbakan was forced to resign and his Welfare Party was shut down in 1998.

These experiences served as a warning for all subsequent governments that the Turkish military perceived itself as the informal guardian of the constitution and that not playing by its rules could result in one's ouster. Erdogan was, of course, aware of this and began systematically re-organizing the military shortly after he took office in 2002 as prime minister (see, e.g. Akça and Balta-Paker 2013).

Since the compliance of Erdogan's government with constitutional rules had started to fall long before 2016, the possibility of a coup was definitely "in the air." But since Erdogan had counted on that possibility, he and his political allies were well prepared and were able to instrumentalize the failed coup to their advantage so much so that there were rumors that the coup might have been staged by Erdogan himself (as, e.g. a couple of years before by Peruvian President Alberto Fujimori in his so-called "autogolpe"). If a playbook for how to use a failed coup to broaden one's own powers was to be written, Erdogan would be an excellent author. He used the coup as a pretense to sack or suspend at least 150,000 from public office and administration including thousands of academics. Close to 60,000 people were imprisoned as a follow-up including leading politicians of the opposition and thousands of journalists. More than 150 media outlets were closed. There are various reports according to which many detainees have been tortured (www.dw.com/en/report-detainees-tortured-under-turkish-state-of-emergency/a-36137826). Yet complaints about this have been dismissed on the grounds that acts committed under an SOE enjoy impunity (https://turkeypurge.com/prosecutor-drops-torture-complaint-due-to-impunity-under-state-of-emergency).

Many organizations, both domestic and international, considered at least some of these measures as incompatible either with Turkish constitutional law or with Turkey's obligations under international law. These include but are not limited to the Turkish Bar Association but also the Venice Commission.

After many prolongations, the SOE was officially ended almost exactly two years after it had been declared. But it is not over yet as many of the measures first implemented during the SOE have been turned into permanent law. To first establish them, Erdogan relied on executive orders. An (incomplete) list of the measures include (www.lexology.com/library/detail.aspx?g=16d960f2-bdf1-4aef-94b0-659605fe0697):

- Organizations linked to the Fethulla Gülen movement have been closed and their rights, assets, and properties confiscated and transferred to the Treasury (but not their obligations).
- Under the Turkish criminal code, the standard term of custody is 24 hours which was extended to up to 30 days under the SOE. After its lifting, suspects can still be detained for up to 12 days without any charges.
- Judges with links to the Gülen movement are removed from office.

Likewise, post-SOE legislation (https://stockholmcf.org/over-40-intl-organisations-call-on-turkey-to-end-state-of-emergency-legislation/)

- grants provincial governors the authority to ban individuals from moving between provinces;
- grants the government the authority to dismiss individuals arbitrarily from academic, public, and judicial service; and
- relaxes certain aspects of judicial review.

Erdogan even managed to get a novel constitution passed during the SOE, which considerably strengthened the powers of the president, that is, his own powers. This constitution further reduces parliamentary control and makes his position as the head of government more secure.

7.4.2 SOE Consequences after Domestic Events

We now move on to deal with our second question. What – if any – are the consequences of an SOE declared after a domestic event for political and civil liberties? We use the respect for human rights indicator developed by Fariss (2014), which was already described in the last chapter. To recap, it combines all available standards-based and events-based indicators available for many countries and several years since 1950. The index effectively captures the latent degree of absence of repression, that is, higher values indicate *less* repression.

For the interpretation of our findings, we propose to focus on columns 5 and 6 of Table 7.5 in which the results for democracies and autocracies are listed separately. The declaration of an SOE subsequent to a domestic event is correlated with a significant drop in the respect for human rights in autocracies but not in democracies. A failed coup does not lead to a significant deterioration with regard to human rights in democracies whereas it does in autocracies that already respect them substantially less.

One way to interpret this finding could be that democratic governments perceive the fact that the coup has failed as evidence of the stability of the institutions at play whereas autocratic governments may interpret it as evidence for discontent implying that there may be more attempts in the future, which autocratic governments could try

Table 7.5 *Consequences for civil liberties*

Sample	All 1	All 2	No causal problems 3	Only democracies 4	Only autocracies 5
			Full baseline included		
Twice-lagged civil liberties	0.788***	0.793***	0.796***	0.802***	0.741***
	(0.018)	(0.018)	(0.017)	(0.026)	(0.022)
Successful coup	-0.188**	-0.175**	-0.176**	-0.393*	-0.176*
	(0.084)	(0.080)	(0.081)	(0.211)	(0.101)
Failed coup	-0.086***	-0.067*	-0.065*	-0.064	-0.074**
	(0.032)	(0.034)	(0.035)	(0.096)	(0.037)
Log conflict index	-0.019***				
	(0.003)				
Domestic SOE	0.089	-0.161***	-0.152***	-0.057	-0.235***
	(0.067)	(0.052)	(0.052)	(0.042)	(0.079)
Succ. coup * SOE	0.089	0.064	0.015	0.323	-0.027
	(0.111)	(0.115)	(0.133)	(0.200)	(0.175)
Fail. coup * SOE	0.019	-0.008	-0.018	-0.231	0.106
	(0.087)	(0.089)	(0.090)	(0.172)	(0.112)
Conflict * SOE	-0.011				
	(0.008)				
Assassinations		-0.014*	-0.014**	-0.014**	-0.018
		(0.007)	(0.007)	(0.007)	(0.013)
General strikes		-0.002	-0.002	-0.009	-0.016
		(0.007)	(0.007)	(0.009)	(0.015)
Guerrilla warfare		-0.001***	-0.001***	-0.001*	-0.001**
		(0.000)	(0.000)	(0.000)	(0.000)
Government crises		-0.046***	-0.046***	-0.023*	-0.056**
		(0.013)	(0.013)	(0.013)	(0.028)
Purges		-0.047**	-0.046**	-0.118**	-0.018
		(0.023)	(0.023)	(0.047)	(0.023)
Riots		-0.005	0.005	-0.002	-0.005
		(0.003)	(0.003)	(0.003)	(0.007)
Revolutions		-0.082***	-0.082***	-0.053*	-0.099**
		(0.027)	(0.028)	(0.028)	(0.041)
Anti-gov. demonstrations		0.001	0.001	0.004**	-0.006
		(0.002)	(0.002)	(0.002)	(0.006)
Assassinations * SOE		0.011	0.009	0.005	0.019
		(0.011)	(0.012)	(0.009)	(0.027)

Table 7.5 *(cont.)*

	All	All	No causal problems	Only democracies	Only autocracies
Sample	1	2	3	4	5
Strikes * SOE		−0.028	−0.035	−0.045	0.037
		(0.036)	(0.039)	(0.041)	(0.054)
Guerrilla * SOE		−0.001	−0.000	−0.004	−0.002
		(0.002)	(0.002)	(0.003)	(0.005)
Gov. crises * SOE		0.013	0.002	−0.024	0.048
		(0.043)	(0.042)	(0.036)	(0.107)
Purges * SOE		−0.059	−0.083	0.003	−0.089
		(0.065)	(0.083)	(0.093)	(0.059)
Riots * SOE		0.007	0.008	−0.022**	0.027
		(0.019)	(0.019)	(0.011)	(0.025)
Revolutions * SOE		0.037	0.047	0.031	0.036
		(0.055)	(0.053)	(0.040)	(0.084)
Demonstrations * SOE		−0.009	−0.009	0.024**	−0.017
		(0.018)	(0.019)	(0.010)	(0.021)
Regime FE	Yes	Yes	Yes	Yes	Yes
Country FE	Yes	Yes	Yes	Yes	Yes
Observations	4206	4206	4186	1880	2326
Countries	99	99	99	71	82
Pseudo R sq.	0.906	0.911	0.914	0.956	0.873
F Statistic	412.26	535.62	533.15	–	958.72

Note: all estimates are conditional fixed effects logit; ***(**) [*] denote significance at $p < 0.01$, ($p < 0.05$), and [$p < 0.10$].

to prevent by tightening the grip on their people. Government crises and revolutions lead to a deterioration of the human rights records in both autocracies and democracies. Interestingly, assassinations and riots combined with an SOE only make things with regard to human rights worse in democracies. The differences between democracies and autocracies are therefore not simple and, as illustrated by the example of India during Indira Gandhi's government, nor is the distinction between the two regime types. Such complications, just as the complications of defining clearly what a domestic event is, need to be kept in mind when interpreting the findings of this chapter.

Indira Gandhi's State of Emergency: 1975–1977

Throughout this book, we have often stressed that SOEs regularly imply an increase in the powers of the executive to the detriment of the other branches of government and – in all likelihood – a reduction in civil and political liberties for all citizens. In this sense, the SOE proclaimed by the Indian government in 1975 is almost too perfect a textbook example: The powers of the executive were increased by enabling Gandhi to rule by decree and allowing her to cancel elections, hence prolonging her term in office. The powers of the judiciary were curtailed by limiting judicial review. Free speech and assembly as well as many workers' rights were reduced. The media were censored and reports on human rights violations abound. In all, more than 110,000 Indians were detained in conjunction with the SOE.

Gandhi had two immediate reasons for calling the emergency on June 25, 1975. There were student protests in Bihar reflecting a more general unhappiness with both the political and economic development of the country. In addition, and probably even more important, the Allahabad High Court had convicted her of corrupt practices regarding the 1971 elections which implied that she was to lose her parliamentary seat and would be barred from running for political office for the next six years. This was on June 12th. Gandhi immediately turned to the Supreme Court hoping that it would overturn the decision. But it did not. Instead, it confirmed the High Court decision on June 24th, one day before the emergency was declared.

But in a sense, the emergency declaration was only the latest move by Gandhi to consolidate and extend her powers. The rigged election of 1971 was just mentioned. But she also managed to pack the Supreme Court in her favor. Already in 1971, she made parliament pass the Maintenance of Internal Security Act (MISA) which was now used to arrest thousands of political opponents.

The declaration itself was done in a tearing hurry. Formally, the president of India can declare after the prime minister has sought the advice of the Council of Ministers. She had not sought the advice of her cabinet arguing that there was an imminent threat to the internal security of the nation. Yet once the SOE was in place, she did not waste any time. The next morning, more than 600 opposition leaders had already been arrested; the press was censored in a highly pragmatic fashion, namely by cutting it off from electricity.

The emergency did more than prolong her own tenure in office and lead to the arrest of more than 110,000. Forced sterilizations went up from 1.3 million in 1975, to 2.6 in 1976 and 8.1 in 1977 (Gupte 2017).

The homes of more than 70,000 people were destroyed by the so-called beautification drive led by Indira Gandhi's son Sanjay (www.opindia.com/2022/04/emergency-sanjay-gandhi-beautification-drive-bulldozed-old-delhi/). One recent account of this episode describes it as "... the Emergency was not a momentary episode but a turning point in the history of Indian democracy" (Prakash 2019, 39).

There are many excellent descriptions of the events surrounding this SOE. Prakash (2019) is the most recent one.

7.5 Conclusions

In this chapter, we have explored two interrelated questions. We have first analyzed, which domestic events are likely to lead to the declaration of an SOE. In a second step, we have asked which events – possibly combined with an SOE – lead to significant changes in the human rights record of a country. Our most general finding is that more domestic events of the types covered in this chapter are correlated with a higher likelihood of observing an SOE being declared. The single events most likely to be accompanied by an SOE are major government crises, riots, and revolutions. Regarding changes in a country's track record with regard to human rights, SOEs declared after a domestic event of the types covered here lead to a deterioration in autocracies, but not in democracies. Successful coups have more negative effects in democracies whereas failed coups have worse consequences on human rights in autocracies.

All of these results should, however, be taken with a grain of salt as the data that we have relied upon to produce them are not very precise. More detailed data are, hence, definitely a desideratum. Two aspects appear particularly noteworthy: Given that all events analyzed here are endogenous to government behavior, explicitly controlling for the policies triggering particular events is desirable. And second: Not all events are born equal; information on their size (as well as frequency of occurrence) is highly desirable.

8 Dealing with Disaster
Analyzing the Emergency Constitutions of the US States

8.1 Introduction

All previous chapters relied on cross-country analysis. Here we propose to change the focus of our analysis: In this chapter, we zoom in on the emergency provisions of a single country, namely the United States. This and the following chapter both deal with emergency provisions in federally constituted countries. This chapter is interested in ascertaining and analyzing the differences in the emergency constitutions of the fifty US states. The next chapter – primarily on India – deals with the relationship between the federal and the state level. Although we change the focus of our analysis, the tools used to analyze state constitutions are the same as those that you are well familiar with by now.

In many countries, the overwhelming majority of emergencies are declared on the municipal or the regional level. In the US and for the period between 1953 and 2001, for example, governors requested on average almost one presidential disaster or emergency declaration a week (Sylves and Búzás 2007, 4). However, governors will not seek presidential declarations after every disaster and every locally declared state of emergency (SOE). Indeed, the declaration of some SOEs varies strongly over time and across states. Figure 8.1 exemplifies this by plotting the share of US counties declaring a state of disaster between 1970 and 2015; the figure also includes the corresponding numbers for Louisiana and Mississippi that tend to be hit by relatively similar natural phenomena. While on average 47 percent of all Louisiana parishes (their parallel to counties) declared a disaster in any year during the period, only 10 percent of Mississippian counties did so. We aim to understand such differences in this chapter.

Here, we analyze the emergency provisions incorporated into the US state constitutions, and not the federal constitution. The US is particularly well suited for such a within-country analysis for a number

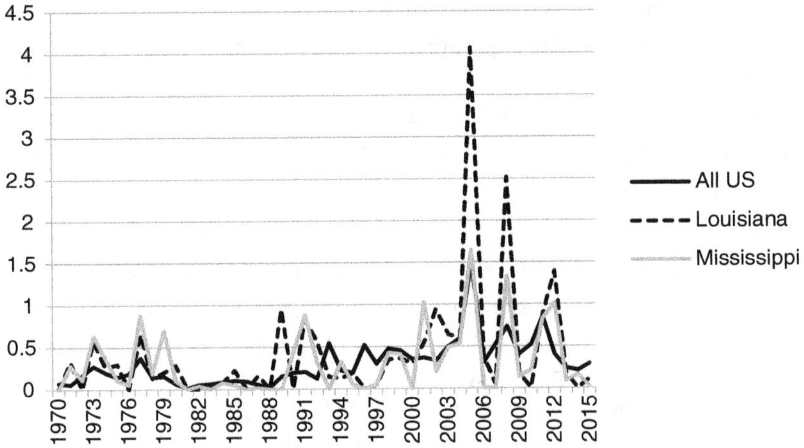

Figure 8.1 Disaster declarations per country, US, Louisiana and Mississippi

of reasons: (1) All fifty states operate under the same legal federal frame, which reduces the need to include control variables. (2) With fifty states, the number of observations is high enough to lend itself to quantitative analysis. (3) Disasters might affect two (or more) states similarly. This therefore constitutes an excellent opportunity to compare the effectiveness of their emergency provisions. (4) Both the availability of data – regarding both disasters and the policy decisions of politicians – as well as their reliability are high. (5) In many other countries, constitutional provisions are not transformed into constitutional reality. In the US, however, we can assume that the de jure provisions will be actually implemented to a very high degree.[1] Our interest lies in analyzing the different emergency provisions that the US states have incorporated into their constitutions. The first step of our analysis is to code all fifty constitutions according to the six variables contained in the Index of Emergency Powers (INEP). This enables us to compare the similarities and the differences between them systematically in the same way as we did in previous chapters regarding cross-country analyses. The second step in our analysis is to rely on cluster analysis. By this, we try to ascertain how similar/dissimilar the various

[1] Analyzing the emergency provisions of state constitutions is, however, no panacea. State governments have far less powers than nation state governments. For example, they cannot call in the military.

state constitutions are. It turns out that forty-nine of the fifty constitutions can be meaningfully grouped into one of six clusters. The only true outlier is the constitution of Texas, which accords considerably less powers to its executive than all other constitutions.

Based on these first two steps in our analysis, a number of follow-up questions almost suggest themselves.

(1) What are the factors driving the differences between state emergency constitutions? Is it proneness to natural disasters? The time period during which the state constitution was passed?
(2) Controlling for the number (and size) of natural disasters occurring in a state, is the emergency constitution a significant factor in explaining the probability that an SOE is declared in a particular state?
(3) Again controlling for the number of natural disasters plus whether an emergency was declared, are the contents of the emergency constitution a significant factor in the effectiveness in which adverse disaster effects are being mitigated?

Starting with Garrett and Sobel (2003), a number of studies, including Sylves and Búzás (2007) and Reeves (2011), have dealt with major political economy aspects involved in disaster and emergency relief provided from the federal to the state level. Key findings are that disaster relief is highly politicized and that the probability of a request from a governor being answered positively by the president depends on a number of political variables such as which party the president belongs to, whether he is currently seeking reelection and so on. The incentive effects of federal disaster relief aid have also been analyzed. On the state level, the sheer possibility of federal disaster relief reduces incentives to invest into disaster preparedness, creating a kind of bailout problem. In this chapter, we are not adding to that literature.

As a consequence of the research just mentioned, one could also inquire into the optimal allocation of powers between the various levels of government when dealing with natural or man-made disasters in the tradition of fiscal federalism (Oates 1972). The normative starting point would be to explore the degree of fiscal equivalence (Olson 1969) or institutional congruence. Intergovernmental grants – such as disaster relief – are usually justified by pointing toward the existence of externalities extending beyond state borders. Such analysis would also ask how best to reduce problems of moral hazard as just discussed. Although highly interesting, this is not the focus of this chapter. In the next chapter, however, we turn to analyze a central issue that all federations face and that they need to handle with particular rigor, namely how to balance the potentially conflicting interests of a state with those of the center. Here, we focus on describing the differences between US state emergency constitutions and mapping their likely consequences.

The rest of the chapter is structured as follows. In Section 8.2, we apply our INEP to the US states. Section 8.3 reports the results of our cluster analysis and a set of simple descriptive statistics. Section 8.4 concludes and spells out a number of follow-up questions that can be tackled with the INEP and the clusters proposed here.

8.2 The INEP for US State Constitutions

8.2.1 Some Details of the State Constitutions

The federal constitution is a very well known document. It is the oldest serving constitution in the world, a very brief document (only 4,582 words), establishing a presidential system with strict separation of powers, and extremely difficult to change. It is complemented by fifty state constitutions.

At least outside the US, the state constitutions are far less well known than the US federal constitution. In many respects, the state constitutions are very different from the federal constitution. A first difference is their longevity: Whereas the federal constitution has been in place for more than 225 years, many of the US states have frequently adopted new constitutions or heavily amended them. At the time of writing, only eighteen states still have their original constitutions. Georgia's current constitution is the ninth in its history, Louisiana's even the eleventh. Second, whereas the federal constitution is built on expressly enumerated powers, the logical flipside is found in the state constitutions. Historically, at least, they have been understood as possessing all those residual powers not explicitly delegated to the national government (Tarr 2000, 7).

State legislatures were not only very powerful in comparision to the US legislature but also vis-à-vis state governments. On the one hand, this was the consequence of dividing the executive into a number of independently elected officials. Tarr (2000, 17) reports that even today, more than two-thirds of the states have at least four independently elected executive officials. On the other hand, the very early state constitutions looked more like parliamentary systems; governors were elected by the legislature and depended on the support of the legislature for their continuation in office (Tarr 2000, 87).

A particular feature of the state constitutions is their explicit treatment of emergencies. While the inclusion of formalized emergency provisions in national constitutions began with the French constitution of 1795, the state constitution of Massachussets included such provisions already in 1780 giving the legislature particular powers of martial law in times of war, invasion, or rebellion (chapter II, art. VII). The state constitutions of New Hampshire (1784) and Vermont (1793) also included similar provisions, but gave the power to declare an emergency to the governor instead of the legislature. All state constitutions now include such provisions but, as we show in the following, within very varied frameworks.

A first difference is the particular conditions that must be met before any government actor – the governor, the legislature, or a collaboration between the two – can call an SOE. The first state constitutions all refer to invasion, insurrection, or rebellion, and the execution of state law as legal conditions for calling an emergency. As of 2023, twenty-six state constititions refer to invasion, seventeen to insurrection or rebellion, and fourteen to "the execution of law." Subsequent constitutions have nevertheless either tended to include more conditions – mostly references to the public peace (eleven cases) or fiscal emergencies (fourteen cases) – or remained vague as to what defines a legal emergency. We assess the conditions in thirty state constitutions to be vague; the remaining twenty with fully specified conditions on average mention 2.8 qualifying circumstances.

In thirty-five cases, we further find that a single actor – typically the governor – can call an SOE on his or her own. They also tend to have substantial approval power such that only six constitutions require some other branch of government, that is, the state congress, to approve the call. Similarly, all but the Texan constitution allow for the dissolution of parliament in an SOE and only three – Maryland, Texas, and Vermont – do not allow for the cancellation of some right that is otherwise constitutionally protected. The constitution of Mississippi is *a priori* the most permissive with article 3 § 4, para 2 (4) stating that the General Assembly (i.e. the Mississippi Congress) is allowed to suspend "all constitutional legislative rules – during emergency caused by enemy attack." However, thirty-eight constitutions mention habeas corpus as a suspendable right, thirty-six allow for the expropriation of property to quarter soldiers, and fourteen constitutions allow the suspension of other rights of which military duty on election day is often mentioned.

8.2.2 An INEP of the State Constitutions

To recall, the INEP that has been introduced in the second chapter and been used throughout this book takes into account: (1) the degree to which the right to declare an SOE is concentrated in a single person – or very few – or limited by multiple veto players; (2) the need to and the degree to which this right is concentrated; (3) how many different situations are explicitly mentioned in the constitution and can be used to justify the declaration of a state of emergency; (4) whether fundamental civil and political rights can be suspended during an SOE; (5) whether parliament can be dissolved during an SOE; and (6) whether the government can introduce censorship of the media and expropriate property during an emergency.

As elsewhere, we refer to the first three variables as the Cost INEP while the last three refer to the powers that government enjoys under an SOE, that is, the Benefit INEP. There is, however, a noteworthy difference compared to the cross-country version of the INEP that you are well acquainted with by now: The first amendment to the constitution explicitly bans censorship, which logically limits the scope of any state measure.

As illustrated by Figure 8.2, the resulting INEP varies between a low of 0.23 in Texas to a high of 0.45 in Georgia and Wyoming. The Cost INEP is smallest for California and largest in Wyoming, in which the constitution's Article 17 § 5 simply states that "the Governor calls out militia." On the benefit side, the Texan constitution is the least permissive by providing absolutely no additional benefits during emergencies while the constitutions of Louisiana and Georgia allow for both expropriation with due compensation and substantial further derogation of basic rights.

The additive index captures that the elements in principle could be substitutes or complements. This is also reflected by the correlations between the five elements of the INEP that vary between –0.14

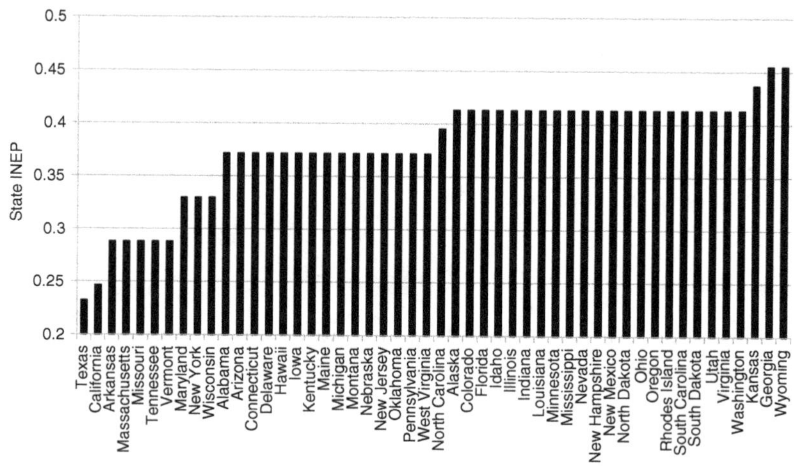

Figure 8.2 State constitution INEP

(declaration powers and conditions) and 0.41 (dissolution powers and rights suspension). Instead of performing a standard statistical analysis, we therefore employ cluster analysis in order to identify commonalities across the emergency constitutions of the fifty state constitutions.

8.3 Cluster Analysis Applied to US State Constitutions

In order to map any similarities or families of emergency constitutions in the US, we apply cluster analysis. We already gave you a couple of paragraphs on how we use it in Chapter 2, so there is no need to repeat that here, as the approach is identical. Tables 8.1 and 8.2 summarize some details, in case you are interested.

In the following, we work with the six-cluster solution as it provides a substantially better balance between precision and parsimony than other solutions. Table 2.1 lists the member constitutions of each of the six clusters as well as the years in which the relevant constitution was implemented. Figure 8.3 illustrates the broad differences in terms of the Cost and Benefit INEPs between the six clusters, in which one needs to recall that Texas is its own cluster.

We begin by outlining which factors characterize the clusters with the cluster averages in Table 8.2. The first obvious thing to note is that the one-state cluster no. 2 – Texas – is considerably different from the rest with the lowest overall INEP, relatively average approval powers

Table 8.1 *Cluster memberships, preferred six-cluster solution*

Cluster	Members
1.	Alaska (1959), Colorado (1876), Florida (1969), Georgia (1893), Idaho (1890), Illinois (1971), Indiana (1851), Kansas (1861), Minnesota (1858), Mississippi (1890), Nevada (1864), New Hampshire (1784), New Mexico (1912), North Dakota (1889), Ohio (1851), Oregon (1859), South Carolina (1896), South Dakota (1889), Utah (1896), Virginia (1971), Washington (1889)
2.	Texas (1876)
3.	Louisiana (1975), Rhode Island (1843), Wyoming (1890)
4.	California (1880), Connecticut (1965), Hawaii (1959), Michigan (1964), New York (1895)
5.	Alabama (1901), Arizona (1912), Maryland (1867), Montana (1973), Nebraska (1875), North Carolina (1971), Oklahoma (1907), Vermont (1793), West Virginia (1872)
6.	Arkansas (1874), Delaware (1897), Iowa (1857), Kentucky (1891), Maine (1820), Massachusetts (1780), Missouri (1945), New Jersey (1948), Pennsylvania (1874), Tennessee (1870), Wisconsin (1848)

Table 8.2 *Characteristics of emergency constitutions, clusters*

Cluster	1	2	3	4	5	6
INEP	0.42	0.23	0.43	0.34	0.36	0.34
Declaration power	1	1	0.67	0.87	0.96	0.42
Approval power	1	0.50	1	0.30	1	1
Conditions	0.50	0.50	1	0.50	0.5	0.5
Dissolution power	1	0	1	1	1	1
Rights suspension	0.68	0	0.78	0.67	0.26	0.64
No. of members	21	1	3	5	9	11

and emergency conditions, and no dissolution rights or suspension of basic rights. Limited declaration powers define the eleven-state cluster no. 6 while limited approval powers are characteristic of cluster 4 as well as Texas. In all other clusters, the declaration of an SOE does not necessarily have to be approved by another branch of government.

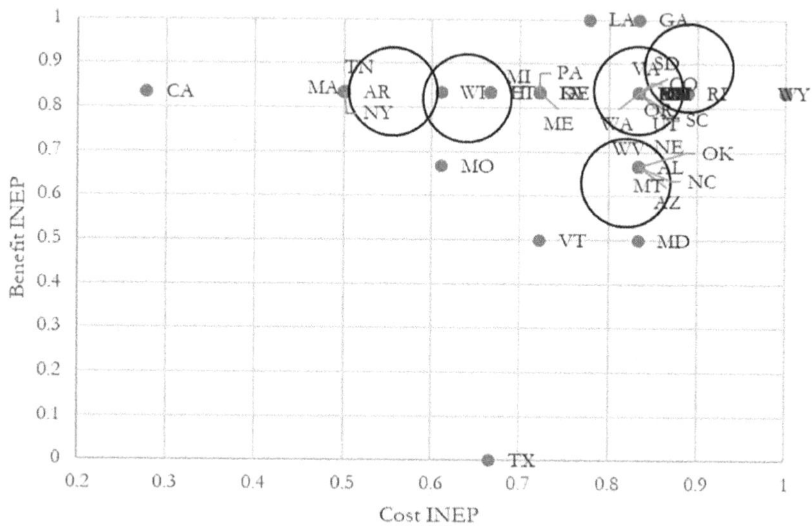

Figure 8.3 Cost and benefit INEPs, six clusters

In terms of conditions, the three constitutions in cluster 3 – Louisiana, Rhode Island and Wyoming – are so permissive as not to clearly define the circumstances that would allow an SOE. Finally, the nine constitutions in cluster 5 resemble the Texan by limiting the number of circumstances that justify an emergency. Only one member – Oklahoma – for example allows calling a fiscal emergency.

8.4 The Factors Determining the Clusters

We are thus able to identify separate clusters or "families" of emergency constitutions in the US. A follow-up question is why constitutional design differs substantially across fifty states that otherwise share an overarching constitutional frame in the form of the US Constitution. Do the clusters reflect objective differences in disaster risk, demographic and economic development, or political or ideological differences? The differences in Table 8.3 provide a number of indications.

We first of all note that CoreLogic's (2014) measure of Natural Hazard Risk (HRS) index is in no way systematically different across the clusters. Despite the apparent differences, the only cluster consisting of states that are geographically smaller is cluster no. 6. Similarly, only the five states in cluster no. 4 were more developed, as measured

Table 8.3 *Further cluster characteristics*

Cluster	1	2	3	4	5	6
Year, const.	1891	1876	1903	1933	1897	1873
Year, state	1852	1845	1831	1844	1847	1810
Population	206,810	212,592	68,696	303,140	381,213	196,559
Urbanization	22.64	9.20	48.20	68.80	24.99	26.01
Pop. density	4.21	0.79	15.54	21.96	9.78	10.16
No. previous	1.76	3.00	3.67	1.60	1.44	1.82
HRS	51.21	60.89	63.05	47.45	45.53	51.58
Area	97,797	268,596	50,579	66,288	62,308	39,128
Trust	31.29	27.54	33.05	30.94	30.79	31.72
D-Nominate 1	0.02	−0.30	0.18	−0.04	−0.10	0.03
D-Nominate 2	0.312	−0.07	0.40	−0.05	−0.01	0.01

by their degree of urbanization and population density, when they implemented their emergency constitutions. Conversely, we find that neither trust nor the age of the constitution matter to cluster placement.

The main determinant turns out to be ideology, although not the standard left-right distinction measured by the first dimension of D-Nominate index (Poole and Rosenthal 2007). The first dimension of the D-Nominate data (D-Nominate 1) represents the standard left-right spectrum on economic matters. The second dimension (D-Nominate 2) instead picks up cross-cutting issues that were politically salient in a given period. In most cases in our dataset, the second dimension represented state positions on slavery and which particular monetary anchor to adopt (the bimetallism debate). D-Nominate two strongly affects cluster placement. In the raw data, the difference between the ideological extremes at the time of constitutional implementation (West Virginia and South Dakota) tends to result in a difference in the INEP of about 0.1 points. This difference is reflected in both the cost and benefit sides of the INEP.

8.5 Do the Differences Matter?

As the final question for which we can provide a tentative answer, we here explore whether the emergency constitutions work as officially intended. In other words, we ask whether states with particular

Table 8.4 *Descriptives, additional disaster data*

	Mean	Standard deviation	Observations
Fatalities (logs)	1.836	1.118	1000
Property damage (logs)	3.603	1.876	1000
Crop damage (logs)	1.392	1.939	1000
Total damage (logs)	3.818	1.956	1000
Log GSP per capita	10.717	0.251	950
Log population size	15.089	1.023	1000
Log state area	10.752	1.098	1000
Log injured	3.107	1.513	1000
Cost INEP	0.761	0.128	1000
Benefit INEP	0.783	0.146	1000

emergency provisions or with emergency constitutions in either of the six families defined by the cluster analysis exhibit lower fatality rates and smaller damage subsequent to natural disasters.

We do so by collecting additional data on the number of fatalities and injured, and the dollar value of damage to property and crops, and total damage resulting from natural disasters between 1995 and 2015. These data derive from the annual reports from the National Oceanic and Atmospheric Administration (NOAA 2017). We couple those with the size of the state population and the geographical area of each state from the US Census (2016) and the real Gross State Product (GSP) per capita, which derive from the US Bureau of Economic Analysis BER (2016). These data are described in Table 8.4.

In all cases, we estimate log-log specifications, that is, we convert all data into logarithms. We control for the number of injured in every year, as a way to capture the size of the underlying natural events while we think of the number of fatalities as an outcome of the emergency efforts. We also include a lagged dependent variable such that all potential effects are identified through the year-to-year changes in disaster fatalities and damage. Thereby, we circumvent the unavoidable causality problem to some extent because emergency constitutions may reflect the relative threat of natural disasters. By identifying effects through changes, the lagged dependent variable effectively captures the typical level of threat, which could have affected the particular design of the emergency constitution while identification is – at least partially – not affected by what may cause simultaneity bias. Doing so in a log-log framework moreover has the benefit that all estimates can be interpreted as elasticities, and that both nationwide changes as well as inflationary bias are all captured by the set of annual fixed effects that we include. All estimates are necessarily random effects (because emergency constitutions do not change over this period).

We report the simple results in Table 8.5. We first of all observe strongly significant persistence, such that disaster characteristics of

Table 8.5 *Disaster consequences*

	Fatalities	Property damage	Crop damage	Total damage
Lagged event	0.202**	0.237***	0.358***	0.282***
	(0.029)	(0.030)	(0.029)	(0.029)
Log GSP per capita	0.086	-0.141	0.417*	-0.086
	(0.108)	(0.213)	(0.241)	(0.213)
Log population size	0.265***	0.283***	0.088	0.278***
	(0.034)	(0.063)	(0.068)	(0.063)
Log state area	0.082***	0.194***	0.168***	0.208***
	(0.021)	(0.042)	(0.048)	(0.043)
Log injured	0.315***	0.419***	0.260***	0.433***
	(0.020)	(0.039)	(0.044)	(0.039)
Log Cost INEP	0.463	0.115	-0.417	0.207
	(0.331)	(0.652)	(0.734)	(0.651)
Log Benefit INEP	-0.476**	-0.808*	-2.268***	-0.877*
	(0.238)	(0.468)	(0.536)	(0.468)
Annual FE	Yes	Yes	Yes	Yes
Observations	949	949	949	949
R squared	0.617	0.475	0.368	0.518
Wald Chi squared	1487.90	835.74	534.44	991.10
Findings with clusters				
Cluster 2	0.181	0.713**	1.859***	0.695**
	(0.176)	(0.346)	(0.398)	(0.346)
Cluster 3	0.188*	0.106	0.036	0.064
	(0.105)	(0.206)	(0.232)	(0.206)
Cluster 4	-0.135	-0.393**	-0.015	-0.376**
	(0.087)	(0.172)	(0.192)	(0.172)
Cluster 5	0.059	0.074	0.110	0.131
	(0.067)	(0.132)	(0.149)	(0.132)
Cluster 6	-0.049	0.029	-0.042	0.031
	(0.067)	(0.131)	(0.147)	(0.131)

Note: ***(**) [*] denote significance at $p < 0.01$, ($p < 0.05$), and [$p < 0.10$]; all regressions include a constant term.

previous years are reflected in those of the present year, and that more encompassing disasters as measured by the number of injured also affect the remaining characteristics. We also see the expected associations with the population and the area of the state, but little influence of how rich the state is.

Most pertinently, our tentative results suggest that states that allocate more benefits to the executive during emergencies have lower fatalities and less damage. Using the cluster solution (in the lower panel), and thus estimating whether emergency constitutions in clusters 2–6 are significantly different from those in the large cluster 1, yields somewhat different findings. They first indicate that the results pertaining to the Benefit INEP are simply due to Texas, in which the emergency constitution allows no benefits at all. Yet they also indicate that while no configuration of emergency provisions clearly affects the fatality rate, emergency constitutions in cluster 4 may be more effective at limiting the economic damage done to property during natural disasters. As such, although these estimates must be interpreted with due care and taken to be quite tentative, they do suggest that the type of emergency constitution chosen by California, Connecticut, Hawaii, Michigan, and New York tends to outperform other types. With this observation – that the choice of emergency constitution may have substantial consequences – we proceed to the conclusions.

8.6 Conclusions and Outlook

We find considerable variation across the fifty constitutions with regard to the rules enabling governments to call an SOE as well as the rules spelling out the additional competences delegated to government after an SOE has been declared.

Drawing on cluster analysis, we identify six different clusters. These can be thought as six different "families" of emergency constitutions. One noteworthy finding regarding these six families is that the Texas constitution depicts a family of its own. In other words, its emergency provisions are very different from those of all other forty-nine states. In Texas, the government enjoys virtually no additional de jure powers after an SOE has been declared.

Inquiring into the factors that determine "family membership" of the emergency constitutions, we find that ideology is key. Interestingly, it is not the well-established left-right divide, but rather cross-cutting issues – such as slavery in the nineteenth century – that were salient at the time the constitution was written.

Finally, we find that "family membership" does matter for how effectively the adverse effects of natural disasters are mitigated by a state government, at least with regard to damage occurring to property. Those constitutions that make the declaration of an SOE contingent upon the approval of the legislature fare significantly better than those that put little or no approval check on a declaration.

9 *Keeping up the Balance between the Federation and the States*[*]

9.1 Introduction

In the preceding chapter, we analyzed a particular aspect of federalism with regard to its emergency provisions, namely the emergency constitutions at the level of the states making up a federation. This was done with regard to the fifty states comprising the United States. In this chapter, the focus is on a different aspect of federations, namely the relationship between the federal level of government and the states. In addition to the design issues of emergency constitutions discussed so far, federations need to deal with an additional one, namely how to allocate the competences regarding emergencies between the center and the states. Imagine a natural disaster just occurred in one of the member states of a federation. Then, who has the power to declare a state of emergency (SOE)? What if the evaluations of the federal government and the government of the state hit by a natural disaster do not align? Who is to pay for costly measures implemented to deal with the consequences of the natural disaster?

After an emergency has occurred, swift government action is often crucial. Temporarily allocating additional competences to the center therefore appears straightforward as time-consuming decision-making processes between center and state governments could be avoided. Yet, if not designed properly, such competences may also be misused by the central government. In essence, these considerations lead us right into the center of a long debate among scholars of federalism: how to deal with the double-problem of centripetal and centrifugal forces explicitly raised by William Riker already in 1964. On the one hand, the center needs to be strong enough to provide all citizens with a set of public goods. On the other, making it too strong would enable

[*] The core of this chapter is a case study on India, exemplifying the particular issues federally constituted nations have with emergencies. The case study was written jointly with Abishek Choutagunta and Shruti Rajagopalan

it to disregard the preferences of citizens in many states and appropriate political rents. But finding an adequate balance is challenging because if there is no functioning device monitoring the behavior of the states, they may produce negative externalities for others by, for example, incurring deficits that they are unable to service leading to the necessity of the center to bail the respective state(s) out. It is this "double dilemma" of federally structured states applied to emergencies, which is at the core of this chapter.

In this book, we have so far focused on two types of event that are often cited to justify the declaration of an SOE, namely natural disasters which we have considered as largely exogenous and man-made turmoil such as riots, general strikes, but also terrorist activities which are, at least in part, endogenous to government behavior. Until now, the implicit assumption has been that man-made turmoil is generated by private actors – and not by representatives of the state. With regard to the topic of this chapter, this assumption may need to be modified. State governments in federations may also endanger the survival of the constitutional order in a variety of ways: they may simply not implement legislation newly passed at the federal level; they may not be fighting secessionist movements to preserve the unity of the nation; or they may even become actively involved in such movements themselves. In a sense, then, man-made emergency situations can also be caused by representatives of the state. So there are really two issues at stake here, namely how to allocate competences between the center and the states with regard to the traditionally discussed events justifying the declaration of an SOE and secondly what provisions to design for the possibility that through their behavior, state representatives themselves endanger the survival of the constitutional order.

In this chapter, we specifically analyze how the tension between centripetal and centrifugal forces plays out in India, the world's largest federal republic. Regarding the federal–state relationship under an emergency, the Constitution of India allows the union (federal) cabinet to dismiss a functioning state government and dissolve the elected state legislature, if the governor of the state appointed by the union cabinet recommends the dismissal which we refer to as "state emergency" in this chapter. This arrangement is also known as "President's rule."

Granting extra powers and discretion to the union government and state governor appointed by the union government during an emergency may result in misuse, as it may motivate union governments to remove state governments formed by rival political parties. By granting the union government this emergency provision, the framers of the constitution wanted to ensure that state governments adhere to the constitution, that is, they wanted to safeguard the unity of the federation (Government of India 1988, p. 6.2.14; Sagar 2016). They were, however, aware of the potential tradeoff between providing strong emergency powers to the union government and the possibility of it being misused for political gain.[1]

The provision has not remained a dead letter. Between 1950 and 2019, it was used 116 times to impose direct union government rule in various states of India. Of the twenty-eight Indian states only two (relatively recently formed) states have never experienced President's rule.[2] Every other state has experienced this kind of union government rule at some point, sometimes for years on end.

In this chapter, we analyze the determinants of the use of President's rule and test the various explanations offered. To do so, we rely on Tsebelis' (2002) veto player theory. Veto players are individual or collective decision-makers whose agreement is required for the change of the status quo. We describe the individual and collective veto players in the Indian federal and parliamentary system, and their relative strengths, to explain the infrequent use of President's rule since the 1990s. We construct a unique panel dataset containing monthly information on the political composition of the state and union-level legislatures and executives with all the potential veto players for forty current and former Indian states between April 1952 and October 2019. Our dataset also contains events that could cause the breakdown of constitutional machinery (i.e. riots and natural disasters).

[1] The Chairman of the Drafting Committee of the Constituent Assembly of India, B.R. Ambedkar (C.A.D. 1949, p. 177) explained: "I do not altogether deny that there is a possibility of these articles being abused or employed for political purposes ... that such articles will never be called into operation and that they would remain a dead letter."

[2] Since the State of Jammu and Kashmir was reconstituted as an administrative division governed by the Indian Union government, that is, Union territory, in August 2019, the total number of states has come down from twenty-nine to twenty-eight. However, for the purpose of this chapter, which looks at the period till 2019, the erstwhile State of Jammu and Kashmir will be counted as a state and not as a Union territory, which has been its status since August 5, 2019. The two states never to experience president's rule are Chhattisgarh formed in 2000 and Telangana formed in 2014.

Our analysis yields three main findings. We first find that in India, the power to invoke state emergency has been politically captured to destabilize the opposition, and not to deal with man-made or natural disasters. We find that union governments invoke it when it is less costly, that is, when confronted with weaker veto players. The likelihood of imposing President's rule is almost exclusively determined by the strength of the mandate of the ruling party in the state legislature; a five percentage point smaller seat share is associated with a 10 percent higher probability of the union government imposing President's rule. Second, coalition governments in states are about three times more likely to experience President's rule than a state government formed by a single party. These findings are in line with Tsebelis (2002) who argues that in parliamentary systems, the veto players are equivalent to the number of political parties.

In many countries, events that may look like real world emergencies are used as the ostensible reason to impose SOEs (for more on this, we refer the reader to Chapter 11, in which we deal with unconstitutional SOEs). Our third finding is that in India, real world emergency situations like communal riots or natural disasters are not significant predictors of President's rule imposition. We observe that the only exogenous shock that consistently influences the likelihood of a President's rule imposition is the death of a state's incumbent chief minister, which causes a power vacuum within the state government leadership, and therefore weakens an important veto player in the office of the chief minister, creating room for politically opportunistic behavior by the union government.

Currently, around 40 percent of the world's citizens live in some two dozen federally constituted states. The problems analyzed in this chapter are thus highly relevant for a major chunk of the world population. In making these issues more concrete, we have decided to make a case study the center of this chapter and hope that the case of India – the world's largest democracy – may serve as a cautionary tale for other federal nations.

The rest of the chapter is organized as follows. Section 9.2 describes Article 356 of the Indian Constitution in a little more detail. Section 9.3 details all the veto players and connects them to the theoretical model. We also develop our hypotheses in this section. In Section 9.4, we describe our data and Section 9.5 presents the results. In Section 9.6, we briefly discuss the results and take a brief look at the relevant provisions in other federally organized countries. Section 9.7 concludes.

9.2 Article 356 (the President's Rule)

9.2.1 Constitutional Context

India is the largest federal republic in the world with its 1.4 billion people in twenty-eight states and eight union territories. The possibility of a federal government undermining states' authority arises because the emergency provision – Article 356 – allows the union government to take over the governance of a state when the latter is not able to carry out its duties "in accordance with the provisions of this Constitution."

India's constitution divides legislative powers into union powers, state powers, and concurrent powers (Schedule VII). However, there are many clauses that enable the union to overrule or undermine the legislative competence and authority of the states enabling legislative centripetalism. One rule establishing the dominance of the federal executive is that the governor of the state, in whom the executive power of the state vests (Article 154) is appointed by the union cabinet and serves at the pleasure of the president (Articles 155–156). The Indian judiciary tends toward centralization as lower courts are bound by the precedent set by higher courts. Additionally, India's Supreme Court determines the policies for appointment and transfer of judges, and overall judicial administration in state high courts.

The origin of Article 356 can be traced back to the Government of India Act 1935. It was included in India's independence constitution while a bloody and violent partition was underway. India's leaders were afraid of potential secession, untamed violent ethnic conflict, and communist revolutions in certain states. This is why the constitution framers decided that the power to intervene when there was a breakdown of law and order, or constitutional governance, would lie with the union government and not the state governor.

9.2.2 Procedure to Invoke Article 356 and Impose President's Rule

In principle, we can think of three ways in which Article 356 can be invoked by the union government: (1) in line with the goal spelled out in the constitution to deal with an emergency; (2) using an emergency as a pretext to increase the power of the union government; or (3) as

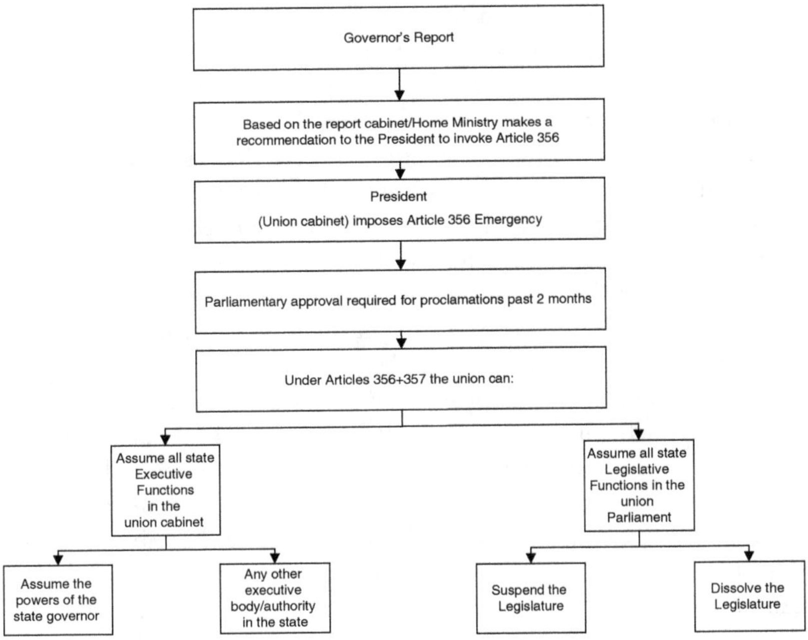

Figure 9.1 Formal procedure of invoking Article 356

a pretext to increase the power of the central government without any emergency occurring. To connect instances in the use of Article 356 with one of these ways, we need to understand the process that determines the incentives of various federal and state actors in invoking Article 356. This will also help resolve the puzzle of why the frequent invocation of President's rule has ebbed since the 1990s.

The formal procedure to invoke Article 356 is depicted in Figure 9.1. The process is kicked off by the appointed governor of a state sending a report to the union cabinet explaining why the state government is unable to function in accordance with the constitution. If the union cabinet concurs with the governor's report and recommends that the president invoke Article 356 in the state, the president has discretionary power to do so. However, the constitution is silent on what constitutes a failure of constitutional machinery or a constitutional emergency. The Sarkaria Commission Report (Government of India 1988), which examined federalism in India and specifically investigated the abuse of President's rule for political purposes in 1988, established a nonexhaustive list of guidelines. This list includes a political crisis or a deadlock where no party can form a government coalition,[3] and an internal subversion where the state government operates contrary to constitutional provisions, ranging from disregarding constitutional norms to plotting violent revolution with a foreign government.[4] The list further mentions a breakdown where the state government is unable to maintain law and order during communal riots, secession, or natural disasters.[5] Lastly, the list mentions noncompliance of a state government with the directions of the union government.[6]

There are several procedural safeguards in place regarding Article 356. The proclamation made under this article is only valid for two months unless it is approved by parliament. After approval, it can be extended for up to six months (Articles 356(3) and 356(4)). However, beyond one year, an extension is not permitted unless there is a national security emergency, and the Election Commission certifies that it is difficult to hold elections to the state assembly (Articles 356(5) and 356(6)). Furthermore, proclamations under Article 356 cannot be extended beyond three years, except in the state of Punjab. There, and only there, it can be extended for up to five years, due to an amendment to Article 356(4).

[3] Political crisis as defined by the Sarkaria Commission arises when: (1) a party or a coalition of parties cannot gain an absolute majority to form the government; (2) a government resigns or is dismissed for losing majority support; or (3) the party with majority refuses to form or continue the government; and all possible alternatives explored by the governor to form a government in such instances have failed.

[4] Internal subversion as defined by the Sarkaria Commission occurs when a state government: (1) conducts its business beyond the constitutional mandate; (2) deliberately brings the government to a standstill or creates a deadlock; (3) functions as a dictatorship; or (4) instigates a violent revolution; and all corrective measures to remedy such distortions have failed.

[5] Physical breakdown as defined by the Sarkaria Commission occurs when a state government refuses or is unable to deal with "internal disturbances" or a natural calamity which paralyzes administration and endangers the security of the State.

[6] Noncompliance with the directive of the union government as defined by the Sarkaria Commission arises when the central government issues constitutional directions, especially when the state government fails to inform the central government of any public disorder threatening the security of the State, and the state government does not comply with such directions despite adequate warning and opportunity, the president can treat such noncompliance as a constitutional emergency.

It is important to note that Article 356 does not authorize the president (and thus the union cabinet) to assume any powers vested in or exercisable by a High Court. The article only grants the president the executive and legislative authority of the state, but no authority over the state judiciary.

In the *SR Bommai* v. *Union of India* judgment of 1991, the Supreme Court placed additional limitations on the union cabinet's authority to use Article 356. This case was initiated by SR Bommai, who was dismissed as chief minister of Karnataka using Article 356. The Court inquired into the following issues after the proclamation of President's rule in a state: (1) whether in fact conditions objectively existed, which rendered it impossible to carry on the governance of the state in accordance with the constitutional provisions; and (2) whether the state's assembly was dissolved only after both houses of parliament approved the proclamation made by the president under Article 356.

The *SR Bommai* judgment determined that, even after obtaining approval from parliament, the issue will be open to review in both the high courts and the Supreme Court to determine independently whether the conditions truly justified the use of power. Once a prima facie case is established, the burden of proof falls on the government/ union cabinet to justify the invocation of Article 356. In the event of such a review, the Supreme Court ruled that the reviewing court is entitled to material evidence in the form of the governor's report to the cabinet, as well as records from the government containing the material on which the cabinet advised the president to invoke Article 356.

The *SR Bommai* judgment also granted courts the authority to order an interim stay on the exercise of power under Article 356, and if the proclamation was declared unconstitutional, the courts had the power to order the revival of the dissolved state assembly and the reinstatement of the dismissed state government. These provisions restrict the union cabinet's (and therefore the president's) authority by giving the judiciary a broad set of powers to reverse the actions of the union cabinet if they are deemed arbitrary and unconstitutional.

9.3 Veto Players and Their Incentives

To understand the operation, implications, and consequences of Article 356, we analyze the incentives of individuals holding positions in or as union cabinet, parliament, governor, president, and so forth.

We assume that political actors are pursuing their self-interest broadly defined. The potential benefit of invoking Article 356 is to increase the power of the union government by bringing a state directly under its rule. Given this benefit, the lower the cost of invoking Article 356, the higher the expected net benefit and in turn the likelihood of its invocation.

According to Tsebelis (2002), a veto player is an individual or collective actor whose agreement is necessary to modify the status quo: in our case, to impose President's rule. Article 356 must be approved by the governor, the president, the union cabinet, and both houses of parliament, and – since 1994 –by the judiciary. These are, hence, the potential veto players. Another key player is the state government, especially the office of the chief minister. We will take their political affiliation explicitly into account as constitutionally separate positions like the union cabinet, or the governor, or the president may not be effective veto players if all of them belong to the same political party.

9.3.1 Union Government (Cabinet)

When the benefits of invoking President's rule in a state outweigh the political and organizational costs, the incumbent union government is expected to declare it. The immediate benefit is that after imposition of President's rule, fresh elections are announced, which the union government party might win. This is especially true because imposition of President's rule makes it more challenging for the destabilized party to win elections immediately after the imposition. In the 116 cases of President's rule imposition studied, the dismissed chief minister was only able to continue in twenty-four cases after the lifting of it. The party that was dismissed using President's rule was able to form the government again in forty-four instances after the lifting of President's rule.[7] Therefore the big benefit to the union government is to destabilize the political trajectory of a state government party in the short term.

But there is also a longer-term benefit: Destabilizing a political rival and capturing a state government also helps increase political

[7] The Indian National Congress party (INC) survived twenty-nine out of the forty-four instances, lending credence to the Brass (1990) dominant party hypothesis.

power at the union level in parliament, as the upper house (Rajya Sabha) represents states proportional to their size. A majority in the upper house is essential to pass constitutional amendments and electing the president.

The union government has two types of cost to consider. The first is the organizational cost of collective decision-making. Parliament is one of the veto players at the union level, and it is bicameral.[8] Passing the motion requires a simple majority of members present and voting in each house of parliament (Article 100(1)). A minimum quorum of one-tenth of the members of the house (Article 100(3)) is also required.

If a government consists of a single party that has the majority in the Lok Sabha (lower house of parliament) and all its cabinet members are from the same political party, then there are fewer effective veto players. A constitutional amendment in 1985 that created an official whip and prohibited legislators from voting against their party whip, further weakened individual parliamentarians as effective veto players. A union cabinet with a strong mandate within parliament is more likely to impose President's rule in a state. Conversely, a coalition government at the union level has more potential veto players and is less likely to impose President's rule in a state.

9.3.2 State Legislature and Chief Minister

The second veto player to consider is the government at the state level. If the state is governed by a coalition, then some actors within the coalition may benefit from the dismissal of the government, if they believe they have a stronger chance of winning a majority in reelection, increasing the likelihood of invoking President's rule. Not all states were formed at the same time, and not all state political parties have the same experience in winning elections and governing a state. If President's rule is invoked by the union government to

[8] Parliament comprises two houses. The Lower House (Lok Sabha) has up to 552 members. The members of the Lower House are directly elected to the Union Legislature through general elections. The union government is directly formed by achieving a majority in the Lower House by a single party or a coalition of parties. The upper house (Rajya Sabha) has up to 250 members. The members of the Upper House are chosen by an electoral college comprising members of State legislatures.

destabilize political rivals in the state, a more experienced political party will be harder to destabilize. The crucial veto player, however, is the state chief minister. The more experienced a chief minister, the less likely that President's rule will be imposed to destabilize his government.

If the incumbent chief minister dies in office, it increases political uncertainty and possibly political instability. This event may, for example, lead to an increase in the likelihood that the union government invokes President's rule under the guise of wanting to reestablish stability, where it is in fact motivated by simple power considerations. The arguments developed so far can be summarized by the following hypotheses:

Hypothesis 1: *The stronger the majority of state governments in the state legislatures, the lower the likelihood of invoking President's rule.*

Hypothesis 1a: *If the state government is in a coalition within the state legislature, it is associated with a higher likelihood of invoking President's rule.*

Hypothesis 2: *If the party forming the government in a given state is not part of the coalition government at the union level, it is associated with a higher likelihood of invoking President's rule.*

Hypothesis 3: *The more years that a party forming the incumbent government has governed the state in the past, the less likely it is that President's rule is imposed.*

Hypothesis 4: *Political uncertainty at the state level caused by the death of important politicians, specifically the death of a chief minister in a state, increases the likelihood of invoking President's rule.*

9.3.3 The Governor

The procedure to invoke President's rule commences with the advice/securing the consent of the governor. The executive power of the state vests in the governor (Article 154), who acts on the advice of the council of ministers with the chief minister as the head, a group also known as the state cabinet (Article 163). Bills passed by the state legislature must be signed by the governor to become acts, but the governor may also reserve a bill for the president's assent. In India, the president appoints governors (Article 155) who hold office at the pleasure of the president (Article 156). Essentially, the union cabinet is responsible for recommending to the president whom to appoint as state governors, making the governor of the state effectively appointed by the union cabinet.

The governor serves at the president's discretion for five years, but their term may not align with the incumbent union government's term. Consequently, the incumbent union government may be working with governors appointed by previous governments, who may even be political rivals. If the governor is an ally of the party (or parties) governing the union, it is easier to get a recommendation from the governor to invoke the rule.

The governor is responsible for appointing the chief minister of the state (Article 164). The convention is that the leader of the largest parliamentary group is invited by the governor to choose the chief minister, but the governor has the final say, and the decision cannot be challenged in the legislature or courts for review (Art. 164(1)).

Regarding the emergency provision, the governor has enormous power and discretion to decide if there is a constitutional crisis caused by a lack of political majority to form a stable government and to recommend to the union cabinet to bring the state under President's rule. Governors who cooperate with the union government may enjoy political benefits such as reappointment, appointments to the upper house of the parliament, positions in the permanent bureaucracy, or positions of power within the party.[9]

Governors have significant discretionary power, and their actions cannot be questioned in court, regardless of whether the emergency or crisis was caused by riots, natural disasters, or political turmoil.[10] The constitution framers intended the governor to be a neutral representative of the federal government (Chatterjee 1992). However, the union cabinet has often appointed partisan individuals (Government of India 1988; Reddy and Joseph 2004) who use their discretionary

9 Of the approximately 550 governors we have in our dataset from 1951 to 2019, we find that governors who were affiliated with any political party have served ~17 percent more months in power.

10 The Supreme Court in *SR Bommai* held that the governor's report in itself was not justiciable, that is, the court would not go into the question of determining the correctness or adequacy of the material, including the governor's report, which would be submitted for the consideration of the President. Even if part of the material is irrelevant, the court is still constrained from interfering as long as there is some material which is relevant to the issuing of the proclamation.

powers, including the invocation of Article 356, to benefit the union cabinet. If the governor was appointed by the current union government or is of the same party as the union government, then despite the separation in constitutional roles, the governor is a much weaker veto player – if he is one at all.

Hypothesis 5: *If the governor of a state was appointed by the incumbent union government, this increases the likelihood of invoking President's rule, c.p.*

9.3.4 The President

The president of India is the head of state, while the prime minister is the head of government. The executive power of the union, and the supreme command of the defense forces of the union vests with the president (Article 53) who is indirectly elected by the upper house of the parliament for a period of five years (Articles 54 and 55).[11] The presidential term need not be synchronous with the union government term. Therefore, it is possible for the union government to govern with a president who was elected during the term of a previous government, and perhaps by political rivals. If the president is a political ally of the governing party, it is easier to secure the president's consent to invoke the rule, making the president a weaker veto player.

Some consider the office of the president a ceremonial position, since the president acts on the aid and advice of the council of ministers. Therefore, the decisions and actions of the president are essentially the decisions and actions of the union cabinet. This extends to Article 356, which, though known as President's rule, is really rule by the union government. In practice, the power lies with the office of the prime minister. The president does not face any direct costs of imposing President's rule, as the decision cannot be challenged in court. Similarly, there are no direct benefits as the president holds the highest office in the country with little possibility of future rewards. However, if the president is a member of or strongly affiliated with a political party, then his decision may promote the interests of that party. If the president, the union cabinet and the governor all belong to the same

[11] The president can only be removed from office by impeachment under the provision in Article 61.

political party, then despite the separation in constitutional roles, they are no longer effective veto players while invoking President's rule, lowering the cost of securing consensus.

However, there is a second possibility. An important incentive for any political party at the union level to invoke President's rule is to capture the state government, which will improve the representation of that party in the upper house which represents states proportional to the size of the state legislature and has twelve eminent members appointed by the president. Since the president is elected by the upper house, which is the council of state legislature representatives, a union government party with higher representation increases the chances of choosing the president in the next election, which also increases power over the twelve presidential appointments. If the incumbent president is already aligned with the union government, there is less incentive to use President's rule to capture more seats in the upper house.

This gives rise to two opposite hypotheses.

Hypothesis 6: *If the President was elected during the term of the incumbent union government, this increases the likelihood of invoking President's rule, c.p.*

Hypothesis 6a: *If the President was elected during the term of the incumbent union government, this decreases the likelihood of invoking President's rule, c.p.*

9.3.5 The Judiciary

In *SR Bommai*, the Supreme Court of India has addressed three main questions: (1) if proclamations of President's rule could be reviewed by the courts; (2) the scope and limits on the powers of the president under Article 356 to dismiss state assemblies and impose President's rule; and (3) the consequences of declaring such a proclamation invalid after parliamentary approval. The majority in *SR Bommai* overruled the 1977 judgment and decided that proclamations under Article 356 could be reviewed by the courts and invalidated if found to be based on improper, *malafide*, or irrelevant grounds. This made the higher judiciary an important veto player.

When reviewing a proclamation, the court examines the material it is based on and whether it is relevant to the decision. The president's power to issue a proclamation is not absolute and must be based on relevant material, such as a governor's report or other information. The presence and reliance on such material are preconditions for issuing a proclamation under Article 356.

Article 74(2) prevents courts from reviewing the advice given by cabinet ministers, but not the material the advice may be based on. Courts can examine if there was any relevant material for the advice given and if the president could have acted on it. One factor is whether the state government had a chance to prove its strength on the floor of the state legislature before President's rule was imposed. In *SR Bommai*, the majority opinion declared the imposition of President's rule in Karnataka unconstitutional because this condition was not met.

The Court decided that the power to review a proclamation and determine its constitutionality would be meaningless if it couldn't grant relief based on the proclamation being unconstitutional. The political impact of the *SR Bommai* ruling is significant: If the proclamation is declared unconstitutional, the court can reinstate the dissolved government even if parliament had approved the proclamation.

Though the language of Article 356 has not changed, *SR Bommai* introduced an additional check on the imposition of President's rule by allowing such decisions to be reviewed by the Court. This decision made it more difficult for the union government to secure consensus for invoking President's rule. Since *SR Bommai*, the judiciary has been an important and strong institutional veto player with the ability to review the invocation of President's rule and reverse it in case it has been invoked on insufficient grounds. This leads to our intuitively obvious hypothesis 7.

Hypothesis 7: *The likelihood of invoking Article 356 has decreased after the Bommai judgment in 1994, c.p.*

9.3.6 Nonpolitical Reasons for Imposing President's Rule

Two types of event, which are not directly related to the strength of the mandate of the union and state governments, may cause the invocation of President's rule. First, events like natural disasters that are not political and are unrelated to the strength of the government in the legislature may lead to President's rule. In this chapter, we treat natural disasters as exogenous events. Second, there is political turmoil, communal riots, and so forth, which we assume to be at least partially endogenous to the policies of state government. Declaring President's rule after an endogenous event is likely to arouse more opposition or backlash from the public than invoking it after an exogenous event and therefore to be politically costlier. If this assumption is correct, then exogenous events might even constitute welcome pretexts to invoke President's rule.

Hypothesis 8: *If the underlying cause of the emergency is a natural disaster, then there is a higher likelihood of invoking President's rule, c.p.*

Hypothesis 9: *If the underlying cause of the emergency is communal riots, then there is a higher likelihood of invoking President's rule, c.p.*

9.4 Data and Empirical Approach

In the previous section, we detailed the various veto players and the incentives of various government actors to impose/block President's rule and the corresponding nine direct implications, which are testable. Since our goal is to understand the relevance of each of the different actors on the likelihood of imposing President's rule, we construct a monthly panel dataset of forty current and former Indian states between April 1952 and October 2019. This fine-grained monthly panel is constructed such that it includes each of the 116 instances of President's rule in each state in every month and year since the founding of the Indian republic. Since the imposition of President's rule can be contemporaneous with other events and variables, we also gather data for them.

9.4.1 Data

We consider and include three broad categories or factors explicitly in the dataset: (1) information on state-level legislative and executive positions; (2) information on union legislative and executive positions; and (3) information on events that may have led to an emergency or the breakdown of constitutional machinery, like riots and natural disasters.[12] This data was compiled using official government sources, accredited news and other information sources. A detailed list of sources on each of the variables is available in Appendix Table A9.1.

Our main outcome variable is binary and indicates whether President's rule was imposed on the particular state in a given month-year. A dataset of all President's rule impositions between 1950 and 2016 was compiled by Shrinivasan (2016), which was an extension of a pre-existing dataset compiled by Sadanandan (2012). Both these studies rely on Lok Sabha records and newspaper reports for recording events. We have extended the dataset until October 2019 relying on newspaper reports as well.

Regarding explanatory variables, we first include the composition of both the state as well as the union legislature. We record the strength of the state government in terms of the percentage of seats held in the legislature by the party (or coalition of parties) in power during the time of a state election via the Election Commission's Statistical Reports (1952–2019) of the general election to the relevant state legislative assembly. We rely on news reports to check for changes in government strength as well as changes in the composition of coalitions until the next election cycle in the state. We collect the same information for the union parliament, which is our second variable of interest, for which we use the Election Commission's Statistical Reports of the general election to the Lok Sabha. For the union level, we also code the composition of the Rajya Sabha (upper house) using information from the Rajya Sabha website.

Data on governors' tenure, including their previous experience as governors of other states is recorded using government (especially Raj Bhawan/governors' offices) websites. We used news reports as well as biographies of the governors to check if they had had any current or previous political affiliations with the parties or the government at the union or the state level. We also record if the governor had any political affiliation and if the governor is politically aligned with the union government. These factors allow us to assess hypotheses 1–6.

[12] In a longer companion paper, written jointly with Abishek Choutagunta and Shruti Rajagopalan, we also include spatial and economic controls. The paper provides a full econometric treatment of the questions dealt with in this chapter.

Regarding violent disturbances within a state leading to an emergency, we first consider communal riots. The data on the riots that occurred between 1952 and 1995 relies on the Varshney-Wilkinson (2006) dataset. This dataset was later extended by Iyer and Shrivatsava (2018) until 2006, and we extended it until October 2019 by using the newspaper archives of the New Delhi edition of the *Times of India*. For political turmoil, we code whether a chief minister dies in office, which we think of as approximately exogenous. Data on such deaths was also collected using newspaper reports of the New Delhi edition of the *Times of India* newspaper.

For purely exogenous emergencies like natural disasters, we use EM-DAT again, an international disaster database which contains event-based disaster damage records for events occurring since 1900 (Guha-Sapir et al. 2020). Within EM-DAT, we only consider naturally occurring extreme events happening in our study's time period within India since the database's technological disasters records might be subject to reporting bias. Extreme events include storms, floods, earthquakes, droughts, landslides, extreme temperature events, epidemics, wildfires, rockfalls, avalanches, and insect infestations. Events are aggregated across states and months. The variables of interest are the occurrence, number of occurrences, and the number of deaths due to these events. We do not consider the total number of people affected and total damage since they contain many missing values for the India sample. The additional data on riots and natural disasters allow us to assess the degree of evidence there is for hypotheses 8 and 9.

Finally, we code the periods before and after the *SR Bommai* case by constructing a categorical variable that captures the period from the beginning of the sample until March 1989 (i.e. before *Bommai)*, the period in which the case was being handled by the Supreme Court (between April 1989 and March 1994), and the post-*Bommai* period starting in April 1994.

The entire dataset includes forty (current and former) state governments observed for 811 consecutive months. Table 9.1 presents summary statistics for our variables. Thus, a fully balanced panel would theoretically contain 32,440 variables. However, since we do not code any political variables for a state if it has merged with another state, or any state government variables if the state is under President's rule, the dataset includes just under 17,000 observations

Table 9.1 *Descriptive statistics*

Variable name	Mean	Minimum	Maximum	Variable type	Observations
State ruling government seat share	57.67	0	100	percentage	18,029
State ruling coalition	0.375	0	1	binary	18,029
Previous state governments of party	2.484	0	10	count	18,056
Union ruling government seat share	54.09	8.471	78.60	percentage	30,010
Union ruling coalition	0.508	0	1	binary	30,010
Previous union governments of party	3.429	0	9	count	30,010
State-union ruling coalition	0.378	0	1	binary	18,056
Governor's previous political affiliation	0.547	0	1	binary	18,657
Governor appointed by center	0.787	0	1	binary	18,663
President appointed by center	0.755	0	1	binary	30,010
Disaster	0.0668	0	1	binary	19,090
Riot	0.0841	0	1	binary	19,090
State chief minister dead and replaced	0.0009	0	1	binary	17,023
President's rule	0.0541	0	1	binary	19,090

for state government variables, and approximately 30,000 observations for central government variables. It is therefore primarily the absence of state government observations that limits the size of the data in the following.

Through the rest of the chapter, we are going to exploit these data in a purely descriptive way. We do so in a series of figures where we explore the likelihood of observing the invocation of President's rule in different circumstances. In all cases, we focus on the invocation of President's rule, not how long it lasts or whether it is prolonged or not.

9.4.2 *The Use of President's Rule*

While the data include a total of 116 instances since 1951 (and four before then) in which President's rule was invoked, covering a total of 1,032 months, some Indian states have been substantially more subject to its use than others. We illustrate this structure of our data in Figure 9.2 where we list all states alphabetically with the number of times that the state has been subject to President's rule. The frequency runs from a single instance in Delhi to nine instances in Uttar Pradesh and Bihar.[13] As such, the typical Indian state has experienced being subject to President's rule three or four times since independence.

However, the application of article 356 has not been stable over time. As we show in Figure 9.3, the union government in particular used President's rule frequently from the mid-1960s after the death of India's first prime minister, Jawaharlal Nehru. The use of President's rule topped in 1977 in which it was invoked against twelve states. This coincided with the election of the first prime minister who was not from the Indian National Congress – Morarji Dessai from the Janata Party. Conversely, after the conclusion of *SR Bommai*, President's rule has been used relatively sparsely with several years without a single instance. Overall, these patterns are suggestive but not evidence of what drives the use of Article 356 of the Indian constitution.

[13] The other states that have only experienced a single instance of President's rule are Travancore–Cochin and Patiala and East Punjab States Union (PEPSU) that were disbanded in 1956, and Arunachal Pradesh and Mizoram, both of which only became states in 1987 after fifteen years as union territories.

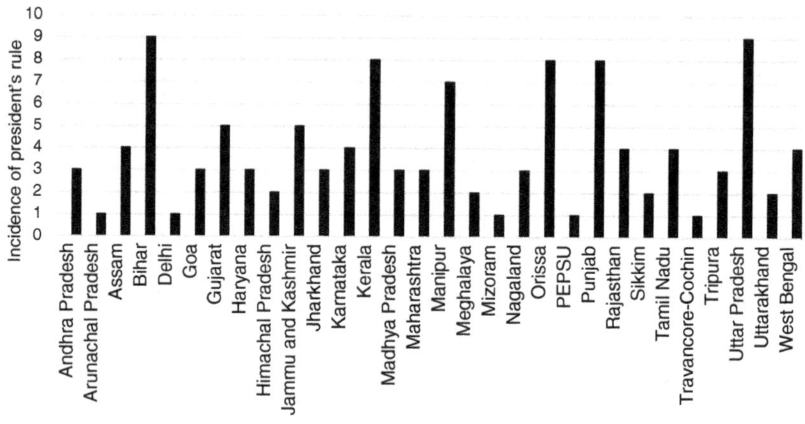

Figure 9.2 State-wise incidence of President's rule (1951–2019)

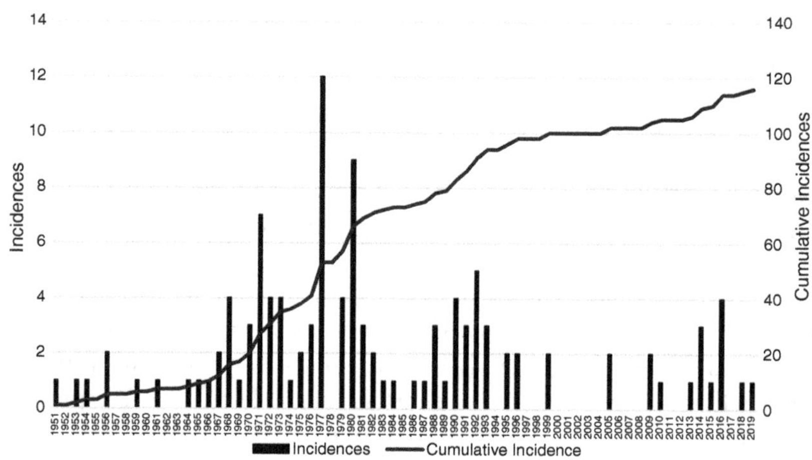

Figure 9.3 Incidences of President's rule by year (1951–2019)

9.5 Patterns around Invocations of the President's Rule

We start by exploring if the party or parties forming the state government are important predictors of invoking President's rule. Hypothesis 1, which states that there will be more invocations of President's rule against coalition governments, finds some support. As Figure 9.4 illustrates, when coalition governments are in power, we observe an 84 percent higher probability of President's rule. Conversely, we see a

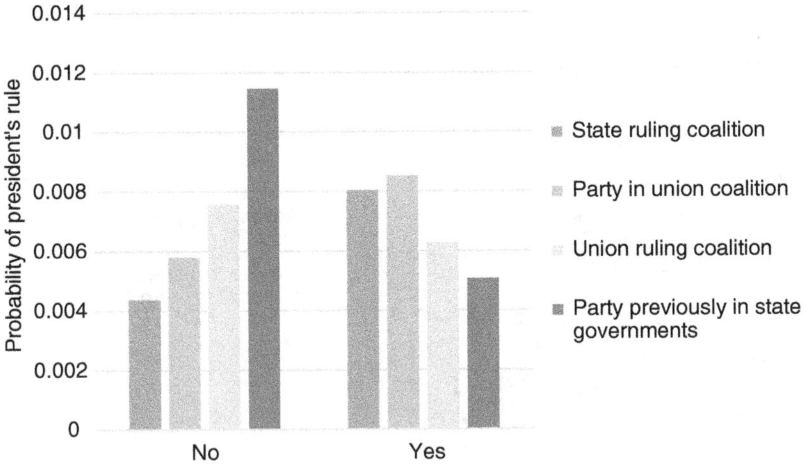

Figure 9.4 State party influence

47 percent higher probability (0.58 versus 0.85 percent) of President's rule being invoked when a party in the state government also forms part of the union coalition, which is contrary to hypothesis 2. We also find no significant evidence that coalition governments at the union level are less likely to invoke President's rule, as the difference between the probabilities with and without is only 21 percent (0.63 versus 0.76 percent). Third, we find evidence in favor of hypothesis 3, as the risk of invoking President's rule more than doubles if the party governing the state has never before governed that particular state (1.11 versus 0.51 percent). The risk is again halved if the party has been in government more than four times. As such, the Indian data suggest that President's rule is primarily invoked against less experienced and established parties, and only rarely against parties with considerable experience in government.

Three of our four hypotheses about the party in power at the state level therefore fit the data, although the differences we observe are relatively moderate. We also find suggestive evidence of three other hypotheses, as we illustrate in Figure 9.5. First, we observe a 43 percent higher probability of President's rule if the governor of a state was not appointed by a party in government at the union level (hypothesis 5). Second, as the figure shows, this is also the case for our test of the competing hypotheses 6 and 6a – are presidents

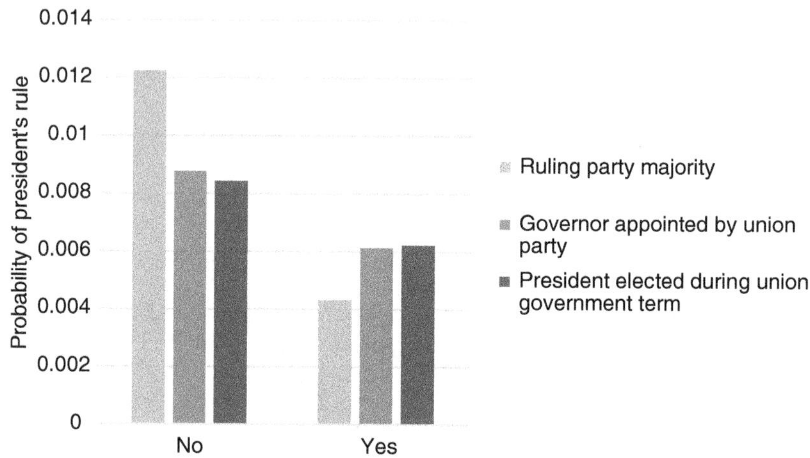

Figure 9.5 Further influences

elected during the term of the incumbent union government more or less likely to invoke President's rule. We find that they are 36 percent more likely if they were not elected during the term of the incumbent (0.84 versus 0.62 percent). Third, the most important predictor of all political factors turns out to be the seat share of the incumbent state government: The likelihood of invoking President's rule is approximately three times higher if the state government does not have a majority as when it does.

However, the data make it evident that these differences are dwarfed by a particular political event: the case in which an incumbent chief minister dies in office (hypothesis 4). While we must emphasize that there have only been seventeen cases since 1948 in which this has happened, the death of a chief minister is associated with a nineteen-fold increase in the likelihood of invoking President's rule! In other words, the factors most clearly associated with the likelihood that President's rule is invoked against a state government are all political in nature, and thus not associated with what was originally considered the events that would justify using Article 356 of the Indian constitution: riots and natural disasters.

As we show in Figure 9.6, neither disasters nor riots are associated with the probability that the union government invokes President's rule. We here illustrate the probability of observing President's rule

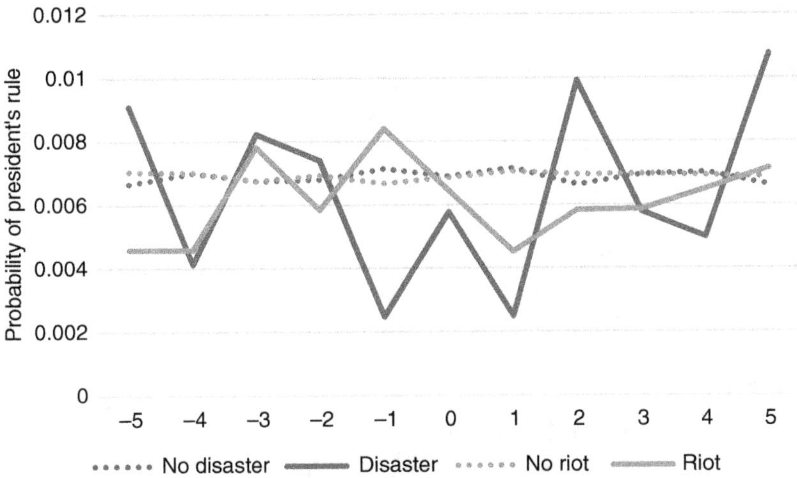

Figure 9.6 Disasters and riots around the President's rule

before and after riots (the blue lines) and natural disasters (the red lines). The logic of the figure is that if riots or natural disasters cause the union government to invoke President's rule in a state – as intended by the constitution – we would likely observe a higher likelihood of President's rule in the months *after* a riot or disaster starts (time 0–5 in the figure) than in the months *prior* to the event (time –5 to –1). However, what we observe is absolutely no difference between the likelihood of President's rule before or after an event, compared to periods without either natural disasters or riots (the dotted lines). In essence, the pattern that ought to exist in the data if Article 356 was used as intended is in no way there.

Finally, we test hypothesis 7 – that the likelihood of invoking Article 356 has decreased after the Supreme Court's *SR Bommai* judgment in 1994 – in Figure 9.7. The clear judgment curtailed the formal de jure options for the union government to invoke President's rule, which we find had substantial consequences. Prior to the *SR Bommai* case, an Indian state had an unconditional 0.96 percent probability of having invoked President's rule against it. This increased slightly to 1.21 percent during the case, although we must emphasize that in the months that the Supreme Court considered it, only four cases occurred. However, after *SR Bommai* was concluded, the probability of invoking President's rule

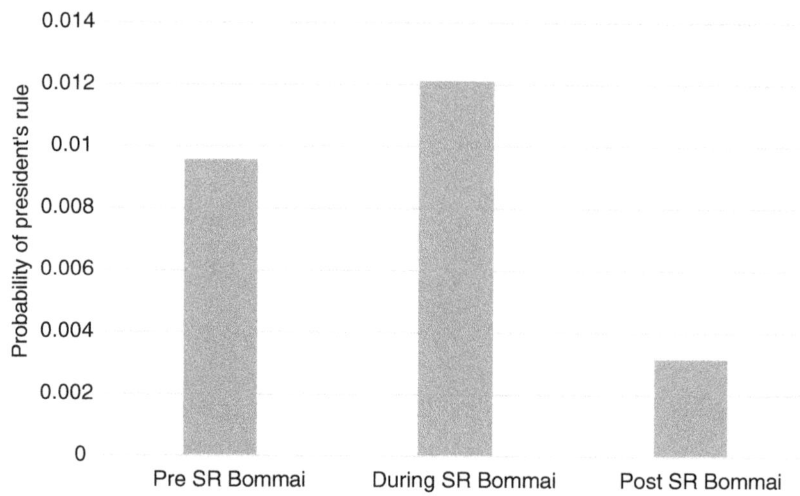

Figure 9.7 President's rule before, during, and after *SR Bommai*

and using Article 356 has dropped to 0.32 percent. In other words, the likelihood that the union government uses this particular constitutional option has decreased to a third of what it was prior to 1994. As we discuss in the rest of the chapter, we take this as quite clear evidence that the Supreme Court effectively curtailed the use of President's rule.

9.6 Discussion

India's constitution is highly centripetal in its design with respect to both the union–state government relationship (Choutagunta et al. 2021) as well as the union–state–local government relationship (Rajagopalan 2016), and in its centralized judiciary. Article 356 – known as President's rule – is, in particular, one of the most misused provisions because of India's poorly designed federal structure. One implication of these results is that the centripetal design of the Indian republic more generally, and specifically Articles 356 and 357, weaken the checks required to maintain a balance between the union and state levels. Because constitutional checks and balances between the union and state governments are weak, there is greater reliance on political relationships to maintain this balance. We find evidence that this theoretical association plays out in Indian politics.

Specifically, we find that the larger the majority of the state government in the state legislature, captured by the higher percentage of seats for a state ruling party, and the more experience it has had forming past governments in the state, the lower is the likelihood of being dismissed through President's rule. We find evidence that it is more likely that the union government invokes President's rule against a coalition state government. And the importance and strength of the chief minister is an important factor, as the death of a chief minister creating political instability is used as a reason to invoke President's rule.

The frequent use of President's rule and its decline since the 1990s has been conflated with the decline of the Indian National Congress Party (Brass 1990; Jain 1994), the rise of coalition politics (Singh 2001), and the increase of regional parties (Sadanandan 2012). We find no evidence supporting Brass (1990) and Jain (1994), on the decline of the dominance of the Indian National Congress. Our results suggest that President's rule is not about any single party at the union level, but the relative strength and weakness of the parties forming state governments. We also find no conclusive evidence for Singh's argument that the coalition governments at the union level are the reason for less frequent use of President's rule. For Sadanandan's argument, on the emergence of strong regional parties reducing the likelihood of President's rule, we find partial support. This is because the seat share of the party ruling the state government is the main factor, irrespective of a regional or national party. We find very strong support confirming Tsebelis' insight, that in parliamentary democracies, it is the strength of political actors that provides the main veto or check. In the case of President's rule, the core issue is that the relative strengths of parties at the different levels of government are required to compensate for India's weak and centripetal federal structure, and in the absence of institutional checks, the politics provides the checks and balances.

While this chapter is focused on the Indian case, it is necessary to explore the degree to which the conclusions here generalize to other societies. India has in recent years grown to become the most populous country in the world and would on that basis alone deserve to be studied in a little more detail. But it turns out that other federations that used to be British colonies have fairly similar provisions.

In our case study on India, we pointed out that the origin of President's rule can be traced back to the Government of India Act of 1935. Upon independence, the former British colony split into two countries, namely India and Pakistan, which is also organized as a federation. It does, therefore, not come as a surprise that Pakistan has provisions very similar to those of India. In fact, Article 234 of the Pakistani constitution is almost identical in wording to the corresponding provision in the Indian constitution. And it is not only the wording that is almost identical but also the misuse of these provisions by the central government of these two countries. Comparing the emergency provisions of India and Pakistan, Sharma (2017, 82) emphasizes the commonalities in their use, writing that they "have been invariably used in Pakistan (as well as in India) as a weapon against the provinces, particularly those governed by parties opposed to the federal government." He adds that the 8th amendment to the 1972 constitution of Pakistan (passed in 1985) gave the president the power to dissolve both the provincial assemblies as well as the federal one and governments on his own initiative. Sharma (ibid., 81) points out that the Article has a varied history. The 13th amendment passed in 1997 did away with its most damaging features that were brought back under the 17th amendment in 2003, only to be cut back again by the 18th amendment which was passed in 2010. The constitutional strength of Pakistan's Article 234 has therefore waned and waxed with the country's democracy.

What is today Malaysia used to be another British colony in Asia, which is also organized as a federation. Its constitutional history has likewise been heavily influenced by the British. Before gaining independence, a constitutional commission was appointed that had the task to make recommendations regarding the constitution's content of the independent state to be. The commission was chaired by Lord Reid and it is usually referred to as the Reid Commission. Regarding emergencies, the Commission recommended that "… the Federal Government should then have power to give directions to any state Government or state officer or authority" (cited in Tan 2010, 159). When the Federation of Malaya became independent in 1957, all the recommendations of the Reid Commission were enacted. Article 150(4) reads: "While a Proclamation of Emergency is in force the executive authority of the Federation shall, notwithstanding anything in this constitution, extent to any matter within the legislative authority of a state and to the giving of directions to the Government of a State or to any officer or authority thereof." This provision has been used to oust the State Chief Minister of Sarawak in 1966 and to prevent the ousting of a state chief minister who had lost a confidence vote in the Legislative Assembly of Kelantan in 1977. Lee (2010, 395) comments on these uses of the emergency provisions: "In both instances, there were serious doubts whether in fact there was a real emergency or an emergency of convenience."

Nigeria is yet another former British colony now organized as a federation. Art. 305 of its 1999 constitution deals with emergencies. Reading Section 4 of that article, one gets the impression that the governor of the state has agenda-setting powers with regard to an SOE as it is he who may request the president to issue such a proclamation. But Section 5 of the same article reads that no proclamation of an SOE shall be issued without the request of the relevant governor "unless the Governor of the States fails within a reasonable time to make a request…" So at the end of the day, it seems to be another top-down organization of emergency powers. Indeed, President Obasanjo relied on this article to declare an emergency in 2004 in Plateau State, in which he suspended the elected Governor Joshua Dariye and the State House of Assembly in the process. In 2006, Obasanjo repeated the exercise in Ekiti State where he removed a sitting governor and his Deputy and replaced them with a retired Army General, Tunji Olurin, for a period of six months (Igwenyi et al. 2019).

What seems noteworthy in this brief overview of how emergencies are organized in former British colonies is that, generally, common law countries do not regulate emergencies on the constitutional level. This is, for example, still true for Canada or Australia. But before granting the former colonies independence, British governments seem to have been extremely concerned with the unity of their newly created federations. The question remains if this is a common feature across federal states.

Germany would appear to be a good example, as the country has a very long history as a federation. Between the tenth century and 1806, it was known as the Holy Roman Empire (of the German Nation) and consisted of dozens of mini-states that often quarreled with each other. To ensure that the decisions of the *Reichstag* or the verdicts of the highest court in the Empire (the *Reichskammergericht*) were implemented in all states, a so-called "Imperial Executive Order" was passed in 1555, which also included military means that could be used against noncomplying member states. During the Weimar Republic, the executive order was used a number of times: In 1923, it was used to dispose the governments of Saxony and Thuringia that consisted of coalitions between social democrats and communists. In 1932, the government of Prussia, led by social democrats, was disposed in the so-called *Preußenschlag*. An equivalent tool can be found in Germany's current constitution, namely the *Bundeszwang*, which has been translated as the "exercise of federal authority over the Länder." According to this, the federal government has the power to enforce its own legislation in a state if that state does not comply with its duties vis-à-vis the federation. In Germany, this article has, however, never been used.

It is well-known that major parts of the Spanish constitution were inspired by Germany's. The analogous provision in the Spanish constitution was applied in October 2017, when the Spanish government dissolved the government of Catalonia.

Other federations know similar instruments: Brazil's constitution, for example, contains a "federal intervention." In its Article 34, the Brazilian constitution stipulates that the union shall not interfere with the states except in a list of enumerated circumstances. Among the list are those that are conventionally mentioned as preconditions for declaring an SOE such as to repel a foreign invasion or put an end to a serious threat to public order. Yet this instrument has been used very rarely. In 2018, Rio was under military intervention because gang wars between groups in different favelas over drugs had gotten violent (http://opiniojuris.org/2018/10/22/the-military-intervention-in-rio-de-janeiro-and-human-rights/) and in January 2023, when newly (re-)elected president Lula da Silva decreed it after attacks on government buildings by supporters of former president Bolsonaro (www.loc.gov/item/global-legal-monitor/2023-01-12/brazil-president-decrees-federal-intervention-in-federal-district-after-attacks-on-government-institutions-and-buildings/?loclr=ealln).

However, the existence of constitutional provisions resembling India's Article 356 is not a universal feature of federal systems. Argentina, which has been constitutionally characterized as a federation since 1853, does not have similar provisions. The US constitution also does not give the president or Congress similar powers, and the semi-federal nation of Belgium has never even had constitutionalized emergency provisions. Yet where they exist, they are likely to create similar problems as in India.

9.7 Conclusions and Outlook

In this chapter, we have focused on a problem regarding the design of emergency constitutions that is particularly prevalent among federations, namely how to organize the relationship between the federal level and the levels of the state. In principle, all the questions regarding the design of emergency constitutions discussed in Chapter 2 need to be answered. Among them are: Who has the power to declare an SOE? Who has the power to declare the end of an emergency? Who has the power to monitor the legality of the means used during an SOE? Who exercises emergency powers? And what (additional) competences does an SOE confer to the emergency government?

In addition to the events that can lead to the declaration of an SOE discussed in previous chapters – natural disasters and man-made turmoil – we broadened our scope and took the possibility into consideration that state actors – in this chapter, state governments – may not comply with their constitutional obligations, which could endanger the survival of the constitutional order and could, therefore, be an additional reason to declare an SOE.

In this chapter, we studied the emergency provisions of the Indian constitution in considerable detail. We saw that the top-down structure of the Indian constitution initially led to the frequent misuse of President's rule there, which was only curbed by a supreme court decision in 1994 and changes in the political landscape of the country. It seems, however, that over time, the possibilities of the most egregious misuses have been effectively curtailed either by way of constitutional amendment (as in Pakistan) or by decisions of the Supreme Court (as in India). In other federations, the possibility to force single states to comply with their federal obligations has been used far less frequently than in India. We treated the cases of Germany, Spain, and Brazil as pertinent counter-examples to India.

This chapter takes a positive approach, that is, we are interested in describing and explaining the use of particular constitutional provisions by utility-maximizing politicians. The primary focus is not on giving advice as to how the current constitutional design could be improved upon, although that does not imply that we cannot flag the importance of properly dealing with these issues. The issue at stake here is, for example, highly relevant for the European Union. A number of papers have pointed out that endowing member states of a federation with the right to exit would increase their bargaining position and would, therefore, be one possible means of curbing the power of the center (see, e.g. Buchanan 1992, Chen and Ordeshook 1994, de Figueiredo and Weingast 2005). Yet we are not aware of a discussion regarding the exact opposite, namely the possibility of forcing a particular state to secede from a federation in case it has repeatedly acted against its obligations as a member of the federation.

Appendix

Table A9.1 *Data sources for Chapter 9*

Variable name	Sources
State ruling government seat share	Election Commission Statistical Reports (1951–2019)
State ruling coalition	News Reports (ProQuest Times of India Archives, Factiva)
Previous state governments of party	Election Commission Statistical Reports (1951–2019) and News Reports
Union ruling government seat share	Election Commission Statistical Reports (1951–2019)
Union ruling coalition	News Reports (ProQuest Times of India Archives, Factiva)
Previous union governments of party	Election Commission Statistical Reports (1951–2019) and News Reports
State-union ruling coalition	Election Commission Statistical Reports (1951–2019) and News Reports
Governor's previous political affiliation	Governor Biographies from Raj Bhawan Websites/News Reports
Governor appointed by center	Governor Biographies from Raj Bhawan Websites
President appointed by center	Election Commission of India, Press Information Bureau
Disaster	EM-DAT
Riot	Database Compiled Iyer and Shrivatsava (2018), Factiva
State chief minister dead and replaced	ProQuest Times of India Archives, Factiva
President's rule	Database Compilation by Rukmini Shrinivasan, Factiva

10 Constitutionalized Media Freedom during Emergencies

Is It Only Window Dressing?

10.1 Introduction

Ever since the time of Edward Burke, the press has been hailed as the "fourth estate," emphasizing its important role both as a government watchdog and a forum wherein possible policy changes can be discussed and advocated. The press can fulfill those important functions only if it enjoys considerable freedom. The responsibilities of the press, and the freedom to fulfill them, are important especially in situations in which the government, other politicians, the civil service or influential special interests have incentives to pursue policies that are not endorsed by the public at large. As is the case for other elements of well-functioning modern institutions, most modern constitutions are intended to do exactly that: protect the press and other media from political control.

Terrorism and terrorist threats have become a salient topic in most Western countries at least since al Qaeda's attacks on New York City and Washington, D.C. in September 2001. Soon afterwards, many politicians and political parties argued that existing legislation failed to provide protection against terrorism; in some countries, governments have introduced wide-ranging anti-terror legislation, which can include the possibility of curtailing media freedom (Dragu 2011). The stated reason typically is that restrictions on the press reduce the likelihood of future terrorist events and increase the chances of apprehending the perpetrators. Since terrorists aim at intimidating audiences beyond that of the immediate victims (Enders and Sandler 2012), media publicity for such events could further the terrorists' cause. This observation is also used as a justification for curbing media freedom, although terrorist incidents may also serve as pretexts justifying restricting the media. Media freedom may be violated for reasons completely unrelated to terrorism or any other tangible threats.

Examples in which terrorist threats serve as justifications for limiting media freedom abound: Singapore, for example, passed a "Public Order and Safety (Special Powers) Act 2018" that allows the ministry of home affairs to ban media coverage of terrorist attacks entirely. Given that the identification of "terrorism" is not always crystal-clear *ex ante*, that law is likely to reduce media freedom in quite a general way. Singapore, on most indicators, already ranks in the bottom quintile of media freedom globally. But such legislation is not confined to countries without traditions of media freedom. The United Kingdom, for example, passed its "counter-terrorism and border security bill" into law on February 12, 2019. The bill was criticized for having extremely worrying implications not only for media freedom, but also for the protection of journalistic news sources (*The Guardian* Oct 25, 2018). After a failed coup in 2016, Turkey closed many news outlets and jailed more than 300 journalists on charges of having aided a terrorist organization.[1]

In those and a number of other cases, legislative action was often justified by referring to a perceived "public demand" for harsher punishments in order to combat terrorism, and a growing acceptance of the need to change the political balance between security and liberty, to the latter's detriment (Dragu 2011). However, the demand for additional legislation may also originate with special interests within the state apparatus, such as the police and intelligence services, or simply result from politicians' own reelection motives if voters reward politicians who appear to be "tough" on terrorism. In general, media freedom is a double-edged sword for governments: On the one hand, it can help alleviate agency slack at lower-level administrative units whose inefficiencies are reported by the press (Egorov et al. 2009). In that sense, media freedom ameliorates principal-agent problems within governments by reducing informational asymmetries. On the other hand, in emotionally charged situations, such as terrorist incidents, the media might criticize governments for not having taken appropriate preventive actions.[2] It has been shown that reelection prospects of governments

[1] As described in more detail in Chapter 7.

[2] Sunstein and Zeckhauser (2011) show that emotionally charged events lead people to be fearful and to neglect adequately taking into account the probability of such events occurring. The likely consequence, namely so-called action bias, would be especially likely if the relevant actors (in our case, the government) expect to be able to claim credit for responding to the threat.

dramatically fall even after a single terrorist incident (Gassebner et al. 2008). To support their reelection efforts, governments can therefore have incentives to curb media freedom after a terrorist attack. Doing so not only curtails civil liberties, but can also have adverse effects on governmental accountability, including corruption and regulatory overreach (Brunetti and Weder 2003; Besley and Prat 2006).

Constitutional constraints are, among other things, designed to protect the governed citizenry against exactly such political actions; changes to statutory law as in Singapore and the United Kingdom must be consistent with the constraints on policymaking defined by the constitution (Buchanan and Tullock 1962). Later scholars have considered the trade-offs between governmental reactions to terrorism and constitutional safeguards for individual freedom (Bernholz 2006). In this chapter, we ask whether constitutional provisions actually protect media freedom in the aftermath of terrorist attacks. Given that civil liberties and media freedom, in particular, might be abridged following terrorist attacks, we ask whether constitutional provisions that are supposed to protect the media are successful in mitigating such restrictions.

Employing a panel dataset of up to eighty-three countries observed between 1993 and 2013, we find a number of unexpected results. First, simple bivariate correlations between levels of realized media freedom and different levels of formal constitutional guarantees of it show that countries *not* explicitly protecting press freedom at all fare best, whereas countries with elaborate formal protections fare worst. Multivariate analysis in which terrorist events are taken into account confirms the informal evidence from simply eyeballing the raw data. When explicitly recognizing the possibility that media freedom might be protected against governmental encroachment by: (1) an independent judiciary (formalized by its constitutional protections); or (2) specific provisions recognizing that states of emergency can be declared (also formalized in the constitution), we find that neither provision mitigates reductions in de facto media freedom following terrorist activities, while their combination may even make encroachments on media freedom more likely.

The rest of the chapter is structured as follows. Section 10.2 briefly summarizes the main insights regarding both the effects of media freedom as well as its determinants. In Section 10.3, we develop a number of hypotheses explaining why media freedom could be curtailed in the wake of a terrorist attack and what provisions might help to counteract that possibility. Section 10.4 describes typical constitutional provisions for protecting media freedom as well as special provisions that enable governments to curtail it in a state of emergency (SOE). That section also presents our measures of both de jure and de facto media freedom. In Section 10.5, we present additional data and our estimation approach. The results are discussed in Section 10.6. Section 10.7 concludes.

10.2 Media Freedom: A Brief Survey

Economic research on both the determinants and the effects of media freedom began relatively late. Regarding its effects, Sen's (1984) contribution was an early study. He observed that, at the time, India had never experienced a famine – and believed that the free Indian press served as a watchdog over the Indian government, incentivizing it to act swiftly to prevent people from starving. Following up on Sen's lead, Besley and Burgess (2001) looked into the actions taken by Indian state governments following food shortages, finding governmental responsiveness to be positively correlated with newspaper circulation. By now, a consensus exists that a free press makes governments more accountable and less prone to corruption (see, e.g. Brunetti and Weder 2003; Chowdhury 2004).

More recent research has studied the relevance of more detailed media characteristics, such as public versus private ownership (Djankov et al. 2003), the effects of media capture by government (Besley and Prat 2006), and the effects of the competitiveness of media markets (Gehlbach and Sonin 2014). Some interest in the determinants of media freedom is evident, with Stier (2015) observing that – quite generally – democracies enjoy more media freedom than autocracies. Within autocracies, he finds that elected autocrats, monarchies, and military regimes have the freest media, whereas communist ideocracies have the least free media. VonDoepp and Young (2012) find that media harassment intensifies when governments confront more uncertainty, such as facing major protests, coups, and conflict onsets, while Bjørnskov et al. (2022) find that only successful coups against democracies result in less media freedom.

Kellam and Stein (2016) are concerned with the reasons for curbing media freedom in presidential democracies. They propose to distinguish between explanations traceable to differences in ideological preferences on the one hand, and different institutional provisions on the other. According to them, left-leaning presidents who act in the context of a conservative media are more likely to curb media freedom than are conservative presidents. Regarding institutional constraints, a decline in media freedom is more likely if the president has stronger executive powers. It is less likely if the constraints on the executive are stronger, and where the judiciary enjoys more independence. Although most of the hypotheses are supported by empirical results, the literature nevertheless is fairly recent and often interested in specific aspects of media freedom, such as the consequences for it of the form of government or media freedom's determinants in specific regions only.

Finally, fascinating evidence has been reported on how important the media are considered to be by the government versus legislators and judges. Peru offers a unique opportunity for answering that question by relying on a specific case, namely Vladimiro Montesinos Torres, the security adviser to former Peruvian president Alberto Fujimori, who documented Fujimori's handing out of bribes in considerable detail. According to McMillan and Zoido (2004), the legislator paid the largest bribe received USD 20,000, the representative of the judiciary (actually not a judge, but the general manager of the judicial power) received USD 55,000, and José Francisco Crousillat of America Television (Channel 4) signed a contract entitling him to USD 9,000,000 (payable in six tranches of USD 1,500,000). If those numbers are interpreted as giving some indication of the perceived relevance of the media vis-à-vis legislators and judges, then favorable reporting is obviously valued highly.

Regarding possible interactions between terrorists, the media, and government, relying on game theory would appear straightforward (Sandler 2014 summarizes the most relevant contributions). Yet the few available studies have focused on the interactions between terrorists and the media, not explicitly including government as a relevant third actor. Rohner and Frey (2007), for instance, work with the reaction functions of both terrorists and the media and find two stable equilibria (a "no attack" equilibrium, consisting of no attacks/no reporting, and an "attack equilibrium" with a maximum number of attacks and maximum news coverage). Rohner and Frey also find an unstable equilibrium (with some attacks and some news coverage). From the point of view of both terrorists and the media, the "attack equilibrium" is preferred to the "no attack" one, an ordering not shared by the public. Based on their model, Rohner and Frey deduce a number of policy proposals that are intended to lessen sensationalist media reporting. Yet for our purposes, government and its incentives would need to be taken explicitly into account, which is not the case in their model.

In a paper inquiring into the effects of media attention on terrorism, Jetter (2017) finds that additional reporting in the *New York Times* encourages more terrorist attacks in the country where the original acts were committed. Digging deeper into the possible relationship between news coverage of terrorist acts and the number of cross-border terrorist events, Asal and Hoffman (2016) propose to separate media freedom from press attention. One group of scholars interested in explaining the determinants of transnational terrorism argues that, given that terrorists aim to generate fear and anxiety in audiences beyond the targeted venue, an absence of domestic media freedom could lead to target substitution, inducing the terrorists to commit violent acts elsewhere. Asal and Hoffman challenge that view, finding that more attention to terrorism in the international press reduces the likelihood of cross-border terrorist attacks. One way of reducing cross-border terrorism therefore could be to encourage the international news media to extend their reporting on countries that have received little attention thus far.

In sum, solid evidence shows that a free media can have important effects on terrorist activities. Furthermore, some evidence shows that favorable reporting in the media is valued highly by governments and that the media is freer in democracies, whereas political uncertainty and general threats to the incumbent government undermine that freedom. Finally, the relationship between the media and terrorists is somewhat symbiotic. In this chapter, we explore a question hardly dealt with to date, namely whether the provisions contained in a country's emergency constitution have an influence on the change in media freedom experienced in the wake of terrorist events.

10.3 Terrorism and Media Freedom: Some Hypotheses

Constitutional provisions constitute the most basic layer of formal law and as such are highly salient. Nonetheless, many instances can be found in which governments are tempted not to comply with law regardless of whether it is statutory or constitutional.[3] Since we assume noncompliance with constitutional constraints to be more visible, we also expect it to be more costly and hence less likely to occur than noncompliance with statutory law. Applied to the question at hand – given that constitutional constraints actually are complied with and function as intended – we expect realized levels of media freedom to be higher and more stable if guaranteed by the constitution.

In the event a terrorist attack takes place, the government might have numerous reasons to curb media freedom. The most benevolent reason would be the belief that extensive reporting of a terrorist incident would make it more difficult for police to arrest the perpetrators, or possibly even incentivize terrorists to carry out additional attacks.[4] Moreover, extensive reporting on the atrocities committed by terrorists could create a "climate of fear" that extends beyond the attack's victims. Given the previously noted finding by Gassebner et al. (2008) that the reelection prospects of governments are lowered significantly by a terrorist incident, less benevolent governments have a strong incentive to constrain reporting about terrorist incidents in order to stay in power. Likewise, a critical press also can pose a threat to incumbents if it helps potential opponents of the current government coordinate anti-government actions, such as demonstrations. Finally, a terrorist incident therefore might simply be a welcome pretext for government to curtail media freedom.[5]

[3] Voigt (2021) surveys the literature that has analyzed the determinants leading to a de jure/de facto gap, that is, the cases in which governments do not comply with formal constitutional constraints.

[4] In many countries, media outlets have adopted guidelines on how (not) to report on terror events, focusing on ethical as well as political concerns. One such example is provided in the editorial guidelines published by the BBC dealing with the language used when reporting terrorism (available at: www.bbc.co.uk/editorialguidelines/guidance/terrorism-language/guidance-full). The UNESCO has published a handbook for journalists entitled "Terrorism and the Media," which is available in many languages and tries to set some standards for reporting (Marthoz 2017).

[5] We note that if government reactions to terrorist attacks are benevolent and meant only to deal with the immediate threat, any reduction in media freedom observed soon after a terrorist attack should be reversed within a reasonable time frame. When, in contrast, government uses terrorist incidents as a welcome pretext for curbing media freedom, it would be unlikely to observe only temporary reductions in press freedom.

In sum, numerous reasons exist for expecting media freedom *in general* to be abridged following a terrorist attack. However, in its attempts to curtail media freedom in such a situation, almost all governments are formally constrained by a variety of constitutional provisions. One is the constitutionally guaranteed protection of freedom of expression already discussed, but as we argue in the following, that protection may interact with at least two more potentially relevant provisions.

First, if government tries to abridge media freedom, although it is constitutionally protected, actual restrictions seem less likely if those affected have standing to take their case to court. If so, it is important that government cannot interfere in the court's decision-making, or – in other words – that the court is independent of the government. We thus expect less reduction in media freedom subsequent to a terrorist attack if media freedom *and* judicial independence are guaranteed constitutionally.

Second, most countries have constitutionalized emergency provisions spelling out: (1) how an SOE can be declared; and (2) what additional competencies the government enjoys once an SOE is in effect. Given that the constitution includes specific emergency provisions, they could have important effects on media freedom. By confining restrictions on media freedom to the emergency period proper, such provisions could help maintain high levels of media freedom in "normal," that is, nonemergency times. Conversely, when the constitutional emergency provisions grant the government power to violate media freedom in emergencies, their existence could also lead to tighter restrictions on the press after a terrorist attack.

We propose to summarize our theoretical conjectures by stating four testable hypotheses. Reductions in media freedom following a terrorist attack are less likely when (1) the constitution explicitly protects media freedom. Such restrictions are, however, more likely when (2) constitutional emergency provisions allow such action simply because all constitution-abiding governments can then curtail media freedom without violating any other constitutional constraint. Abridgment of media freedom is less likely when (3) an independent judiciary can credibly enforce constitutional protections of media freedom (and constitutional emergency provisions do not allow curbing it). Finally, (4) reductions in media freedom are most likely when emergency provisions permit them *and* the judiciary is not independent from government.

10.4 Constitutional Provisions to Safeguard Media Freedom

10.4.1 Measuring de jure Protection of Media Freedom

Before presenting the indicators referring to media freedom that we have adopted for quantifying a number of relevant constitutional provisions, a definition of media freedom is in order. Freedom of expression is a broad concept, encompassing both freedom of the press and other types of media. In Article 19 of the Universal Declaration of Human Rights (UN 1948), it is defined as a "right to freedom of opinion and expression; this right includes freedom to hold opinions without interference, and to seek, receive, and impart information and ideas through any media regardless of frontiers." In the following, we take that definition as our starting point for both measurement and interpretation of our findings.

We focus herein on the protection of media freedom as defined by the constitution and not merely by statutory law. Given that it may be in the interest of a parliamentary majority to repress the media, for example, following a terrorist attack, the same majority can change or revoke any statutory protection for the media. As such, statutory protection of media freedom is no less fragile than ordinary political promises. Many constitutions treat freedom of the press and other media as part of the even broader concept of freedom of speech. Only a minority of constitutions separate freedom of speech from media freedom explicitly, supplying another reason for relying on a broad term; more specific ones could cause us to overlook relevant constitutional provisions.

Paragraph 77 of the Constitution of Denmark, for example, states that "Any person shall be entitled to publish his thoughts in printing, in writing, and in speech, provided that he may be held answerable in a court of justice. Censorship and other preventive measures shall never again be introduced." The Danish constitution thus makes it abundantly clear that the media are free of any censorship. The First Amendment to the US Constitution provides similarly unambiguous protection from any form of censorship by establishing that "Congress shall make no law ... abridging the freedom of speech, or of the press."

Both the Danish paragraph 77 and the US Constitution's First Amendment are examples in which the constitution makes clear that censorship is unconstitutional in all circumstances. However, most constitutions include a set of emergency provisions that allow restrictions on the press and other media during emergencies. While protecting freedom of speech under normal circumstances, the emergency provisions of the French constitution, for example, allow for substantial government-mandated restrictions on the press when an SOE has been declared.[6]

Such cases are easily coded, but a number of other cases require some judgment calls. The protection of media freedom in Bermuda's Constitution Order of 1968 is such a case. Paragraph 9 of that order states that: "(1) Except with his consent, no person shall be hindered in the enjoyment of his freedom of expression, and for the purposes of this section the said freedom includes freedom to hold opinions and to receive and impart ideas and information without interference, and freedom from interference with his correspondence." However, section (2) of the same paragraph effectively allows for legislation that contravenes section (1) when it is deemed reasonable:

> in the interests of defence, public safety, public order, public morality or public health; or for the purpose of protecting the rights, reputations and freedom of other persons or the private lives of persons concerned in legal proceedings, preventing the disclosure of information received in confidence, maintaining the authority and independence of the courts, regulating telephony, telegraphy, posts, wireless broadcasting, television or other means of communication or regulating public exhibitions or public entertainments; or that imposes restrictions upon public officers or teachers, except so far as that provision or, as the case may be, the thing done under the authority thereof is shown not to be reasonably justifiable in a democratic society.

We adopt a conservative approach to coding media freedom by treating the foregoing list as an indication that media freedom can be curbed with relative ease within the bounds of the constitution. As such, if doubt exists about whether the constitution actually protects media freedom, or if additional provisions, such as is the case in Bermuda's Constitution Order, which in principle provides government with constitutional means to curb it, we code press freedom

[6] Article 16 of the French constitution, which outlines its emergency provisions, allows the president, after due consultation, to "take measures required by these circumstances" and merely limits these measures to those that "provide the constitutional public authorities as swiftly as possible, with the means to carry out their duties."

as not protected. While we therefore code Denmark and the United States with scores of 1, indicating full media freedom, we code Bermuda as a 0. Our main source of information is the Comparative Constitutions Project (CCP) (Elkins et al. 2009), which provides carefully coded information on constitutional provisions for most countries in the world until 2013.

Assessed in 2012, of the eighty-three countries in our full sample, sixty-two have constitutions that protect media freedom under normal circumstances, of which twenty-two allow restrictions in some kind of emergency. Conversely, sixteen either have no constitutional provisions or their provisions are unclear; only five have what we consider as providing no protections for media freedom.[7] We combine that information with whether or not media freedom is protected in general in order to create a dummy variable effectively capturing whether the press is not protected during emergencies, which also includes circumstances in which no protection is granted outside of emergencies.[8]

We recognize that whenever the constitution permits limits on media freedom, either by being unclear or – as in the case of Bermuda – by stipulating circumstances in which the government can claim that restrictions are constitutional, it is up to a court to interpret the constitution and thus define the de jure limits within which the government can act. Similarly, even if the constitution explicitly bans any censorship or other limits on media freedom, a government with sufficient influence over court decisions and courts' de facto interpretations of the constitution may still be able to introduce legislation that restricts media freedom without facing constitutional repercussions. We therefore also develop a measure of high court independence in the following, based similarly on the way independence is defined in the constitution.

[7] The five are Bermuda, Ecuador, Honduras, Montenegro, and Turkey. Four of the countries are, incidentally, also countries in which the constitution provides particularly strong protections for the independence of judges sitting on high courts. The exception is Bermuda. We coded the Bermudan constitution ourselves, as that country is not included separately in the CCP because of its status as a British dependency.

[8] In principle, we could have coded whether general constitutional protection of media freedom operates outside of declared SOEs. However, our first tests revealed no empirical significance associated with general protections of media freedom. Our measure therefore can be interpreted as the protections accorded to press freedom during states of emergency.

10.4.2 Measuring de jure High Court Independence

We measure judicial independence using information contained in the CCP to create an index of constitutional protections for the political independence of nations' high courts (Elkins et al. 2009). Our measure is the unweighted average of four indicators: (1) Does the constitution contain an explicit declaration regarding the independence of the central judicial branch of government? (2) Are judicial decisions rendered by the highest ordinary court final, or can they be challenged politically? (3) Is the government involved in nominating or approving the high court's chief justice? (4) Is the government involved in nominating or approving other members of the high court? The first two indicators are coded directly in the CCP; we assign a score of 1 if the constitution provides such explicit protection, 0.5 if the language is unclear, and 0 if the constitution provides no protections for the judiciary. For the third and fourth indicators, we assign similar scores if, alternately, the head of state, the head of government, or the government/cabinet is involved in the nomination of the chief justice/other members; if the same officials are involved in the approval of nominations of the chief justice/ other members; and if the chief justice/other members are limited in terms of party affiliation, gender, or religion. We normalize the full measure to a 0–1 scale, with larger values indicating more de jure independence.

Within our sample, minimum independence is 0.125, while the maximum is a perfect 1, with an average of 0.57 (the value for Bermuda).[9] We note that, in general, the partial correlation between constitutional protections for media freedom and high court independence is small (r =–0.17). The same is the case for de jure independence of the high court and a de facto measure that we use throughout in the following. That de facto measure is the average of assessments of independence

[9] Interestingly, Denmark is an excellent example of the disconnect between de jure and de facto independence; it is among the countries with the lowest de jure independence scores. However, in practice, the nomination and appointment of judges to the Danish courts is separated completely from government or politics. The process is instead handled by a committee of the Danish Court Administration, over which neither the minister of justice nor any other politician has instructive or discretionary power. As such, the Danish High Court is one of several examples of countries with very limited constitutional, but substantial de facto independence.

of the high courts and lower-level courts in the Varieties of Democracy database (Coppedge et al. 2016).

As the data make clear, the cross-sectional correlation between the de jure and the de facto measures of judicial independence in recent years (2008–2012 averages) is negative at –0.19.[10] The lack of any clear association between the de jure status and de facto judicial independence provides a first reason to doubt whether constitutional status actually ties the hands of the other branches of government. If not, the de jure measure of high court independence may instead reflect historical problems with limiting political interference. It thus is an open question whether constitutional provisions actually provide de facto protections for media freedom when politicians have incentives to renege on them. In the following, we provide a first answer to that question.

10.4.3 *Measuring de facto Protection of Media Freedom*

Constitutional protection of media freedom, as described in Section 3.1, refers to the letter of the law – in this case the constitution. However, it is well known that the actual extent of freedom enjoyed by the media might diverge substantially from what a constitution stipulates. Over the years, various organizations have produced indices that are meant to indicate the level of media freedom as implemented in practice. Two of those organizations focus on journalists' freedom, security, and personal safety, namely *Reporters without Borders* and the *Committee to Protect Journalists*. *Freedom House*, a New York based NGO interested in political, economic, and civil freedoms has published a Freedom of the Press indicator ever since 1980, although the continuous indicator that we use here has been available only since 1993. The index covers 199 countries and territories and is based on a relatively minimalist, negative definition of press freedom that, for example, does not incorporate any consequences of

[10] A very similar pattern arises when using the alternative measure of judicial independence from Linzer and Staton (2015). Gutmann and Voigt (2020) inquire into the reasons explaining the puzzling negative correlation. They find that high-trust societies often manage to arrive at strong de facto judicial independence without recording it in any formal law. In a sense, then, they find that formal legislation is a (very imperfect) substitute for social trustworthiness.

press action, specify any particular political roles played by the media, or requires the media in general to abide by any form of quality criteria (Becker et al. 2007). Given both its breadth as well as its frequent use, we rely on Freedom House's index here; Appendix A provides a detailed description.[11]

The Freedom House (2017) index of media freedom is coded on the basis of a number of questions and is distributed between 0 and 100, with lower scores indicating more freedom. As such, the index, which has been available since 1993, is a measure of press freedom's absence. Since 2001, the index has been decomposable into three constituent sub-indices on media laws and regulations as well as the political and economic environments. The index thus captures both political and de facto legal limits on media freedom, such as those created by governments attacking or closing media, bringing it under direct state control as well as potential restrictions created, for example, by the media's ownership structure. We reverse and rescale the index such that the largest average values we observe – the most free countries – score at approximately 0.94 to 0.95 (in Scandinavia and Switzerland) and the least free – that is, the countries with the most restricted media – for example, Azerbaijan (0.24), Belarus (0.15), and Cuba (0.06), score closer to zero. We do so such that both de jure and de facto measures are distributed on approximately similar scales, making the interpretation of effects straightforward.

10.5 Control Data and Empirical Strategy

To identify the effects of terror events on media freedom, we rely on two separate measures of terrorism: the logarithm of the number of terrorist events in a given country to measure their frequency, and the logarithm of the number of individuals killed in those events, as a measure of their severity. Those data all are taken from the Global Terrorism Database (GTD 2018). We follow standard practice and count only the events that satisfy three criteria: (1) the attack has a

[11] The Varieties of Democracy Project also contains a variable on media freedom. We refrain from using it here because it is not always clear whether the focus is on a country's de jure or de facto media environment. Similarly, we refrain from using the alternative measure from *Reporters without Borders* owing to its more restricted coverage of countries and years.

political, socioeconomic, or religious motive; (2) the attack is intended to coerce, intimidate, or send a message to an audience wider than the immediate victims; and (3) the attack exceeds the boundaries set by international humanitarian law. In subsequent tests, we also draw data on events directed specifically against a government or police/military forces, and attacks in which the terrorists were armed with police- or military-grade weapons or attacked multiple targets.

Although the GTD covers most countries in the world, we restrict the present sample to a total of 60,649 episodes from eighty-three countries that satisfy a particular set of criteria. The sample is thus slightly larger, but comparable to what we use in Chapter 6. We first require that each country entering the sample has either democratic political institutions or formal constitutional rules that resemble those of Western democracies, and is not surrounded by countries that do not satisfy the same criteria. In other words, all countries in the sample have constitutions that de jure define the political system as democratic. Had we included societies with markedly different political institutions, wherein political processes, for example, are governed by single individuals, single tribes, or single undisputed regimes (as in communism or theocracy), we would not expect political independence to have the effects predicted by established public choice or political economy thinking. Second, in order to be able to compare constitutional efficacy, we require that the constitutional histories of the countries in our sample rest on similar foundations. In practice, our sample-selection methodology means that we exclude countries in which constitutional development starts with a first constitution written under the influence of the Soviet Union or similar intellectual tradition after World War II. Our sample thus includes Latin American countries that implemented their first constitutions simultaneously with most European countries, along with the Caribbean countries in which constitutional development rests on an even older British colonial tradition. Finally, we require that countries in the sample have sufficiently entrenched constitutions whose basic provisions remain stable over time. That criterion means that we exclude most countries in Asia and Africa, where the constitutional order is frequently suspended and where regime transitions are often accompanied by nontransparent interim constitutions. Both of those features and the general lack of constitutional persistence in many societies beyond the Western tradition imply substantial uncertainty in constitutional interpretation.

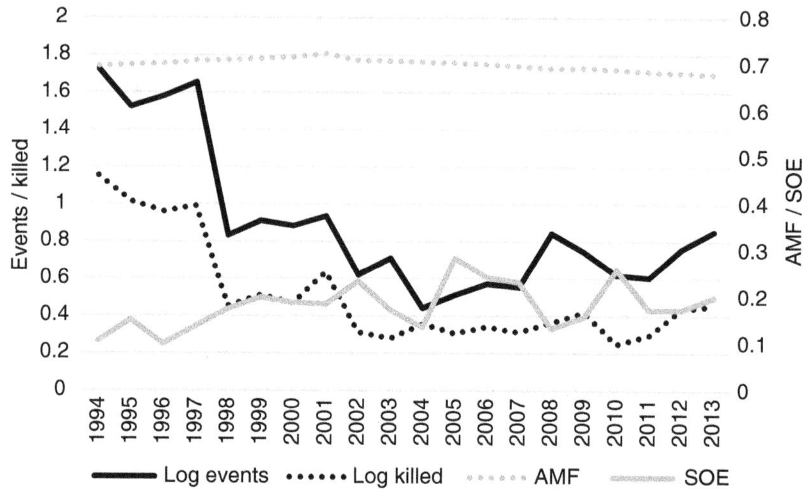

Figure 10.1 Developments, 1994–2013
Note: The left–hand y-axis pertains to the log of the number of terrorist events and the log to the number killed in those events per year. The right-hand y-axis pertains to the average media freedom (AMF) and the share of countries that declared at least one state of emergency (SOE) per year.

The eighty-three countries potentially entering our sample thus cover Europe, the Americas, and Australasia, which ensures that their formal political institutions are similar, such that regular politics, political reactions and the role of the constitution are formally structured in similar ways. In the estimated models, this sample drops to a maximum of seventy-eight countries owing to restricted availability of specific control variables.

Figure 10.1 illustrates the development over time of our two measures of terrorism – the average number of events and the average number of deaths per event – and the average level of media freedom (AMF) as well as the share of countries that in each year declared an SOE. As is clear in the figure, de facto media freedom has remained quite stable over time within our sample, reaching a high in 2001 and declining slightly thereafter. Conversely, terrorism fell substantially in the 1990s and shows only a slight increase in the new millennium, despite an actual increase in the likelihood that countries declare SOEs.

Figure 10.2 depicts average media freedom across four groups of countries, based on their constitutional provisions: countries with

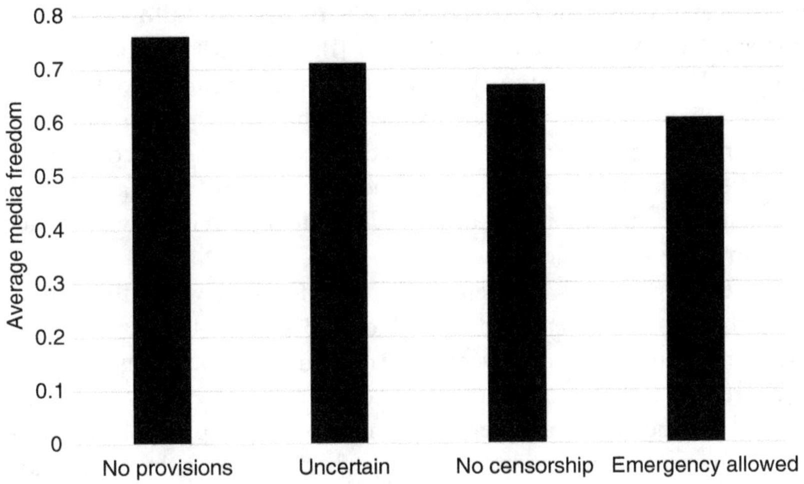

Figure 10.2 Media freedom differences, constitutional provisions

no provisions protecting media freedom; countries with uncertain provisions; countries that provide clear constitutional protections; and lastly countries that allow censorship and restrictions of media freedom during SOEs. Interestingly, the average level of de facto media freedom follows a sequence with countries without any formal protections having the highest average levels of media freedom, followed by those with uncertain provisions and then countries with clear protections in place. Finally, countries that do provide some constitutional protections for the media, but allow that freedom to be violated during emergencies exhibit the weakest media freedoms, on average. Table A10.1 in the appendix lists all countries in the sample, along with their overall media freedom averages, terrorism experiences (both variables), censorship, and constitutional independences of their high courts.

Our basic model looks like this:

$$\text{De facto } mf_{it}+1=a + b^{*}terror_{it}+ c^{*}\text{de jure } mf_{it}+ d^{*}\text{de jure } JI_{it} + e^{*}allowance_{it}+ f^{*}X_{it}+ g^{*}D_{i}+ h^{*}I_{t}+ u_{it}$$

Our baseline model is estimated alternately with two measures of terrorism (number of attacks or number of people killed) to ascertain the extent to which de jure media freedom (de jure mf) predicts de facto freedom (de facto mf), conditional on whether regular constitutional provisions or emergency provisions allow restrictions (allowance), the independence of the judiciary (de jure JI), and a set of controls, X. Variable D_i is a set of country fixed effects and I_t annual fixed effects; u_{it} is the error term. Since we hypothesize that terror events have less of a dampening effect on de facto media freedom when accompanied by either constitutionalized guarantees of (de jure) media freedom or constitutional guarantees of an independent judiciary, we interact them in some specifications.

The ensuing results are reported in Table 10.2, while the results of further tests are reported in Table 10.3. In the latter, we either add a triple interaction between all terrorism and both constitutional measures, or test the interaction between constitutionally guaranteed judicial independence and terrorism in two subsamples split according to emergency provisions – that is, whether or not the emergency provision allows limits on media freedom during such extraordinary times. In both tables, we also report all main estimates with a sample only including observations from democratic country-years in order to make sure that our results are not driven by autocracies or anocracies.

We keep our specification quite parsimonious and include only a few control variables (the X vector). First, we add the logarithms of population size and real (purchasing-power parity) GDP per capita (both variables are from the Penn World Tables, mark 9; see Feenstra et al. 2015). From the GDP data, we also calculate a dummy for recessions that takes the value of 1 if the year-to-year growth rate is negative. Second, we enter a dummy for whether a coup attempt – failed or successful – was reported in a given year; we get the information for that variable from the database in Bjørnskov and Rode (2020). We also follow previous research in adding a few features of the country's political institutions and enter the Herfindahl-Hirschmann index of legislative fractionalization (of the lower house in bicameral systems), because political fractionalization per se may work as a veto institution creating de facto judicial independence. Following Kellam and Stein (2016), who found that in presidential systems, left-leaning governments are more likely to reduce media freedom than right-wing governments, we enter a measure of the political ideology of the incumbent government as an explanatory variable. In addition, we include a dummy for whether a terrorist attack occurred during a parliamentary election year, as governments might be particularly sensitive to critical media reports when they are trying to be reelected. We derive those observations from the background database of Berggren and Bjørnskov (2017) and add a set of regime fixed effects from Bjørnskov and Rode's (2020) update of Cheibub et al. (2010), thereby capturing differences between parliamentary, weak presidential, and fully presidential democracies, and civilian autocracies, military dictatorships, and absolutist monarchies.

Finally, we enter a full set of country, regime, and year fixed effects such that all results are driven by within-country variation relative to those explained jointly by international factors. The fixed effects imply that we are controlling for stable differences in threat levels, and international threat changes over time that are common to all countries in our sample. They also capture a set of other approximately time-invariant potential influences, such as social trust, historical experience and religious differences (cf., Engerman and Sokoloff 2008; Hillman and Potrafke 2018; Bjørnskov 2019).

As the fixed effects thus also capture long-run differences in constitutional histories and terrorist threats, we mainly see two potential sources of endogeneity. First, our estimates may be biased if country-specific changes in media freedom are known and foreseeable by terrorists, and that terrorists have clear interests in exploiting them before they are implemented. We cannot dismiss this problem, but note that the process of introducing constitutional changes tends to be very lengthy and that such changes are relatively rare in democracies. A second potential cause for endogeneity bias in our setting is that changes in media freedom could affect the likelihood of terrorist events, and could also affect the death tolls of those events indirectly if changes in media freedom reflect changes in underlying institutional quality or capacity (cf. Hoffman et al. 2013). While we do not believe either of those possibilities to be serious concerns because institutional quality tends to be very stable over time in relatively developed countries – and particularly so in democracies – the potential reactions of terrorists to institutional change might give rise to a positive bias (overestimation of the true effect) if restrictions on media freedom lead to more terrorist events, and a negative bias (underestimation) if they work in the intended way and lead to fewer events. One could argue further that the threat of terrorism could affect the de jure status of media freedom, making the estimates of our constitutional measures subject to endogeneity bias. However, given how rarely constitutions change and that provisions regulating media freedom and emergencies change even less frequently (as shown in Chapter 2), both the

Table 10.1 *Descriptive statistics*

Variable	Average	Standard deviation	Observations
Press freedom	0.698	0.211	1971
Log no. of events	0.908	1.316	1971
Log no. of killed	0.538	1.234	1971
Target: Government	0.393	0.767	1971
Target: Police/military	0.336	0.827	1971
Type: Heavily armed	0.789	1.226	1971
Constitutional independence	0.574	0.210	1663
de facto independence	1.078	1.308	1827
Emergency allowance	0.164	0.296	1706
Log population	1.898	1.781	1761
Log GDP per capita	9.691	0.759	1761
Recession	0.181	0.385	1743
Coup	0.001	0.032	1971
Legislative fractionalization	0.363	0.185	1771
Government ideology	0.102	0.328	1771
Election year	0.273	0.446	1888

country-specific threat as well as the constitutional provisions are close to being time-invariant. They are therefore subsumed in the country fixed effects and are not a source of endogeneity bias. As such, and following Nizalova and Murtazashvili's (2016) logic, the interaction terms and thus the heterogeneity of effects are free of endogeneity bias. In other words, our interacted results can still be interpreted as causal, as long as constitutional changes are rare, slowly implemented, and not affected directly by immediate changes in terrorist threats.

All data are summarized in Table 10.1, while, as noted, Table A10.1 in the appendix summarizes the main constitutional and terrorist data as country averages.

10.6 Main Results

We report our main results in Table 10.2, noting first that despite the relatively limited variability of media freedom – our dependent variable – in many countries, the specification does a decent job of

Table 10.2 *Main results, Freedom House index (2017)*

	Log no. of events					Log no. killed				
Terrorism measure:	1	2	3	4	5	6	7	8	9	10
Log population	−0.212**	−0.209**	−0.206**	−0.165**	−0.166***	−0.217***	−0.211***	−0.209**	−0.169**	−0.169**
	(0.081)	(0.082)	(0.081)	(0.079)	(0.079)	(0.079)	(0.081)	(0.080)	(0.078)	(0.078)
Log GDP per capita	0.051	0.048	0.049	0.055	0.055	0.051	0.048	0.049	0.054	0.054
	(0.0041)	(0.034)	(0.034)	(0.039)	(0.039)	(0.041)	(0.035)	(0.035)	(0.040)	(0.040)
Recession	0.019**	0.011*	0.012*	0.015**	0.015**	0.019**	0.012**	0.013**	0.016**	0.016**
	(0.008)	(0.006)	(0.006)	(0.007)	(0.007)	(0.008)	(0.006)	(0.006)	(0.007)	(0.007)
Coup	0.040	0.000	−0.002	−0.010	−0.009	0.033	−0.007	−0.008	−0.015	−0.015
	(0.056)	(0.029)	(0.029)	(0.031)	(0.034)	(0.056)	(0.032)	(0.031)	(0.032)	(0.031)
Legislative fractionalization	−0.008	−0.007	−0.007	−0.009	−0.009	−0.006	−0.005	−0.004	−0.008	−0.008
	(0.068)	(0.061)	(0.061)	(0.059)	(0.059)	(0.058)	(0.061)	(0.061)	(0.059)	(0.059)
Government ideology	0.035	0.036	0.034	0.026	0.026	0.035	0.035	0.034	0.026	0.026
	(0.044)	(0.039)	(0.039)	(0.037)	(0.038)	(0.044)	(0.039)	(0.039)	(0.038)	(0.038)
Election year	0.000	0.002	0.002	0.002	0.002	0.001	0.003	0.003	0.002	0.002
	(0.002)	(0.002)	(0.002)	(0.002)	(0.002)	(0.002)	(0.002)	(0.002)	(0.002)	(0.002)
Terrorism	−0.007*	−0.007**	0.007	−0.006	−0.005	−0.008**	−0.007***	0.008	−0.005*	−0.005
	(0.004)	(0.004)	(0.007)	(0.004)	(0.004)	(0.003)	(0.003)	(0.006)	(0.003)	(0.003)
Con court independence		0.144*	0.156**				0.150*	0.155**		
		(0.077)	(0.078)				(0.078)	(0.079)		
de facto court independence		0.067**					0.067***			
		(0.016)					(0.016)			

Table 10.2 (*cont.*)

	Log no. of events					Log no. killed				
Terrorism measure:	1	2	3	4	5	6	7	8	9	10
Terrorism * court independence			−0.023**					−0.023**		
			(0.011)					(0.009)		
Emergency allowance				0.016	0.018				0.017	0.017
				(0.021)	(0.022)				(0.021)	(0.021)
Terrorism * emergency					−0.002					−0.001
					(0.007)					(0.007)
Annual FE	Yes	Yes	Yes	Yes	Yes	Yes	Yes	Yes	Yes	Yes
Country FE	Yes	Yes	Yes	Yes	Yes	Yes	Yes	Yes	Yes	Yes
Regime FE	Yes	Yes	Yes	Yes	Yes	Yes	Yes	Yes	Yes	Yes
Observations	1665	1457	1457	1486	1486	1665	1457	1457	1486	1486
Countries	78	71	71	72	72	78	71	71	72	72
Within R squared	0.216	0.357	0.359	0.337	0.337	0.218	0.356	0.359	0.336	0.336
F statistic	3.06	4.47	4.88	4.40	4.51	3.64	5.17	7.24	4.77	4.73
Only democracies										
Terrorism	−0.001	−0.003	0.009	−0.001	−0.000	−0.003	−0.004	0.008	−0.003	−0.003
	(0.003)	(0.003)	(0.008)	(0.003)	(0.003)	(0.002)	(0.002)	(0.006)	(0.003)	(0.003)
Constitutional independence		0.128	0.136				0.131	0.135		
		(0.091)	(0.091)				(0.091)	(0.092)		
de facto independence										

	(1)	(2)	(3)	(4)	(5)	(6)	(7)	(8)	(9)	(10)
Terrorism * constitution			−0.018					−0.019**		
			(0.012)					(0.009)		
Emergency allowance				0.032*	0.034*				0.032*	0.032*
				(0.018)	(0.019)				(0.018)	(0.018)
Terrorism * emergency					−0.003					0.000
					(0.008)					(0.008)
Observations	1551	1348	1348	1377	1377	1551	1348	1348	1377	1377
Countries	74	67	67	68	68	74	67	67	68	68
Within R squared	0.238	0.319	0.320	0.291	0.291	0.239	0.319	0.321	0.292	0.292
F statistic	–	–	–	–	–	–	–	–	–	–

Note: ***(**) [*] denote significance at $p < 0.01$, ($p < 0.05$), and [$p < 0.10$].

explaining the within-country variation. However, we find only three significant control variables: countries that are more populous are likely to see less media freedom while we find that media freedom tends to improve during recessions and, moreover, that de facto court independence is significant when it is entered. Conversely, we find weak evidence that more formal judicial independence ("constitutional court independence") is conducive to greater media freedom (columns 2 and 7), and that constitutionalized emergency provisions allowing restrictions on media freedom during SOEs are correlated systematically with slightly higher levels of media freedom (columns 4 and 9). Throughout, we find very similar, but slightly less precise estimates when we restrict the sample to observations from democracies only; those results are reported in the lower panel of the table.

What is most important is that we find that terrorism is on average associated with reductions in de facto media freedom (columns 1, 2, 6, and 7). Doubling the number of terrorist attacks or the numbers killed in those attacks is associated with a deterioration in actual media freedom of approximately one-half of a standard deviation. Yet as we note in the discussion of theoretical considerations, reasons exist for suspecting that the average association hides considerable heterogeneity across constitutional characteristics. In columns 3 and 8, we therefore interact our terrorism measures with the constitutional independence of the high courts. In both cases, we find that the estimated effects of terrorism increase in the level of courts' constitutional independence and become significant as that independence strengthens. At the maximum index value of 1, that is, the most careful constitutional protection of the independence of the high courts that we observe, the estimate is 0.156 in column 3 and 0.150 in column 7; the former is significant at the 5 percent level, while the latter is significant at the 1 percent level.

In Figure 10.3, we plot the logged number of deaths during terrorist events, conditional on the de jure independence of the judiciary (i.e. those results reported in column 8). The figure illustrates how the association between terrorism and media freedom starts around zero for countries with very weak constitutional judicial independence and declines with the formal de jure level of court independence. The association becomes significantly negative at an index value exceeding approximately 0.6, as indicated by the 95 percent confidence interval illustrated by the dotted lines. As such, the result is also politically

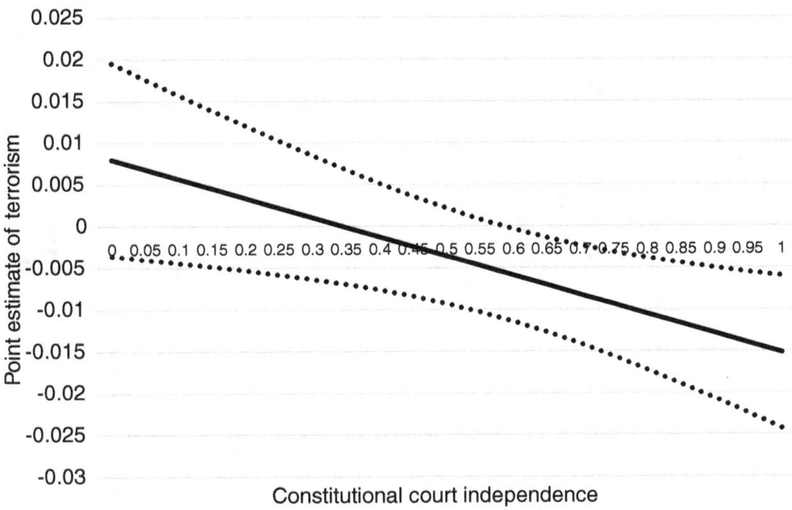

Figure 10.3 Effects of terrorism, conditional on court independence

relevant as the constitutionally guaranteed independence of the judiciary is above that level in three-fourths of the countries in our sample.

In columns 5 and 10 of Table 10.2, we enter an interaction between terrorism and whether or not the emergency provisions allow the suspension of media freedom during such times. In both cases, we find that terrorism is insignificant when the emergency provisions do not allow for censorship, but significant when they do: The estimate conditional on allowing censorship in column 5 is –0.007 and the corresponding estimate in column 10 is –0.006; both are significant at the 5 percent level. We thus do not find evidence of a significant difference in the size of the estimate, but a much more precisely estimated effect in countries where the emergency provisions allow the government to curtail media freedom.

In Table 10.3, we therefore take a further step toward identifying the constitutional conditions under which terrorist attacks lead to reductions in media freedom. We do so by introducing a triple interaction between our two terrorism measures, the index of constitutional independence, and the dummy capturing whether the emergency provisions allow press restrictions during SOEs.

We find that a terrorist event occurring in a country that allows restrictions on media freedom during an SOE and that enjoys a high

Table 10.3 *Specific results*

	Log no. of events			Log no. killed		
	1	2	3	4	5	6
			Full baseline included			
Terrorism	–0.004	–0.006	0.023*	–0.003	–0.004**	0.002
	(0.008)	(0.008)	(0.013)	(0.002)	(0.002)	(0.007)
Con court independence	0.156**	0.139*	–0.027	0.159**	0.148*	–0.057
	(0.079)	(0.073)	(0.131)	(0.080)	(0.076)	(0.140)
Terrorism * court independence	–0.004	–0.004	–0.037**	–0.008	–0.009	–0.008
	(0.012)	(0.014)	(0.014)	(0.006)	(0.006)	(0.007)
Emergency allowance	0.002			0.003		
	(0.023)			(0.023)		
Terrorism * emergency	0.046*			0.042*		
	(0.024)			(0.022)		
Terrorism * emergency * court independence	–0.071**			–0.064**		
	(0.035)			(0.031)		
Annual FE	Yes	Yes	Yes	Yes	Yes	Yes
Country FE	Yes	Yes	Yes	Yes	Yes	Yes
Regime FE	Yes	Yes	Yes	Yes	Yes	Yes
Observations	1456	1088	369	1456	1088	369
Countries	71	65	32	71	65	32
Within R squared	0.363	0.335	0.518	0.363	0.336	0.514

F statistic	5.85	6.29	–	7.81	6.85	–
Only democracies						
Terrorism	0.001	–0.006	0.023*	–0.002	–0.004**	0.005
	(0.008)	(0.008)	(0.013)	(0.002)	(0.002)	(0.016)
Constitutional independence	0.135	0.103	–0.025	0.136	0.111	0.124
	(0.092)	(0.076)	(0.149)	(0.093)	(0.079)	(0.323)
Terrorism * const. independence	–0.004	0.003	–0.037**	–0.001	–0.003	0.008
	(0.013)	(0.014)	(0.015)	(0.005)	(0.005)	(0.017)
Emergency allowance	0.019			0.019		
	(0.019)			(0.019)		
Terrorism * emergency	0.030*			0.031*		
	(0.018)			(0.016)		
Terrorism * emergency * independence	–0.049**			–0.051**		
	(0.022)			(0.019)		
Observations	1347	1017	331	1347	1017	331
Countries	67	61	30	67	61	30
Within R squared	0.325	0.349	0.506	0.326	0.351	0.500
F statistic	–	–	–	–	5.48	

Note: ***(**) [*] denote significance at $p < 0.01$, ($p < 0.05$), and [$p < 0.10$]. The results in columns 2 and 5 are obtained in a subsample of observations for which the emergency provisions do not allow for restrictions of media freedom during states of emergency; the estimates in columns 3 and 6 are obtained for a subsample of observations for which the emergency provisions do allow for restrictions of media freedom during states of emergency.

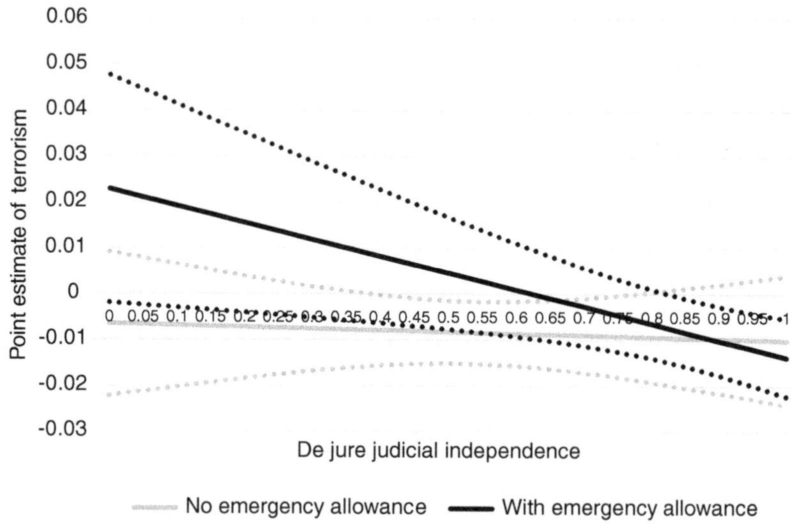

Figure 10.4 Effects of terrorism, triple interacted conditions

degree of formal court independence is likely to lead to a considerable decline in actual media freedom. That reduction is slightly more pronounced when terrorist events are captured by their numbers (column 1) than by their severities (column 4); we illustrate those differences in Figure 10.4. While we find no evidence of significant effects on the number of events in countries with no emergency provisions and no or little constitutional protections, we find significant effects for more severe events, captured by the number of victims killed by terrorists. Yet the triple interaction indicates that terrorist attacks lead to much larger reductions in de facto media freedom in countries where the emergency provisions allow for press restrictions and the constitution more clearly protects the independence of the courts. While the results also appear to indicate that emergency provisions per se lead to more media freedom, that result must be interpreted as significant only when the constitutional independence of the courts is very limited, which is only the case for four years in a single country: Portugal in the years immediately before democratization in the mid-1970s.

In columns 2–3 and 5–6 in Table 10.3, we substantiate our results by restricting the sample to observations in which the emergency provisions do not allow for restricting media freedom (columns 2 and 5) or observations in which they do (columns 3 and 6), which allows us to determine if the results differ depending on the basic characteristic of the emergency provisions. We observe that while media freedom is unaffected by the number of terrorist events when the constitution does not allow restraints during emergencies, events do lead to some abridgment of press freedom when it does, and when the constitution ostensibly protects the independence of the high courts. Conversely, we find that more severe attacks, that is, those that lead to more people being killed, are associated with further restrictions when the constitution does not allow limits in emergencies. When it does, we find no evidence that terrorist events lead to restrictions on media freedom.

In further tests, which we report in the appendix, we separate terrorist events based on whether they are directed specifically against the government or military/police forces and we separate the attacks in which the terrorists used heavier arms and those involving multiple targets. In the former type, politicians or public officials are targeted directly, which may, for personal reasons, make them more likely to react, while heavily armed attacks may also pose more serious threats to the incumbent regime. We nevertheless find no significant differences across those specific types of terrorist events, and quite weak effects when focusing on the small number of attacks involving multiple targets; we therefore refrain from further comment. In further tests (not shown), we also conclude that the main results are not driven by, for example, Israel, which has been in a continuous SOE, and that our results are independent of whether the government actually declared an SOE or not. The main results in Table 10.3 are thus robust to intuitive tests and appear generalizable under the specific constitutional conditions identified in the table.

10.7 Conclusions and Outlook

In this chapter, we look into the consequences of terrorist attacks for media freedom. More specifically, we ask whether constitutional guarantees of free media mitigate the (expected) downturn in media freedom following a terrorist attack and thus whether a specific kind of constitutional protection (in this case of the media) actually does lead to stronger protections. Put differently, we employ terrorist attacks as "stress tests" of the relevance of constitutional safeguarding of media freedom.

The results are quite sobering. As expected, more and, in particular, more severe terrorist events lead to reductions in media freedom. That effect is independent of the specific way of accounting terrorist activities (the number of incidents versus their severity). When the independence of the highest court as specified in the constitution is taken explicitly into account and is interacted with our terrorism variables, it turns out that terrorist events (no matter how accounted for explicitly) become significant in explaining restrictions of media freedom, the stronger are the constitutional guarantees of high court independence. In other words, in robust constitutional systems, terrorist attacks lead to substantial reductions in media freedom. Legal scholars have discussed the possibility that constitutional restrictions on government do not bind governmental hands, ever since James Madison expressed his concern that constitutional rights and other limits on government behavior would create mere "parchment barriers" in Federalist No. 48 (Levinson 2011 discusses the "puzzle of constitutional commitment" from a legal scholar's point of view). It seems not only that Madison's concerns have been vindicated with regard to media freedom, but that other parchment barriers nominally ensuring the independence of the judiciary interact perniciously with de jure media protections.

Most constitutions contain explicit emergency provisions. They regulate the conditions under which government is allowed to declare an SOE and what additional powers it has under those conditions. Based on a dummy variable indicating whether government is allowed to tinker with media freedom during an SOE, we find that provisions allowing for curtailing media freedom in those times are indeed associated with less de facto media freedom.

Interacting terrorist events with both de jure court independence and emergency provisions – which we introduce in order to allow for heterogeneous effects that depend on constitutional performance and the potential unconstitutionality of restricting media freedom – indicates that terrorist attacks lead to much larger reductions in de facto media freedom in countries where the emergency provisions allow such restrictions and the constitution more clearly protects the independence of the courts.

A remaining question is the transmission channel reflected in our findings. We prefer to remain agnostic, as we see two interpretations that both are consistent with our empirical results. First, it is possible to interpret the findings as evidence that politicians limit media freedom in order to protect citizens from further terrorist attacks. However, such an interpretation requires that politicians believe that curbing media freedom is an effective way of enhancing the citizenry's security. We note that little evidence exists supporting such a belief although politicians may still hold it (as mentioned in Chapter 6). A benevolent interpretation of the effects also would imply that the restrictions on the press will be temporary, to be lifted once the imminent terrorist threat has passed. Yet we observe that changes in de facto media freedom tend to persist. That observation leaves open two options that are both consistent with the overall findings.

First, an interpretation in which the findings reflect opportunistic political behavior is consistent with the results. Leading politicians as well as some government agencies have an interest in gaining additional power and avoiding criticism, and substantial de jure constitutionalization of the judiciary may reflect a state in which such influence can be enforced through formal mechanisms (Dragu 2011). However, we must emphasize that that interpretation is difficult to reconcile with the evidence that terrorist attacks as well as emergency reactions to such attacks appear unpopular with most voters (Gassebner et al. 2008).

A second, alternative interpretation, nevertheless, is also consistent with the findings. If one interprets substantial constitutionalization as reflected in our de jure index of judicial independence as an indication of the independence of government agencies in total, a side effect of independence may be a lack of political or bureaucratic coordination across agencies. That interpretation implies that the results can be explained by multiple agencies all reacting to terrorist threats in an uncoordinated manner. As such, substantial abridgments of media freedom are a result of a bureaucratic overreaction similar to the tragedy of the commons or voracity effects (cf. Tornell and Lane 1999), and not political opportunism.

To sum up the results, we find that governments' inclinations to reduce media freedom after a terrorist event cannot easily be prevented by constitutionally protecting judicial independence or by specific emergency provisions. At least some of the constitutional provisions that ostensibly protect the media therefore appear to be mere window dressing that governments can exploit during and after terrorist events. In other words, at least some governments might have an interest in terrorist incidents occurring because attacks allow them to repress the media and apparently do it within constitutional bounds protected by an ostensibly independent high court.

Our findings thus point toward two interesting questions for future research. First, what makes governments and other political actors constitutionalize media freedom and adopt other features of the institutional framework in the first place? Second, do reductions in media freedom occur in isolation or are they accompanied by restrictions on other civil liberties? In other words, while we find limits on media freedom under specific constitutional circumstances, do those effects generalize to other repressive government actions?

Appendix

Appendix A10.1 The Press Freedom Measure

We use the Freedom House (2017) measure of press freedom as our measure of media freedom, which conceptually is based on Article 19 of the Universal Declaration of Human Rights. The index is scored by expert coders at Freedom House on twenty-three methodology questions that aim to cover the multiple ways in which governments and private actors can place pressure and limits on the flow of information to the public and the ability of the media to operate freely and without potential repercussions. The twenty-three questions cover three separate elements: the legal, political, and economic environments of the media. Recent editions offer three separate subindices: (1) the extent to which media freedom is restricted by laws and regulations and their de facto enforcement in practice; (2) the extent to which media content is subject to political control, which includes editorial independence, absence of censorship, information availability, and the de facto freedom of journalists to perform their jobs; and (3) the extent to which economic characteristics, such as the industrial and ownership structure of the media, impediments to production, distribution and advertisement, and possible corruption can limit the media's freedom. The overall index of press freedom thus includes expert assessments of a broad array of mechanisms through which government and private actors could influence the media's freedom.

Appendix A10.2 Additional Tables

Table A10.1 ***Country averages***

Country	Press freedom	Censorship	Log killed	Log events	Const. independence
Albania	0.48	0.00	0.40	0.69	0.60
Antigua and Barbuda	0.63	1.00	0.00	0.00	0.25
Argentina	0.61	0.85	0.33	1.01	0.60
Armenia	0.40	1.00	0.43	0.47	0.60
Australia	0.88	1.00	0.12	0.71	0.44
Austria	0.85	1.00	0.13	0.68	0.57
Azerbaijan	0.24	0.05	0.42	0.56	0.60
Bahamas	0.89	1.00	0.03	0.09	0.51
Barbados	0.87	1.00	0.00	0.00	0.41
Belarus	0.15	0.00	0.17	0.34	0.62
Belgium	0.94	0.00	0.12	0.59	0.76
Belize	0.81	1.00	0.00	0.07	0.51
Bolivia	0.69	0.75	0.12	0.51	0.63
Bosnia and Herzegovina	0.48	1.00	0.52	1.33	0.13
Brazil	0.65	0.60	0.79	1.08	0.60
Bulgaria	0.67	0.00	0.44	0.74	0.84
Canada	0.87	1.00	0.07	0.95	0.13
Chile	0.76	0.75	0.14	1.45	0.60
Colombia	0.45	0.80	5.28	4.76	0.63
Costa Rica	0.87	0.00	0.16	0.10	1.00

Table A10.1 *(cont.)*

Country	Press freedom	Censorship	Log killed	Log events	Const. independence
Croatia	0.57	0.35	0.23	0.58	0.88
Cuba	0.06	1.00	0.14	0.32	0.50
Cyprus	0.83	1.00	0.12	0.60	0.32
Czech Republic	0.84	0.65	0.16	0.48	0.60
Denmark	0.94	0.00	0.00	0.24	0.38
Dominica	0.84	1.00	0.00	0.03	0.38
Dominican Republic	0.67	0.20	0.19	0.32	0.61
Ecuador	0.56	1.00	0.20	1.06	0.72
El Salvador	0.61	0.00	0.43	0.42	0.63
Estonia	0.86	0.00	0.10	0.29	0.85
Finland	0.93	0.95	0.12	0.14	0.69
France	0.81	1.00	0.73	3.33	0.63
Georgia	0.46	1.00	1.63	1.88	0.60
Germany	0.89	0.00	0.62	1.99	0.60
Greece	0.71	0.35	0.34	3.09	0.60
Grenada	0.83	1.00	0.00	0.00	0.13
Guatemala	0.44	0.00	1.12	1.22	0.63
Guyana	0.75	1.00	0.34	0.28	0.57
Honduras	0.49	1.00	0.86	0.76	0.63
Hungary	0.75	1.00	0.16	0.48	0.93
Iceland	0.93	0.25	0.00	0.03	0.13

Ireland	0.88	1.00	0.25	1.17	0.72
Israel	0.74	1.00	3.28	3.51	0.00
Italy	0.73	0.35	0.19	1.84	0.38
Jamaica	0.89	1.00	0.24	0.26	0.79
Japan	0.83	0.00	0.25	0.97	0.92
Korea, Republic of	0.74	0.00	0.03	0.27	0.82
Latvia	0.81	0.15	0.07	0.36	0.63
Lithuania	0.83	0.35	0.03	0.16	0.60
Luxembourg	0.93	0.00	0.00	0.07	0.35
Macedonia	0.54	0.00	0.50	1.03	0.75
Malta	0.85	1.00	0.03	0.07	0.35
Mexico	0.49	0.00	2.15	1.82	0.82
Moldova	0.44	0.00	0.09	0.26	0.63
Montenegro	0.65	0.88	0.04	0.13	0.80
Netherlands	0.91	1.00	0.21	0.73	0.38
New Zealand	0.93	1.00	0.00	0.28	0.13
Nicaragua	0.57	0.35	0.53	0.63	0.60
Norway	0.96	1.00	0.25	0.28	0.25
Panama	0.65	0.00	0.33	0.42	0.69
Paraguay	0.47	0.00	0.34	0.71	0.60
Peru	0.55	0.55	2.39	1.79	0.63
Poland	0.79	0.15	0.05	0.42	0.79
Portugal	0.88	0.00	0.05	0.16	0.88
Romania	0.59	0.45	0.00	0.07	0.38
Russia	0.32	0.00	5.03	4.42	0.60

Table A10.1 *(cont.)*

Country	Press freedom	Censorship	Log killed	Log events	Const. independence
Serbia	0.50	0.30	1.00	1.61	0.75
Singapore	0.35	1.00	0.03	0.03	0.35
Slovak Republic	0.75	1.00	0.19	0.38	0.82
Slovenia	0.79	1.00	0.03	0.17	0.63
Spain	0.82	0.00	1.52	3.10	0.60
Suriname	0.76	1.00	0.00	0.09	0.35
Sweden	0.95	1.00	0.07	0.61	0.25
Switzerland	0.94	0.00	0.20	0.64	0.63
Taiwan	0.79	1.00	0.20	0.46	0.60
Trinidad &Tobago	0.78	1.00	0.14	0.34	0.57
Turkey	0.42	1.00	3.78	3.69	1.00
Ukraine	0.47	0.10	0.31	0.96	0.88
United Kingdom	0.84	1.00	1.75	3.67	0.47
United States	0.88	1.00	1.78	3.12	0.35
Uruguay	0.77	0.00	0.00	0.24	0.38
Venezuela	0.42	0.00	0.58	1.17	0.66

Note: Press freedom is the index of press freedom in Freedom House (2017); Censorship refers to Freedom House's subindex of censorship; log killed and log events are the logarithms to the number of killed and the number of events in GTD (2018); and const. independence is our index of constitutional protection of the independence of the high court. All numbers are averages across all years of the sample.

Table A10.2 *Results, different types of attack*

	Log no. of events							
	Government		Police/military		Heavily armed		Multiple targets	
Target/type	1	2	3	4	5	6	7	8
	Full baseline included							
Terrorism	−0.004	0.005	−0.003	−0.004	−0.003	0.006	−0.006	0.012
	(0.004)	(0.013)	(0.004)	(0.017)	(0.003)	(0.008)	(0.008)	(0.017)
Constitutional const.	0.125	0.129	0.126	0.125	0.124	0.134	0.124	0.125
independence	(0.091)	(0.091)	(0.092)	(0.090)	(0.092)	(0.093)	(0.092)	(0.091)
Terrorism * independence		−0.013		0.000		−0.012		−0.016
		(0.022)		(0.031)		(0.015)		(0.036)
Emergency allowance	0.020	0.019	0.021	0.017	0.020	0.018	0.020	0.022
	(0.018)	(0.018)	(0.018)	(0.019)	(0.018)	(0.019)	(0.018)	(0.018)
Terrorism * emergency		0.044*		0.065**		0.037*		0.000
		(0.024)		(0.031)		(0.019)		(0.028)
Terrorism * emergency *		−0.071**		−0.079**		−0.056**		−0.039
independence		(0.031)		(0.039)		(0.024)		(0.042)
Annual FE	Yes	Yes	Yes	Yes	Yes	Yes	Yes	Yes
Country FE	Yes	Yes	Yes	Yes	Yes	Yes	Yes	Yes
Regime FE	Yes	Yes	Yes	Yes	Yes	Yes	Yes	Yes

Table A10.2 *(cont.)*

	Log no. of events							
	Government		Police/military		Heavily armed		Multiple targets	
Target/type	1	2	3	4	5	6	7	8
Observations	1347	1347	1347	1347	1347	1347	1347	1347
Countries	67	67	67	67	67	67	67	67
Within R squared	0.322	0.327	0.321	0.324	0.321	0.327	0.321	0.328
F statistic	–	–	–	–	–	–	–	

Note: The results in columns 2 and 5 are obtained in a subsample of observations for which the emergency provisions do not allow for restrictions of media freedom during states of emergency; the estimates in columns 3 and 6 are obtained for a subsample of observations for which the emergency provisions do allow for restrictions of media freedom during states of emergency. We define the specific types of terrorism events in the following way: "Government" and "Police/military" refer to attacks against government and government facilities, and against the policy or the military, respectively. "Heavily armed" attacks are defined as terrorism events in which the perpetrators used heavier arms than handguns, and "Multiple targets" refers to events in which several attacks were targeted on the same day. All are coded according to event-specific information in GTD (2018).

11 *Unconstitutional States of Emergency*[*]

11.1 Introduction

In this chapter, we ask to what degree formal emergency provisions are complied with by governments. The chapter thus aims at identifying a possible gap between de jure provisions and de facto reality. Based on a novel dataset that identifies 115 out of 853 analyzed states of emergency (SOEs) as unconstitutional, we take first steps toward identifying the reasons that lead governments to violate constitutional rules. Due to the particular structure of the data, this chapter is largely confined to correlational analysis and we therefore cannot claim that our findings are fully causal. We find that political turmoil is more likely to be followed by an unconstitutional emergency than natural disasters. Autocratic governments are more likely to renege upon the constitution than democratic governments. Finally, bicameral systems are more likely to suffer from unlawful SOEs than unicameral ones. If domestic events induce government to declare an SOE, an unconstitutional one is particularly likely if the constitution requires emergency approval from a second chamber of parliament.

In Chapter 5, we show that, as a consequence of an SOE declared subsequent to a natural disaster, more people die when the government enjoys more benefits under the emergency constitution. This is an indication that emergency constitutions are often misused.

In addition to contributing to the literature on constitutional emergency provisions, this chapter also contributes to a small but fast-growing literature inquiring into the factors that determine whether governments comply with constitutional provisions or not.

The rest of the chapter is organized as follows. In the next section, we develop a number of theoretical conjectures regarding the conditions

[*] The article on which this chapter is based was written in collaboration with Mahdi Khesali.

under which governments are particularly likely not to comply with the respective emergency constitutions. Section 11.3 introduces a novel and unique dataset. In Section 11.4, we provide empirical evidence of when governments choose to declare unlawful SOEs after which we discuss the results and conclude.

11.2 Framing the Issue

We frame this issue by first spelling out possible ways of unconstitutional government behavior related to emergencies and then inquire into possible reasons to do so.

11.2.1 Types of Unlawful Government Behavior

We distinguish three phases during which unlawful behavior can occur:

(1) the declaration of an SOE can be unconstitutional;
(2) the acts chosen by the executive during an SOE can be unconstitutional;
(3) the way in which the SOE is prolonged can be unconstitutional.

It is, of course, possible that two or even all three types of noncompliance with the constitution occur in sequence.

Referring to phase one, at least four such ways can be distinguished. First, it is possible that the executive calls an SOE without any accompanying event. Second, the executive might declare an SOE due to a type of reason not specifically mentioned in the constitution. Third, an SOE may be unconstitutional if it is declared by a government actor who does not have the competence to declare an SOE. Finally, an SOE may be unconstitutional even if it is declared by the "correct" actor, but formal conditions (such as the consent of parliament) stated in a constitution are not complied with.

Referring to the second phase, governments can overstep their competences in a variety of ways. They could, possibly even with benevolent intentions, be too active in their rescue missions following a natural disaster by, for example, relying on the military domestically, ignoring binding budget constraints, having rescuers transgress or expropriate private property and thus disrespecting private property rights, and so forth. A second way in which governments can overstep their competences is in strengthening their own position by weakening the opposition: possible means include the dissolution of parliament, postponing elections, and suppressing media freedom (as we explore in Chapters 10 and 12). A third possible way is to weaken other veto players such as the judiciary by, for example, suspending judicial review during an SOE or by creating entirely new courts. A fourth possible way – which might be difficult to delineate in practice from the last two just named – is to strengthen the position of the executive by creating new ministries, relying more heavily on executive decrees and so on.

Finally, unconstitutional behavior can also occur in prolonging an SOE. Many constitutions define a maximum length during which an SOE can be upheld. The most famous of these provisions dates back to republican Rome where the time of the dictator ran out automatically after six months. Should government wish to extend the emergency beyond the maximum length provided for in the constitution, it needs to seek approval by the bodies laid down in the constitution. Government can therefore behave unconstitutionally by either not seeking approval before prolonging an SOE or by prolonging it despite not getting approval from the relevant actor(s).

The baseline for ascertaining unconstitutional behavior of the executive branch is the underlying emergency provisions contained in a country's constitution. In this chapter, we take these provisions as data. But of course, these are not simply given but the consequence of choices made by some constitutional assembly. We analyze both the factors leading to the inclusion of emergency provisions in a country's constitution and the specific type of emergency constitution chosen in Chapters 2 and 3.

11.2.2 Theoretical Considerations

We now move on to discuss possible reasons for why the executive might rely on potentially unconstitutional means. We start from the assumption that the relevant decision-makers act in order to remain in office. In established democracies, this implies seeking reelection and in autocracies it means preventing any potential competitor from becoming too strong. But would-be autocrats might also misuse an emergency as a welcome pretext for getting rid of democratic institutions (as argued by Lührmann and Rooney 2021).

To structure the analysis further, we keep up the distinction between natural disasters and domestic turmoil already used in previous chapters. Among natural disasters, we largely follow the classification already used in Chapter 5 and include biological events (such as malaria or the COVID-19 pandemic), geophysical ones (such as earthquakes), hydrological ones (such as floods), and climatological events (such as droughts). Domestic turmoil, in turn, encompasses mass demonstrations, general strikes, but also assassinations (successful and attempted), and terrorist acts.

We choose this binary categorization because natural disasters are exogenous events beyond the control of governments.[1] Domestic turmoil, in turn, is highly endogenous to government behavior: demonstrations, but also terrorist acts, are often a response to government policies. This distinction is analytically useful for at least two reasons. First, endogeneity and reverse causality are much less of a concern with regard to natural disasters than domestic turmoil. Second, precisely because of the exogenous nature of natural disasters, citizens' reactions to executives violating the constitution might differ from their reactions to executives violating the constitution as a reaction to domestic political turmoil.[2]

Unconstitutional SOEs conducted by executives aiming at safeguarding or even extending their own powers to the detriment of other political actors and the population at large are, on the other hand, much more likely to be caused by domestic turmoil. While natural events cannot reasonably be blamed on the government, domestic events can, giving the incumbents a political incentive to safeguard their position. We use this conceptual framework to propose a number of hypotheses.

1 This refers to the events, but not necessarily to the effects of such events. An earthquake in a region with lax construction regulation or underenforced regulation might, for example, cause more fatalities than the same earthquake in a country with strict construction regulation (Escaleras et al. 2007).

2 As a reader, you may suspect that some events potentially causing the declaration of an SOE are not covered by this binary classification. This could be events such as financial crises, external wars, but also man-made disasters such as the fallout of nuclear power plants or the explosion of chemical factories. In our dataset, there are, however, very few such cases, which is why we constrain the analysis to the two categories just described.

Hypothesis 1: *Executives not respecting the constraints of the constitution during "normal" times are unlikely to respect them during an SOE.*

It might be that their unconstitutional behavior has become a sort of a habit which they will not deviate from after an SOE has been declared. The question then becomes: Why would executives that do not respect the constitution under "normal" circumstances declare an SOE in the first place? A possible reason is that declaring an SOE accords an aura of legitimacy to their behavior.

A government's decision to declare an SOE is heavily influenced by the institutional setting prevailing in a country. In Chapter 4, we analyze the triggers that lead governments to declare an SOE and find that it is crucial to distinguish between natural disasters on the one hand and political turmoil on the other.

Further, autocracies are more likely than democracies to declare an SOE following domestic turmoil whereas no such association can be uncovered with regard to natural disasters. Precisely because domestic turmoil is likely a response to government behavior, it is more threatening to the survival of government. This leads to our second hypothesis.

Hypothesis 2: *Governments will exhibit a higher propensity to renege on constitutional constraints as a consequence of political turmoil than natural disasters.*

Moving on to situations under which the declaration of an SOE is unconstitutional (i.e. referring to phase 1 as introduced earlier), we expect:

Hypothesis 3a: *The more constraints the constitution contains regarding the issuance of an emergency declaration, the more likely it is that the emergency will be declared in contravention of the constitutional constraints.*

Closely related, we expect:

Hypothesis 3b: *Executives in countries with a bicameral legislature are more prone to overstep their competences in declaring an SOE than executives in countries with an unicameral legislature because getting the consent of two houses is more cumbersome than securing the consent of a single chamber.*

Once an SOE has been declared, the executive chooses the means for fighting the emergency (referring to hypotheses of phase 2). And again, it has the choice between relying on means allocated to it under the constitution or to overstep the constitution and to rely on means not in accordance with the constitution.

Hypothesis 4: *The fewer additional competences are allocated to the executive during an SOE, the higher the probability of noncompliance.*

We now move on to the third phase of SOEs in which the executive branch can violate the constitution by not ending it on time.

Hypothesis 5: *The executive is likely to prolong an SOE unconstitutionally to the extent that not doing so represents a likely future threat to the government's survival in office.*

In addition to these hypotheses, we propose to control for a number of potentially confounding influences. If current economic growth is negative, large parts of the population are likely to be unhappy with their government. A natural disaster can be the focal point (Schelling 1960) to kick off anti-government demonstrations to which government is likely to answer by nonconstitutional means.

Finally, we control for whether a constitution is democratic or autocratic. Given that autocrats declare an SOE, we would expect:

Hypothesis 6: *Autocracies will renege more frequently than democratic regimes because many monitoring mechanisms relied upon in democracy are weak or entirely absent.*

11.3 Data

11.3.1 The Dependent Variable

To be able to analyze the determinants that make governments overstep their constitutionally determined competences, a complete list of SOEs – both constitutional and unconstitutional – is needed. The starting point of our analysis is the dataset assembled by Hafner-Burton et al. (2011), which we updated until 2017 and already described in Chapter 4. Making sure that the states of emergency ending up in our dataset all pertain to the national level gives us a universe of 853 cases that occurred between 1949 and 2017.

Then, the unconstitutional SOEs needed to be separated from the constitutional ones. To identify a de jure/de facto gap, government behavior is evaluated relying on the constitution in place in the respective country.[3] To separate lawful from unlawful behavior, we took three steps: We first relied on both legal and journalistic documents provided by two commercial providers, namely Factiva and Lexis/Nexis, combining the search terms "state of emergency" and "unlawful."[4]

Second, we consulted the annual reports of international NGOs that are concerned with basic human rights and political/civil freedom more generally. The reports provided by Freedom House proved to be particularly useful. Third, to determine unconstitutional behavior in phase three, we calculated the length of an SOE in days and compared it to the maximum length stipulated in the constitution. In case the actual length exceeded the constitutionally stipulated length, we searched for information reporting about extensions passed through parliament, and so forth. In case no such information was found, the respective SOE was coded as unconstitutional.

Decisions on whether a particular behavior of the executive is in line with the constitution or a breach of it are always subjective. The question thus is whose evaluation to take into account and whose evaluation to discard. Our search via both Factiva and Lexis/Nexis does not rely exclusively on court decisions but includes evaluations of law professors, NGOs, and journalists reporting on the states of emergency. We deem such a rather broad take to be justified because relying exclusively on courts is likely to give us far too few unlawful states of emergency as the actual independence of courts from the executive is low in many countries.

Relying on Factiva and Lexis/Nexis essentially means that we rely on reports that ran in major newspapers with the vast majority of

[3] Some constitutions read as if they were to make their governments immune from acting unlawfully under an SOE. In 1981, the Malaysian constitution was amended to make the proclamation of an emergency, its continued operation, any emergency ordinance, and continuation in force of those ordinances nonjusticiable (Ramraj 2010, 40). The Pakistani constitution contains a very similar clause (Kalhan 2010, 97).

[4] Although one of our search terms is "unlawful" we also refer to this behavior as "unconstitutional." This is warranted since out of a total of 115 identified cases of such behavior, only three involved noncompliance with statutory law.

Table 11.1 *(Unconstitutional) States of emergency according to both regime type and potential causes*

	Democracies	Autocracies
Natural Disaster	271 (8)	68 (6)
Domestic Turmoil	241 (41)	245 (56)

Note: The first number in each cell indicates the respective number of declared SOEs. In parentheses, we report the number of SOEs that were reported as unconstitutional.

them appearing in English and the richest countries of the world. This is likely to have resulted in some underreporting of SOEs – and correspondingly their unlawfulness – in quite a few countries of the global south. In addition, coverage also depends on the degree to which the domestic press is allowed to report freely as domestic reports are often the initial clues for foreign newspapers to report on events. Finally, both the coverage of events taking place in far-away countries as well as the digitization of newspapers – which is a precondition for inclusion in these databases – is subject to a time-trend. According to our dataset, the vast majority of unlawful SOEs took place post 1990. In all likelihood, it is not the disrespect for constitutional constraints that increased since, but rather the degree of searchable reports.

Table 11.1 splits both constitutional as well as unconstitutional states of emergency with regard to two dimensions, namely democracies versus autocracies on the one hand, and natural disasters versus domestic political turmoil on the other. The numbers before the brackets indicate the overall number of SOEs, the numbers in brackets the number of unconstitutional ones. Whereas in democracies, the numbers of SOEs triggered by political turmoil and natural disasters are almost equally split, autocracies are almost four times as likely to declare an emergency as a consequence of domestic turmoil than of a natural disaster. This may, of course, indicate that autocracies are more likely to experience political turmoil. Yet unconstitutional SOEs are much more likely to be caused by domestic turmoil in both autocracies and democracies, a finding in line with hypothesis 2.

There are a number of reasons to assume that our dataset underestimates the number of unconstitutional SOEs. Quite a few countries

Table 11.2 *Unconstitutional behavior during the various phases*

	All	Natural disasters	Political turmoil	Only demo-cracies	Only auto-cracies
Phase 1 (declaration)	19*	1	16	6	13
Phase 2 (behavior during SOE)	65	4	60	28	38
Phase 3 (temporal extension)	37*	9	30	20	19
Sum**	115	14	97	51	64

*Two man-made cases are dropped out of the analysis (because of low number of observations).[5]

**These phases overlap in several cases. At times, sums do not add up due to missing information.

have been relying on long-standing SOEs, lasting many years or even decades, among them Egypt, Jordan, Sri Lanka, and Syria. With regard to some of them, not a single news report was found claiming that government behavior was unconstitutional. This was the case with regard to Jordan and Syria, but also Zimbabwe (which was under an SOE between 1980 and 1990). Moreover, awareness regarding a government's noncompliance with basic human rights seems to be higher than with regard to procedural provisions also determined by the constitution. It might therefore be that violations of the latter type remain unreported.

In addition to regime type and potential causes, Table 11.2 contains information regarding the phase(s) during which government reneged on constitutional constraints. The overwhelming majority of noncompliance happens during the SOE (with sixty-five reported cases). Constitutional noncompliance in declaring an SOE is reported nineteen times, and noncompliance because an emergency was extended violating the constitution occurred thirty-nine times. These categories overlap slightly, as we find six cases where the constitution

[5] The first case refers to economic problems and occurred in Sierra Leone in 1988 and the second one refers to Trinidad and Tobago in 1990 where the official reason for the SOE was to fight crime caused by drug gangs.

was violated during both the declaration and under the state of emergency and three cases where it was violated during the emergency as well as in an extension of it. Finally, in one case – the Central African Republic in 1981 – the constitution was violated in all three phases. The other four columns allow a more fine-grained distinction with regard to the events having triggered an SOE (natural disasters vs. political turmoil) as well as the type of regime (democracies vs. autocracies).

11.3.2 Explanatory Variables

In the following, we divide our explanatory variables into economic variables, judicial institutions, political institutions, ideological factors, and variables relating to the emergency constitution. Throughout, we control for two factors: average income and whether the country is a democracy. Information on income, which we capture by purchasing-power adjusted GDP per capita, as well as the rest of the economic variables, derive from the Penn World Tables (Feenstra et al. 2015). The remaining economic variables are trade volumes (as percent of GDP), a recession variable that takes the value 1 if growth in a given year was negative, and the investment price and the cost of government spending, both of which are measured relative to the overall price level. The investment price variable captures the price of capital goods relative to consumer goods, and we think of it as a proxy for the impact of emergency restrictions on capital and business owners; with a higher investment price, capital owners will suffer larger losses when being restricted by an SOE. Likewise, the price level of government spending effectively captures the budgetary impact of increasing government spending.

Our source for form of government is Cheibub et al. (2010) as updated by Bjørnskov and Rode (2020). They not only separate democracies and autocracies but also include information on two characteristics of the political institutions: whether the political system is presidential and data to separate unicameral from bicameral legislatures.

We include data on the degree to which the constitution is being complied with by the executive in general. This allows us to ascertain whether governments not complying with the constitution under an SOE are generally low compliers. These data derive from the

Varieties of Democracy (V-DEM) dataset, which is based on country expert ratings and measure the year preceding an SOE. Our two variables capture whether members of the executive respect the constitution (the variable called v2exrescon) and the likelihood that the executive and legislature comply with high court decisions (v2juhccomp). V-DEM creates a continuous latent variable out of expert ratings on a scale from "members of the executive never violate the constitution" to they do so "whenever they want to, without legal consequences" (see Pemstein et al. 2020 for the construction of the latent variable).

Turning to the ideological data, we ask whether the ideological position of the governing party plays any role (in the case of coalition governments the largest party in government). We retrieve that information from the Database of Political Institutions (Scartascini et al. 2018), which contains an indicator which codes whether the party is right-wing (a score of 1), center (2), left-wing (3), or not codable (0). In most cases where the ideological position is not codable, the party is effectively nonprogrammatic, populist, nationalist, or a reflection of pure power politics (cf. Cruz and Keefer 2015).[6]

Finally, turning to the constitutional data, we rely on the Index of Emergency Powers (INEP), well-known to you by now (and described in detail in Chapter 2). We also use two specific components of the overall indices on their own: whether declaring an SOE requires approval from a second chamber, and the number of conditions that justify a declaration, as it provides direct information on the conditions that would make an SOE unconstitutional.[7]

Table 11.3 contains the relevant descriptive statistics of the variables. Given that our dependent variable is binary, we run a set of simple logit estimates to reveal systematic structures in the data. We do so for both the full sample, for all SOEs declared on the basis of a domestic event (by far the most common type), and for all SOEs declared in democracies, which informs about the degree to which democratic polities are different. An appendix also includes a set

[6] In a few cases, parties without ideology in the Database of Political Institutions are regional or separatist parties. We do not code these parties as we have no cases in which the party of the executive was regional or separatist.

[7] We are able to single out these two elements of the INEP, as they are not conceptually overlapping with most other components.

Table 11.3 *Descriptive statistics*

	Mean	Standard deviation	Observations
Unlawful	0.063	0.244	853
Natural	0.400	0.490	847
Domestic	0.574	0.495	847
Man-made	0.027	0.163	846
Democracy	0.628	0.483	853
GDP per capita	9,931	8,933	783
Negative growth	0.331	0.471	782
Government price level	0.863	0.449	783
Investment price level	1.301	0.957	783
Trade volume	0.417	0.307	783
Presidential	0.691	0.462	853
Bicameral	1.427	0.502	793
Nationalist/populist government	0.105	0.306	822
Left-wing government	1.451	1.260	822
High court compliance	0.416	1.244	815
Respect of executive for constitution	0.421	1.178	814
Cost INEP	0.494	0.116	775
Benefit INEP	0.436	0.225	775
Second chamber approval	0.303	0.459	782
Conditions index	0.339	0.215	811

of simpler tests in which we divide the respective sample into two equally large subsamples, one representing cases where the attribute (e.g. income per capita) is below the mean, and the other cases where it is above the mean. When using dummy variables, the sample split is along the lines of the defining criterion (a country has a presidential form of government or not). We then use these subsamples and calculate the proportion of unlawful SOEs among them. Should the difference in proportion between the two subsamples be significant at the 95 percent level, we report them in the figures. All differences, including the insignificant cases, for the first three cases are also listed in Appendix Table A11.1.

Before presenting our main results, a note on challenges regarding causal inference. First, there is amazingly little systematic structure in the data, which is why we refrain from employing more advanced econometric models. Second, in analyses of this type, potential endogeneity is always a major concern. Political turmoil is likely to be a consequence of government behavior while SOEs are often reactions to such turmoil, that is, government reactions to consequences of government decisions. In that sense we are, indeed, likely to have endogeneity and the estimates are likely to be biased.

It nevertheless makes sense to reflect in what ways the estimates are likely to be biased. Governments who have not complied with the constitution all along or governments who plan to behave unconstitutionally after political turmoil might refrain from declaring an SOE altogether. As this, in turn, implies that we would not observe anything with the tools currently employed, it would mean that the relevant endogeneity works against finding any significant results and all results found are rather conservative estimates.[8]

Any attempt at alleviating the nonrandom sampling problem would itself yield a biased sample. We therefore aim for describing simpler patterns in the data and in many cases refrain from making causal claims.

11.4 What Is Common to Unlawful SOEs?

We begin by illustrating the overall use of SOEs and the likelihood that they are unlawful in two world maps. Figure 11.1 shows the density of SOEs across the world and thus illustrates where our 853 events took place, while Figure 11.2 shows where the 115 unlawful SOEs that we identify typically occurred. As both maps show, most events took place in Africa and Asia although a substantial number is reported for European and Latin American countries.

[8] This issue is closely connected with the problem of our nonrandom sample as governments not having abided by the constitution while running an SOE have not been randomly drawn. Unfortunately, implementing a Heckman two-step model to correct for nonrandom sampling cannot be applied here because the procedure requires large amounts of data. Moreover, applying the Heckman correction in our case implies estimating the probability of observing an SOE given that a potentially triggering event has been detected. The requirement of such models that one can relatively precisely identify the selection stage defeats our purpose, because some SOEs are declared without any such event ever having taken place.

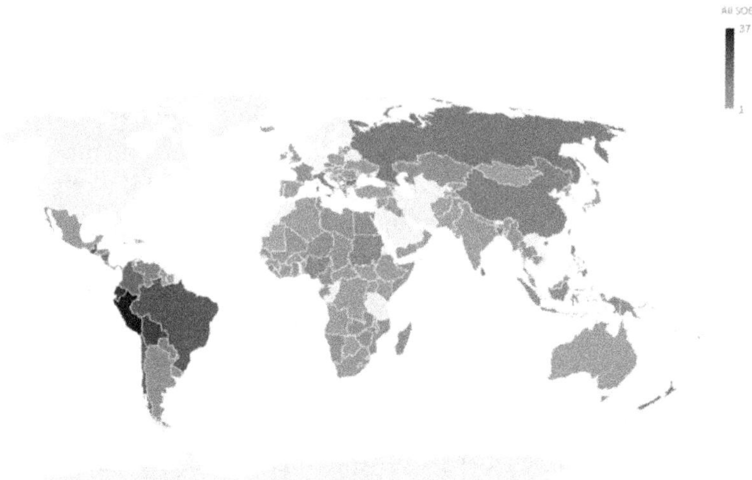

Figure 11.1 Frequency of state of emergency

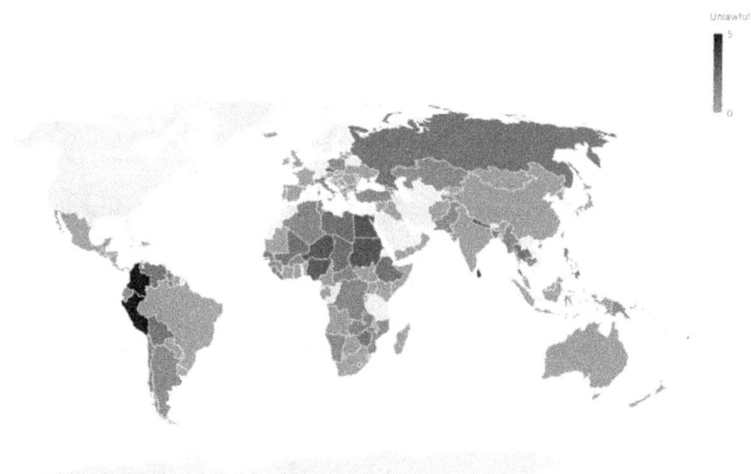

Figure 11.2 Frequency of unlawful state of emergency

11.4.1 Descriptive Differences

One of the clearest common features in unlawful SOEs is that the majority of the events are due to political turmoil – ninety-seven of the 115 unlawful SOEs we identify are declared for such reasons.

We find only fourteen cases in which an unlawful emergency declaration was justified by natural disasters and five in which the cause was man-made disasters. Regarding the duration of SOEs, of the observations with full information, 63 percent ended exactly at their maximum allowable duration. Only 15 percent are ended before their constitutionally demanded expiry, while 22 percent are lawfully extended beyond that date. For unlawful SOEs, in turn, the corresponding numbers are 13, 21, and 66 percent. Lawful SOEs last 115 days on average while the average duration of unlawful SOEs is 321 days. The difference in lengths is statistically significant at the 1 per cent level.

11.4.2 Main Results

Findings for the full sample are shown in Table 11.4. Throughout, we find that democracies are substantially less likely than autocracies to behave unlawfully in the context of an SOE (cf. hypothesis 6). Calculating the odds ratio from the output in column 1 suggests that the probability of observing an unlawful SOE in a democracy is about 75 percent of the probability in an autocracy. We also find that unlawful SOEs are less likely in richer countries.

Turning to the specific groups of explanatory variables, we find suggestive evidence of four variables: relative investment price levels, presidential systems, bicameral political systems, and the need for emergency approval from a second chamber. While investment prices are negatively correlated with the likelihood of observing an unlawful SOE, the remaining variables are positively correlated with this likelihood. However, when tested against each other (not shown), only presidentialism and having a bicameral system remain statistically significant. They are also practically meaningful as the odds ratio of having a presidential system (relative to a parliamentary) suggests that unlawful SOEs are approximately 70 percent more likely in presidential systems. Likewise, unlawful SOEs are approximately 50 percent more likely in bicameral systems, a finding consistent with hypothesis 3b.

We present comparable results in Table 11.5 where we focus only on domestic turmoil, which includes ninety-seven of the 115 unlawful SOEs. We first note that this change renders income insignificant

Table 11.4 *Empirical results*

	1	2	3	4	5	6	7
Log GDP per capita	–0.275**	–0.321**	–0.219*	0.217*	–0.273**	–0.299**	–0.336***
	(0.117)	(0.129)	(0.122)	(0.131)	(0.117)	(0.128)	(0.124)
Democracy	–0.849***	–0.908***	–0.752***	–0.999***	–0.854***	–1.110***	–1.060***
	(0.228)	(0.233)	(0.262)	(0.237)	(0.237)	(0.244)	(0.252)
Trade volume		–0.180					
		(0.403)					
Inv. price		–0.322*					
		(0.186)					
Gov. price		–0.196					
		(0.239)					
Recession		–0.176					
		(0.232)					
High court compliance			0.071				
			(0.111)				
Executive respect			–0.178				
			(0.121)				
Presidential				0.547*			
				(0.293)			
Bicameral				0.398*			
				(0.226)			
Left-wing					–0.128		
					(0.087)		

	(1)	(2)	(3)	(4)	(5)	(6)	(7)
Nationalist/populist					−0.312		
					(0.347)		
Cost INEP						1.467	
						(1.038)	
Benefit INEP						0.368	
						(0.515)	
Conditions index							0.089
							(0.561)
Second chb. app.							0.593**
							(0.243)
Observations	783	782	774	724	776	718	715
Pseudo R sq	0.047	0.057	0.050	0.062	0.053	0.066	0.070
LR Chi squared	29.17	35.36	30.81	34.54	32.55	38.74	40.67

Note: All results are obtained by a logit estimator with all regressions including a constant term. Numbers in parentheses are standard deviations. ***(**) [*] denote significance at $p < 0.01$, ($p < 0.05$), and [$p < 0.10$].

Table 11.5 ***Empirical results, domestic events only***

	1	2	3	4	5	6	7
Log GDP per capita	–0.067	–0.168	–0.042	–0.043	–0.062	–0.049	–0.127
	(0.135)	(0.150)	(0.138)	(0.153)	(0.135)	(0.155)	(0.148)
Democracy	–0.520**	–0.662***	–0.629**	–0.717***	–0.469*	–0.917***	–0.788***
	(0.248)	(0.256)	(0.292)	(0.261)	(0.258)	(0.277)	(0.278)
Trade volume		0.146					
		(0.410)					
Inv. price		–0.479**					
		(0.224)					
Gov. price		–0.049					
		(0.216)					
Recession		–0.409					
		(0.253)					
High court compliance			0.141				
			(0.123)				
Executive respect			–0.060				
			(0.132)				
Presidential				0.236			
				(0.319)			
Bicameral				0.532**			
				(0.251)			
Left-wing					–0.135		
					(0.099)		

	(1)	(2)	(3)	(4)	(5)	(6)	(7)
Nationalist / populist					−0.206		
					(0.402)		
Cost INEP						2.688**	
						(1.356)	
Benefit INEP						−0.007	
						(0.554)	
Conditions index							0.277
							(0.636)
Second chb. app.							0.700***
							(0.273)
Observations	450	449	446	394	445	392	390
Pseudo R sq	0.013	0.034	0.016	0.031	0.018	0.035	0.039
LR Chi squared	5.74	15.46	7.20	12.37	7.89	14.51	16.05

Note: All results are obtained by a logit estimator with all regressions including a constant term. Numbers in parentheses are standard deviations. ***(**) [*] denote significance at $p < 0.01$, ($p < 0.05$), and [$p < 0.10$].

Table 11.6 *Empirical results, democracies only*

	1	2	3	4	5	6	7
Log GDP per capita	−0.344*	−0.350	−0.079	−0.364*	−0.329*	−0.205	−0.442**
	(0.178)	(0.219)	(0.216)	(0.194)	(0.185)	(0.194)	(0.189)
Democracy	-	-	-	-	-	-	-
Trade volume		0.616					
		(0.615)					
Inv. price		0.104					
		(0.228)					
Gov. price		−1.184**					
		(0.587)					
Recession		0.154					
		(0.356)					
High court compliance			0.228				
			(0.229)				
Executive respect			−0.622**				
			(0.281)				
Presidential				0.129			
				(0.393)			
Bicameral				0.441			
				(0.331)			
Left-wing					0.033		
					(0.144)		

Nationalist / populist					0.708		
					(0.688)		
Cost INEP						1.796	
						(1.755)	
Benefit INEP						−1.801*	
						(0.964)	
Conditions index							−0.066
							(0.901)
Second chb. app.							0.724**
							(0.342)
Observations	491	491	485	489	484	476	475
Pseudo R sq	0.012	0.0341	0.030	0.019	0.016	0.028	0.029
LR Chi squared	3.62	9.08	8.76	5.48	4.57	7.95	8.42

Note: All results are obtained by a logit estimator with all regressions including a constant term. Numbers in parentheses are standard deviations. ***(**) [*] denote significance at $p < 0.01$, ($p < 0.05$), and [$p < 0.10$].

throughout the table while democracy remains statistically significant and practically important. Of our explanatory variables, four retain significance: the relative investment price levels, bicameral political systems, the Cost INEP measure, and the need for emergency approval from a second chamber. The positive correlation between the difficulty of lawfully declaring an SOE and the likelihood of observing an unlawful one is in line with hypothesis 3a. Testing these variables against each other again, we find robust support for two of the four: the relative investment price level and having a bicameral system. While unlawful SOEs appear about 60 percent more likely in bicameral systems, having a higher investment price level reduces the likelihood considerably.

Our final tests in which we repeat the analysis based on a sample of democratic countries only is reported in Table 11.6. We here find only fragile evidence for an effect of income while the main explanatory variables appear to be the relative price level of government spending, executive respect for the constitution, the Benefit INEP, and whether emergency declarations require approval from a second chamber. Higher benefits for the executive under an SOE are, hence, associated with a lower probability of an unlawful SOE, a finding in line with hypothesis 4.

Repeating our robustness exercise for the democratic-only subsample reveals support for three explanatory variables (not shown). While income remains very far from significance, the cost of government spending appears to substantially drive down the likelihood of unlawful SOEs, as does executive respect for the constitution, as assessed by experts in the year preceding the emergency, a finding predicted by hypothesis 1. Conversely, requiring second chamber approval more than doubles the likelihood that an SOE is going to be unlawful. As we find this result for the complete sample as well as for two different subsamples, we consider it robust (and in line with hypothesis 3b).

As such, comparing results across Tables 11.4 and 11.6 can provide some information about differences between democracies and autocracies. Of the results in Table 11.4, the effects of relative investment prices and presidentialism are clearly driven by the autocracies in our sample while the results pertaining to the relative price level of government spending, executive respect for the constitution, and second chamber approval are exclusively driven by the democracies in our full sample.

Overall, we thus find that apart from being a full democracy, specific economic, judicial institutional and features of the emergency constitution all affect the likelihood of observing unlawful SOEs. In all cases, the results are easily interpretable as consequences of either economic or political costs of keeping an SOE within constitutional bounds.

11.5 Conclusions

This chapter analyzes the determinants that make executives behave unconstitutionally with regard to an SOE. It distinguishes between unconstitutionality in declaring, running, and ending SOEs. Interestingly, the vast majority of nonconstitutional SOEs occur subsequent to domestic turmoil and not subsequent to a natural disaster.

We find that autocrats are a lot more likely not to comply with constitutionalized emergency provisions as are executives that have not respected the constitution even prior to the triggering event. Poor countries are significantly more likely to suffer from an unlawful emergency than rich countries, even when they are democratic. Following domestic turmoil, countries that are in recession are particularly prone to experience a nonconstitutional state of emergency. Finally, when the focus is exclusively on democracies, then executives from "nonprogrammatic parties" are far more likely to implement an unconstitutional SOE than nonnationalist executives.

Unfortunately, we are unable to test all our hypotheses due to data constraints. Given the finding by Lührmann and Rooney (2021) that SOEs often open a slippery slope toward democratic backsliding, we suspect that at least in some cases the measures implemented during an SOE survive its end and become standard practice. To ascertain whether this really is the case, more fine-grained data are needed. Given that exactly two thirds of all unlawful SOEs remain in place too long, it seems not only warranted to do more research on this aspect but also to ask what means can be implemented to reduce this particular kind of unconstitutional behavior.

Appendix

Table A11.1 *All simple differences*

	Full sample			Democracies			Domestic events		
Democracy	0.20	0.09	$p < 0.01$	0.03	0.17	$p < 0.01$	0.22	0.17	$p < 0.12$
Presidential	0.11	0.15	$p < 0.10$	0.09	0.09	$p < 0.72$	0.19	0.20	$p < 0.71$
Bicameral	0.12	0.15	$p < 0.29$	0.09	0.10	$p < 0.50$	0.17	0.24	$p < 0.07$
Population	0.12	0.15	$p < 0.35$	0.08	0.09	$p < 0.62$	0.18	0.23	$p < 0.15$
GDP per capita	0.18	0.09	$p < 0.01$	0.11	0.07	$p < 0.08$	0.22	0.18	$p < 0.18$
Trade	0.16	0.11	$p < 0.03$	0.12	0.06	$p < 0.02$	0.21	0.19	$p < 0.68$
Investment price	0.14	0.13	$p < 0.74$	0.09	0.09	$p < 0.86$	0.22	0.18	$p < 0.26$
Government costs	0.17	0.09	$p < 0.01$	0.13	0.05	$p < 0.01$	0.22	0.18	$p < 0.38$
Recession	0.13	0.14	$p < 0.79$	0.08	0.10	$p < 0.49$	0.10	0.30	$p < 0.01$
Social trust	0.11	0.14	$p < 0.28$	0.08	0.09	$p < 0.87$	0.16	0.21	$p < 0.18$
Rule of law	0.15	0.12	$p < 0.26$	0.09	0.09	$p < 0.88$	0.18	0.22	$p < 0.26$
HC compl.	0.15	0.12	$p < 0.19$	0.09	0.09	$p < 0.81$	0.22	0.16	$p < 0.16$
Exec. compl.	0.18	0.09	$p < 0.01$	0.12	0.06	$p < 0.02$	0.22	0.17	$p < 0.20$
Right-wing	0.13	0.16	$p < 0.40$	0.09	0.2	$p < 0.08$	0.19	0.19	$p < 0.88$
After 1990	0.11	0.14	$p < 0.24$	0.12	0.09	$p < 0.49$	0.11	0.26	$p < 0.01$
SOE conditions	0.14	0.13	$p < 0.60$	0.08	0.12	$p < 0.11$	0.16	0.25	$p < 0.02$
Cost INEP	0.15	0.13	$p < 0.52$	0.09	0.11	$p < 0.55$	0.23	0.21	$p < 0.62$
Benefit INEP	0.15	0.13	$p < 0.29$	0.09	0.09	$p < 1$	0.22	0.21	$p < 0.79$

12 *The COVID-19 Pandemic, States of Emergency, and Reliance on Executive Decrees*

12.1 Introduction

By May 10, 2020, ninety-nine governments, equal to almost precisely half of all sovereign governments, had declared a state of emergency (SOE) due to the arrival of a new Corona virus, called COVID-19 or SARS-COV-2. The Italian government was the first to declare an SOE on January 31, 2020 and many other governments followed suit during March 2020. Such a wave of SOE declarations is completely novel. As we reported in Chapter 4, between 1985 and 2014, the governments of at least 137 countries declared an SOE at least once. This number – spread over a period of 30 years – appears almost dwarfish compared to the Corona-induced wave, which occurred in less than four months. As virtually all countries were affected by the virus at approximately the same time, governments were all trying to fight the virus, and their responses can be easily compared. This is akin to a natural experiment and constitutes a very rare setting enabling us to compare the determinants of declaring an SOE across virtually all countries in the world.

Alluding to both particular crises as well as governments' responses to them, Reinhart and Rogoff (2009) entitled their book on centuries of financial crisis management *This Time Is Different.* Although during most crises, it is claimed that this time is really different, they showed that things weren't so different after the financial crisis of 2008–09 and that history does seem to repeat itself. In this chapter, we ask a similar question: If hundreds of thousands are going to die and millions to lose their jobs, shouldn't one assume that governments call an SOE because they want to save lives? Although emergency provisions have been misused time and again in the past, shouldn't one expect that this time really is different?

Calling an SOE typically implies a shift in the balance of powers toward the executive to the detriment of the other government branches, but also to the detriment of citizens who enjoy fewer civil liberties. Sometimes, elections are postponed, parliaments are shut down, and if the courts are prevented from hearing cases, a judicial review of emergency measures applied by government is often close to impossible. There are already plenty of examples of the misuse of emergency provisions during the 2020–22 pandemic. Casual observation seems to indicate that we had no reason to worry less this time around:

- Parliaments unable to meet in a number of countries due to the pandemic. The government of Mauritius, for example, suspended its national assembly (Budoo 2020), and the Thai government turned down the request of its parliament for an extraordinary session (Tonsakulrungruang and Leelapatana 2020). Four days before declaring an SOE, the Serbian government prohibited gatherings of more than 100 people. Based on that decision, it argued that the parliament could not meet – with the consequence that the SOE was not confirmed by the Serbian parliament, which it is required to do according to the Serbian constitution (Cavdarevic 2020). Not to be controlled by parliament seemed to be a desirable state of affairs for many governments.
- Court operations were suspended in many countries. Without doubt, this was often done to protect both parties involved in court cases as well as judges and court personnel. Yet there are also cases in which the closing of courts simply meant that government policies could not be challenged in court anymore. This was the case in Bangladesh (Hoque 2020) and Nigeria (Abdulrauf 2020), among others. In Egypt, an amendment was passed that allows military courts to investigate any case discovered by a military officer. In other words, civilians can now be tried in front of military courts again (Ellaboudy 2020).
- In a number of countries, the military was brought in to enforce government measures. This was, for example, the case in Iran (Alasti 2020) as well as in democratic Malaysia and Denmark (Andersen and Bjørnager 2020; Balasubramaniam 2020). Domestic operations of the military always entail the danger that the military will remain an important player even after the SOE has been lifted.
- Journalists were not only targeted in repressive societies such as Belarus, where authorities on May 6 removed the official accreditation of Russia's Channel One that had reported on the spread of

> COVID-19 virus in the country (CPJ 2020). In the United Kingdom, police threatened the journalist James Delingpole with fines if he reported on a protest against the government's corona lockdown in London's Hyde Park. The event was recorded by several people and went viral on Twitter. Similarly, the South African government since mid-March 2020 prevented epidemiologists and other health experts from commenting on COVID-19 without coordinating with the National Institute for Communicable Diseases. In the Philippines, President Duterte refused to renew the license of the most popular Philippine television channel ABS-CBN (BBC 2020).

These are casual observations, and many more could be listed. Making judgments on a limited number of examples can be misleading – and even dangerous. This is why we are aiming at a more systematic analysis here. In this chapter, we first inquire into the factors that provoked governments to declare an SOE in 2020. If declarations were clearly driven by the desire to save lives, things would be different this time. If, on the other hand, emergency declarations were motivated by political economy factors, things would not be so different after all. And indeed, we find that things were not so different. We then ask how governments used the extra powers that they enjoyed after declaring an SOE. Here, we focus on one policy measure that does not rely on contentious evaluations regarding various health-related policy measures namely how governments have behaved toward the media. This is why we ask to what degree media freedom was upheld even after an SOE was declared. We find that the protection of journalists – and free expression more generally – does not seem to be high on the agenda of many governments, thus echoing our findings from Chapter 10 in which we find that SOEs declared subsequent to terrorist events are likely to decrease media freedom even if it is protected in a country's constitution.

In addition to SOEs, very little is known about the factors determining the use of executive decrees in general. We hypothesize that some governments use them as an alternative to calling an SOE. We find that this is, indeed, the case with regard to reactions to COVID-19. The use of executive decrees has rarely ever been analyzed on a cross-country level. This chapter is a very first in that direction. It is certainly desirable to employ similar analyses with regard to other policy measures.

The rest of the chapter is structured as follows. Section 12.2 spells out a number of hypotheses regarding the COVID-19 pandemic as a possible cause for declaring an SOE. In Section 12.3, we describe our data and the estimation approach, and Section 12.4 contains the estimates. Section 12.5 concludes.

12.2 Hypotheses

Following directly from the dismal record of governments regarding their use of emergency powers described in Chapters 5 and 6 in particular, we hypothesize that this time is not different. Formulated differently:

Hypothesis 1a: *The less difficult it is for government to declare an SOE, the more likely that an SOE has been declared in relation to COVID-19.*

And analogously:

Hypothesis 1b: *The more benefits a government enjoys after having declared an SOE, the more likely an SOE has been declared in relation to COVID-19.*

If, however, this time really is different, then we would expect the state of public health with regard to COVID-19 to be the main determinant for declaring an SOE. These hypotheses are competing, and we run a horse race to see which hypothesis is more consistent with the data.

In the literature on the determinants of calling SOEs, executive decrees have nevertheless played no role so far. We propose to change that here based on the conjecture that governments having at their disposal far-reaching executive decree powers have fewer reasons to resort to SOEs, *ceteris paribus*. Carey and Shugart (1998, p. 9) define decree power as "the authority of the executive to establish law in lieu of action by the assembly." Power-maximizing executives that have been granted far-reaching decree powers by their country's constitutions might, therefore, consider decrees and SOEs as substitutes. We conjecture that executives enjoying far-reaching decree powers will, indeed, be less likely to call an SOE. Argentine President Fernández, for example, did not declare an SOE during the pandemic but issued some fifty emergency decrees instead (Gargarella 2020). The Indian government declared a tough nation-wide lockdown based on executive decrees only. An SOE was not declared – and parliament was not involved at any time (Bhatia 2020). In both countries, SOEs are extremely unpopular due to previous cases in which emergency powers have been blatantly misused, which might explain why governments relied upon their decree powers as a substitute.

In our analysis of declaring a COVID-related SOE, we propose to control for three aspects, namely, the quality of political institutions, the level of economic development, and the capacity of the health system. The quality of political institutions can be ascertained in a variety of ways such as the degree to which the rule of law and press freedom are realized. In our context, the distinction between democratic and autocratic forms of government seems to be crucial. We assume that constitutions of democratic countries put more constraints on the executive than constitutions of autocratic countries. If the decision to declare an SOE is driven by the additional benefits associated with it, it follows directly that democratic governments have more incentives to declare an SOE.

The expected effect of controlling for the level of economic development is not entirely clear: During the pandemic, many governments have resorted to lockdowns, shutdowns, quarantine, and the like. For people in poor countries without a full-blown welfare state, such measures can easily spell disaster. This leads us to expect that poorer countries are less likely to declare an SOE. However, one may also argue that people in richer societies are better able to avoid risks of contagion that are endemic to poorer societies, and thus may not have a need for government-mandated lockdowns. Conversely, the effect of capacity in the health system is straightforward if government behavior is consistent with official justification of it. Many executives explicitly argued in March 2020 that a lockdown and other measures were necessary for a short while to protect hospitals and other parts of the health system from exceeding their capacity limits.

Governments do not enjoy getting criticized, a fact which holds for both democratic as well as autocratic governments. Disasters may therefore serve as a welcome pretext to curtail media freedom. Governments hope to get away with arguments such as "curtailing media freedom only prevents rumors and false information to spread," which could lead to additional uncertainty among the population. As a consequence of the pandemic, a number of countries have, indeed, passed legislation making the spreading of "fake news" a criminal offense although leaving the definition of "fake" an open question. We therefore hypothesize that:

Hypothesis 2: *Governments that declared an SOE also run more events against journalists.*

12.3 Data and Estimation Approach

The central variable of this study is if and when countries declared an SOE. We coded this variable ourselves based on international news reports where we require at least two independent sources in order to code the onset of an SOE. We compared our list to one compiled by the Centre for Civil and Political Rights. Figure 12.1 documents the cumulative number of countries that had declared an SOE between January 31, 2020, and April 10, 2020. The first is Italy, which declared an SOE on January 31st with effect from the next day.

Next, we obtained events against journalists from the Eurozine/Index database, which was updated daily during the spring and summer of 2020. The database is maintained at Eurozine, a network of European cultural journals that also publish an online magazine, and

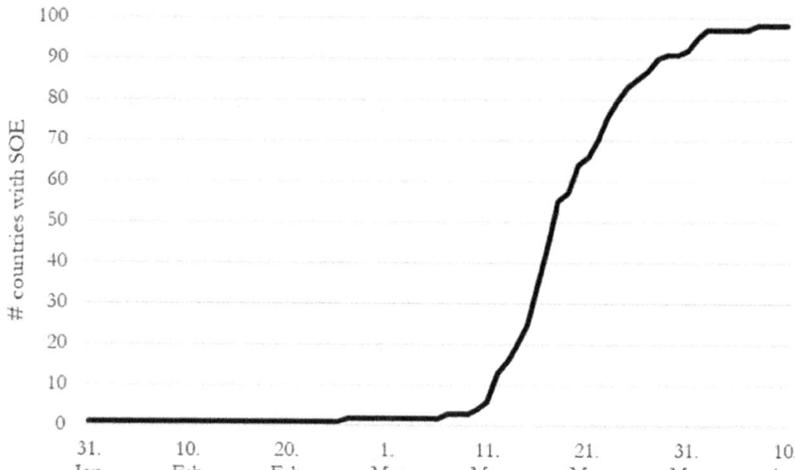

Figure 12.1 Emergency declarations

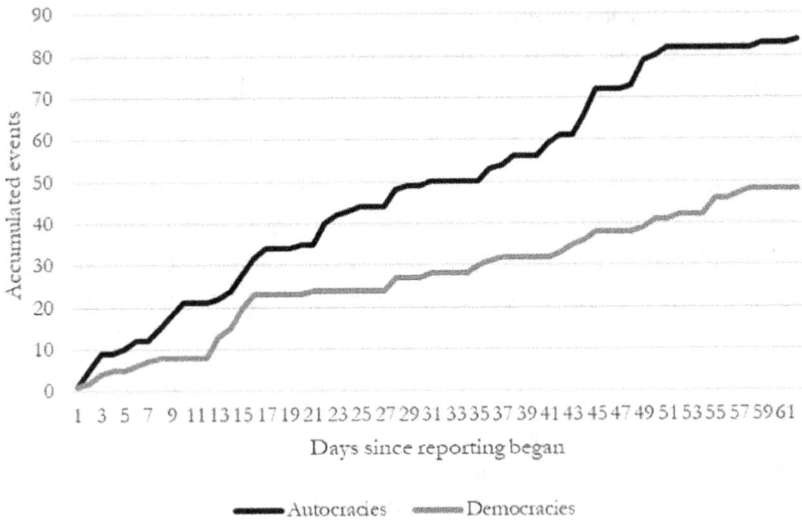

Figure 12.2 Repressive events against journalists and media

rests on daily reports on events against journalists from members of the network. The database covers a number of events against journalists, of which we only include the detention or arrest of journalists, journalists being prevented from reporting, new legislation that restricts media freedom, government U-turns on media policy (signals that government may with some probability no longer tolerate critical media), restrictions on social media, and crackdowns on so-called fake news. We supplement these data with a full confirmation of these events and our own media search for similar events since February 1, 2020, making sure that they were not related to other emergencies at the same time. The number of reported events against journalists is depicted in Figure 12.2, in which we distinguish between democracies and autocracies.

We supplement these data with information on a number of features. To code the power of governments to resort to executive decrees without having to declare an SOE, we create a new indicator, constitutionalized decree powers. It is based on a number of variables provided by the Comparative Constitutions Project (Elkins et al. 2009), coded such that the indicator can take on values between 0 and 2 with higher values indicating more government powers. A score of 0 means that no political actor has decree power while a score of 2 means that both the head of state and the head of government separately have full decree powers not constrained by parliament.

With respect to institutional and economic data, we employ the dichotomous democracy indicator from Bjørnskov and Rode (2020), the rule of law indicator from the Worldwide Governance Indicators (World Bank 2021), the Reporters Without Borders (2020; RSF) index of violations of press freedom, and the logarithm to real GDP per capita and population size from the CIA (2020). We included these on the basis of the following expectations: Democracies are expected to be more likely to declare an SOE because the power differential between normal and emergency times is larger than for autocracies. A high score in the rule of law indicates that governments have complied with abstract rules and that general rules are taken seriously in a high scoring country. This is why we expect governments with a high score to be less likely to declare an SOE. The media is free to discuss and criticize government behavior in countries that do well with regard to press freedom. Given that governments do not enjoy being criticized for limiting citizens' civic freedoms, we expect governments in countries scoring well with regard to press freedom prior to the pandemic to be less likely to declare an SOE. We report that governments of more populous countries are not only more likely to declare an SOE but also to reduce civil liberties once an SOE has been declared (as described in Chapter 5). This is why we include it here too. In analyses of events against journalists, we effectively compare the number of events with the "normal" situation in the country and with periods without an SOE.

In addition, we add the number of hospital beds per one thousand inhabitants as a measure of the capacity in the health system, thus providing a direct test of the official justification of most executive action in early 2020; the data are from the World Bank (2021). Finally, data on the number of people diagnosed with COVID-19, and the number of deaths associated with COVID-19 are from Our World In Data (Roser et al. 2020), which was also updated on a daily basis through the COVID-19 pandemic. Our health data covers January 1st through May 10th, and we use the logarithm to the days since January 1st, the logarithm to the official number of infected, and a dichotomous indicator capturing whether any infections were observed on or before a given date.

In both estimates, we employ a logit estimator as both outcome variables are dichotomous; we employ random effects as a number of our main variables of interest are time-invariant within our relatively short time period. With SOE as the dependent variable, countries drop out of the sample once they have declared an SOE. While we only find 132 events against journalists, which may be considered a small number relative to the total number of observations, we do not believe it is sufficiently small to warrant the use of a rare events estimator or some form of rare events correction. Given that this type of correction might be needed, our estimators are likely to be conservative. Our unit of observation are country days. All variables are described in Appendix Table A12.1.

12.4 Results

In this section, we first analyze the factors that lead governments to declare an SOE before turning to the question of whether declaring an SOE has any effects on the number of recorded events against journalists.

12.4.1 Factors Leading Governments to Declare

As described above, the general question is whether the declaration of an SOE is primarily driven by the state of public health with regard to COVID-19 or alternatively by the political attractiveness of calling an SOE. With regard to the state of public health, Table 12.1 shows that the (log) number of people affected make the declaration of an SOE more likely, but that neither the number of days passed since the first person infected was identified nor the question whether anybody was infected are significant determinants. We proxy the quality of the political system by the levels of democracy, the rule of law, and press freedom. It turns out that countries enjoying a high level of the rule of law as well as a high level of press freedom are less likely to declare an SOE, whereas neither the level of democracy nor the level of economic development are significant predictors for declaring an SOE. We also find no evidence that declaring an SOE is related to the capacity of the health system.

According to the results reported in Table 12.1, the difficulty of declaring an SOE as measured by the Cost INEP was not a predictor for the wave of declarations in the spring of 2020. The additional powers that accrue to a government once it has declared an SOE as

Table 12.1 *Determinants for declaring an SOE*

	1	2	3
Democracy	-0.371	-8.442*	–
	(1.022)	(3.859)	
Rule of law	-4.232**	-4.336**	-4.934**
	(0.892)	(0.922)	(1.322)
RSF press freedom	-0.279**	-0.294**	-0.153
	(0.058)	(0.062)	(0.085)
Log GDP per capita	0.374	0.122	1.413
	(0.632)	(0.678)	(1.053)
Log population size	-0.720*	-0.796*	-1.277**
	(0.339)	(0.369)	(0.465)
Log hospital beds	0.045	0.065	-0.036
	(0.585)	(0.596)	(0.742)
Log days since start	0.306	0.364	0.205
	(1.064)	(1.119)	(1.162)
Log infected	1.066**	1.128**	1.367**
	(0.238)	(0.246)	(0.314)
Any infected	1.789*	1.722	1.409
	(0.867)	(0.884)	(1.103)
Cost INEP	3.518	-7.927	6.059
	(3.312)	(5.578)	(3.775)
Benefit INEP	8.148**	7.714**	10.148**
	(1.962)	(2.529)	(2.815)
Cost at Democracy		15.455*	
		(6.747)	
Benefit at Democracy		2.094	
		(3.521)	
Observations	9665	9665	5896
Countries	158	158	95
Log likelihood	-371.563	-369.905	-257.545
Wald Chi squared	53.04	55.71	38.83

Note: **(*) denote significance at $p < 0.01$ and ($p < 0.05$). Estimates are obtained with a random effects logit estimator and include a constant term.

indicated by the Benefit INEP are, however, highly significant. The interaction term in Column 2 even suggests that the effect of additional powers may be slightly stronger in democracies. As hypothesized above, the political attractiveness of gaining substantial discretionary

Table 12.2 ***Probability of SOE declaration depending on emergency as well as decree powers***

		Decree index	
		Low	High
Benefit INEP	Low	0.79 (0.18)	0.41 (0.45)
	High	0.79 (0.57)	0.60 (0.20)

Note: Numbers in parentheses pertain to autocracies.

power is, thus, not limited to autocratic governments. The last column of Table 12.1 refers to democracies only. By and large, democratic governments are driven by the same factors as autocratic ones. If anything, the amount of additional benefits a government enjoys once it has declared an SOE may play a more important role in democracies in comparison to autocracies such that democracies with particularly permissive emergency constitutions are indistinguishable from autocracies in emergencies.[1] We also asked whether extensive decree powers can be used by a government as an alternative to declaring an SOE. Governments – no matter whether democratic or autocratic – were significantly more likely to declare an SOE if decree powers were low and the benefits from declaring high than when decree powers were high and the benefits from declaring low. We summarize these findings in Table 12.2, where we show the probability that democracies (autocracies in parentheses) have declared an SOE, given that they are above or below the median of emergency powers and decree power.

[1] Beyond the variables included in Table 12.1, we also asked if the generalized level of trust is associated with SOE declarations. It turns out that high trust democracies are significantly less likely to declare an SOE, but this result might be entirely driven by the Scandinavian countries. We did not include trust in the main models because the data are available for significantly fewer countries than those included in Table 12.1. These results are available upon request. The measure of social trust used in them follows the standard in the literature by using the dichotomous question of whether people believe that most people can be trusted. The data derive from the World Values Survey as well as the Barometer surveys.

Taken together, these results are perfectly in line with previous findings: Governments – no matter whether democratic or autocratic – are more likely to declare an SOE if this conveys more benefits to them and allows them to increase their competences to the detriment of both the other branches of government as well as citizens at large. In that sense, things have not been different this time. However, declaring an SOE does not automatically entail negative consequences for citizens. Therefore, we ask how governments have used their additional powers during the pandemic. We refrain from analyzing and evaluating the consequences of short-term measures such as quarantine, lockdown, or efforts to track and trace individuals; this is the topic of a specialized literature with which we do not engage. Rather, we are interested in trends that might very well have effects outlasting the current pandemic by, for example, changing policies and de facto institutions.

12.4.2 Effects on Media Freedom

As a consequence of the pandemic, a number of countries have passed legislation making the spreading of "fake news" a criminal offense although leaving the definition of "fake" an open question. We therefore ask whether there is a significant association between events against journalists and SOEs.[2]

Our operational definition of "events against journalists" includes new legislation to restrict media freedom, detention or arrest of journalists, journalists not allowed to report, and crackdowns on "fake news." Table 12.3 shows that fewer such events are expected in democracies, but are more likely in larger countries and after anyone had been infected. Conversely, we do not find any clear association with the stage of the pandemic (as measured by the number of days since December 31, 2019) or how many people were infected. Importantly, a government that had declared an SOE was no more likely to stage such events than governments that had not declared.

It remains a possibility that passing fresh legislation curtailing media freedom is a precondition for observing events against

[2] There are various measures for media freedom. Unfortunately, none of them were available for 2020 at the time of writing, which is why we resort to the number of events directed against journalists.

Table 12.3 ***Determinants of events against journalists***

	1	2	3
Democracy	−1.635**	–	0.496
	(0.379)		(1.218)
SOE	0.405	0.765	0.422
	(0.295)	(0.546)	(0.293)
Rule of law	−0.140	−0.307	−0.123
	(0.222)	(0.587)	(0.222)
RSF press freedom	−0.000	0.025	0.004
	(0.014)	(0.041)	(0.014)
Log GDP per capita	0.227	0.092	0.236
	(0.170)	(0.506)	(0.168)
Log population size	0.680**	0.787**	0.664**
	(0.105)	(0.218)	(0.108)
Log days since start	0.423	0.087	0.403
	(0.423)	(1.474)	(0.422)
Log infected	−0.032	0.012	−0.029
	(0.055)	(0.146)	(0.056)
Any infected	1.661*	–	1.645*
	(0.753)		(0.753)
Cost INEP	−0.099	−3.405	0.910
	(0.743)	(1.881)	(1.313)
Benefit INEP	0.210	0.215	0.466
	(0.553)	(1.253)	(0.643)
Cost with SOE			−3.459
			(2.345)
Benefit with SOE			−1.122
			(1.195)
Observations	11,344	6174	11,344
Countries	162	99	162
Log likelihood	−510.909	−145.349	−509.223
Wald Chi squared	89.10	46.49	92.53

Note: **(*) denote significance at $p < 0.01$ and ($p < 0.05$). Estimates are obtained with a random effects logit estimator and include a constant term.

journalists. Table 12.4 counts the number of events against journalists, taking into account whether any such legislation has been passed (both before and after possible events). According to the numbers reported in the table, it seems fairly irrelevant whether a country first

Table 12.4 *Sequence of events against journalists*

		De facto changes		
		None	First	Second
De jure changes	None	–	27 (13)	–
	First	8 (1)	–	5 (3)
	Second	–	7 (5)	–

Note: Numbers in parentheses refer to democracies.

introduced new legislation or not. Finally, a specific result is worth mentioning: When we only look at one particular category among the events against journalists, namely journalists arrested, and how often autocracies resort to such behavior, we find that 16 percent of those autocracies whose emergency provisions convey few benefits to the government have arrested journalists, compared to 52 percent of those autocracies conveying many benefits. This difference is significant at the one per cent level. Clearly, the contents of emergency constitutions do seem to matter also in autocracies, while we find no clear differences among democracies. Note that the likelihood of arrests in democracies and autocracies with few emergency benefits does not differ significantly.

In describing and evaluating government action during the pandemic, some other scholars have drawn conclusions somewhat different from ours. We take up two such views here and begin with Pozen and Scheppele (2020) who are concerned with what they refer to as "executive under-reach." They position this notion in direct opposition to executive overreach, in other words, the evaluation arrived at in this study.

Pozen and Scheppele (2020) are concerned with (heads of) governments who are not sufficiently active in protecting their populations against the pandemic – based on the implicit assumption that lockdowns were effective in combating the COVID pandemic – and explicitly refer to Brazilian president Bolsonaro and US president Trump. In principle, such an evaluation is completely compatible with ours: that there are many governments that overreach does, of course, not exclude some governments that under-reach. More to the point, under-reach is not necessarily equivalent with the decision not to declare an SOE. We insist that there exist many potentially effective policy options below the declaration of an SOE.

In a paper entitled "The Bound Executive: Emergency Powers during the Pandemic," Ginsburg and Versteeg (2021) argue that legislatures, courts, and subnational government units have played an important role in constraining national executives and that the claim of executive overreach might, therefore, be overblown. It is definitely true that in many countries, these actors have behaved as veto players who have monitored the executive and also constrained it somehow. We are less optimistic in interpreting the overall evidence, however. The simple fact that in many countries, the respective top courts have dealt with dozens of suits in which the executive was held to have overstepped its competences can not only be interpreted as evidence in favor of the constraining role of the judiciary, but also in the frequent attempts of the executive to broaden its competences to the detriment of citizens' freedoms.

12.5 Conclusions and Outlook

Summing up, it seems safe to conclude that this time is not different. As under previous natural disasters, democratic and autocratic governments alike have behaved like power-maximizers during at least the first wave of the COVID-19 pandemic. We find that the discretionary power they gain during emergencies is the main determinant of whether they declared an SOE, while the severity of the epidemic is irrelevant. As mentioned in the introduction, this is also likely to be the first study that asks whether executives perceive executive decrees as substitutes of states of emergency and use them accordingly. With regard to COVID-19, we show that this is, indeed, the case. Future research should ask whether this insight also holds with regard to states of emergency not related to the pandemic. We also observe that those executives that have declared an SOE as a consequence of the pandemic may be likely to misuse these powers against journalists and the media. The danger, as under previous disasters, is that some of the measures now implemented are likely to outlast the current pandemic and weaken the rule of law and democracies for many years to come. In fact, in many countries the ultimate victim of the corona virus may be the separation of powers and freedom of expression.

What implications follow from these results? This question is pressing as Lührmann and Rooney (2021) observe that the declaration of an SOE often initiates a process of democratic backsliding. Getting rid of emergency constitutions entirely is no adequate answer. As reported in Chapter 4, countries without an emergency constitution are more likely to declare an SOE than countries having incorporated emergency provisions into their constitutions, *ceteris paribus*. More generally speaking, incorporating emergency provisions into the constitution makes government behavior more predictable, independently of the reduced likelihood of declaring.

To reduce the likelihood that the contemporaneous use of emergency provisions will have long-term repercussions on the separation of powers and the rule of law more generally, it seems to make sense to include a number of provisions into emergency constitutions. First, states of emergency should only be allowed for a limited time clearly spelled out in the provisions. Second, any legislation passed under an SOE should automatically cease to be valid with the end of the emergency. To keep it beyond the emergency phase, legislation should be subject to broad public discussion and pass the conventional parliamentary readings again. Both these insights were realized in the Roman Republic more than two millennia ago but appear to have been forgotten in the meantime. Third, the judiciary could be allocated the power of ex post–judicial review. On the one hand, experience with such provisions is not entirely encouraging. On the other, apex courts have increasingly demonstrated their willingness to constrain governments in their behavior, so allocating them with the competence to review government behavior promises to make executives more rule abiding in their implementation of an SOE. Regardless of one's ideological position and constitutional preferences, the dramatic use of SOEs during the COVID-19 pendemic should force all political actors as well as the media and academics to reassess the use of emergency powers.

Appendix

Table A12.1 ***Descriptive statistics***

	Mean	Standard deviation	Observations
SOE	0.277	0.447	13527
Events against journalists	0.009	0.096	11371
Democracy	0.642	0.479	13527
Rule of law	0.169	1.026	13527
RSF press freedom	33.108	15.270	13527
Log GDP per capita	9.687	1.128	13527
Log population size	16.394	1.752	13527
Log hospital beds	0.786	0.890	13403
Log days since start	4.186	0.728	13527
Log infected	3.872	3.380	13490
Any infected	0.748	0.434	13526
Cost INEP	0.525	2.094	13527
Benefit INEP	0.393	0.223	13527

13 *Returning to the Status Quo Ante?*[*]

13.1 Introduction

As noted elsewhere in this book, the main purpose of declaring a state of emergency (SOE) is often held to be to return to the status quo as rapidly and fully as possible. Natural disasters such as hurricanes, earthquakes, and floods cause substantial physical and economic damage. The same is sometimes the case for man-made disasters, including such diverse events as pollution disasters, insurgencies, and violent coup attempts.

Yet emergencies often also cause major institutional and political disruptions. As shown in previous chapters, these disruptions may include reducing civil liberties, reducing media freedom, reducing the protection of property rights by allowing expropriation, and increasing regulatory control. To understand the medium- and long-term consequences of SOEs, it is necessary to understand how fast – and if at all – countries return to the status quo ante. In other words, are institutional setbacks during emergencies permanent or transitory, and to which extent?

This chapter deals with these questions by exploring the speed with which countries return to the institutional quality and protection of civil liberties they exhibited prior to an emergency. Across 850 emergencies around the world, we find that a fair share of countries return to their status quo ante very rapidly. However, our results also indicate that in countries with particular political characteristics, the return to the status prior to the emergency can be very lengthy and may not happen de facto.

[*] This chapter is written with considerable inspiration from Emily Johnson's master's thesis *Understanding States of Emergency: Path to the Status Quo Ante* from the University of Hamburg in 2022, which we jointly supervised. We are grateful to Emily for allowing us to reuse much of her research.

13.2 Returning to the Status Quo Ante: Definitions and Incentives

When considering why some societies return faster than others to the status quo ante after emergencies, we must define what is meant by status quo ante. This is complicated by the fact that the status quo emerges from a conceptually complex process full of interdependent choices made along separate dimensions (Buchanan 2004). It is therefore not a simple condition decided upon by the incumbent or a former executive but can better be thought of as a multi-dimensional "balance sheet." This balance sheet both includes economic development and distribution (not least the stock of physical capital), the health status of the population, political institutions, and the legal and policy framework.

In this chapter, we focus on the institutional framework as it defines and limits behavioral options for all members of society (cf. North 1990). Regarding the status quo ante, we explicitly take the quality of legal institutions, the protection of civil liberties, and the relative absence of government repression immediately prior to a declared SOE into account. In other words, we focus on the effects that SOEs have on the quality of legal institutions and two consequences of reduced quality: repression and weaker civil liberties.

As indicated elsewhere in this book, SOEs often undermine civil liberties and most emergency constitutions actively allow the executive to do so during an SOE. When an SOE is declared, the legislature may for example not need to be consulted to impose restrictions such as curfews, constraints on domestic movement, or limitations of the freedom of expression. Judicial attitudes may also tend to shift toward helping to uphold restrictions imposed by the executive instead of protecting citizens' rights, and thereby lead to fewer constraints on the executive in practice (Hafner-Burton et al. 2011). As we discuss in Chapter 14, legal scholars often assert that temporarily derogating civil and political rights may allow the executive branch to more effectively deal with an emergency at hand. Ignatieff (2013) describes it as the "lesser evil" compared to a lengthy and destructive emergency, given that short-term derogations, in practice, reduce casualties and lessen the time required to return to the status quo ante. However, in natural disasters, this tends not to be the case as we show in Chapter 5.

Our main focus in this chapter is on the return to the status quo ante, that is, what happens *after* the immediate disaster or domestic event that justified an SOE has occurred. Whether the government is democratically elected or not, our theoretical starting point is – contrary to much legal thinking on the topic – that the primary motivation of politicians is to gain and stay in power. As noted in several chapters, the declaration of an SOE may therefore be grounded in a desire to remain in power. Likewise, an SOE for entirely justifiable and constitutional reasons can be used as a vehicle to stay in power or maximize the chances of winning a coming election, or simply increase the power of the incumbent government.

We therefore expect that the more power the constitution grants the executive branch during an emergency, the less incentive will the executive have in giving up the SOE and the additional power it enjoys. This power might, for example, be used to benefit special interests or to campaign for reelection.[1] It may also be used for numerous other purposes that would be impossible to steer through parliament in non-emergency times. The incumbent executive therefore has little incentive in returning to the status quo ante but will most likely want to maintain a long period with reduced checks and balances, reduced media freedom, and more discretionary power than under normal circumstances to the extent that the constitution actually grants it additional power. It may even extend these privileges past the framework of the emergency constitution through amendment of statutory law so that once the emergency formally ends, it has more capacity than before the declaration. This leads us to our first testable hypothesis.

Hypothesis 1: *The more power is granted to the executive by the constitution, the longer will it take to return to the status quo ante.*

However, emergency constitutions also regulate the ease with which an SOE can be declared. These components of the constitution give rise to two opposite incentives. First, if it is easy to call an SOE, government may return to the status quo ante quickly because the additional discretionary power granted during an SOE is relatively easy to reestablish in a subsequent emergency. Second, constitutions that

[1] The New York Post reported in December 2020 under the title “Billions in foreign aid, pet projects stuffed into COVID relief bill” that that the 2.3 trillion USD COVID-19 relief bill included 15 billion USD in support of live entertainment venues such as Broadway, as well as numerous other special interests (Nelson 2020). The report was subsequently discussed in the US Congress and criticized by both parties.

make declaration fairly easy also often make prolonging emergencies comparatively easy. This second element thus makes it easier for governments to prolong a status of weakened checks and balances and repression and therefore return only slowly to the status quo ante – if at all. This leads us to two opposing hypotheses.

Hypothesis 2a: *The easier it is to call an SOE, the faster will society return to the status quo ante.*

Hypothesis 2b: *The easier it is to call an SOE, the slower will society return to the status quo ante.*

In addition to the constitutional restrictions, the particular shape of the status quo ante may affect the time it takes to reestablish it. On the one hand, we expect that better institutions will objectively make it easier to reestablish the status quo ante. Boudreaux et al. (2023), for example, suggests that governance institutions moderate the effects of natural disasters. Their theoretical argument is that good institutions support entrepreneurial activity that is central to rebuilding society and reestablishing the status quo ante economic situation. In addition, high-quality, independent judiciaries are more likely to be able to protect themselves from being undermined than politically dependent judiciaries in autocracies.

On the other hand, the better the institutions, the more they restrict political action and repression, and the more they enforce citizens' civil liberties, the more does the executive stand to "gain" from declaring an SOE. In other words, declaring an SOE in a society with poor institutions is unlikely to allow the executive particularly more de facto discretionary power, while in one with good institutions, the power gain will be substantial. We therefore also expect that the better the pre-emergency institutions are, and the better citizens' civil liberties are protected, the longer will it take to return to the status quo ante. This leads us to our third hypothesis.

Hypothesis 3: *The better the pre-emergency institutions, the longer will it take society to return to the status quo ante.*

Finally, we also expect effects to be particularly strong in democracies. While one might argue that politicians and the executive in strongly coup-proofed autocracies in principle can derogate citizens' rights and intervene in judicial decisions without risking consequences, the same is not the case in democracies. Most democracies differ from most autocracies by being characterized by relatively strong veto institutions that restrict politicians' power to affect institutions (cf., Tsebelis 2002). In such circumstances, declaring an SOE implies a much larger change in political institutions and the "rules of the game" by significantly lifting barriers to politics. This leads us to our final testable hypothesis.

Hypothesis 4: *Effects of institutions and emergency provisions are more pronounced in democracies.*

13.3 Data and Empirical Strategy

In order to assess how emergency constitutions affect the time needed to return to the status quo ante, and test our hypotheses, we employ four different indicators. For each, we create a count variable starting in the year of an SOE and counting each year until the level of the indicator just prior to the SOE is reached again. This allows us to estimate a duration model, as is regularly done in, for example, studies of consequences of unemployment policy. Our four indicators are the Fariss indicator of government repression, the civil liberties index from the *Varieties of Democracy* project, the overall rule of law index from the same source, and real GDP per capita from the Penn World Tables, which serves as a comparison to the institutional measures; sources are Fariss (2014), Coppedge et al. (2016), and Feenstra et al. (2015).

The repression indicator from Fariss (2014), which we also use elsewhere, combines all standards-based and events-based indicators available for a large group of countries since 1950; we use the data starting in 1970. The index captures the latent degree of absence of repression, that is, higher values indicate less repression. We rescale the index to a scale from 0 to 1 in order to ease comparability with the other two indicators. The civil liberties index is a broad indicator formed of separate subindices capturing the existence of property rights, protection from forced labor, freedom of religion and repression of religious organizations, and freedom of foreign and domestic movement (private civil liberties), freedom from political killings and torture (physical violence), and freedom from government censorship, harassment of journalists, media self-censorship, freedom of discussion, absence of party ban and barriers to political parties, opposition parties' autonomy, and free civil society entry and exit and absence of repression (political civil liberties). Finally, the rule of law index is also a composite index consisting of measures of compliance with high court decisions, compliance with the judiciary, high and lower court independence, executive respect for the constitution, the existence of rigorous and impartial public administration and transparent laws with predictable enforcement, access to justice for citizens, judicial accountability, and five different indicators measuring the relative absence of corruption, theft, and embezzlement in the public sector and politics.

We combine these data with real GDP per capita, trade volumes (as percent of GDP) and population size from the Penn World Tables, mark 10 (Feenstra et al. 2015), and dummies capturing whether a failed or successful coup occurred in a country in a given year, and a dummy for the existence of electoral democracy. The latter data are from Bjørnskov and Rode's (2020) dataset on regime types and regime changes with the democracy indicator based on a minimalist conception of democracy. As in previous chapters, we supplement these data with the Cost and Benefit INEP measures of the ease of calling an SOE and the additional constitutional power given to the executive branch during emergencies; see Chapter 2 for details. All data are summarized in Table 13.1.

Table 13.1 ***Descriptive statistics***

Variable	Mean	Standard deviation	Observations
Count, repression	8.863	9.405	1859
Count, civil liberties	6.936	7.452	1585
Count, rule of law	9.576	9.700	1980
Count, GDP per capita	10.111	10.117	840
Initial repression	0.465	0.262	1789
Initial civil liberties	0.633	0.243	1513
Initial rule of law	0.462	0.262	1886
Failed coup	0.020	0.148	10984
Successful coup	0.015	0.126	10984
Log population	2.304	1.472	7105
Log GDP per capita	8.980	1.225	8322
Recession	0.269	0.444	8146
Trade volume	0.565	0.832	8451
Democracy	0.518	0.499	10928
Cost INEP	0.466	0.113	7234
Benefit INEP	0.355	0.226	7234

Our empirical approach in this chapter is dictated by the fact that we have count variables: Our focus is on the number of years it takes to reestablish the status quo ante. As such, we estimate a duration model capturing the likelihood that a country remains in a state of more repression/poorer civil liberties or rule of law/lower real GDP per capita. To do so, we use a random-effects parametric survival model in which we assume that survival is exponentially distributed.

Throughout, we add decadal fixed effects which, for example, pick up effects of the Cold War prior to 1990, and after the 9/11 terrorist attacks and changes in terrorism policy after 2001. We also interact the INEP measures as well as direct measures of the status quo ante – the pre-SOE repression, civil liberties, rule of law, and GDP per capita – with our democracy indicator in order to assess whether effects are larger in democracies as a direct test of hypothesis 4.

13.4 The Raw Data

We begin by providing an impression of the raw data. This is not only important to justify our empirical assumption of exponentially distributed data – which they rather clearly are – but also to give readers a sense of the scope of the problem.

Starting with the Fariss indicator of government repression, which we have used in other chapters, we find that of a total of 416 SOEs for which we have full data, 249 (60 percent) did not result in any increase in repression. Conversely, we also observe that after forty-four events (11 percent), it took a decade or longer to return to the pre-SOE level of repression. Using the V-Dem civil liberties index as an alternative indicator, we find that 374 of 502 (75 percent) did not experience any decline in the protection of formal civil liberties. We also see that after forty-seven events (9 percent), that is, a similar share and in most cases the same events as using the Fariss indicator, it took a decade or longer to return to the civil liberties that citizens enjoyed prior to the SOE.

These developments are visible in Figure 13.1, in which we plot the frequency of the years to status quo ante, given that an SOE results in either an increase in repression or a decline in the respect for citizens' civil liberties. As the figure illustrates, in the majority of cases reestablishment takes one or two years; in 80 percent of all cases, repression is back to "normal" after two years. Reestablishing civil liberties takes

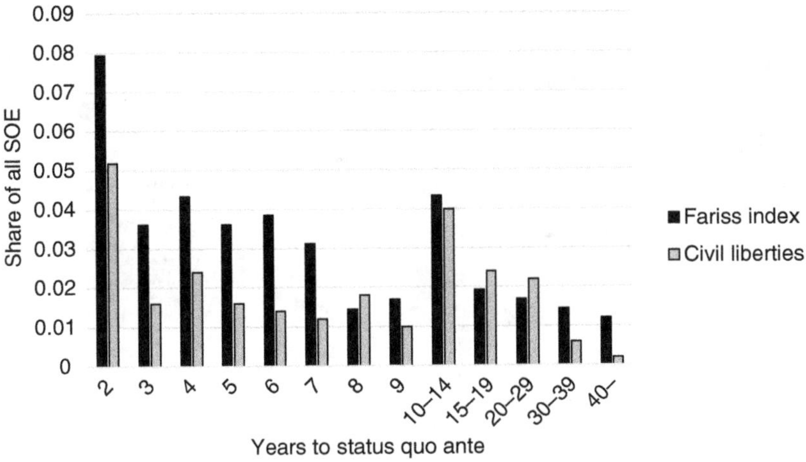

Figure 13.1 Number of years to status quo ante

one or two years in 52 percent of all cases and exceeds 80 percent after four years. As such, to the extent that the indicators are sufficiently precise to make such claims, it appears that direct repression declines more rapidly than other more subtle ways of violating civil liberties during and after an emergency.

In other words, in the majority of cases we find that the status quo ante remains, or at least is reestablished so rapidly that we cannot measure any decline with the available data. This is also reflected in Figure 13.2, which illustrates the average shape of repression around an SOE, depending on whether it was declared in a democracy or autocracy – depicted by black and gray lines, respectively, and whether the SOE was lawful or not – in full or dotted lines (see Chapter 11). The Fariss index increases in all cases prior to the SOE (cf., Fariss 2019), and only declines marginally in the year of the SOE when autocracies declare lawful SOEs. The only group in which the average country experiences a clear increase in repression (a decline in the index) is autocracies that declare SOEs and where either the declaration or the regime's behavior during the emergency is unlawful.

These patterns are even more pronounced when we focus on the rule of law and average income. The patterns around the rule of law resemble government repression closely with 82 percent of all emergencies playing out without a decline in the quality of the legal system

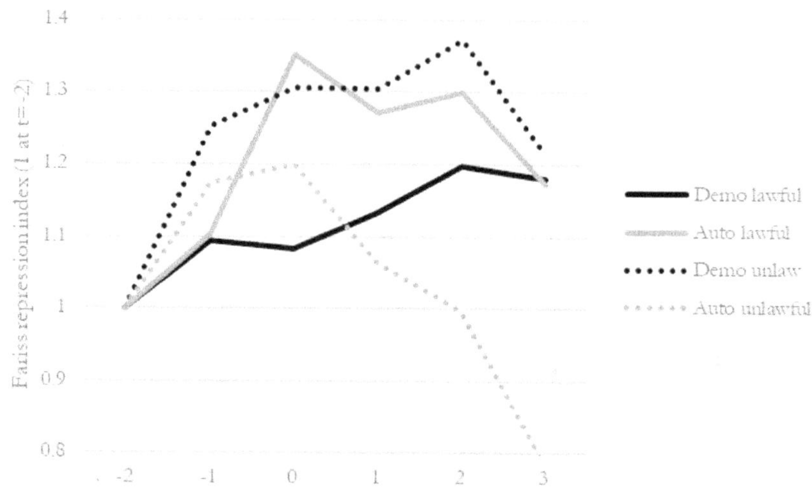

Figure 13.2 Typical developments of repression around SOE

that is visible within a year. Income losses are even less likely, as we find that real GDP per capita only declines in 10 percent of our cases. This is potentially important as we use the income dynamics around SOEs as a comparison to institutional changes in the following.

13.5 Empirical Results

We report the results of estimating the determinants of the duration of a decline in repression and the respect for civil liberties in Table 13.2. Focusing first on the control variables, we find only four instances in which they are significant when we use the Fariss repression index. When not directly controlling for the initial level of repression, that is, the specific status quo ante, we find that trade volumes increase the duration of the repression increase. We also find that successful coups actually shorten the duration of direct repression but do not affect the duration of a decline in respect for civil liberties.[2] When controlling

[2] This ambiguity reflects an ambiguity in the literature on coups. While it is clear that institutional quality declines after most coups, as recently shown by Bennett et al. (2021), some coups evidently result in democratization (cf., Derpanopoulos et al. 2016; Thyne and Powell 2016). The degree to which coups are good for democracy and when they result in democratization remains an open and highly contentious question.

Table 13.2 *Duration of repression increase after SOE*

Indicator	1 Fariss repression	2 Fariss repression	3 V-Dem civil liberties	4 V-Dem civil liberties
Failed coup	0.994 [0.698; 1.418]	1.002 [0.704; 1.427]	1.261 [0.812; 1.958]	1.299 [0.839; 2.013]
Successful coup	0.568** [0.359; 0.899]	0.617** [0.380; 0.999]	0.982 [0.497; 1.943]	0.974 [0.495; 1.919]
Log population	0.908 [0.795; 1.037]	0.902 [0.784; 1.039]	0.941 [0.825; 1.074]	0.921 [0.810; 1.047]
Log GDP per capita	0.903 [0.759; 1.073]	0.726*** [0.599; 0.879]	0.927 [0.784; 1.098]	0.872 [0.735; 1.033]
Recession	0.949 [0.817; 1.103]	0.955 [0.819; 1.112]	0.983 [0.831; 1.164]	0.997 [0.841; 1.182]
Trade volume	1.577** [1.011; 2.460]	1.242 [0.781; 1.975]	1.092 [0.697; 1.712]	0.930 [0.594; 1.458]
Democracy	0.958 [0.386; 2.381]	0.422 [0.143; 1.250]	0.621 [0.239; 1.615]	0.202 [0.054; 0.752]
Initial repression		3.837*** [1.269; 11.593]		1.696 [0.644; 4.468]
Cost INEP	0.496 [0.094; 2.604]	0.405 [0.079; 2.081]	0.332 [0.071; 1.555]	0.385 [0.085; 1.743]
Benefit INEP	1.030 [0.472; 2.248]	0.829 [0.364; 1.886]	0.512 [0.217; 1.211]	0.508 [0.217; 1.188]
Cost INEP * Democracy	0.665 [0.112; 3.954]	1.182 [0.196; 7.125]	3.764 [0.573; 24.742]	4.122 [0.653; 26.022]
Benefit INEP * Democracy	2.658** [1.098; 6.430]	2.629** [1.039; 6.644]	2.820** [1.062; 7.487]	2.531* [0.963; 6.654]
Initial repression * Democracy		2.865* [0.986; 8.328]		4.329** [1.149; 16.302]
Decadal FE	Yes	Yes	Yes	Yes
Observations	1203	1192	944	927
Countries	113	112	114	113
Wald Chi squared	89.53	123.35	108.83	129.90
Log likelihood	−3510.829	−3462.919	−2429.585	−2362.974

Note: The estimates are hazard ratios and the intervals in brackets are the 95 percent confidence intervals of the hazard ratios. All regressions include a constant and decade fixed effects.

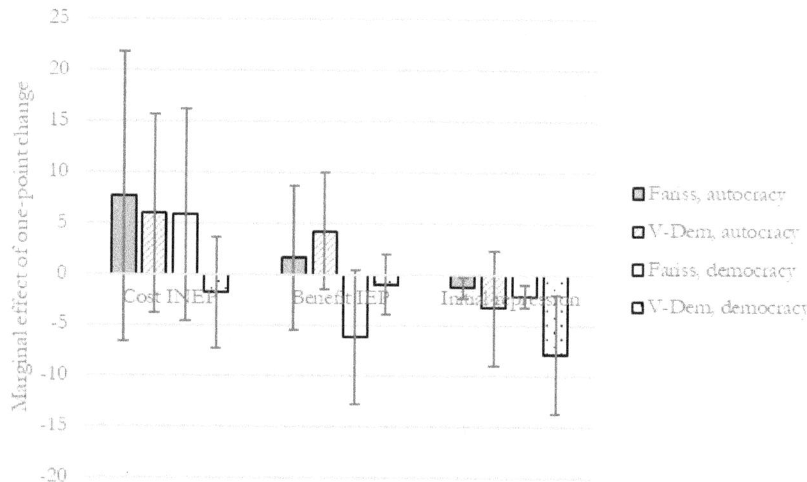

Figure 13.3 Marginal duration effects, repression in autocracies and democracies

for the initial level, we find that SOEs in societies with little repression cause longer periods with more repression during and after the SOE, but shorter durations in richer societies. However, we fail to find similar differences when focusing on civil liberties.

Turning to the question of whether constitutionalized emergency powers make a difference, we find clear evidence that they do. Using the Fariss index, we find that a higher Benefit INEP is associated with longer duration – that is, a longer period with more repression after an SOE has been declared – and particularly so in democracies. As we illustrate in Figure 13.3, we also find larger effects of the Benefit INEP when the initial level of repression was low, in which case we also observe a longer duration in which civil liberties are less respected, and larger effects when the country is democratic at the onset of an SOE. Conversely, we do not find evidence that the Cost INEP significantly affects duration. Overall, focusing on repression and civil liberties, we therefore find evidence in favor of hypotheses 1, 3, and 4.

We reestimate the associations using two alternative indicators: the rule of law and real GDP per capita. The point of the exercise in Table 13.3 is that we ought to find similar patterns around declines in the rule of law after an SOE while there is little reason to expect that declines in average incomes follow similar patterns if our estimates reflect institutional changes caused by discretionary policy. Successful

Table 13.3 *Duration of declines in rule of law and GDP after SOE*

	1	2	3	4
Indicator	V-Dem rule of law	V-Dem rule of law	GDP per capita	GDP per capita
Failed coup	1.017	1.136	0.965	1.009
	[0.717; 1.443]	[0.696; 1.856]	[0.622; 1.498]	[0.546; 1.864]
Successful coup	0.566**	0.627	1.694*	1.517
	[0.358; 0.895]	[0.305; 1.289]	[0.998; 2.874]	[0.729; 3.156]
Log population	0.924	0.909	0.945	1.091
	[0.807; 1.059]	[0.769; 1.073]	[0.790; 1.129]	[0.893; 1.333]
Log GDP per capita	0.855*	0.639***	1.587***	59.134***
	[0.721; 1.014]	[0.508; 0.806]	[1.289; 1.952]	[19.252; 181.629]
Recession	0.935	0.955	1.535***	2.297***
	[0.808; 1.081]	[0.735; 1.118]	[1.266; 1.862]	[1.660; 3.179]
Trade volume	1.723**	1.204	0.753	0.832
	[1.112; 2.672]	[0.613; 1.989]	[0.402; 1.410]	[0.448; 1.548]
Democracy	1.023	0.263**	1.751	3.855
	[0.409; 2.553]	[0.069; 0.987]	[0.543; 5.647]	[0.109; 136.747]
Initial RoL / GDP		2.665		0.021***
		[0.634; 11.211]		[0.006; 0.072]
Cost INEP	0.382	0.435	0.974	0.425
	[0.073; 2.007]	[0.065; 2.906]	[0.109; 8.648]	[0.026; 7.097]
Benefit INEP	1.042	0.624	0.669	0.702
	[0.475; 2.289]	[0.199; 1.958]	[0.262; 1.711]	[0.243; 2.026]
Cost INEP * Democracy	0.604	1.856	0.446	0.708
	[0.100; 3.637]	[0.189; 18.224]	[0.041; 4.887]	[0.026; 19.173]
Benefit INEP * Democracy	2.554**	4.056**	0.786	0.530
	[1.052; 6.198]	[1.110; 14.812]	[0.265; 2.333]	[0.119; 2.356]
Initial RoL / GDP * Democracy		3.164		0.908
		[0.710; 14.089]		[0.612; 1.347]
Decadal FE	Yes	Yes	Yes	Yes
Observations	1272	643	521	231
Countries	114	99	79	60
Wald Chi squared	104.20	81.22	108.03	151.44
Log likelihood	−3800.386	−3462.919	−1580.5388	−663.833

Note: The estimates are hazard ratios and the intervals in brackets are the 95 percent confidence intervals of the hazard ratios. All regressions include a constant and decade fixed effects.

coups are followed by less durable declines in the rule of law, and hence a rapid return to the status quo ante, while the reverse is the case for average income (see Bjørnskov 2022; Grier et al. 2023). We also find that richer countries return faster to the status quo ante respect for the rule of law, emphasizing the role of wealth for institutional stability, but more slowly to their pre-SOE average income. Most pertinently, we find that the more permissive the emergency constitution is – the higher the Benefit INEP is – the longer is the period in which the rule of law is worse than prior to the SOE.

We do not find this pattern around income declines, underlining our interpretation that our findings are caused by active policy choices and not simple wealth changes. As such, we can dismiss the worry that what we find is simply a reflection of general crises. We see how a repression measure and two directly related indicators follow similar patterns of decline and recovery to the status quo ante following an SOE, but not incomes.

13.6 Discussion and Conclusions

When declaring an SOE, most governments gain additional discretionary power to use during the emergency. Although there is no clear consensus, many legal scholars argue that these powers are important and necessary to deal with emergencies – a question that we address in other chapters of this book – but must seize once it is over. Yet, although the emergency per se may be over, emergency policies and institutional changes may persist longer after an earthquake, terrorism attack, or coup is over. How long such changes persist is the topic of this chapter.

We here find that countries in which the constitution grants the executive branch substantial discretionary power once it has declared an SOE are slower in reestablishing the status quo ante: The more power the executive gains in an emergency, the longer does it take to get back to the (lower) level of government repression and (higher) level of civil liberties that citizens enjoyed prior to the emergency. This is particularly the case for democracies, and particularly the case when the pre-SOE status was characterized by little repression and strong protection of civil liberties. The finding from Chapter 5 that societies in which the emergency constitution grants the executive branch more power suffer more deaths during natural disasters serves as a sinister background to grasping these particular results.

One way to think of these findings is in terms of institutional resilience: How much does it take to push the institutional framework more or less permanently in a nonbenevolent direction? In his recent book, Brunnermeier (2021) specifically thinks of resilience as the capacity of a system to revert to the mean. There are different ways to apply this concept of resilience to our topic: exploring how quickly societies get from an SOE to calling it off again; how effectively societies deal with emergencies; and how quickly and stably societies get back to the status quo ante.

A starting point is that in many emergencies, the question is not how to get rescue efforts or other initiatives going, but one of how to get from an unconstitutional state of affairs to a constitutional state of affairs. Declaring an SOE can therefore be a way to legalize and legitimize initiatives to address the emergency that have already begun, and which in many cases may violate statutory legislation as well as regular constitutional rules. Elsewhere in this book, we ask if these actions are effective – and as we show in Chapter 5, this is evidently not the case in the context of natural disasters – and if they are constitutional.

Yet Brunnermeier also emphasizes that part of the institutional resilience of a society – regardless of the background for the emergency and the specific actions government takes – is the ability to get back to the pre-SOE state of affairs in an orderly and quick way. Our chapter speaks to this particular aspect of resilience in a particular way. We find that the time it takes to return to the status quo ante is longer when institutional quality is better, when the country is a democracy, and when the emergency constitution grants the executive more power. The sum of these three factors lends itself to specific interpretation: The more power the executive stands to gain during an emergency relative to the de facto situation prior to declaring an SOE, the longer does it take to reestablish the status quo ante.

In other words, resilience in this context is strongly negatively associated with the power given to the executive. If anything, our estimates regarding the importance of constitutional powers are biased downward because executives who do not gain any real additional power after declaration may choose not to declare a constitutional emergency at all. Resilience may therefore be even higher in countries such as the three Scandinavian countries that never declare an SOE (see Chapter 4).

Our main findings are thereby entirely consistent with public choice theory emphasizing that politicians primarily aim at maximizing power and staying in office. The perhaps most worrying aspect, from a democratic political point of view, is that the duration effects we find in this chapter are strongest in societies that otherwise have the strongest institutions – democracy, better rule of law, and limited repression. They therefore serve to emphasize the dangers associated with emergencies, and particularly with granting the executive relatively wide-ranging, unconstrained emergency powers.

14 Contracting for Catastrophe

Legitimizing Emergency Constitutions by Drawing on Social Contract Theory

14.1 Motivation

In this book, we have analyzed many different aspects of states of emergency (SOEs) and the emergency constitutions often underlying them. We have analyzed the design of emergency constitutions, the factors that make governments use them, the various effects that SOEs have, the specific issues related to SOEs under federal constitutions, as well as their misuse. Regarding the type of analysis, all the previous chapters have one thing in common, namely that the analysis has been positive: We described and explained things, but did not try to justify anything on a moral or philosophical basis. But this is exactly what we are up to now: We ask how the existence of emergency constitutions could possibly be justified – given our knowledge of the often undesirable side effects that unravel once an SOE is declared.

Many academic treatises order things exactly the other way round: They start by legitimating exercises and only then proceed to have a look at the – often unpleasant – empirical facts. In his famous Feuerbach thesis, Karl Marx states that philosophers have only explained the world but that it would be crucial to change it. We beg to differ: changing the world presupposes that we know how the world works. In other words, positive knowledge should preceed normative thinking – and this is why this chapter is placed after all the chapters analyzing things from a descriptive and explanatory angle.

Emergency constitutions are invoked when the stakes arguably are very high. If their institutionalization is inadequate, catastrophe can result. As cited in previous chapters, Loveman (1993) argued that the emergency constitutions prevalent in Latin America during the nineteenth century prepared the ground for the emergence of populist and military regimes in the twentieth century because those constitutions allocated wide-ranging powers to the military that could easily be misused. Under emergencies, the numbers of innocent detainees and wrongly convicted people are often particularly high. The thousands of US citizens of Japanese descent that were detained during World War II in the US provide a pertinent and cautionary example.

In this chapter, we ask two questions. First, can the passing of an emergency constitution be legitimized by drawing on social contract theory? Second, if it can, then what constitutional emergency rules would well-informed rational citizens consent to? To answer these questions, we draw on a social contract framework as commonly used by economists, and most prominently so by Buchanan (1975). We argue that arguments conventionally probed in favor of emergency constitutions are not entirely convincing and propose a novel justification for them. In times of unforeseen catastrophic events, both citizens and politicians tend to overreact, which may induce political decision-makers to implement policies that are not suitable to face the respective challenge. In such situations, emergency constitutions may serve as a commitment device, protecting both citizens and politicians from their time-inconsistent preferences and action bias.

The remainder of the chapter is organized as follows. Section 14.2 first defines the term emergency constitution, and then describes central aspects of emergency constitutions in a bit more detail. Section 14.3 contains both a brief sketch and critique of the literature that justifies emergency clauses. Section 14.4, the core of the chapter, first discusses a number of reasons why rational individuals would hesitate to sign on to constitutionalized emergency provisions, and then advances a novel justification in their favor. Section 14.5 concludes.

14.2 Emergency Constitutions: The Relevant Dimensions

As we have done throughout this book, we describe an emergency constitution as a set of constitutional provisions that, under specific circumstances, empower governments to take action beyond the previously fixed constitutional constraints. At the same time, it limits governments' use of extra powers, for example, by defining core basic rights, which can never be derogated, or determining a maximum period of time during which government can resort to any additional powers delineated by the constitution. Throughout this book, we have noted more than once that emergency constitutions always contain a paradoxical element: A constitution defines the limits of state action whereas one of its parts – the emergency constitution – creates the foundations for suspending some of the limits created by the same document.

Historically, the primary rationale given by those who enacted emergency power provisions has been that those provisions would serve to ensure the survival of the state. This rationale primarily refers to external threats such as war. Yet over time, emergency powers have been broadened considerably to be used during civil wars, revolutions, general strikes, and subsequent to terrorist attacks.[1] Often, a distinction is made between a French – and subsequently continental – approach to emergencies (*état de siège*), and a British approach originating from martial law (e.g. by Rossiter 2009, especially in chapter X). Two aspects in particular make them distinct from one another: the identity of the actor authorized to monitor the state of emergency, and the degree of judicialization. Under a state of siege, monitoring would primarily fall to the legislature, whereas it would fall on the judiciary under martial law. Whereas the state of siege is legally anticipated, martial law could be characterized by "the absence of statutory foresight for its initiation and use" (ibid., 141).

If the constitution is interpreted as "constituting" the state, then representatives of the state should be bound to the provisions of the constitution at all times, no matter whether normal or exceptional. This position can also be called monism, and implies the absence of any emergency rules. Under monism, citizens coordinate their behavior under a single set of rules, the rule of law applies to exceptional as well as to normal times, and basic human rights are not weakened during times of emergency. This view has been ascribed to both Leibniz and Condorcet, but also to Constant.

The alternative to monism is dualism, which comes in at least two types (Ferejohn and Pasquino 2004).[2] According to the first, government behavior can and should be subjected to the constitutional order no matter whether the state of the world is "normal" or "exceptional." Under dualism, however, the relevant constitutional order to be applied depends on whether the state of the world is "normal"

[1] Interestingly, this "broadening over time" seems to repeat itself as it already took place in Rome. A number of researchers (Lintott 2009, 111; Straumann 2016, 72f.) argue that, at least originally, the Roman dictatorship was confined to external threats and could not be applied to fight domestic unrest. A similar broadening occurred again in the twentieth century as described in more detail in Chapter 2.

[2] They also distinguish between monist and dualist conceptions but would group my first dualist conception into the monist camp.

or "exceptional." Under this version of dualism, the competence of deciding on the concrete state of the world and, hence, on the *modus operandi* of the constitution is crucial, yet it does not lead "outside" the rule of law and constitutional provisions.

The competence to decide on what state of the world applies is crucial also in the second type of dualism. Yet adherents of the second version of dualism hold that SOEs cannot be (or should not be) constitutionalized. Those who believe that they cannot be constitutionalized usually argue that human foresight is too limited to spell out the constraints under which government should operate under these conditions (most famously Schmitt 1922, 14). Those who believe that it should not be constitutionalized argue that this could be the best means to safeguard long-term constitutional fidelity (e.g. Gross 2003).[3] This position also appears paradoxical: precisely because the rule of law is highly valued, it is proposed to be suspended temporarily. But this kind of dualism is silent on how to return to the desired state of affairs and the existence of situations in which politicians ought not to be bound by basic constitutional rules which appears rather incompatible with constitutionalism and the rule of law proper.[4] At base, thinkers who share this position must necessarily assume that there are situations in which the rule of law is antithetical to efforts to sustain order in society. Figure 14.1 is a simple mapping of the approaches to emergency constitutions just discussed.[5]

Under monism, no rules to regulate an SOE, which we may call power-conferring rules, are needed.[6] This is also true of the

[3] Gross proposes to call this the "extra-legal measures model." It would inform "public officials that they may act extralegally when they believe that such action is necessary for protecting the nation and the public in face of calamity, provided that they openly and publicly acknowledge the nature of their actions." Apparently, no (constitutionalized) actor is charged with monitoring if public officials have "openly and publicly" acknowledged the nature of their actions. In other words, the status of this provision remains unclear.

[4] An advantage of hardcore dualism could be that it is clear from the outset that the emergency government cannot produce any legislation that will be valid beyond the state of emergency.

[5] This is, of course, only one of many possible mappings. Loevy (2016) proposes to distinguish between the extralegal Lockean model, the neo Roman model of dictatorship, and the rule-of-law model of legality. In addition, she refers to four other mappings (in footnote 19).

[6] This does not exclude the possibility that specific competences are allocated to government on the basis of statutory law. It was mentioned in the

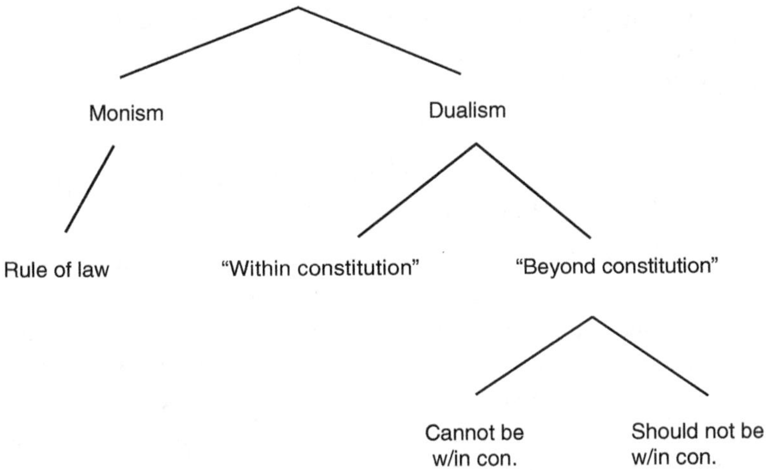

Figure 14.1 A conceptualization of emergency constitutions

second kind of dualism, at least regarding the kind and extent of competences that politicians have at their disposal. Since we are interested in the possibility of justifying an emergency constitution, only the first kind of dualism is of further interest here; we are explicitly not interested in an emergency constitution that effectively gives the executive branch a *carte blanche*. Some of the relevant institutional aspects have been discussed in previous chapters, but as we are interested in normative analysis here we take them up again – but "wearing a different pair of glasses" if you will. The relevant institutional aspects that need to be dealt with under the first kind of dualism include:

(1) What are the necessary conditions for an SOE?
(2) What (additional) competences does an SOE confer on the emergency government?
(3) Who has the power to declare an SOE?

introduction that today, some 90% of all countries dispose of an emergency constitution as defined here. The remaining 10 percent have passed statutory legislation to deal with emergencies. In fact, many – if not most – countries having emergency constitutions also rely on statutory law in addition to their constitutional provisions. An example are public health laws on whose basis many governments imposed quarantine on their populations during the COVID pandemic, often without declaring an SOE. Counterterrorist legislation is another area in which much statutory law exists.

(4) Who has the power to declare the end of an emergency?
(5) Who has the power to monitor the legality of the means used during an SOE?
(6) Who exercises emergency powers?

In the following paragraphs, we briefly sketch the relevance of these aspects as well as potential institutional choices.

Ad (i): Emergency constitutions can be narrow or broad in the sense that they allow the declaration of an SOE only for a small or for a large number of events. If the constitution is precise in describing the events, this can lead to a low probability of an SOE being called.

Ad (ii): The probability of an SOE being declared is determined not only by the conditions named in the emergency constitution but also by the additional competences that it confers on a government under an SOE. One would expect constitutions conferring substantial additional powers on government to be attractive for government. Such constitutions might also be attractive for government if they can be easily misused: The right to dissolve parliament may, for example, be misused simply to prolong one's own stay in office.

Ad (iii): No matter how precisely the necessary conditions are defined, the power to decide must be allocated to some actors by power-conferring rules. At base, the question can be reduced to the degree of separation of powers in the declaration of SOEs. On the one hand, one can imagine a constitution that allocates the power to declare an emergency exclusively to the head of the executive and no one needs to approve. This would be equivalent to a very low degree in the separation of powers. This is, for example, the case in Kazakhstan. On the other hand, one can imagine that more than one constitutional actor must be involved in the declaration and more than one actor must approve it.[7] In Liberia, for example, the head of state declares but both chambers of parliament need to approve the declaration of an SOE. An intermediate solution could be that some other branch needs to be consulted; if its advice is not followed, this might increase the

[7] Throughout the chapter, we will refer to this as separation of powers. Alternatively, one could also refer to the number of veto players, that is, the number of actors whose consent is needed to make a specific decision.

political costs of declaring an emergency in terms of a reduction in perceived legitimacy.[8]

Ad (iv): Another important institutional issue is the power to end an SOE. One possibility (famously used by the Romans) is to have it expire automatically. Here, too, the separation of powers is central. Acknowledging that every SOE entails the danger of misuse with the possibility of developing into permanent autocracy, it seems to make sense to allocate the power to end an SOE to a constitutional actor other than the actor endowed with the exercise of emergency powers. Ackerman (2004) proposes a "supermajoritarian escalator": the longer the emergency lasts, the more inclusive the parliamentary majority necessary to sustain it.

Ad (v): It seems natural to think of the judiciary as monitoring the legality of the means used. Yet many scholars believe that speed is of the essence in emergency situations and that judicial review should be postponed (most prominently, of course, John Locke). Others, such as Ackerman (2004) or Dyzenhaus (2006), point to the dismal record of the judiciary in constraining government action under emergency.

Ad (vi): Conferring emergency powers on the head of the executive may be another natural assumption. Other provisions are, however, possible. They include not only the head of the military, but also technocrats. The French version of an SOE, the *état de siège*, implies an expansive delegation of powers to the military (Rossiter 2009, chapter VI).

We now turn to different types of emergency constitutions as discussed in the literature. Ferejohn and Pasquino (2004) have proposed to distinguish between a "neo-Roman" and a "legislative model" of emergency powers that has close connections to the distinction between a monist and a dualist conception of legal orders. In Rome, government in normal times was led by two consuls. During SOEs, which could be declared only by the Senate, the consuls would appoint a single dictator who could not be an active consul himself, but instead was recruited solely for the purpose of leading the emergency government for a maximum term of six months (Rossiter 2009, chapter II).

8 Additionally, the necessary majorities can be taken into account. As already shown by Buchanan and Tullock (1962) a high supermajority in one chamber can be equivalent to two simple majorities in two chambers.

The dictator's emergency powers differed from the powers of the consuls in that the dictator's decisions were not subject to the veto powers of other magistrates nor to the intercession of the tribunes.[9] The Roman institutions were, hence, built on a dualist conception. Some modern constitutions do vest an elected president with extraordinary powers, the main difference to ancient Rome, of course, being that the dictator had to be a person who was not part of government during normal times. As examples of the Neo-Roman model, Ferejohn and Pasquino (2004) name the Weimar Republic and the current French Constitution.

The "legislative model," by contrast, is characterized by the legislature passing statutes to fight the emergency. It is, however, built on a monist notion of the legal order. Ferejohn and Pasquino (2004, 215–217) cite the complex of laws passed by the British parliament in recent decades against terrorism and the PATRIOT Act in the US, but also the various laws passed in the 1970s and 1980s in both Italy and Germany to deal with terrorism. The dualist approach implies the vesting of extraordinary powers that will be divested after the SOE has ended. It also implies that any legislation produced during the emergency for the purpose of fighting the emergency, will be invalid after it has ended. This is different if an emergency is fought by passing ordinary legislation.[10] In other words, monism entails the danger that civil liberties will not merely be derogated for a fixed period of time but will be suspended for good. It would, of course, be interesting to compare the effects of the neo-Roman with those of the legislative model, but this must be left to another paper since we are here interested only in the possibility of justifying an emergency constitution.

Our inquiry into the possibility of establishing justification for an emergency constitution is based on two aspects. The first aspect asks whether an emergency constitution is the most suitable means to reach a certain end. It draws on available social science in making this judgment. The second one asks whether an emergency constitution can

[9] Both Lintott (2009) and Straumann (2016) point out that many features that were taken for granted regarding the institution of dictatorship might not be historically accurate. Straumann, in particular, takes pains to uncover the historical evolution of the institution between its inception in 494 BC and its abolishment in 44 BC.

[10] It is true that some legislative measures are passed with a sunset clause, or are not renewed.

be justified in the sense of being recognized as legitimate by all those living under an emergency constitution. The first of these aspects is dealt with in the next section of the chapter whereas the second aspect occupies center stage in Sections 4 and 5.

14.3 Justifying Emergency Legislation: A Brief Sketch of the Contractarian Literature

Much recent discussion has defended or even praised Locke's prerogative which can be interpreted as a proposal to deal with emergency situations in an extralegal way (Lazar 2009 but also Pasquino 1998 and Casson 2008). This is why we briefly summarize and critically discuss Locke's approach in this part of the chapter.[11]

Before discussing Locke's argument, it makes sense to look at Machiavelli's thoughts because it was he who "rediscovered" the institutions used in ancient Rome for emergencies (although Machiavelli was, of course, not a contractarian). In the *Discourses on Livy*, Machiavelli writes: "... those Republics which in urgent perils do not have resort either to a Dictatorship or a similar authority, will always be ruined in grave incidents" (Discourses, Book 1, chapter XXXIV). Machiavelli reveals himself as a great admirer of the Roman institutions. The Roman model plays a central role in the justification of emergency constitutions to this very day (see, e.g. Rossiter 2009 or Ferejohn and Pasquino 2004). Ever since Machiavelli, two arguments have been frequently used to justify them: the lack of time to respond to an emergency using the established procedures, and the incompleteness of "the laws" due to restrictions of the human capacity to anticipate the future.

Regarding the first argument, many philosophers and political theorists argue that speed is of the essence in emergencies and that no time must be wasted in such situations. Since collective decision-making requires more time than individual decision-making, in order to speed up the decision-making process, one individual should make all the important decisions. This argument can, for example, be found in Machiavelli (2009) who presents it as a two-step argument: (1) collective bodies take

[11] A very detailed description complemented by an in-depth evaluation of both the strengths and the weaknesses of Locke's approach can be found in Fatovic (2009, 38–82).

more time than individual persons to deliberate and decide; and (2) the separation of powers slows things down even more. Interestingly, the costs of the simplified decision-making endorsed via emergency constitutions (e.g. in terms of bad decisions) are seldom discussed although Machiavelli is clearly aware of the potential costs, warning that relying on "the extraordinary method" could serve as pretext for evil objectives (ibid.). Harrington (1992), who writes about the dangers of "unnatural haste," is certainly the exception.

Regarding the second argument, Locke maintains that the executive is in need of discretion as legislators are unable to foresee every possible contingency (*Two Treatises on Government*, II, §160). With this, we have hit Locke's famous prerogative which is to apply to circumstances not foreseen by the legislators including SOEs (Locke does not use this term but speaks of "accidents and necessities" [ibid.]). In §160 of his Second Treatise, Locke describes prerogative as the "power to act according to discretion, for the public good, without the prescription of the law, and sometimes against it." Casson (2008, 954) summarizes Locke's point as follows: "Prerogative is a power that exists beyond written law, yet it is constrained by constitutional authorization. It is in this sense that Pasquino (1998, 19) can assert that Locke provides us with 'a systematic constitutional theory of extralegal power.'" This position is difficult to reconcile with Locke's statement quoted earlier: "without the prescription of the law, and sometimes against it."

John Locke is hailed as a proponent of constitutionalism and the rule of law. This is why his reliance on the prerogative has been criticized by many as it seems incompatible with the rule of law. Fatovic (2009, chapter two) tries to reduce the seeming incompatibility by reminding us of the paramount importance that Locke attributes to natural law. According to Locke, the laws of nature are "permanent, unvarying, inerrant, and inviolable" whereas human laws are "historically contingent, changing, fallible, and potentially breakable" (ibid., 61). The overarching goal of natural law is "the preservation of society, and (as far as is consistent with the public good) of every person in it" (II, § 134). It is the natural law that is to constrain the executive in its use of the prerogative. Since natural law and civil law can deviate from each other, it is the function of the executive to ensure that natural law will be complied with, if need be by relying on the prerogative. This position takes the perceptability of the natural law for granted.

Locke conceives of two mechanisms to constrain the executive in its use of the prerogative, namely (1) virtue, and (2) the right to resistance by the governed. His view of virtue is instrumental in the sense that he thinks princes to be virtuous because they are afraid of being punished, for example, by being removed from power. Locke is, however, aware that the right to resistance may not be perfectly reliable to prevent tyrannical misuse of the prerogative, writing that "many misuses will be born by the people without mutiny or murmur" (II, §225).

To this day, Locke is often mentioned as having developed a convincing justification for emergency provisions; Casson's (2008) explicit defense of Locke at the expense of Schmitt is only one example of this. Our own reading of Locke is nonetheless much more critical. From a twenty-first century perspective, informed by both empirical evidence on how emergency powers have been used and a public choice perspective modeling governments as maximizing their own utility, the Lockean treatment of the "public good" is not convincing. True, the pursuit of the public good is mentioned as a condition for the legitimacy of prerogative powers, but who is to be the judge on government behavior? Locke even wants to make the scope of prerogative powers a function of the character of the individual wielding it (Fatovic 2009, 41). This begs the question who is to judge the government's character? As just cited in the last paragraph, Locke himself was not entirely convinced of the reliability of the right to resistance as a mechanism to keep government in check.[12]

Social contract theory received another boost almost exactly eighty years after Locke had published his *Two Treatises*. Rousseau (2019) is an excellent representation of some of the arguments regarding SOEs that are still quoted today. His two main arguments are speed and the incompleteness of legislation. In *The Social Contract*, he deals with the latter issue writing: "A thousand cases can arise for which the Lawgiver did not provide, and it is a very necessary foresight to sense that one cannot foresee everything" (IV, 6, 1).

[12] Poole (2009) is yet another twentieth-first century perspective on Locke asking about the role of the prerogative in our age of statutes. He observes that the movement from prerogative to statute in crisis lawmaking is undertheorized and laments that formerly royal authority now exists "in a murky gray area between the authority of the legislature and the power of the executive" (ibid., 254).

But he still held that only the greatest danger, namely when the existence of the country is at stake, could justify the temporary nonapplication of the laws. He was very optimistic regarding the recognition of such situations ("in these rare and obvious cases"). He sketched two models of government under emergency, depending on the "nature of the danger." The first and more moderate model would not entail a change in the laws, only in the way they are administered. The second model, on the other hand, suggests nominating a supreme ruler "who shall silence all the laws and suspend for a moment the sovereign authority." In such cases, there would be "no doubt about the general will." He traces both models back to Rome, but insists that Rome borrowed the second model from Alba. To prevent the misuse of emergency powers, Rousseau proposed to impose a number of limitations on them. One such limitation was that the dictator was not allowed to legislate (IV, 6, 4). He also insists that the time period allocated to a dictator be "a very brief term that can never be extended" (IV, 6, 11).

Today, Rouseaus's assertions seem optimistic and even naïve. They are optimistic because he seems convinced that the evaluation of the concrete situation will be more or less unanimous (stating that there is "no doubt about the general will"), and they are naïve because he wants the "most worthy" to be entrusted with the special powers. Locke, unfortunately, remains completely silent on procedure, that is, rules according to which a normal state can be transferred into an exceptional one, and then returned back to a normal state. With hindsight, Rousseau's assertions also appear optimistic and naïve because – as we have shown in particular in Chapter 5 – emergency provisions have not only been misused frequently but have served as a welcome instrument of would-be autocrats to put their countries on a path away from the rule of law and democracy (Lührmann and Rooney 2021).[13]

Of course, there are philosophers who were convinced that societies are able to frame rules of such generality that no emergency constitution is necessary; these include Tocqueville and Constant. Instead of summarizing their arguments here, we instead emphasize

[13] With regard to the COVID pandemic, there are voices claiming that emergency constitutions are not misused but rather underused (Pozen and Scheppele 2020), echoing Rousseau's claim that the office of dictator was underused, rather than misused in Rome (IV, 6, 8 and 9).

Scheppele's (2004) point that the standards for legitimizing SOEs should be higher under republican forms of government than under monarchies. Many of the justifications summarized here were written with some sort of prince in mind. In a modern constitutional democracy, some of these arguments therefore no longer hold.

14.4 A Novel Justification of Emergency Constitutions

A social contract argument, used both to justify the existence of the state and to legitimize specific constitutional rules, has been popularized among economists by James M. Buchanan (1975). According to him, the purpose of the contractarian approach is justificatory in the sense that

> it offers a basis for normative evaluation. Could the observed rules that constrain the activity of ordinary politics have emerged from agreement in constitutional contract? To the extent that this question can be affirmatively answered, we have established a legitimating linkage between the individual and the state. (1987, 249)

In this section, we ask whether the observed emergency constitutions could have emerged from agreement in constitutional contract. This section is divided into four parts. We begin by rehearsing the economic perspective on the social contract view. We then set out the basic assumptions used for the justificatory exercise. The third part presents a number of reasons why rational individuals are unlikely to consent to an emergency constitution. The fourth part revisits this notion of consent, and finds some reasons why rational individuals might very well agree to constitutionalized emergency provisions.

14.4.1 The Economic Take on the Social Contract

In their *Calculus of Consent*, Buchanan and Tullock (1962) note that consent is scarce and that this fact would justify an economic analysis of constitutions. In the *Limits of Liberty*, Buchanan (1975) offers a rationale for leaving the state of nature or anarchy behind and moving on to a constitutional state. This move would shift realized utility levels of all those living in that state outward and closer to the utility frontier. The utility that can be realized in the state of nature has the important function of serving as a fallback option. No rational individual would ever accept a constitution under which her (expected) utility would be lower than under the state of nature.

Here, we are primarily interested in the question of whether unanimous consent to a particular part of the constitution – the "emergency constitution" – appears plausible. This does not mean that questions of implementation should be set aside lightheartedly, which is why we ask to what degree the emergency constitution – if it can be legitimized at all – can be expected to be self-enforcing. Self-enforceability would be high if political actors have incentives to control each other.

The "original social contract" is a disarmament contract that endows the representatives of the state with immense power that could easily be misused. The institutional setup requires that the probability of misuse is somehow contained. The separation of powers, both horizontally and vertically, is the most important such institutional device. Holding elections at regular intervals could be another one. But democracy also entails numerous dangers such as the tyranny of the majority. One means to contain those dangers is the inclusion of basic human rights in the social contract.

In this context, basic human rights can be given a very simple rationale. Negative rights can be interpreted as creating protected domains that not even the state is allowed to trespass, and can be thought of as part of the original contract. In short, individuals are only willing to disarm themselves on the understanding that they are endowed with protected domains into which the state will not enter. For democratically organized states, this implies that negative rights limit the possible scope of majority decision-making. If rights are really basic, even large majorities are bound by them and cannot simply ignore them, nor infringe upon them. Negative rights can thus also be interpreted as a device to protect minorities against current majorities, or as "veto rights." In this sense, they give the holders of these rights the right to behave in a certain way, even if an overwhelming majority would prefer them not to act in that way.

One argument for justifying basic human rights could be that individuals who choose a basic legal framework from behind a veil of uncertainty are uncertain about their own individual position in the future. They might belong to a minority and might not be willing to submit to the will of the majority. If enough individuals consider this probability to be sufficiently large, they have an incentive to create basic human rights. Human rights can thus be interpreted as insurance against adverse effects on one's own utility given that one finds oneself to be with the minority. This is, of course, only one of many possible justifications for basic human rights. But it is based on economic reasoning: Being forced not to behave according to one's preferences is utility-reducing and costly. Agreement to basic human rights can thus be the result of a calculus based on exchange.

To sum up, it has been shown that the social contract approach can be given an economic logic.[14] This was shown in particular with regard to negative basic rights (Buchanan and Tullock 1962). In all likelihood, an emergency constitution would enable a government to derogate from some of these basic rights. Whether rational individuals are likely to agree to such derogation is, of course, the central question that will be taken up in the third part of this section.

14.4.2 Assumptions

Here, we are primarily concerned with the amount of information that the individuals choosing – or not choosing – their emergency constitution have. The Rawlsian veil of ignorance has been criticized for assuming that the choosing individuals "know everything in general but nothing in particular" (Cooter as cited in Buchanan 1977, 205) in the sense that they are perfectly informed about cause-effect relationships of many institutions, but have no clue regarding their own selves. The question thus is: How much do we know "in general," or rather, how much knowledge do we assume that those who are choosing their basic rule-set have at their disposal?

Speaking of the "veil of uncertainty," Buchanan and Tullock (1962, 78f.) assume that people know who they are today but they are uncertain about the future and their future selves. Whatever merits the Rawlsian veil of ignorance approach may have, we side with Buchanan and Tullock and assume that individuals are familiar with emergency measures taken as a reaction to prior emergencies. We know the consequences of Art. 48 of the Weimar Constitution, we know how

[14] The economic rationale underlying rights is spelled out in much more detail in Mueller (1991). Drawing on decision-making costs as introduced by Buchanan and Tullock (1962, chapter 6), he shows that there could never be a need to define constitutional rights if all decision-making costs were zero. But of course, they never are.

US citizens of Japanese descent were treated during World War II, we know that many suspects have been detained in Guantanamo as a consequence of 9/11. Moreover, we know the current state of technology, and we also know the costs of the measures enacted as a consequence of, for example, 9/11. Finally, we assume that people also know whether their country is disaster-prone. Formulated differently, we want to assume that the insights regarding the effects of emergency constitutions as spelled out over various chapters in this book are known to all of the decision-makers behind the veil. All the information the decision-makers are assumed to have is based on previous events; they are, hence, not endowed with any clairvoyant capacities.

Further, we assume that the entire rest of the constitution has already been agreed upon. On the one hand, this assumption is a deviation from the approach chosen by Buchanan where the constitution is chosen in its entirety. On the other hand, it simplifies the analysis as the number of decisions to be taken simultaneously is dramatically reduced.

14.4.3 *Trying to Justify an Emergency Constitution*

Given the assumptions just discussed, would rational individuals opt in favor of an emergency constitution? As we have seen in the last section, the two most frequently offered justifications for an emergency constitution are the need for speed and the impossibility to cover all future contingencies under general constitutional rules.

The argument that the life of a nation could be threatened because its constitutional organs are not fast enough in making decisions comes in two varieties. The first one claims that collective decision-making is much slower than individual decision-making. The second argument holds that in times of crises, making decisions could be impossible because parliament is not in session, legislators could not meet, and so forth.

Let us address them in turn. The first variant does not seem to be convincing: If the life of the nation is threatened, both the legislature as well as the executive are likely to act more cooperatively than in nonemergency times and to agree on some measures immediately. Just remember the passing of counterterrorist legislation after 9/11. The US PATRIOT Act, which is more than 300 pages long was, passed a mere forty-five days after the events. Other countries were almost as quick: the British parliament passed the Anti-terrorism, Crime and Security

Act on November 19th and received royal assent on December 14th, and the Canadian Anti-terrorism Act became law after having received royal assent four days later.[15] But if the survival of the nation is at stake, unusually high levels of cooperation are not confined to the legislature. During World War I, Britain had a coalition cabinet – at base completely alien to a majoritarian electoral system – which was created to enhance government's legitimacy. A War Cabinet was created specifically to speed up decision-making (described in Rossiter 2009, chapter XI). Yet executive acts that need not be authorized by the legislature – such as certain executive decrees – still require less time than any kind of cooperation across government branches.

The second argument claims that in times of crises decision-making could simply be impossible, for example, because parliament is not in session. Whereas the first argument cannot be dismissed lightly, this one is not convincing in the twenty-first century anymore. In monarchies, in particular, parliament was often only in session at the behest of the monarch. During the nineteenth century, it was not uncommon for a country's parliament to be in session only for two or three months every year. But this is no longer the case. During the pandemic of 2020, many parliaments, for example, created the option to assemble only virtually, that is, online.

The argument that constitutional rules being passed today could be insufficient or inappropriate for tomorrow's emergencies has been made by Schmitt (1922, 6f.).[16] Today, terrorism is often described as a qualitatively new phenomenon that old constitutions would be ill-equipped to deal with. This argument is unconvincing for two reasons. First, terrorism has been around at least since Spanish guerilla

[15] Legislation as a reaction to the coronavirus was also very quick. In most non-Asian countries, the virus began to spread in February 2020. Here are some examples for when legislatures passed relevant laws: Canada, March 25th; France, March 23rd; Ireland, March 20th; Italy, February 23rd (a decree law); Poland, March 2nd; and Ukraine, March 17th (all information from www.lexology.com/library/detail.aspx?g=d75c6657-a3f7-4312-b341-7ba8da835fd8; assessed on March 17, 2021).

[16] "The precise details of an emergency cannot be anticipated, nor can one spell out what may take place in such a case, especially when it is truly a matter of an extreme emergency and of how it is to be eliminated. The precondition as well as the content of jurisdictional competence in such a case must necessarily be unlimited. From the liberal constitutional point of view, there would be no jurisdictional competence at all. The most guidance the constitution can provide is to indicate who can act in such a case."

fighters were fighting Napoleon's army in the early nineteenth century. Second, the average life-span of constitutions is less than twenty years (Elkins et al. 2009, 129–146). In other words, the phenomenon of terrorism is much older than almost all constitutions in place today.[17] Flipped around, on average, each society has had the chance to modernize its emergency provisions every twenty years over the course of more than two centuries. The probability of constitutions being completely outdated and out of sync with contemporaneous threats appears, hence, rather low.

One important trait of constitutional rules is their generality, which makes them applicable to a wide variety of situations that could not possibly have been foreseen at the time they were passed. This can even be interpreted as a pragmatic rationale for making rules as general as possible. Granted, our imagination may fall short of imagining the concrete issues at stake for extreme and highly improbable contingencies – and the COVID-19 pandemic comes to mind immediately – but does this justify special rules that are only applicable during times of emergency?

In sum, it is unclear how to justify a dualistic approach to the constitution that differentiates between normal and extraordinary times. Yet many constitutions do, and so does international law. So let us analyze the rationale offered in favor of the possibility to derogate from a number of basic human rights, such as freedom of assembly and association, freedom of movement, freedom of speech, and electoral self-determination. Unfortunately, such a rationale is rarely made explicit. At base, derogation clauses seem to imply that respect for human rights is a sort of luxury that is too costly to afford in times of crises.[18] This position is, of course, at odds with the argument here

[17] Over the last couple of decades, we have seen enormous technological changes that have substantially affected our lives, including personal computers and the world wide web. Many pieces of legislation have been passed to deal with new issues arising from the use of these technologies. But we are not aware of an argument that would demand constitutional change as a consequence of these developments. The question hence is: Are the developments supposedly threatening the life of a nation of such a different quality to justify constitutional changes?

[18] The position that basic rights are luxury goods is also shared by Rossiter, whose study remains the most influential on constitutional dictatorship. He writes: "Civil liberties, free enterprise, constitutionalism, government by debate and compromise – these are strictly luxury products …" (2009, 5).

developed: Basic human rights are not a luxury good but a precondition for unanimous consent to the disarmament contract. One reason for calling them basic is precisely their nonderogability.

Among economists, such a complete refusal of any trade-offs regarding basic human rights might not be the norm. An alternative take that is often used by legal scholars would ask whether derogations from human rights are at all proportionate. But to prevent us from falling back into a more conventional welfare-based type of analysis, the question is not answered with reference to any traditional welfare standard but by asking whether a hypothetical member of the constitutional assembly would be willing to forgo the benefits of a strict protection of constitutional rights in favor of some possible benefits regarding a particular emergency situation. If one can imagine that all members of a constitutional assembly – or even all members of society – are ready to forgo some constitutional rights protection in favor of some benefits regarding an emergency, we would have established a legitimating link between individual citizens and an emergency constitution.

Before the issue of proportionality can be meaningfully addressed, we must nevertheless pose another question: Is the suspension of any right at all part of a suitable way of successfully dealing with the emergency?

During World War II, the US detained many citizens of Japanese descent, predominantly on the West Coast. The Supreme Court held this practice to be constitutional.[19] Their detention was equivalent to the suspension of many aspects of due process or *habeas corpus*. In hindsight, it seems more than questionable whether this disrespect for human rights improved the odds of the US winning the war, winning it faster, or causing fewer casualties. In that sense, the measure was unsuitable. With this knowledge available today, it is questionable whether rational individuals would be in favor of allowing the possibility of softening due process during times of emergency.[20]

This is a single example. But the suitability question can be raised on a more general level: Terrorist attacks are most likely to be prevented if friends and family of would-be terrorists turn to the police to warn

[19] *Korematsu* v. *United States* 323 US 214 (1944).

[20] Wu (2002) summarizes the findings of the report of the US Commission on Wartime Relocation and Internment of Civilians (1983) by stating that "the internment had been motivated by wartime hysteria, racial prejudice, and failure of political leadership – not military necessity."

them of planned attacks. Walsh and Piazza (2010) argue that this is less likely if the police are known not to comply with physical integrity rights. In Chapter 6, we show that increases in repression levels subsequent to a terrorist attack lead to more, rather than fewer, terrorist incidents. We hence present evidence that some measures made possible by emergency constitutions are unsuitable to fight terrorism. But suitability is not even a sufficient criterion, it is merely a necessary one. Given that a measure is suitable, it also needs to be proportionate.

To illustrate the case of proportionality let us assume, hypothetically, that the detention of 800 Muslims would lead to the identification of one active member of the so-called Islamic State and the detention was somewhat suitable. But the measure would imply that 799 innocent people were detained. This case is, of course, not only hypothetical as up to almost 800 Muslims were held by the US in its Guantanamo detention camp. Would this be proportionate? To frame the question in terms of a constitutional assembly: Would I agree to live in a country that can detain a very high number of innocent people? Suppose I were a member of a minority group, would I consent to the possibility of being detained for an indefinite period knowing how people of Japanese descent were treated before? Given that the answer is no, no consent for the derogation of human rights in times of emergency can be assumed.[21]

Summing up, many considerations seem to speak against emergency provisions that allow the government to derogate from basic human rights. Moreover, the time pressure argument frequently offered in

[21] There have been various attempts to evaluate the policy reactions of the US government to 9/11 in terms of cost-benefit analyses. Mueller and Stewart (2011), for example, observe that the increase in expenditures on US domestic homeland security over the decade since 9/11 is in excess of one trillion dollars, that is, 100 billion dollars on an annual basis. Note that this number does not refer to total costs but only to increases in costs. Further note that it only refers to domestic expenditures and does not cover the costs of the interventions in Afghanistan and Iraq. The authors find that for these expenditures to be cost effective, they would have to deter 1,667 otherwise successful Times-Square type attacks per year or equivalently four such attacks every single day of the year! Blalock et al. (2009) deal with the unintended consequences of tougher regulation. Air travelers who do not want to lose time at the airport navagating tough controls might switch to the car for short distance travel. It is estimated that this substitution behavior caused 327 additional driving deaths per month in late 2001. Although the effect weakened over time, the authors estimate that as many as 2,300 driving deaths may be attributable to the attacks.

favor of shifting powers away from the legislature (and the judiciary) to the executive is not convincing in the twenty-first century. But the shift in competences and the possibility of government intruding into the private sphere of its citizens are the two core elements of emergency constitutions.[22] Viewed like this, attempting to legitimize them on the basis of social contract theory seems futile.

14.4.4 Another Attempt to Justify Emergency Constitutions

An attack like 9/11 can make many people very angry. Just having experienced an extreme condition can lead them to demand drastic measures. Once calmed again, it might turn out that these measures were extremely costly, disproportionate or even outright unsuitable. If, subsequent to a terrorist attack, voters demand tougher counterterrorism policies, governments are likely to supply them because they want to be reelected. These policies might, however, be unsuitable as they can induce additional alienation between government and communities from which terrorists might emerge. If entire communities get alienated, their members are unlikely to report suspicious activities, which could actually make terrorist incidents more, rather than less, likely.

Rational citizens might, hence, want to protect themselves against succumbing to the danger of "action bias" too easily.[23] Action bias has been described as a consequence of probability neglect: Since many individuals focus on the bad outcome of an event and not on its likelihood of ever occurring again, they overreact. Action bias can be observed in individual behavior (not taking the subway to the airport any more after an attack on a subway) but also in demands that government show a tough response. Since action bias is a very prominent reaction, governments have incentives to react strongly to keep their own popularity levels high.

22 It is possible to reframe the argument in a more continuous fashion. The economic justification of basic human rights refers to the protection of minorities. If there were completely homogeneous societies without any kind of minority, this sort of justification would not have bite. One could, hence, reframe the argument such that the justification of emergency constitutions becomes more difficult the more heterogeneous the respective society.

23 The term "action bias" was coined by Patt and Zeckhauser (2000) and first applied to environmental issues. In the meantime, it has been applied to other areas including terrorism (see Sunstein and Zeckhauser 2011).

We have thus arrived at Ulysses and the Sirens, one of the most basic allegories in constitutional political economy. In more modern language, people know that they are subject to problems of time inconsistency. In "normal times," they know that a carefully crafted reaction to any problem promises the highest return. Yet confronted with an emergency, they tend to overreact and fall prey to action bias, which could also be called the "we-need-to-do-something-now fallacy." If, in a calm mood, they anticipate this possibility and realize its potentially huge costs, they may want to take care to implement precautions against it in the constitution. Here, the constitution could serve as a commitment device that prevents politicians from giving in to the tempting voices of the Sirens (in this case their potential voters). Possible ways to institutionalize such precautions include the requirement that legislation can only be passed after so many readings in parliament, that a minimum amount of time must pass between readings, and so on.

So if constitutions are seen as a commitment device, and members of society believe they are subject to the "we-need-to-do-something-now fallacy," then this constitutes a strong argument in favor of including emergency provisions into a country's constitution.[24] Notice that its function is entirely different from the one perceived by Ackerman (2004). For him, it served primarily as an enabling device (reassuring that government was acting) whereas here, it serves to constrain government ("don't do anything you might regret tomorrow"). If this argument and the evidence presented earlier are considered jointly, a number of implications follow:

- The hurdles for invoking an SOE should be high, implying that various actors need to agree. Only if there is broad consensus across factions that the country is challenged by an emergency should it be possible to switch from the "normal" to the "emergency state." The high hurdles are to protect the country against governments that try to misuse the emergency provisions to their own advantage.
- The attempt to exactly specify the conditions under which an SOE can be invoked is of little use when uncertainty is genuine. Whether cyber war attacks are sufficiently serious to be included into the constitution is hard to predict. Rather than specifying the conditions, increasing the

[24] The BBC sitcom *Yes Minister* famously described action bias in the political sphere as a situation where: "We must do something. This is something. Therefore, we must do this."

number of actors who need to agree seems more sensible. The actors that need to consent would depend on the specific constitutional tradition. Beyond the chambers of parliament, they could include a court, expert bodies, but possibly also the citizens if the country has a strong tradition in direct democracy (and time allows).

- The additional benefits a government enjoys after declaring an SOE should be strictly limited. It is unclear why dissolving a parliament could ever help to resolve an emergency more effectively.
- This also holds for the possibility to derogate from basic human rights. There is evidence that many such derogations are unsuitable and hence ineffective.
- Measures passed under an SOE should automatically cease to be valid once the SOE is over.
- All decisions connected to the declaration of an SOE and the policy decisions taken under it should be subject to judicial review.

Since there is evidence that emergency constitutions do affect government behavior, spelling out the constraints as precisely as possible does promise to have the intended effects. Involving all branches of government at some point also increases the chances that the emergency provisions will be self-enforcing since representatives of each branch can be expected to guard their own interest against intrusions from either of the other branches.

Constitutionalizing emergency provisions implies a clear separation between normal and emergency times. Under a monist legal order, newly created legislation often survives the emergency proper and becomes part of the permanent legal order. Measures reducing civil rights can therefore lead to a perpetual decline in the level of basic human rights. If measures passed under an SOE are only valid until the end of the SOE, a dualist order of the first kind might be better able to safeguard civil rights over time. In addition to the institutional safeguards just spelled out, rational individuals are therefore likely to demand that measures passed under an SOE become automatically void once the emergency is over.

Human foresight is limited. Catastrophic events not foreseen by anybody may require swift government action. But acknowledging the human tendency to overreact would make rational individuals favor an emergency constitution that not only enables governments to react swiftly but tries to minimize the possibilities of misuse at the same time. Once it has been shown that a dualist approach can be justified, the question becomes: What kind of emergency constitution? We hope we have shown that the involvement of a high number of veto players is desirable, and not just because it increases the chances of the self-enforceability of an emergency constitution. While the consent of many players for declaring a state of emergency seems desirable, relatively few benefits should be offered to the government under an SOE. And finally, the *ex post* accountability of government should make forward-looking governments more careful in the choice of policy options.

14.5 Outlook: Toward an Economics of Emergency Constitutions

This chapter has been confined to a single question, whether emergency constitutions can be justified from a strictly individualistic perspective. The question has been answered in the affirmative, but with important caveats.

The question dealt with in this chapter is a normative one. The fact that constitutional provisions that put few constraints on government have become the norm over the course of the last five or six decades is a positive observation. The divergence between our justificatory exercise and political reality is easy to explain. For many emergency constitutions, (hypothetical) consent is hard to imagine in practice. Instead, their creation is likely to have been in the interests of the ruling elites.[25] Emergency constitutions may be very valuable for ruling elites even if they are never actually used; the mere hint at the possibility of using them might already be sufficient reason for the opposition to moderate its behavior.

Some follow-up questions come immediately to mind:

(1) Is the presumption that constrained dualism strictly limits the application of laws passed during SOEs to emergency periods empirically correct? Are there systematic differences in both the kind as well as the quantity of anti-terror legislation passed by countries following either of the two main models described in this chapter?

[25] This is, of course, not a new argument. Regarding the Roman emergency constitution, Montesquieu (1989) noted that the dictatorship was a means by which the plebeians could be intimidated.

(2) Implicitly, we have assumed throughout that the decision to incorporate emergency provisions into a constitution takes place in an environment where the entire remaining text of the constitution follows well-established rule-of-law principles, and has a high chance of being implemented according to the letter of the law. But assume we are dealing with a newly independent state or a fledgling new regime. In that case, it might very well be possible that emergency constitutions are misused by governments in order to stabilize their position. It might, hence, be necessary to add an important qualifier to the normative argument here developed.

15 *The Future of States of Emergency*

15.1 Introduction

Most chapters of this book are entirely positive. We have been interested in the reasons behind differences in emergency constitutions across time and space, the factors leading governments to declare a state of emergency (SOE), the effectiveness of SOEs in reestablishing the status quo ante and the conditions under which governments are likely to overstep constitutional constraints.

Given the ambivalent record of emergency constitutions, it seems only natural to ask whether they should not be discarded altogether. This normative question was taken up in the last chapter. There, we put emergency constitutions in the context of social contract theory as developed by economists and argued that emergency constitutions could serve as a commitment device of societies, binding their politicians and themselves to prevent overreactions after a disaster – natural or man-made – has occurred.

This concluding chapter serves two main purposes. The Index of Emergency Powers (INEP) has accompanied us through almost all chapters. In the next section, we simply depict all cases in which either the benefit or the cost version of the INEP were shown to be significant. The message of this entire exercise is clear: Emergency constitutions do channel the behavior of politicians.

The second purpose of this chapter is to speculate a bit about the future of emergency constitutions. We do this by relying on two different perspectives. We first ask whether current trends such as climate change make the modification of emergency constitutions desirable. This section focuses, hence, on events possibly making changes in emergency constitutions desirable. The subsequent section then asks whether other players such as international organizations or independent agencies at the nation-state level should be granted any emergency powers. It thus focuses on actors.

We end this outlook by asking to what degree the strengthening of societal resilience can be interpreted as a substitute for or a complement to emergency regimes.

15.2 A Very Brief Synthesis of Our Findings

This is a long book analyzing constitutional emergency provisions from many different angles. It is easy to get lost in all the detailed results we have presented over the fourteen preceding chapters. As a workhorse for many of our analyses, we have relied on the INEP that has both a cost and a benefit variant. Based on the INEP, we find both a number of characteristics of emergency constitutions that have changed over recent decades as well as a number of effects.

Our findings first document that while emergency constitutions differ substantially across countries, these differences do not follow the usual categorization of regime types: On average, emergency constitutions are remarkably similar in democracies and autocracies.

Second, we find clear evidence that constitutional change over the last two or three decades has resulted in more competences being

Table 15.1 *Overview of effects*

	SOE declaration	Cost INEP	Benefit INEP
Natural disasters		More SOEs	More deaths
Terrorism	Increased repression	More SOEs (in Muslim countries)	More events, fewer SOEs Exacerbates repression effect
Domestic		Conflict leads to SOEs with high costs	
Pandemic		More SOEs in democracies	More SOEs
Overall effects			Longer time to status quo ante More unlawful SOEs when second chamber approves

allocated to the executive branch. This change is partly the result of new constitutions in formerly communist countries, and partly the result of constitutional change in developing countries.

Turning to the results of differences across emergency constitutions, our empirical exploration shows that SOE declarations are systematically misused for political reasons. While we do observe some intended positive consequences, the effects of declarations and allocating more power during emergencies are often negative. We summarize our overall findings in Table 15.1.

Taking these findings into account, we now move on to ask whether it is desirable to add more events to emergency constitutions that would justify the declaration of an SOE. A particular focus will be on climate change and effects that climate change may be inducing such as migration.

15.3 Possible Trends

15.3.1 Climate Change Causing More Natural Disasters?

It has almost become something of a commonplace: Climate change increases not only the number of natural disasters but also their severity. If that is true, one might think about possible consequences for emergency regimes. If climate-induced natural disasters become a lot more common, then the question is whether the tools used to fight their consequences should not be normalized in the sense that these tools can be used even without having declared an SOE. If, on the other hand, both the occurrence of climate change-induced natural disasters as well as their effects have remained more or less unpredictable, it would seem to make sense to keep the toolkit reserved for states of emergency. It might then, however, be a question of whether additional tools should be included in the SOE toolkit.

The central question thus is the connection between climate change and the natural disasters that could possibly be induced by it. Although a new commonsense on this connection seems to have emerged, the evidence is not so clear-cut. We rely here on various reports of Swiss Re, one of the world's largest reinsurance companies. To stay in business, it is vital for reinsurance companies to evaluate the additional threats caused by climate change as precisely as possible.

In one of its reports, Bevere and Gloor (2020) write: "We expect warmer temperatures will lead to growing frequency of severe weather events, and that these will make an increasing contribution to rising losses in the coming decades." The uncertainty regarding possible tipping points is one reason for the difficulty in answering the question. Swiss Re (ibid.) refers to reenforcing feedback loops as particularly problematic and names permafrost thaw and an increase in wildfire activity as examples. In a more recent report, Guo et al. (2021) go one step further and estimate the potential loss of economic value due to climate change. According to that report, the world might lose 10 percent of its total economic value by mid-century if climate change stays on the currently anticipated trajectory. This would be a huge amount. Given that poorer countries are hit hardest (as many predict), this could, indeed, induce migration waves of large proportions.

Yet how trustworthy are these estimates? As mentioned earlier, the survival of reinsurance companies depends on the accuracy of their estimates regarding risks. Then again, they may want to promote climate change mitigation policies to reduce uncertainty, which will make setting premiums easier for them and thus reduce their transaction costs.

It is noteworthy that in one of the two reports just cited (Bevere and Gloor 2020), Swiss Re argues that the rise in losses due to natural disasters that have occurred until today is mainly due to past economic growth, which implies that more valuable assets have been created whose destruction now causes higher losses, and to denser urbanization, which implies that more people will be affected per square kilometer hit by a natural disaster. Swiss Re estimates that these two factors are responsible for some 55 percent of the growth in economic losses between 1980 and 2019. For emerging economies, this number is estimated to be 70 percent. An additional factor is general population growth, as it increases the expected number of people affected for every natural disaster.

However, the empirical evidence is not so clear. To study the changes in terms of fatalities and income lost, Formetta and Feyen (2019) think of disaster risk as composed of three components: (1) hazard, (2) exposure, and (3) vulnerability. To take account of these three factors, they express fatalities as a proportion of the entire population and economic losses as a percentage of GDP and find "a clear decreasing trend in both human and economic vulnerability, with global average mortality and economic loss rates that have dropped by six and a half and nearly five times, respectively, from 1980–1989 to 2007–2016."

Based on these estimates and predictions, modifications of emergency constitutions do not seem to be justified. Before advocating modifications in emergency constitutions, other questions would need to be dealt with too. One is the predictability of disasters: If they have become more predictable (both with regard to their occurrence and their effects), it might make sense to endow governments with the necessary tools in the realm of regular powers implying a "normal" state of affairs. A completely different aspect is the question of whether climate change increases the spread of pathogens and in turn pandemics? If that is the case, provisions for health-induced pandemics may need to be fine-tuned. The COVID-19 pandemic showed that many emergency constitutions were apparently not written with health-related disasters in mind (Hodge et al., 2020).

These two aspects definitely deserve closer scrutiny. But based on what we know today, a broadening of emergency constitutions due to climate change does not seem warranted at this stage.

15.3.2 Climate Change Causing Violent Conflict?

During the course of this book (and in Chapters 6 and 13 in particular), we have shown that as a consequence of SOEs human rights – and the rule of law more generally – may suffer. In addition, we have shown that the recovery of such rights – the time it takes to reestablish the status quo ante – is affected by the emergency constitution. We have also seen that natural disasters give less reason to be concerned than terrorist acts and other instances of domestic turmoil such as mass demonstrations, general strikes, and even armed conflict. But it has been argued that climate change may function as a "threat multiplier" making various kinds of domestic turmoil more likely. The question thus is: Does climate change increase the probability of such events?

Here again, the available empirical evidence seems anything but clear-cut. Buhaug (2015, 269) offers a succinct summary: "Ten years of generalizable quantitative research on climate change and armed conflict appears to have produced more confusion than knowledge … The most immediate insight gained from quantitative research on climate and conflict is that the two phenomena are not connected in the simple and direct manner as sometimes portrayed."

Buhaug (ibid.) then moves on and offers some reasons for the unsatisfactory state of our knowledge: Empirical analyses usually do not match well with theoretical arguments; the quantitative literature is generally weak on theory; identified patterns often come along with post hoc "explanations"; the causal frameworks discussed in abstract theory are usually too complex for empirical testing; and most empirical work relates to short-term changes in weather patterns or to extreme weather events, but not to climate change.

A Case Study: Civil War in Syria Caused by Climate Change?

Many people take it for granted that one – if not the central – reason for the civil war in Syria that has been raging since 2011 and that has had millions of people displaced within the country and made millions of them international refugees is climate change. This explanation has been used by Barack Obama, John Kerry, Bernie Sanders, and Prince (now King) Charles among others.

Most people who support this evaluation seem to have a three-step sequence in mind: (1) anthropogenic emissions were crucial in causing a serious drought before 2010; (2) the drought led to domestic migration; which (3) caused unrest which led to the civil war. Selby et al. (2017) have analyzed the evidence in support of these three steps. Here is a very brief summary of their findings: While Northeast Syria experienced very low rainfall between 2006 and 2009, this was not true for other Syrian regions. In addition, the drought in the northeastern part of the country is unlikely to have been caused by climate change.

Regarding the second step (namely domestic migration), Selby et al. (2017) find that it is not as unusual, as claimed by some. And in all likelihood the migration observed during the crucial years was not induced by the drought but rather by political decisions of the regime. The Assad regime had removed both fuel and fertilizer subsidies which made the survival of farmers very challenging and may have caused many to move westward. In addition, most agricultural production in the Northeast was not heavily dependent on rainfall as it was irrigation based. The authors conclude that the resulting unrest was not primarily a consequence of the drought but rather due to socioeconomic and political reasons.

De Chatel (2014) makes a very similar case arguing that the uprisings were not caused by climate change but by the inadequate policies of the Syrian government. In summary, the Syrian case seems inadequate as an example of climate change leading to domestic conflict.

Buhaug is definitely not alone in his critique. Bernauer et al. (2012) criticize that many analyses are simply not differentiated enough ("… it would be helpful to know what kinds of environmental changes have what kinds of influences on what kinds of conflict") but suspect that two indirect effects may be relevant, namely those via economic performance and migration.

In sum, the evidence regarding the effects of climate change on armed conflict is clearly unclear. Before any advice regarding possible changes in emergency constitutions can be given, more research unveiling the exact transmission channels – to the degree that they exist – is definitely needed.

15.3.3 Anticipating Novel Events – Such as Cyberwar?

Climate change seems to be one of the megatopics of our time. As we have seen in the previous two sections, as of today, there is little reason to adjust emergency constitutions as a consequence of climate change though. But how about other events threatening societies' infrastructure and maybe even their survival?

Predicting the effects of novel – or even completely unknown – events seems to be closer to science fiction than to empirically grounded science. Yet it does make sense to try to anticipate the possible effects of some possible events – and to think about how governments could best react to the ensuing challenges. Events that are mentioned as possible future challenges include cyberwar, cyberterrorism, and other forms of large-scale internet failures but also geo-engineering gone wrong, bio-engineering gone wrong, and artificial intelligence gone wrong.

As far as we know today, cyberwar is the most manifest type of danger among the possibilities just named. It has been evaluated that Russia prepared the invasion of Ukraine in 2022 by deploying more destructive malware "than the rest of the world‘s cyberpowers combined typically use in a given year."[1] By doing so, Russia rendered the computer systems of multiple government, military, and critical infrastructure sectors inoperable. The satellite of the internet provider KA-SAT was knocked off with negative consequences for military, intelligence, and police units.

[1] Nato Assistant Secretary David Cattler, as cited in *The Economist*, November 30, 2022, page 14.

But this is only the most recent important case of cyber warfare. Given the various experiences with cyber warfare, it seems that the protection of critical infrastructure should get high priority such that the emergencies that can be a consequence of cyber warfare never materialize. As of today, it is difficult to identify any concrete need to modify existing emergency constitutions. It seems, rather, a priority to increase technological resilience first.

15.4 Possible Modifications in Legalized Emergency Regimes

Until now, our focus has been on the question of whether particular events – known or only imagined – make modifications in existing emergency constitutions desirable. Our answer to this question has been that of today, there is little reason to amend emergency constitutions as a consequence of these events. This is why we now shift our attention from events to actors and now ask: Should emergency provisions be extended to actors presently not enjoying any extra powers during an SOE?

We discuss this question in two sections here: The first section deals with the question of whether international organizations should be given emergency powers while the second section asks whether (domestic) independent regulatory agencies such as central banks should be allocated emergency powers.

15.4.1 Should International Organizations be Endowed with Emergency Powers?

We propose to discuss this question with a focus on the European Union (EU) as it is by far the most advanced international organization. That said, it is more appropriately recognized as a supranational organization implying that any possible insights with regard to the EU may not be directly applicable to other international organizations.

Carl Schmitt (1922) famously stated that "sovereign is he who decides on the exceptional case." Now, thinking about an emergency constitution for the EU seems awkward as it is a club of sovereign nation states but not sovereign itself. Moreover, it is not based on a formal constitution and giving it an emergency constitution before it even has a firmly established constitution seems to put the cart before the horse. Yet from an economic point of view, any foundational document can be deemed an organization's constitution no matter the name accorded to the document, implying that the Treaty of Lisbon can be interpreted as the EU's constitution.

Once a disaster – or other event conventionally justifying the declaration of an SOE – assumes a multinational character, it seems only straightforward to think about multinational responses. With a focus on the EU, Kreuder-Sonnen and White (2022) recently proposed to think of four different types of exceptionalism that may become relevant. Here are their four types:

(1) *Supranational emergency politics*; these would be based on European institutions expanding their discretion. An example includes the Troika that monitored the behavior of the Greek government (among others) during the financial crisis in 2010 and the subsequent years.
(2) *Multilateral emergency politics*; these take place when the member states expand their discretion collectively. Examples include the creation of the European Financial Stability Facility (EFSF) or the European Stability Mechanism, although both only apply to members of the euro zone.
(3) *Unilateral emergency politics*; these are observed when one or more member state suspends or abrogates EU rules. The so-called migration crisis of 2015 was met by a number of member states simply ignoring the Dublin regulation of the EU, which contains clear rules for which EU member state is responsible for the examination of applications for asylum.
(4) *Domestic emergency politics*; the most conventional way of running SOEs.

In the remainder of this section, the primary focus will be on the first two types. With regard to the last two types, an important question is how the EU can ensure compliance with its rules, which is certainly also an important issue but not our focus here.

Over the last dozen years or so, the EU has been subject to a number of severe crises such as the euro crisis which began in 2008, the refugee crisis of 2015, and the COVID-19 pandemic of 2020/2021. The Treaty of Lisbon does not contain any explicit emergency provisions, yet the EU expanded its powers in a number of ways during each of these crises. Kreuder-Sonnen (2021) goes further than this and claims that the EU exceeded its powers de facto in numerous ways.

According to him, five traits stand out, namely (1) self-empowerment, (2) rule circumvention, (3) rule bending, (4) domination, and (5) judicial deference. His claims are that the EU Commission and Council of Ministers empowered themselves without consulting member states, circumvented or at least bent formal rules set down in treaties, dominated member states, and failed to defer to judicial decisions.

The EU always insists on its members being countries respecting the rule of law. Unfortunately, the types of behavior outlined by Kreuder-Sonnen (2021) are hardly compatible with the rule of law, thereby shedding some doubt on the priority accorded to rule of law standards. The question thus is whether the introduction of explicit emergency provisions could improve the degree to which the EU complies with generally accepted rule-of-law standards. Moreover, explicit emergency provisions may have the advantage of reducing uncertainty and making EU policy decisions more predictable.

The analysis by Kreuder-Sonnen (2021) that the EU has exceeded its powers in numerous ways during the last crises immediately raises the question why such exceedance has not been stopped by anyone. To answer that question, it makes sense to take the preferences of the relevant actors explicitly into account while keeping in mind that EU institutions are not characterized by a clear separation of powers that apply to most democratic countries.

During the various recent crises, leading European politicians have learned that they are able to overstep the constraints of the European treaties and enact policy instruments and policy measures that will likely become permanent. Formally amending the treaties has become almost impossible as the unanimous consent of all EU member states is necessary. In such a situation, the possibility to amend the treaties de facto by making some emergency measures permanent is politically a very attractive option. In all likelihood, explicit emergency provisions would limit such competences, which is why leading European politicians are likely to be against it.

In such a situation at the nation-state level, one would hope that constitutional veto players would raise their voices and step in. Primary candidates are the nation-state parliaments as well as the judiciary. At the level of the EU, such hopes may be in vain as most relevant actors seem to be pro-integrationist. In principle, both the European Parliament as well as the Court of Justice of the EU are capable of assuming the role of veto players and constraining the policies that can be implemented by the Commission. But due to their inherent interest in expanding the powers of the EU, they are unlikely to do so.

Under the current rules, then, the Council and the Commission have the discretion to make emergency measures permanent. From the point of view of an impartial spectator, the prospect of having some sort of permanent emergency is very unwelcome and probably the strongest reason in favor of explicit emergency provisions at the European level. At the same time, the exact same observation leads us to predict that such emergency provisions are unlikely to be adopted any time soon as they would reduce the discretionary leeway of those who would need to push their introduction.

15.4.2 The Role of (Domestic) Independent Regulatory Agencies in Emergencies

Over the last couple of decades, independent regulatory agencies have been established in many countries. They have often been given considerable decision-making power (Jordana et al., 2018 is an overview). These agencies may play an important role in dealing with emergencies. Competition rules, for example, may be deemed too strict after an economic crisis, emission standards too strict and so forth.

In the last section, we focused on the most advanced international organization, namely the EU. In this section, we focus on the question of whether, under an SOE, the mandate of central banks should be modified as central banks have been granted formal independence in a large number of countries. Here, too, we will refer to the central bank of the EU as an example.

Before dealing with the normative aspects of the question, let's do some stocktaking. Analyzing current constitutions, we identified fifteen constitutions that mention central banks and their mandates in connection with emergencies. More than half of these (namely eight) are Latin American countries (Bolivia, Brazil, Chile, the Dominican Republic, El Salvador, Guatemala, Honduras, and Paraguay), two are successor states of the Soviet Union (Georgia and Tajikistan), one used to be part of Yugoslavia (North Macedonia), two are located on the Arab peninsula (Bahrain and Yemen) and one is in West Africa (Liberia). It is noteworthy that no country in Western Europe, North America, or East Asia has explicitly included emergency-based provisions.

The most frequently mentioned event types that justify some deviation from the standard mandate are war (including the threat of war, foreign invasion, or rebellion) and natural or public disasters. Given one of these events, the central bank is then allowed to directly finance government, which it is not allowed to do in normal times. As emergencies are frequently connected with important financial challenges and recovery/reconstruction measures after both wars and natural disasters are likely to be very costly, such exceptions do seem to have some plausibility.

Yet such exceptions may also create undesirable incentives. Suppose a government is keen on being financed by its central bank, which is prohibited under normal times but legal after the declaration of an emergency. This possibility may constitute sufficiently strong incentives for some governments to declare an SOE.

The European Central Bank (ECB) is special in the sense that its mandate is not based on some nation-state constitution but on the Treaty of Lisbon, that is, on the quasi-constitution of a supranational organization. The ECB has been an important part of the EU's policy responses to a number of recent crises: its Pandemic Emergency Purchase Program (PEPP), for example, has the function to "counter the serious risks to the monetary policy transmission mechanism and the outlook for the euro area posed by the coronavirus (COVID-19) outbreak" (www.ecb.europa.eu/mopo/implement/pepp/html/index.en.html). With a total cost of €1,850 billion, the program, which was terminated in March 2022, was a huge undertaking without any clear constitutional backing.

15.5 Possible Modifications beyond Emergency Regimes: Strengthening Resilience

So far, very few – if any – convincing arguments in favor of important changes to emergency constitutions have been identified in this chapter. But societies do need to cope and prepare for emergencies, in particular as the probability of natural disasters occurring seems to be on the rise.

As a consequence of the pandemic, resilience has become a new buzzword. Traditionally, the word referred to the capacity of individuals to withstand major challenges in their lives. Here, we are not concerned with individuals being resilient, but with resilience on the societal level which should, in turn, increase individual resilience. If societies are able to anticipate disasters and adopt both behavioral norms and policy decisions accordingly, this will increase resilience – and possibly make the extension of emergency powers superfluous. In other words, we propose to think of resilience as a substitute to far-reaching emergency provisions. Central to our thinking are avoiding moral hazard and similar public choice problems, and the need to use decentralized local knowledge when building resilience and effective emergency responses.

Moral hazard may become a real problem when central government provides some form of emergency insurance, which weakens the incentives of local government and individuals to do so themselves. This mechanism, which is often referred to as a Peltzman effect, was important during the COVID-19 pandemic as stricter public regulation weakened citizens' compliance with individual safety recommendations (Henk et al. 2023). This aspect emphasizes that emergency resilience must focus on empowering individuals and that excessive government action may entail the opposite.

Sobel and Leeson (2006, 56) emphasize a second problem, which they prefer to call a "tragedy of political commons," which occurs "when too many individuals and groups have access to the decision-making process with overlapping powers of obstruction." Their main argument is that layers of bureaucracy may imply that emergency responses are very slow to materialize and may never happen. In addition, layered bureaucracies and series of veto players may often entail a bias against action, which Sobel and Leeson argue can create Type II errors in handling emergencies.

However, they also note the opposite problem in what they term "glory seeking" by politicians and other officials. Sobel and Leeson's description of glory seeking is a version of the broader concept of action bias, which is a serious concern in special circumstances (Patt and Zeckhauser 2000) and which we already referred to in the last chapter. The problem has both a psychological and a political aspect. Psychologically, Patt and Zeckhauser argue that people tend to believe that "doing something" is always better than doing nothing, as they ignore unintended side effects and less immediately visible consequences. The political aspect of the problem comes about because voters are likely to reward politicians for doing well in unique circumstances, but not to punish them for doing poorly or directly causing problems. For both reasons, politicians and officials are likely to commit Type I errors and overdue emergency efforts. Politicians in addition may tend to ignore longer-run unintended consequences and engage in myopic emergency policy, when some or most of the consequences will occur after the next election.

Another part of effective emergency policy and resilience is the full use of knowledge and in particular decentral and local knowledge. Pennington (2021) focuses on this aspect by employing Hayek's distinction between simple and complex phenomena. His attempt to understand the nature of the challenge facing policymakers in responding to emergencies, and specifically pandemics, shows that while government action may be justifiable, policymakers face a fundamental problem: It is likely to be impossible to systematically distinguish good from bad policy responses. Pennington (2021, 217) finds that the very "*emergency* nature of the situation severely limits the scope for policymakers to avoid large scale errors and to learn in a sufficiently timely manner."

Finally, although numerous expert committees have produced lots of reports evaluating policy measures from various angles, the policy choices made by government invariably involve tough tradeoffs between public health concerns on the one hand and individual liberty, education and economic production on the other. The problem here is that no single "best" tradeoff exists because not only societies, but also single individuals, can reasonably disagree on what their preferred tradeoff is. The inherent problem is one of aggregating individual preferences to find some form of "public will" or public opinion, which is known to be impossible under general conditions (Arrow 1951).

Overall, these problems appear to be endemic to emergency policies and thus also to the design of optimal emergency constitutions. Considerable local and individual autonomy is required in order to make the most of local and dispersed knowledge, as well as getting the tradeoffs approximately right for a majority of citizens. Good policy may also include some form of keeping memories of emergencies alive in order to, among other things, reduce problems of probability neglect (cf., Sunstein 2002). However, these are only ideas on how to solve a major problem, the severity of which the findings of this book serve to underline.

15.6 Concluding Remarks

With these considerations, you have finally arrived at the very end of a very long book. Now, it is common practice to use concluding sections (or even entire chapters) not only for summing up the various insights that the rest of the book has offered, but also to flag missing knowledge and to point out some directions for future research. This book is no exception.

The overall insight in this book is that although emergency constitutions do have some intended consequences, it is the problematic side effects and political misuse that dominate the findings. Our findings also raise a number of additional questions that may be worth dealing with in future research. We here mention only a few obvious examples.

We find that most of the challenges regarding the rule of law as a consequence of SOEs have not been caused by SOEs declared in the wake of natural disasters but rather those declared in conjunction with terrorist events and domestic turmoil. One question we leave for future research thus is whether natural disasters lead to an increase in domestic turmoil events. If that is the case, they could, hence, be considered a "deep" cause for the issues connected with them, including the overstepping of constitutional constraints as discussed in Chapter 11.

Second, we note that if disasters occur more frequently and are more predictable, it might make sense to extend governments' constitutional competences such that they are able to fight them without needing to declare an SOE. This would hence imply modifying the relationship between a "normal state of affairs" and an SOE. However, if the frequency or severity of natural disasters has not increased, but the number of SOEs declared on their behalf has (cf., Lomborg 2020), then we are left with a situation that does not point toward more powers, but lends itself to analytical scrutiny from a public choice/political economy approach.

A final example is analysis of the economic and social consequences of both natural disasters and domestic events such as coups and other conflicts. Tanzi (2022, 140), for example, encourages the development of what he calls "disaster economics" as a new subdiscipline of economics and political science to study such questions. Thinking about such a discipline, Tanzi discusses the possibility to regard "uncertainty" as a new kind of market failure, which government ought to alleviate. This perspective raises the question of governments spending too much on risk mitigation when they instead ought to spend more on the mitigation of uncertainty. However, Tanzi's perspective also raises new political perspectives, as uncertainty can also be analyzed as a government failure, and thus a phenomenon that would caution against state action.

After writing a book about the topic, we could continue with other examples of possible extensions, further development, and new questions. Yet at the end of the day, we emphasize Knight's (1921) distinction between risk and uncertainty, which defined what is now often known as Knightian uncertainty. This distinction may be important to understand the special nature of emergencies: While risk can be calculated as the probability of events and their severity is known – and individuals and firms can therefore insure themselves against it – emergencies entail Knightian uncertainty where the lack of real, quantifiable knowledge about the event makes both insurance and detailed policy-making logically impossible. Despite decades of research, it is, for example, still not possible to predict with any precision when an earthquake or hurricane will happen and how damaging it will be. The entire topic must, as we have attempted throughout the book, be approached with considerable epistemological humility.

Effective constitutional emergency provisions must therefore be highly general rules that are adapted to a given society while leaving limited room for the kind of political misuse we have found in this book. We can neither predict emergencies, nor tell politicians exactly what to do or which emergency provisions to adopt. However, our findings are consistent with Benjamin Franklin's warning about asking government to do too much:

They who can give up essential liberty to obtain a little temporary safety deserve neither liberty nor safety. (Benjamin Franklin)

References

Abadie, A., Gardeazabal, J. (2008). Terrorism and the world economy. *European Economic Review* 52(1):1–27.

Abdulrauf, L. (2020). *Nigeria's Emergency (Legal) Response to COVID-19: A Worthy Sacrifice for Public Health? VerfBlog,* 2020/5/18, https://verfassungsblog.de/nigerias-emergency-legal-response-to-covid-19-a-worthy-sacrifice-for-public-health/, https://doi.org/10.17176/20200518-133659-0

Abrahams, M. (2008). What terrorists really want – terrorist motives and counterterrorism strategy. *International Security* 32(4):78–105.

Acemoglu, D., Robinson, J., Torvik, R. (2013). Why do voters dismantle checks and balances? *Review of Economic Studies* 80:845–875.

Acemoglu, D., Ticchi, D., Vindigni, A. (2010). A theory of military dictatorships. *American Economic Journal: Macroeconomics* 2(1):1–42.

Ackerman, B. (2004). The emergency constitution. *Yale Law Journal* 113(5):1029–1091.

Aghion, P., Algan, Y., Cahuc, P., Shleifer, A. (2010). Regulation and distrust. *The Quarterly Journal of Economics* 125(3):1015–1049.

Akça, İ., Balta-Paker, E. (2013). Beyond military tutelage? Turkish military politics and the AKP government. Chapter 4 in Canan-Sokullu, E. (ed), *Debating Security in Turkey. Challenges and Changes in the Twenty-First Century*. New York: Lexington Books, pp. 77–92.

Alasti, S. (2020). *The Iranian Legal Response to Covid-19: A Constitutional Analysis of Coronavirus Lockdown, VerfBlog,* 2020/4/24, https://verfassungsblog.de/the-iranian-legal-response-to-covid-19-a-constitutional-analysis-of-coronavirus-lockdown/, https://doi.org/10.17176/20200424-164907-0

Ambedkar, B. R. (1949). Constituent assembly debates, August 4, 1949, Vol. IX:177.

Amnesty International (2017). Dangerously Disproportionate. The Ever-Expanding National Security State in Europe. Available at: www.amnesty.org/en/latest/campaigns/2017/01/dangerously-disproportionate/

Amnesty International. (2018). Spain: Counter-terror law used to crush satire and creative expression online. Press release, Amnesty International, March 13. Available at www.amnesty.org/en/latest/news/2018/03/

spain-counter-terror-law-used-to-crush-satire-and-creative-expression-online/ (accessed November 2018).

Andersen, J. J., Aslaksen, S. (2013). Oil and political survival. *Journal of Development Economics* 100(1):89–106.

Andersen, S., Bjørnager, J. A. (2020). Soldater nervøse over minkindsatsen. *Berlingske Tidende*, November 16.

Arrow, K. (1951). *Social Choice and Individual Values*. New Haven: Yale University Press.

Asal, V., Hoffman, A. M. (2016). Media effects: Do terrorist organizations launch foreign attacks in response to levels of press freedom or press attention? *Conflict Management and Peace Science* 33(4):381–399.

Atkeson, A., Kopecky, K., Zha, T. (2020). Four stylized facts about Covid-19. NBER Working Paper Series, Working Paper 27719.

Bäck, H., Debus, M., Dumont, P. (2011). Who gets what in coalition governments? Predictors of portfolio allocation in parliamentary democracies. *European Journal of Political Research* 50(4):441–478.

Balasubramaniam, R. R. (2020). *Covid-19: Malaysia and the Return of Rule by Law, VerfBlog*, 2020/5/16, https://verfassungsblog.de/covid-19-malaysia-and-the-return-of-rule-by-law/, https://doi.org/10.17176/20200516-133138-0

Ban, C. (2021). Central banking in pandemic times. *Global Perspectives* 2(1):24188.

Bandyopadhyay, S., Sandler, T., Javed Younas, J. (2018). Trade and terrorism: A disaggregated approach. *Journal of Peace Research* 55(5):656–670.

Banks, A. S. (2004). *Banks' Cross-National Time-Series Data Archive*. Binghamton, NY: Databanks International [distributor].

Barrett, P., Chen, S. (2021). Social repercussions of pandemics. IMF Working Paper 21/21.

BBC. (2020). Philippines top broadcaster ABS-CBN denied new licence. BBC News, 10 July. www.bbc.com/news/world-asia-53360925

BEA. (2016). US Bureau of Economic Analysis. Online databases; data available at www.bea.gov/ (accessed October 2016).

Beck, T., Clarke, G., Groff, A., Keefer, P., Walsh, P. (2001). New tools in comparative political economy: The database of political institutions. *World Bank Economic Review* 15(1):165–176.

Becker, L. B., Vlad, T., Nusser, N. (2007). An evaluation of press freedom indicators. *International Communication Gazette* 69:5–28.

Beckmann, K. B., Dewenter, R., Thomas, T. (2017). Can news draw blood? The impact of media coverage on the number and severity of terror attacks. *Peace Economics, Peace Science and Public Policy* 23(1): 1–16.

Bendavid, E., Oh, C., Bhattacharya, J., Ioannidis, J. P. A. (2021). Assessing mandatory stay-at-home and business closure effects on the spread of COVID-19. *European Journal of Clinical Research* 51: e13484.

Bennett, D. L., Bjørnskov, C., Gohmann, S. F. (2021). Coups, regime transitions, and institutional quality. *Journal of Comparative Economics* 49(2): 627–643.

Berggren, N., Bjørnskov, C. (2017). The market-promoting and market-preserving role of social trust in reforms of policies and institutions. *Southern Economic Journal* 84:3–25.

Bernauer, T., Böhmelt, T., Koubi, V. (2012). Environmental changes and violent conflict. *Environmental Research Letters* 7(1):015601.

Bernholz, P. (1979). Freedom and constitutional economic order. *Zeitschrift für die gesamte Staatswissenschaft/Journal of Institutional and Theoretical Economics* (H. 3), 510–532.

Bernholz, P. (2006). International political system, supreme values and terrorism. *Public Choice* 128(1): 221–231.

Bernholz, P. (2013). Independent central banks as a component of the separation of powers. *Constitutional Political Economy* 24(3):199–214.

Berrebi, C., Ostwald, J. (2011). Earthquakes, hurricanes, and terrorism: Do natural disasters incite terror? *Public Choice* 149(3):383–403.

Besley, T., Burgess, R. (2001). Political agency, government responsiveness and the role of the media. *European Economic Review* 45(4–6):629–640.

Besley, T., Prat, A. (2006). Handcuffs for the grabbing hand? Media capture and government accountability. *American Economic Review* 96(3):720–736.

Besley, T., Robinson, J. A. (2010). Quis custodiet ipsos custodes? Civilian control over the military. *Journal of the European Economic Association* 8(2–3):655–663.

Bevere, L., Gloor, M. (2020). *Natural Catastrophes in Times of Economic Accumulation and Climate Change*. Zürich: Swiss Re Institute.

Bevere, L., Schwartz, M., Sharan, R., Zimmerli, P. (2018). Natural catastrophes and man-made disasters in 2017: A year of record-breaking losses. Swiss Re Institute.

Bhatia, G. (2020). *An Executive Emergency: India's Response to Covid-19, VerfBlog,* 2020/4/13, https://verfassungsblog.de/an-executive-emergency-indias-response-to-covid-19/ https://doi.org/10.17176/20200413-153127-0

Bjørnskov, C. (2019). The political economy of trust. Chapter 32 in Congleton, R., Grofman, B., Voigt, S. (eds.), *Oxford Handbook of Public Choice*, Vol. 1. Oxford: Oxford University Press, pp. 628–648.

Bjørnskov, C. (2020). Why do military dictatorships become presidential democracies? Mapping the democratic interests of autocratic regimes. *Public Choice* 185:21–43.

Bjørnskov, C. (2021). Did lockdown work? An economist's cross-country comparison. *CESifo Economic Studies* 67(3):318–331.

Bjørnskov, C. (2022). Coups and economic crises. IFN working paper 1449, IFN, Stockholm.

Bjørnskov, C., Rode, M. (2020). Regime types and regime change: A new dataset on democracy, coups, and political institutions. *Review of International Organizations* 15:531–551.

Bjørnskov, C., Voigt, S. (2014). Constitutional verbosity and social trust. *Public Choice* 161(1–2):91–112.

Bjørnskov, C., Voigt, S. (2022). Notstandsverfassungen: Wortfülle kulturell tradiert. In: G. Pehnelt (ed.), *Fragen unserer Zeit: Festschrift für Andreas Freytag zum 60*. Geburtstag. Berlin: Logos Verlag, pp. 33–44.

Bjørnskov, C., Gutmann, J., Freytag, A. (2022). Coups and the dynamics of media freedom. *Economic Modelling* 116, 106025.

Bjørnskov, C., Voigt, S., Khesali, M. (2022). Unconstitutional states of emergency. *Journal of Legal Studies* 51(2):455–481.

Blalock, G., Kadiyali, V., Simon, D. (2009). Driving fatalities after 9/11: A hidden cost of terrorism. *Applied Economics* 41:1717–1729.

Boudreaux, C. J., Iha, A., Escaleras, M. (2023). Natural disasters, entrepreneurship activity, and the moderating role of country governance. *Small Business Economics* 60(4):1483–1508.

Bove, V., Nisticò, R. (2014a). Military in politics and budgetary allocations. *Journal of Comparative Economics* 42(4):1065–1078.

Bove, V., Nisticò, R. (2014b). Coups d'état and defense spending: A counterfactual analysis. *Public Choice* 161(3–4):321–344.

Brambor, T., Clark, W. R., Golder, M. (2006). Understanding interaction models: Improving empirical analyses. *Political Analysis* 14:63–82.

Brandt, P. T., Sandler, T. (2010). What do transnational terrorists target? Has it changed? Are we safer? *Journal of Conflict Resolution* 54(2):214–236.

Brass, P. R. (1990). *The Politics of India since Independence*. New York: Cambridge University Press.

Briggs, D. C. (2004). Causal inference and the Heckman model. *Journal of Educational and Behavioral Statistics* 29:397–420.

Brophy-Baermann, B., Conybeare, J. A. (1994). Retaliating against terrorism: Rational expectations and the optimality of rules versus discretion. *American Journal of Political Science* 38:196–210.

Brunel, S. (2015). Eruption du Cotopaxi, une catastrophe utile? *Le Monde* August 18.

Brunetti, A., Weder, B. (2003). A free press is bad news for corruption. *Journal of Public Economics* 87(7):1801–1824.

Brunnermeier, M. K. (2021). *The Resilient Society*. Princeton, NJ: Princeton University Press.

Buchanan, A. (1992). Self-determination and the right to secede. *Journal of International Affairs* 347–365.

Buchanan, J. M. (1975). *The Limits of Liberty – Between Anarchy and Leviathan*. Chicago: University of Chicago Press.

Buchanan, J. M. (1977). *Freedom in Constitutional Contract: Perspectives of a Political Economist.* College Station: Texas A & M.

Buchanan, J. M. (2004). The status of the status quo. *Constitutional Political Economy* 15(2):133–1444.

Buchanan, J. M., Tullock, G. (1962). *The Calculus of Consent: Logical Foundations of Constitutional Democracy.* Ann Arbor: University of Michigan Press.

Budoo, A. (2020). *Rescuing Human Rights in Mauritius During the COVID 19 Tsunami, VerfBlog,* 2020/4/22, https://verfassungsblog.de/rescuing-human-rights-in-mauritius-during-the-covid-19-tsunami/ https://doi.org/10.17176/20200422-182625-0

Buhaug, H. (2015). Climate–conflict research: Some reflections on the way forward. *WIREs Climate Change* 6(3): 269–275.

Buhaug, H., Nordkvelle, J., Bernauer, T., Böhmelt, T., Brzoska, M., Busby, J. W., ... Von Uexkull, N. (2014). One effect to rule them all? A comment on climate and conflict. *Climatic Change* 127(3):391–397.

Carey, J. M., Shugart, M. S. (Eds.). (1998). *Executive Decree Authority.* Cambridge: Cambridge University Press.

Casson, D. (2008). Emergency judgment: Carl Schmitt, John Locke, and the paradox of prerogative. *Politics & Policy* 36(6):944–971.

Cavdarevic, I. (2020). *Serbia and Covid-19: State of Emergency in a State in Disarray, VerfBlog,* 2020/5/12, https://verfassungsblog.de/serbia-and-covid-19-state-of-emergency-in-a-state-in-disarray/, https://doi.org/10.17176/20200513-013341-0

Central Intelligence Agency. (2020). *CIA World Factbook.* Langley: Central Intelligence Agency.

Chatterjee, S. (1992). *Governor's Role in the Indian Constitution.* New Delhi: Mittal Publications.

Chaudhry, R., Dranitsaris, G., Mubashir, T., Bartoszko, J., Riazi, S. (2020). A country level analysis measuring the impact of government actions, country preparedness and socioeconomic factors on COVID-19 mortality and related health outcomes. *EClinical Medicine* 25, art. 100464.

Cheibub, J. A., Limongi, F. (2002). Democratic institutions and regime survival: Parliamentary and presidential democracies reconsidered. *Annual Review of Political Science* 5(1):151–179.

Cheibub, J. A., Gandhi, J., Vreeland, J. R. (2010). Democracy and dictatorship revisited. *Public Choice* 143:67–101.

Chen, Y., Ordeshook, P. C. (1994). Constitutional secession clauses. *Constitutional Political Economy* 5:45–60.

Chilton, A., Versteeg, M. (2020). *How Constitutional Rights Matter.* Oxford: Oxford University Press.

Choutagunta, A., Manish, G. P., Rajagopalan, S. (2021). Battling COVID-19 with dysfunctional federalism: Lessons from India. *Southern Economic Journal* 87(4):1267–1299.

Chowdhury, S. K. (2004). The effect of democracy and press freedom on corruption: An empirical test. *Economics Letters* 85(1):93–101.

Cingranelli, D., Richards, D. (2004). The Cingranelli-Richards (CIRI) Human Rights Database. Downloadable from ciri.binghamton.edu, last assessed June 2018.

Clinton, R. L. (1994). Game theory, legal history, and the origins of judicial review: A revisionist analysis of Marbury v. Madison. *American Journal of Political Science* 38(2):285–302.

Clokie, H. Mcd. (1947). Emergency powers and civil liberties. *Canadian Journal of Economics and Political Science* 13:384–394.

Cole, S., Healy, A., Werker, E. (2012). Do voters demand responsive governments? Evidence from Indian disaster relief. *Journal of Development Economics* 97(2):167–181.

Conrad, J., Milton, D. (2013). Unpacking the connection between terror and Islam. *Studies in Conflict and Terrorism* 36(4):315–336.

Coppedge, M., Lindberg, S., Skaaning, S-E., Teorell, J. (2016). Measuring high level democratic principles using the V-Dem data. *International Political Science Review* 37:580–593.

CoreLogic. (2014). CoreLogic identifies US States at highest risk of property damage loss from natural hazards. Available at www.corelogic.com/about-us/news/corelogic-identifies-us-states-at-highest-risk-of-property-damage-loss-from-natural-hazards.aspx (assessed in October 2016).

CPJ. (2020). Belarus cancels 2 journalists' accreditations after covering COVID-19 deaths. Committee to Protect Journalists, May 8. https://cpj.org/2020/05/belarus-cancels-2-journalists-accreditations-after/

Crassweller, R. D. (1966). *Trujillo: The Life and Times of a Caribbean Dictator*. New York: Macmillan.

Cruz, C., Keefer, P. (2015). Political parties, clientelism, and bureaucratic reform. *Comparative Political Studies* 48:1942–1973.

Davenport, C. (1996). "Constitutional promises" and repressive reality: A cross-national time-series investigation of why political and civil liberties are suppressed. *Journal of Politics* 58(3):627–654.

De Châtel, F. (2014). The role of drought and climate change in the Syrian uprising: Untangling the triggers of the revolution. *Middle Eastern Studies* 50(4):521–535.

De Figueiredo Jr, R. J., Weingast, B. R. (2005). Self-enforcing federalism. *Journal of Law, Economics, and Organization* 21(1):103–135.

De Haan, J., Bodea, C., Hicks, R., Eijffinger, S. C. (2018). Central bank independence before and after the crisis. *Comparative Economic Studies* 60(2):183–202.

De la Calle, L., Sánchez-Cuenca, I. (2012). Rebels without a territory: An analysis of nonterritorial conflicts in the world, 1970–1997. *Journal of Conflict Resolution* 56(4):580–603.

Deligiannis, T. (2012). The evolution of environment conflict research: Toward a livelihood framework. *Global Environmental Politics* 12(1):78–100.

Deng, F. (2010). Post-disaster reconfiguration of property rights in a transition economy. *Post-Communist Economies* 22(2):193–206.

Derpanopoulos, G., Frantz, E., Geddes, B., Wright, J. (2016). Are coups good for democracy? *Research and Politics* 3(1):1–7.

Di Lonardo, L. (2019). The partisan politics of counterterrorism: Reputations, policy transparency, and electoral outcomes. *Political Science Research and Methods* 7(2):253–269.

Diebel, M. (2019). *"Die Stunde der Exekutive" – das Bundesinnenministerium und die Notstandsgesetze 1949–1968*. Bonn: Bundeszentrale für politische Bildung.

Djankov, S., McLiesh, C., Nenova, T., Shleifer, A. (2003). Who owns the media? *Journal of Law and Economics* 46(2):341–382.

Dragu, T. (2011). Is there a trade-off between security and liberty? Executive bias, privacy protection, and terrorism prevention. *American Political Science Review* 105:64–78.

Dragu, T., Polborn, M. (2014). The rule of law in the fight against terrorism. *American Journal of Political Science* 58:511–525.

Dreze, J., Sen, A. (1990). *Hunger and Public Action*. Clarendon Press.

Drury, C., Olson, R. (1998). Disasters and political unrest: An empirical investigation. *Journal of Contingencies and Crisis Management* 6:153–161.

Dugan, L., Chenoweth, E. (2012). Moving beyond deterrence: The effectiveness of raising the expected utility of abstaining from terrorism in Israel. *American Sociological Review* 77(4):597–624.

Dyzenhaus, D. (2006). *The Constitution of Law. Legality in a Time of Emergency*. Cambridge: Cambridge University Press.

Egorov G., Guriev, S., Sonin, K. (2009). Why resource-poor dictators allow freer media: A theory and evidence from panel data. *American Political Science Review* 103:645–668.

Eichengreen, B. (2018). *The Populist Temptation: Economic Grievance and Political Reaction in the Modern Era*. Oxford: Oxford University Press.

Eldor, R., Melnick, R. (2004). Financial markets and terrorism. *European Journal of Political Economy* 20(2):367–386.

Elkins, Z., Ginsburg, T., Melton, J. (2009). *The Endurance of National Constitutions*. Cambridge: Cambridge University Press.

Elkins, Z., Ginsburg, T., Melton, J. (2014). The content of authoritarian constitutions. Chapter 7 in Ginsburg, T., Simpser, A. (eds.), *Constitutions in Authoritarian Regimes*. Cambridge: Cambridge University Press, pp. 141–164.

Ellaboudy, A. (2020). *Emergency Law Amendments to Fight Covid-19 in Egypt: Putting the Poison in the Honey, VerfBlog,* 2020/5/19, https://verfassungsblog.de/emergency-law-amendments-to-fight-covid-19-in-egypt-putting-the-poison-in-the-honey/ https://doi.org/10.17176/20200519-133749-0.

EMDAT. (2019). *EM-DAT: The International Disaster Database*. Database and codebook, Centre for Research on the Epidemiology of Disasters – CRED, Université Catholique de Louvain. Available at www.emdat.be/ (accessed March 2019).

Encyclopædia Britannica. (2018). Censorship. Online encyclopedia, accessed at www.britannica.com/topic/censorship#ref358885 (accessed January 2018).

Enders, W., Sandler, T. (1993). The effectiveness of antiterrorism policies: A vector-autoregression-intervention analysis. *American Political Science Review* 87(4):829–844.

Enders, W., Sandler, T. (2012). *The Political Economy of Terrorism*. Cambridge: Cambridge University Press.

Enders, W., Sandler, T., Gaibulloev, K. (2011). Domestic versus transnational terrorism: Data, decomposition, and dynamics. *Journal of Peace Research* 48(3):319–337.

Engerman, S. L., Sokoloff, K. L. (2008). Debating the role of institutions in political and economic development: Theory, history, and findings. *Annual Review of Political Science* 11:119–135.

Epifanio, M. (2011). Legislative response to international terrorism. *Journal of Peace Research* 48(3):399–411.

Escaleras, M., Anbarci, N., Register, C. (2007). Public sector corruption and major earthquakes: A potentially deadly interaction. *Public Choice* 132:209–230.

Fariss, C. J. (2014). Respect for human rights has improved over time: Modeling the changing standard of accountability. *American Political Science Review* 108(2):297–318.

Fariss, C. J. (2019). Yes, human rights practices are improving over time. *American Political Science Review* 113(3):868–881.

Fatovic, C. (2009). *Outside the Law – Emergency and Executive Power*. Baltimore: Johns Hopkins University Press.

Feenstra, R. C., Inklaar, R., Timmer, M. P. (2015). The next generation of the Penn World Table. *American Economic Review* 105(10):3150–3182.

Ferejohn, J., Pasquino, P. (2004). The law of the exception: A typology of emergency powers. *International Journal of Constitutional Law* 2(2):210–239.

Ferejohn, J., Weingast, B. R. (1992). A positive theory of statutory interpretation. *International Review of Law and Economics* 12(2):263–279.

Finn, J. E. (1991). *Constitutions in Crisis: Political Violence and the Rule of Law*. Oxford: Oxford University Press.

Fish, M. S., Kroenig, M. (2009). *The Handbook of National Legislatures: A Global Survey*. Cambridge: Cambridge University Press.

Formetta, G., Feyen, L. (2019). Empirical evidence of declining global vulnerability to climate-related hazards. *Global Environmental Change* 57:101920.

Freedom House. (2017). *Freedom in the Press 2017: Press Freedom's Dark Horizon*. Washington, DC: Freedom House.

Friedrich, C. (1968). *Constitutional Government and Democracy – Theory and Practice in Europe and America*. Waltham et al.: Blaisdell Publishing Company, 4th ed.

Gallup. (2018). *Gallup World Poll*. Database available at www.gallup.com/consulting/worldpoll/24046/About.aspx (accessed February 2019).

Gandhi, J. (2008). Dictatorial institutions and their impact on economic growth. *European Journal of Sociology* 49(1):3–30.

Gargarella, R. (2020). *The Fight Against COVID-19 in Argentina: Executive vs Legislative Branch, VerfBlog,* 2020/5/01, https://verfassungsblog.de/the-fight-against-covid-19-in-argentina-executive-vs-legislative-branch/, https://doi.org/10.17176/20200501-133308-0.

Garrett, T. A., Sobel, R. S. (2003). The political economy of FEMA disaster payments. *Economic Inquiry* 41(3):496–509.

Gassebner, M., Luechinger, S. (2011). Lock, stock, and barrel: A comprehensive assessment of the determinants of terror. *Public Choice* 149(3–4):235–261.

Gassebner, M., Jong-A-Pin, R., Mierau, J. O. (2008). Terrorism and electoral accountability: One strike, you're out!. *Economics Letters* 100(1):126–129.

Gehlbach, S., Sonin, K. (2014). Government control of the media. *Journal of Public Economics* 118: 163–171.

Gemenne, F., Barnett, J., Adger, W. N., Dabelko, G. D. (2014). Climate and security: Evidence, emerging risks, and a new agenda. *Climatic Change* 123(1):1–9.

Ginsburg, T., Versteeg, M. (2021). The bound executive: Emergency powers during the pandemic. *International Journal of Constitutional Law* 19(5):1498–1535.

Ginsburg, T., Elkins, Z., Blount, J. (2009). Does the process of constitution-making matter? *Annual Review of Law and Social Science* 5(5) (February): 201–223.

Gleditsch, N. P. (2012). Whither the weather? Climate change and conflict. *Journal of Peace Research* 49(1):3–9.

Goemans, H. E., Gleditsch, K. S., Chiozza, G. (2009). Introducing Archigos: A dataset of political leaders. *Journal of Peace Research* 46(2):269–283.

Government of India. (1988). Commission on Centre-state Relations, Vol I and II, Delhi: Government of India Press.

Grier, K., Grier, R., Moncrieff, H. J. (2023). Uncertain times: The causal effects of coups on national income. Paper presented at the annual conference of the Public Choice Society, Seattle, March 16–18.

Gross, O. (2003). Chaos and rules: Should responses to violent crises always be constitutional? *Yale Law Journal* 112:1011–1134.

GTD. (2018). *Global Terrorism Database Codebook: Inclusion Criteria and Variables*. College Park, MD: University of Maryland. Database available at www.start.umd.edu/gtd/ (accessed October 2018).

Guha-Sapir, D., Below, R., Hoyois, P. (2014). EM-DAT: International Disaster Database. Université Catholique de Louvain, Brussels. Available at www.emdat.be.

Guha-Sapir, D., Below, R., Hoyois, P. (2020). *EM-DAT: The CRED/OFDA International Disaster Database*. Database, Université Catholique de Louvain.

Guo, J., Kubli, D., Saner, P. (2021). *The Economics of Climate Change: No Action Not an Option*. Swiss Re Institute.

Gupte, P. R. (2017). India: "The Emergency" and the politics of mass sterilization. *Education About Asia* 22(3):40–44.

Gutmann, J., Voigt, S. (2015). The rule of law and constitutionalism in Muslim countries. *Public Choice* 162(3–4):351–380.

Gutmann, J., Voigt, S. (2020). Judicial independence in the EU: A puzzle. *European Journal of Law and Economics* 49(1): 83–100.

Hafner-Burton, E., Helfer, L., Fariss, C. (2011). Emergency and escape: Explaining derogations from human rights treaties. *International Organization* 65(4):673–707.

Hair, J. H. jr., Andersen, R. E., Tatham, R. L., Black, W. C. (1998). *Multivariate Data Analysis* (5th ed). New Jersey: Prentice Hall.

Harrington, J. (1992). *The Commonwealth of Oceana*. Cambridge: Cambridge University Press.

Hartman, J. F. (1981). Derogation from human rights treaties in public emergencies. *Harvard International Law Journal* 22:1–52.

Henisz, W. (2012). The Political Constraint Index (POLCON) dataset. Available at https://mgmt.wharton.upenn.edu/faculty/heniszpolcon/polcondataset/

Henk, K., Rosing, F., Wolff, F., Frenzel, S. B., van Dick, R., Erkens, V. A., Häusser, J. A., Mojzisch, A., Boer, D. (2023). An examination and extension of the Peltzman effect during the Covid-19 pandemic. *Current Research in Ecological and Social Psychology* 4, art. 100091.

Heritage Foundation. (2016). *2016 Index of Economic Freedom*. The Heritage Foundation and the Wall Street Journal, Washington DC.

Heston, A., Summers, R., Aten, B. (2012). Penn World Tables version 7.1. Philadelphia: Center for International Comparisons of Production, Income and Prices, University of Pennsylvania.

Higgs, R. (1987). *Crisis and Leviathan*. New York: Oxford University Press.

Hillman, A. L., Potrafke, N. (2018). Economic freedom and religion: An empirical investigation. *Public Finance Review* 46(2):249–275.

Hodge Jr, J. G., Piatt, J. L., Carey, E., Reinke, H. N. (2020). COVID's constitutional conundrum: Assessing individual rights in public health emergencies. *Tennessee Law Review* 88(4):837–887.

Hoffman, A. M., Shelton, C., Cleven, E. (2013). Press freedom, publicity, and the cross-national incidence of transnational terrorism. *Political Research Quarterly* 66:896–909.

Hoque, R. (2020). *Bangladesh's Unofficial Emergency: Managing the COVID-19 Crisis by Notifications, VerfBlog,* 2020/5/06, https://verfassungsblog.de/bangladeshs-unofficial-emergency-managing-the-covid-19-crisis-by-notifications/, https://doi.org/10.17176/20200506-133738-0.

Horne, F. (2017). State of Emergency Ends in Ethiopia. Available at: www.hrw.org/news/2017/08/07/state-emergency-ends-ethiopia.

Hsiang, S. M., Burke, M., Miguel, E. (2013). Quantifying the influence of climate on human conflict. *Science* 341(6151):1235367.

Huber, J. D., Martinez-Gallardo, C. (2008). Replacing cabinet ministers: Patterns of ministerial stability in parliamentary democracies. *American Political Science Review* 102(2):169–180.

Ignatieff, M. (2013). *The Lesser Evil: Political Ethics in an Age of Terror*. Princeton: Princeton University Press.

Igwenyi, B. O., Nwogbo-Egwu, C. C., Igwe, C. A. (2019). Nigerian governors get jittery when "State of Emergency" is mentioned: A juristic overview of S. 305 of the constitution of the federal republic of Nigeria, 1999 as amended. *Beijing Law Review* 10(5):1346–1355.

Ishak, P. (2019). Autocratic survival strategies: Does oil make a difference? *Peace Economics, Peace Science, and Public Policy* 25(2):1–22.

Iyer, S., Shrivastava, A. (2018). Religious riots and electoral politics in India. *Journal of Development Economics* 131:104–122.

Jain, S. K. (1994). *Party Politics and Centre-state Relations in India*. New Delhi: Abhinav Publications.

Jetter, M. (2017). The effect of media attention on terrorism. *Journal of Public Economics* 153:32–48.

Jones, S. G., Libicki, M. C. (2008). *How Terrorist Groups End: Lessons for Countering al Qa'ida*. Rand Corporation.

Jordana, J., Fernández-i-Marín, X., Bianculli, A. C. (2018). Agency proliferation and the globalization of the regulatory state: Introducing a data set on the institutional features of regulatory agencies. *Regulation & Governance* 12(4):524–540.

Kahn, M. (2005). The death toll from natural disasters: The role of income, geography, and institutions. *Review of Economics and Statistics* 87(2):271–284.

Kalhan, A. (2010). Constitution and 'extraconstitution': Colonial emergency regimes in postcolonial India and Pakistan, In Ramraj, V., Thiruvengadam, A. (eds.), *Emergency Powers in Asia: Exploring the Limits of Legality*, Cambridge: Cambridge University Press, pp. 89–120.

Keefer, P., Stasavage, D. (2002). Checks and balances, private information, and the credibility of monetary commitments. *International Organization* 56:751–774.

Keith, L. C. (2012). *Political Repression – Courts and the Law*. Philadelphia: University of Pennsylvania Press.

Keith, L. C., Poe, S. C. (2004). Are constitutional state of emergency clauses effective? An empirical exploration. *Human Rights Quarterly* 26(4):1071–1097.

Kellam, M., Stein, E. A. (2016). Silencing critics: Why and how presidents restrict media freedom in democracies. *Comparative Political Studies* 49(1):36–77.

Klomp, J., Bulte, E. (2013). Climate change, weather shocks, and violent conflict: A critical look at the evidence. *Agricultural Economics* 44(s1):63–78.

Knight, F. (1921). *Risk, Uncertainty, and Profit*. Boston, MA: Hart, Schaffner & Marx.

Kreuder-Sonnen, C. (2019). *Emergency Powers of International Organizations: Between Normalization and Containment*. Oxford University Press.

Kreuder-Sonnen, C. (2021). Does Europe need an emergency constitution? *Political Studies* 71(1):125–144.

Kreuder-Sonnen, C., White, J. (2022). Europe and the transnational politics of emergency. *Journal of European Public Policy* 29(6): 953–965.

Krieger, T., Meierrieks, D. (2017). How to deal with international terrorism. In Eger, T., Oeter, S., Voigt, S. (eds.), *International Law and the Rule of Law under Extreme Conditions*. Tübingen: Mohr Siebeck, pp. 223–47.

Krishnarajan, S., Rørbæk, L. L. (2020). The two-sided effect of elections on coup attempts. *Journal of Conflict Resolution* 64(7–8):1279–1306.

La Porta, R., Lopez-de-Silanes, F., Shleifer, A. (2008). The economic consequences of legal origins. *Journal of Economic Literature* 46(2):285–332.

Laframboise, N., Loko, B. (2012). Natural Disasters: Mitigating Impact, Managing Risks. IMF Working Paper 12/245.

Lazar, N. C. (2009). *States of Emergency in Liberal Democracies*. Cambridge: Cambridge University Press.

Lee, H. F. (2018). Measuring the effect of climate change on wars in history. *Asian Geographer* 35(2):123–142.

Lee, H. P. (2010). Constitutionalised emergency powers: A plague on Asian constitutionalism? In Ramraj, V. Thiruvengadam, A. (eds.), *Emergency Powers in Asia*. Cambridge: Cambridge University Press, pp. 393–411.

Leeson, P. T. (2008). Media freedom, political knowledge, and participation. *Journal of Economic Perspectives* 22:155–169.

Leeson, P. T., Sobel, R. S. (2008). Weathering corruption. *Journal of Law and Economics* 51(4):667–681.

Leon, G. (2014). Loyalty for sale? Military spending and coups d'état. *Public Choice* 159(3):363–383.

Levinson, D. J. (2011). Parchment and politics: The positive puzzle of constitutional commitment. *Harvard Law Review* 124(3):657–746.

Lintott, A. (2009). *The Constitution of the Roman Republic*. Oxford: Oxford University Press.

Linzer, D. A., Staton, J. K. (2015). A global measure of judicial independence, 1948–2012. *Journal of Courts and Law* 3:223–256.

Loayza, N., Olaberría, E. (2012). Natural disasters and growth: Going beyond the averages. *World Development* 40(7):1317–1336.

Locke, J. (1824). *The Work of John Locke in Nine Volumes. Volume 4: Economic Writings and Two Treatises of Government* (12th ed). London: Rivington.

Loevy, K. (2016). *Emergencies in Public Law*. Cambridge: Cambridge University Press.

Lomborg, B. (2020). *False Alarm: How Climate Change Panic Costs Us Trillions, Hurts the Poor, and Fails to Fix the Planet*. New York: Basic Books.

Londregan, J. B., Poole, K. T. (1990). Poverty, the coup trap, and the seizure of executive power. *World Politics* 42:151–83.

Loveman, B. (1993). *The Constitution of Tyranny. Regimes of Exception in Spanish America*. Pittsburgh: University of Pittsburgh Press.

Lührmann, A., Rooney, B. (2021). Autocratization by decree: States of emergency and democratic decline. *Comparative Politics* 53:617–649.

Machiavelli, N. (1531/2009). *Discourses on Livy*. Oxford: Oxford University Press.

Maddison, A. (2008). *Statistics on World Population, GDP and Per Capita GDP, 1-2008 AD*. Online database. Accessed December 16, 2016. www.ggdc.net/MADDISON/oriindex.htm.

Maerz, S. F., Lührmann, A., Lachapelle, J., Edgell, A. B. (2020). Worth the sacrifice? Illiberal and authoritarian practices during Covid-19. V-Dem Working Paper 110, University of Gothenburg.

Mainwaring, S., Liñán, A. P. (1997). Party discipline in the Brazilian constitutional congress. *Legislative Studies Quarterly* 22(4):453–483.

Marshall, M. G., Jaggers, K. (2010). *Polity IV Project: Political Regime Characteristics and Transitions, 1800–2008: Dataset Users' Manual.* Maryland: University of Maryland.

Marthoz, J. P. (2017). *Terrorism and the Media: A Handbook for Journalists.* New York: UNESCO.

Martin, L. W., Stevenson, R. T. (2001). Government formation in parliamentary democracies. *American Journal of Political Science* 45(1):33–50.

Masciandaro, D. (2020). COVID-19 helicopter money, monetary policy and central bank independence: Economics and politics. BAFFI CAREFIN Centre Research Paper, (2020-137).

McMillan, J., Zoido, P. (2004). How to subvert democracy: Montesinos in Peru. *Journal of Economic Perspectives* 18(4):69–92.

Meierding, E. (2013). Climate change and conflict: Avoiding small talk about the weather. *International Studies Review* 15(2):185–203.

Melnick, R., Eldor, R. (2010). Small investment and large returns: Terrorism, media and the economy. *European Economic Review* 54(8):963–973.

Mirza, D., Verdier, T. (2008). International trade, security and transnational terrorism: Theory and a survey of empirics. *Journal of Comparative Economics* 36(2):179–194.

Montesquieu, C. (1989). *The Spirit of the Laws.* Cambridge: Cambridge University Press.

Mueller, D. S. (1991). Constitutional rights. *Journal of Law, Economics, and Organization* 7(2):313–333.

Mueller, J., Stewart, M. G. (2011). *Terror, Security, and Money: Balancing the Risks, Benefits, and Costs of Homeland Security.* Oxford: Oxford University Press.

Nelson, S. (2020). Billions in foreign aid, pet projects stuffed into COVID relief bill. New York Post, December 2020.

Neumayer, E. (2012). Do governments mean business when they derogate? Human rights violations during notified states of emergency. *Review of International Organizations* 8(1): 1–31.

Nizalova O. Y., Murtazashvili, I. (2016). Exogenous treatment and endogenous factors: Vanishing of omitted variable bias on the interaction term. *Journal of Econometric Methods* 5:71–77.

NOAA (2017). *Billion-Dollar Weather and Climate Disasters.* Report, National Oceanic and Atmospheric Administration. Data retrieved from www.ncei.noaa.gov/access/billions/time-series (accessed July 2023).

Noorani, A. G. (2011). President rule: Limits & checks. *Frontline* 8(12): 14–17.

North, D. C. (1990). *Institutions, Institutional Change and Economic Performance*. Cambridge: Cambridge University Press.

Noy, I. (2009). The macroeconomic consequences of disasters. *Journal of Development Economics* 88(2):221–231.

Oates, W. (1972). *Fiscal Federalism*. New York: Harcourt Brace Jovanovich.

Olson, M. (1969). The principle of "Fiscal Equivalence": The division of responsibilities among different levels of government. *American Economic Review* 59(2): 479–487.

Pasquino, P. (1998). Locke on King's prerogative. *Political Theory* 26(2):198–208.

Patt, A., Zeckhauser, R. (2000). Action bias and environmental decisions. *Journal of Risk and Uncertainty* 21(1):45–72.

Peduzzi, P., Dao, H., Herold, C. (2005). Mapping disastrous natural hazards using global datasets. *Natural Hazards* 35:265–289.

Peltz, P. (2020). No Evidence for Autocratization by Decree: A rejoinder. Available at SSRN: https://ssrn.com/abstract=4410418.

Pemstein, D., Marquardt, K. L., Tzelgov, E., Wang, Y., Medzihorsky, J., Krusell, J., Miri, F., Römer, J. von (2020). The V-Dem measurement model: Latent variable analysis for cross-national and cross-temporal expert-coded data. V-Dem Working Paper 21, 5th edition.

Pennington, M. (2021). Hayek on complexity, uncertainty and pandemic response. *Review of Austrian Economics* 34:203–220.

Pepinsky, T. (2014). The institutional turn in comparative authoritarianism. *British Journal of Political Science* 44(3):631–653.

Piazza, J. A., Walsh, J. I. (2009). Transnational terror and human rights. *International Studies Quarterly* 53:125–148.

Pinkovskiy, M., Sala-i-Martin, X. (2016). Lights, camera ... income! Illuminating the national accounts-household surveys debate. *The Quarterly Journal of Economics* 131(2): 579–631.

Poe, S., Tate, N., Keith. L. C. (1999). Repression of human rights to personal integrity revisited: A global cross-national study covering the years 1976–1993. *International Studies Quarterly* 43:291–313.

Poole, K. T., Rosenthal, H. (2007). *Ideology and Congress*. New Brunswick, NJ: Transaction Publishers.

Poole, T. (2009). Constitutional exceptionalism and the common law. *International Journal of Constitutional Law* 7(2):247–274.

Pozen, D. E., Scheppele, K. L. (2020). Executive underreach, in pandemics and otherwise. *American Journal of International Law* 114(4):608–617.

Prakash, G. (2019). *Emergency Chronicles: Indira Gandhi and Democracy's Turning Point*. Princeton: Princeton University Press.

Qian, Y., Weingast, B. R. (1997). Federalism as a commitment to reserving market incentives. *Journal of Economic Perspectives* 11(4):83–92.

Rajagopalan, S. (2016). Constitutional change: An economic analysis. In Choudhry, S., Khosla, M., Mehta, P. B. (eds.), *Oxford Handbook of the Indian Constitution*. Oxford: Oxford University Press.

Rajagopalan, S. (2021). Interest groups repairing unconstitutionality: India's Ninth Schedule. *Journal of Legal Studies* 50(S2): S151–S178.

Ramraj, V. (2010). The emergency powers paradox. In Ramraj, V., Thiruvengadam, A. (eds.), *Emergency Powers in Asia: Exploring the Limits of Legality*, Cambridge: Cambridge University Press, pp. 21–55.

Reddy, K. J., Joseph, J. V. (2004). Executive discretion and Article 356 of the Constitution of India: A comparative critique. *Electronic Journal of Comparative Law* 8(1):13–14.

Reeves, A. (2011). Political disaster: Unilateral powers, electoral incentives, and presidential disaster declarations. *Journal of Politics* 73(4):1142–1151.

Reinhart, C. M., Rogoff, K. S. (2009). *This Time is Different: Eight Centuries of Financial Folly*. Princeton: Princeton University Press.

Reporters without Borders. (2020). World press freedom index. Database and report, Paris: Reporters without Borders.

Richards, D., Clay, C. (2012). An umbrella with holes: Respect for non-derogable human rights during declared states of emergency, 1996–2004. *Human Rights Review* 13:443–471.

Rogers, J. R. (2001). Information and judicial review: A signaling game of legislative judicial interaction. *American Journal of Political Science* 45(1):84–99.

Rohner, D., Frey, B. S. (2007). Blood and ink! The common-interest-game between terrorists and the media. *Public Choice* 133(1–2):129–145.

Rosen, L. (2000). *The Justice of Islam: Comparative Perspectives on Islamic Law and Society*. Oxford: Oxford University Press.

Roser, M., Ritchie, H., Ortiz-Ospina, E. Hasell, J. (2020). Our World in data: Coronavirus pandemic (COVID-19). Available at https://ourworldindata.org/coronavirus (accessed May 5, 2020).

Ross, M., Mahdavi, P. (2015). Oil and gas data, 1932–2014. *Harvard Dataverse, 2.*

Rossiter, C. (2009). *Constitutional Dictatorship – Crisis Government in the Modern Democracies*. New Brunswick: Transaction Publishers.

Rousseau, J-J. (2019). *The Social Contract and other Later Political Writings*, edited and translated by Victor Gourevitch, 2nd edition. Cambridge: Cambridge University Press.

S. R. Bommai v. Union of India AIR 1994 SC 1918

Sadanandan, A. (2012). Bridling central tyranny in India: How regional parties restrain the federal government. *Asian Survey* 52(2):247–269.

Sagar, R. (2016). Emergency powers. In Choudhry, S., Khosla, M., Mehta, P. B. (eds.), *The Oxford Handbook of the Indian Constitution*. New Delhi: Oxford University Press.

Sandler, T. (2011). New frontiers of terrorism research: An introduction. *Journal of Peace Research* 48(3):279–286.

Sandler, T. (2014). The analytical study of terrorism: Taking stock. *Journal of Peace Research* 51(2):257–271.

Sarkaria, R. S. (1988). *Commission on Centre-state Relations: Report*. New Delhi: Ministry of Home Affairs, Government of India.

Scartascini, C., Cruz, C., Keefer, P. (2018). The database of political institutions 2017. Database and codebook, the World Bank, Washington DC.

Scheffran, J., Brzoska, M., Kominek, J., Link, P. M., Schilling, J. (2012). Disentangling the climate-conflict nexus: Empirical and theoretical assessment of vulnerabilities and pathways. *Review of European Studies* 4(5): 1–13.

Schelling, T. C. (1960). *The Strategy of Conflict*. Cambridge: Harvard University Press.

Scheppele, K. L. (2004). Law in a time of emergency: States of exception and the empttations of 9/11. *University of Pennsylvania Journal of Constitutional Law* 6:1001–1083.

Schmitt, C. (1922). *Politische Theologie*. Berlin: Duncker & Humblot.

Selby, J., Dahi, O. S., Fröhlich, C., Hulme, M. (2017). Climate change and the Syrian civil war revisited. *Political Geography* 60:232–244.

Sen, A. (1984). Food Battles: Conflicts in the access to food. *Food and Nutrition* 10:81–89.

Sharma, P. R. D. (2017). Comparative federalism with reference to constitutional machinery failure (emergency) in India and Pakistan. *BRICS Law Journal* IV(2):71–94.

Shor, E. (2011). Constructing a global counterterrorist legislation database: Dilemmas, procedures, and preliminary analyses. *Journal of Terrorism Research* 2(3):249–277.

Shrinivasan, R. (2016). President's rule: A story of over 100 chapters. *The Hindu, January 29, 2016*.

Shugart, M. S. (1998). The inverse relationship between party strength and executive strength: A theory of politicians' constitutional choices. *British Journal of Political Science* 28:1–29.

Singh, M. P. (2001). Towards a more federalized parliamentary system in India: Explaining functional change. *Pacific Affairs* 74(4):553–568.

Skarbek, E. (2014). The Chicago Fire of 1871: A bottom up approach to disaster relief. *Public Choice* 160(1):155–180.

Sobel, R. S., Coyne, C. J. (2011). Cointegrating institutions: The time-series properties of country institutional measures. *Journal of Law and Economics* 54(1):111–134.

Sobel, R. S., Leeson, P. T. (2006). Government's response to Hurricane Katrina: A public choice analysis. *Public Choice* 127(1–2):55–73.

Spinoza, B. de (1670/1891). *The Chief Works of Benedict de Spinoza,* translated from the Latin, with an Introduction by R.H.M. Elwes, vol. 1 Introduction, Tractatus-Theologico-Politicus, Tractatus Politicus. Revised edition (London: George Bell and Sons, 1891). 2.11.2017. http://oll.libertyfund.org/titles/1710

Stier, S. (2015). Democracy, autocracy and the news: The impact of regime type on media freedom. *Democratization* 22(7):1273–1295.

Straumann, B. (2016). *Crisis and constitutionalism: Roman political thought from the fall of Rome to the Age of Revolution.* Oxford: Oxford University Press.

Strömberg, D. (2007). Natural disasters, economic development, and humanitarian aid. *Journal of Economic Perspectives* 21(3):199–222.

Sunstein, C. R. (2002). Probability neglect: Emotions, worst cases, and law. *Yale Law Journal* 112(1):61–107.

Sunstein, C. R. (2003). Terrorism and probability neglect. *Journal of Risk and Uncertainty* 26(2/3):121–136.

Sunstein, C. R., Zeckhauser, R. (2011). Overreaction to fearsome risks. *Environmental and Resource Economics* 48(3):435–449.

Sylves, R., Búzás, Z. I. (2007). Presidential disaster declaration decisions, 1953–2003: What influences odds of approval? *State & Local Government Review* 39(1):3–15.

Tan, K. (2010). From Myanmar to Manila: A brief study of emergency powers in Southeast Asia. In Ramraj, V., Thiruvengadam, A. (eds.), *Emergency Powers in Asia.* Cambridge: Cambridge University Press, pp. 149–186.

Tanzi, V. (2022). *Fragile Futures: The Uncertain Economics of Disasters, Pandemics, and Climate Change.* Cambridge University Press.

Tarr, G. A. (2000). *Understanding State Constitutions.* Princeton: Princeton University Press.

Theisen, O. M., Gleditsch, N. P., Buhaug, H. (2013). Is climate change a driver of armed conflict? *Climatic Change* 117(3):613–625.

Thyne, C. L., Powell, J. M. (2016). Coup d'état or Coup d'autocracy? How coups impact democratization, 1950–2008. *Foreign Policy Analysis* 12(2):192–213.

Tonsakulrungruang, K., Leelapatana, R. (2020). *Health Before Rights and Liberties: Thailand's Response to COVID-19, VerfBlog,* 2020/5/08, https://verfassungsblog.de/health-before-rights-and-liberties-thailands-response-to-covid-19/ https://doi.org/10.17176/20200508-133133-0.

Tornell, A., Lane, P. R. (1999). The voracity effect. *American Economic Review* 89(1):22–46.

Tsebelis, G. (1995). Decision making in political systems: Veto players in presidentialism, parliamentarism, multicameralism and mMultipartyism. *British Journal of Political Science* 25(3):289–325.

Tsebelis, G. (2002). *Veto Players. How Political Institutions Work.* Princeton: Princeton University Press.

Tummala, K. K. (1996). The Indian union and emergency powers. *International Political Science Review* 17(4):373–384.

United Nations. (1948). *Universal Declaration on Human Rights.* New York: The United Nations.

United States Department of State. (2017). *International Religious Freedom Report for 2017.* Washington, DC: United States Department of State, Bureau of Democracy, Human Rights, and Labor.

US Census. (2016). US Census Bureau. Database; dData available at www.census.gov/ (accessed October 2016).

Uslaner, E. M., Davis, J. R. (1975). The paradox of vote trading: Effects of decision rules and voting strategies on externalities. *American Political Science Review* 69(3):929–942.

Vanberg, G. (2001). Legislative-judicial relations: A game-theoretic approach to constitutional review. *American Journal of Political Science* 45(2):346–361.

VanDoepp, P., Young, D. J. (2012). Assaults on the fourth estate: Explaining media harassment in Africa. *Journal of Politics* 75(1):36–51.

Varshney, A., Wilkinson, S. (2006). *Varshney-Wilkinson Dataset on Hindu-Muslim Violence in India, 1950–1995, Version 2.* Inter-University Consortium for Political and Social Research ICPSR.

Voigt, S. (2020). *Constitutional Economics. A Primer.* Cambridge: Cambridge University Press.

Voigt, S. (2021). Mind the gap – analyzing the divergence between constitutional text and constitutional reality. *International Journal of Constitutional Law* 19(5):1778–1809.

Voigt, S., Gutmann, J., Feld, L. (2015). Economic growth and judicial independence, a dozen years on: Cross-country evidence using an updated Set of indicators. *European Journal of Political Economy* 38:197–211.

Volden, C., Carrubba, C. J. (2004). The formation of oversized coalitions in parliamentary democracies. *American Journal of Political Science* 48(3):521–537.

Vreeland, J. R. (2008). The effect of political regime on civil war: Unpacking anocracy. *Journal of Conflict Resolution* 52:401–425.

Walsh, J. I, Piazza, J. A. (2010). Why respecting physical integrity rights reduces terrorism. *Comparative Political Studies* 43(5):551–577.

White, J. (2022). Constitutionalizing the EU in an age of emergencies. *Journal of Common Market Studies* 61(3):781–796.

Williamson, S. (2019). Elections, legitimacy & compliance in authoritarian regimes. Working paper, Stanford University.

Wintrobe, R. (1990). The tinpot and the totalitarian: An economic theory of dictatorship. *American Political Science Review* 84(3):849–872.

Wintrobe, R. (2019). Are there types of dictatorship? Chapter 15 in Congleton, R., Grofman, B., Voigt, S. (eds.), *The Oxford Handbook of Public Choice*, Vol. 2. Oxford: Oxford University Press, pp. 286–310.

World Bank. (2021). World development indicators. Online database, the World Bank: Washington DC.

Wright, C. (2014). Executives and emergencies: Presidential decrees of exception in Bolivia, Ecuador, and Peru. Documentos de Trabaja IELAT No. 60. Available at https://ebuah.uah.es/dspace/bitstream/handle/10017/19987/executives_wright_IELATDT_2014_N60.pdf?sequence=1&isAllowed=y

Wu, F. (2002). Profiling in the wake of September 11: The precedent of the Japanese American internment. *Criminal Justice* 52–59.

Index

Page numbers in italic refers to figure and table.

www.ingramcontent.com/pod-product-compliance
Lightning Source LLC
LaVergne TN
LVHW011659200926
848484LV00004B/997
9781009372084